The Derecognition of States

This book is the first comprehensive study of the derecognition of states in world politics. It offers a global and comparative outlook of this unexplored diplomatic practice, guided by an innovative conceptual framework and informed by original empirical research. The book delves into the intricate processes, justifications, and effects surrounding state derecognition. It offers original insights from five aspirant states that have experienced withdrawal of recognition, namely Taiwan, Western Sahara, Abkhazia, South Ossetia, and Kosovo. The book argues that state derecognition is a highly contested and unstable practice that has less to do with the unfulfillment of the conditions of statehood by the claimant than with the advancement of the self-interest of the former base state and derecognizing state. The derecognition of states is not a rule; rather, it is an exception in international diplomacy, driven by political expediency and incompatible with original rationales for granting recognition. The book demonstrates that the derecognition of states plays a far more significant role than previously recognized in shaping the reversal dynamics of secession and state creation and impacting regional peace, geopolitical rivalries, and the international order. This book addresses a notable gap in international relations, diplomatic studies, and international law, making it a valuable contribution to our understanding of these complex dynamics.

Gëzim Visoka is Associate Professor of Peace and Conflict Studies in the School of Law and Government at Dublin City University, Ireland.

The Derecognition of States

Gëzim Visoka

University of Michigan Press
Ann Arbor

Copyright © 2024 by Gëzim Visoka

(cc) BY-NC

This work is licensed under a Creative Commons Attribution-NonCommercial 4.0 International License. *Note to users*: A Creative Commons license is only valid when it is applied by the person or entity that holds rights to the licensed work. Works may contain components (e.g., photographs, illustrations, or quotations) to which the rightsholder in the work cannot apply the license. It is ultimately your responsibility to independently evaluate the copyright status of any work or component part of a work you use, in light of your intended use. To view a copy of this license, visit http://creativecommons.org/licenses/by-nc/4.0/

For questions or permissions, please contact um.press.perms@umich.edu
Published in the United States of America by the
University of Michigan Press
Manufactured in the United States of America
Printed on acid-free paper
First published October 2024

A CIP catalog record for this book is available from the British Library.

Library of Congress Cataloging-in-Publication Data

Names: Visoka, Gëzim, author. | Michigan Publishing (University of Michigan), publisher.
Title: The derecognition of states / Gëzim Visoka.
Description: Ann Arbor [Michigan] : University of Michigan Press, 2024. | Includes bibliographical references (pages 245–279) and index.
Identifiers: LCCN 2024024779 (print) | LCCN 2024024780 (ebook) | ISBN 9780472077090 (hardcover) | ISBN 9780472057092 (paperback) | ISBN 9780472904693 (ebook other)
Subjects: LCSH: State, The. | Recognition (International law)—Political aspects. | Self-determination, National. | Sovereignty.
Classification: LCC JZ1316 .V56 2024 (print) | LCC JZ1316 (ebook) | DDC 320.1—dc23/eng/20240705
LC record available at https://lccn.loc.gov/2024024779
LC ebook record available at https://lccn.loc.gov/2024024780

DOI: https://doi.org/10.3998/mpub.11703277

The University of Michigan Press's open access publishing program is made possible thanks to additional funding from the University of Michigan Office of the Provost and the generous support of contributing libraries.

Contents

LIST OF ILLUSTRATIONS	vii
PREFACE AND ACKNOWLEDGMENTS	ix
1 Introduction: Statehood and Derecognition in World Politics	1
2 Conceptualizing State Derecognition	34
3 The Process of State Derecognition	69
4 The Rationales for State Derecognition	114
5 The Effects of State Derecognition	162
6 Conclusion: Rethinking State Derecognition	209
APPENDIX	237
REFERENCES	245
INDEX	281

Digital materials related to this title can be found on the Fulcrum platform via the following citable URL: https://doi.org/10.3998/mpub.11703277

Illustrations

FIGURES

Figure 2.1. The Conceptual Framework   56
Figure 2.2. The Actors of State Derecognition   58
Figure 2.3. The Process of State Derecognition   60

TABLES

Table 1. Taiwan   238
Table 2. Western Sahara (Sahrawi Arabic Democratic Republic)   242
Table 3. Abkhazia   244
Table 4. South Ossetia   244
Table 5. Kosovo   244

Preface and Acknowledgments

This book examines the derecognition of states in theory and practice. Since this is the first book solely focused on the derecognition of states, the arguments and claims presented are inductive inferences and contingent generalizations drawn from observing contemporary state practice and discourse. It is exploratory and aims to systematically examine the contemporary state practices and discourses of state derecognition. The book aims not only to probe whether states can withdraw the recognition of other states but also to go a step further and identify the conditions that enable the presence of this contested diplomatic practice in world politics. It offers a critical and cross-case comparison of the process, rationales, and effects of state derecognition. The book argues that state derecognition is a highly contested and unstable practice that has less to do with the unfulfillment of the conditions of statehood by the claimant than with the advancement of the self-interest of the derecognizing state. The derecognition of states is not a rule; rather, it is an exception in international diplomacy driven by political expediency and incompatible with the original grounds for recognition.

Inevitably, the unexplored nature of state derecognition makes this book a foundational study upon which other normative and empirical studies could develop conceptual, theoretical, and empirical perspectives on this subject. By offering original analysis and tracing contemporary state practices, the book aims to add conceptual and empirical nuances to the dominant legal, normative, and area-specific views on the recognition and derecognition of states. By disentangling the complex diplomatic, economic, and geopolitical linkages and trans-scalar factors that shape decisions of states and diplomats to withdraw recognition, the book aims to enrich further existing accounts

x • *Preface and Acknowledgments*

in diplomatic studies about the role of great power politics, normative institutions, international organizations, and foreign policy contested states. By exploring five case studies, namely Taiwan, Western Sahara, Abkhazia, South Ossetia, and Kosovo, which have unique sociohistorical trajectories, different geographical locations, statehood capacity, and great power support, the book enriches comparative analysis of the diplomatic standing of these aspiring states. In addition, by exploring the rationales and politics behind derecognizing states, the book offers new perspectives on the foreign policy of postcolonial states and the instrumentalization of international recognition for domestic interests.

Scholarly work is frequently a building block that incorporates the conclusions and observations of earlier research, or it can be an unanticipated rupture from the planned research trajectory. This book shares both orientations. While editing the *Routledge Handbook of State Recognition* together with my esteemed colleagues John Doyle and Edward Newman, I wanted to include a chapter on the derecognition of states, but we were unable to find an appropriate author who had written exclusively and authoritatively on the subject. Driven by many questions to which I couldn't find the answers in the existing literature on state recognition, I conducted preliminary research on state derecognition, which was published as a chapter in this handbook. Although this preliminary work provided satisfactory answers, the abundance of empirical data and the prevalence of state derecognition in contemporary world politics convinced me that this topic needs a more in-depth and serious investigation. Subsequently, it took me five years to write this book, coinciding with the most research-intense period of my career while juggling parenting and family obligations.

In writing this book, I am in debt to many friends and colleagues who have offered much-needed personal encouragement, intellectual guidance, and research assistance. First and foremost, I am enormously grateful to my former PhD students Dr. Liridona Veliu-Ashiku and Dr. Ramesh Ganohariti, for their research assistance in different stages of the project. I am also grateful to Professor John Doyle, Professor Donnacha Ó Beacháin, Professor Iain McMenamin, Dr. Ken McDonagh, and many other colleagues at Dublin City University for supporting this book project in various ways and at different stages. I am grateful to Professor James Summers for inviting me to present parts of this book to Lancaster Law School in November 2021 and Ms. Leonora Kryeziu for inviting me to present the book to the Prishtina School of Politics in 2020. Special gratitude goes to the esteemed scholars Professor Ryan Griffiths, Professor Bruno Coppieters, and Professor

Jure Vidmar, who have read the full manuscript and provided valuable and constructive feedback.

Similarly, I have benefited from numerous conversations on the subject with Mr. Muhamet Brajshori, Professor Oliver P. Richmond, Professor Annika Björkdahl, Professor Edward Newman, Dr. Vjosa Musliu Dr. Adem Beha, and Dr. Ramadan Ilazi. I am also grateful to Ms. Azra Naseem and Ms. Mary Hashman for carefully reading and copyediting the entire manuscript. Finally, I am enormously thankful to Dr. Elizabeth Sherburn Demers for considering this project and expertly seeing this book through the review and publication at the University of Michigan Press. Similarly, I am grateful to Ms. Haley Winkle and Danielle Coty-Fattal, who have offered invaluable support and assistance throughout the publication process. Last, I thank my family for their much-needed love, care, and patience while I was writing this project.

Dublin
January 2024

1 ✦ Introduction

Statehood and Derecognition in World Politics

In August 2018, El Salvador switched its recognition from Taiwan to China. By pushing for withdrawal of recognition, China aggressively tried to isolate Taiwan internationally and push against Western geopolitical interests worldwide. Other countries, such as Burkina Faso, the Dominican Republic, Panama, São Tomé and Príncipe, and the Solomon Islands have also switched sides to China in response to lucrative economic and security incentives. Withdrawal of recognition is raising tensions between China and Taiwan and has become one of the sources of contention between China and the United States. Around the same time, in another region of the world, Serbia undertook a similar campaign for the derecognition of Kosovo. Between 2017 and 2023, Serbia convinced over twenty states to suspend or entirely withdraw recognition of Kosovo (see Table 5 in the appendix). This move not only undermined the European Union–led talks to normalize relations between these two countries, but also escalated ethnic tensions in the region and brought back to the surface geopolitical rivalries between global powers in the Balkans. Similarly, Morocco has actively lobbied for the derecognition of the Sahrawi Arabic Democratic Republic (SADR) to legitimate the four-decade occupation of Western Sahara. As a result of this campaign, Morocco has convinced over forty countries to end diplomatic ties with SADR, which has increased regional tensions in North Africa. The separate yet relatable events raise a number of important questions. Why do states withdraw the recognition of other states? Can states legitimately withdraw recognition of other states they once deemed to have fulfilled statehood criteria? Does international derecognition result in the dismantling of statehood? This book offers a comprehensive and critical outlook on the politics and effects of state derecognition in world politics.

Diplomatic recognition plays a vital role in the ability of new states to function as sovereign and independent states and have relatively equal access, rights, and obligations in the international system (Crawford 2007; Coggins 2014; Griffiths 2017). Within the scholarly and policy community, there are deep divisions on who has the right to self-determination and statehood, under what circumstances new states gain diplomatic recognition, and whether recognition, nonrecognition, or derecognition has a constitutive or constraining effect on independent statehood (Visoka 2022). Recognition is widely defined as an acknowledgment of entitlement to and effective performance of sovereignty statehood in practice, and it can be expressed in multiple forms, such as through bilateral or collective channels, in explicit or implicit means, or in de facto and de jure forms (Visoka, Doyle, and Newman 2020). On the other hand, nonrecognition refers to the withholding of granting recognition for various reasons, and this can take the form of either remaining impartial and neutral on the status of the claimant entity or siding with the base state and defending its claims to sovereignty and territorial integrity over a contested entity (Caspersen 2020). Scholarly work on international law, diplomatic studies, international relations, political sciences, and area studies has already addressed many ambiguities, tensions, and dilemmas surrounding state recognition and nonrecognition. However, so far we still have a limited engagement with and knowledge of the quintessential question: whether recognition can be revoked or withdrawn.

State derecognition as a concept and practice has multiple meanings and invocations. While, in general, derecognition of states entails the withdrawal, revocation, or retraction of recognition of the international legal sovereignty of a state, by default it can also imply the re-recognition of the sovereignty and authority of the former base state over the contested territory or derecognized state (Visoka 2020b). In other words, derecognition can imply rescinding recognition prior to the consent of the state the claimant entity has seceded from. However, in the absence of accepted rules governing the recognition or derecognition of states, the suspension, freezing, or withdrawal of recognition tends to take place even when the factual presence of original conditions of recognition and the effectiveness and legitimacy of the statehood of the claimant state are still intact.

Despite its significant impact, state derecognition is not a common diplomatic practice. Subject to derecognition are mainly a limited number of states that have declared independence or claimed a statehood continuing without the consent of the former base state and exist as de facto states satisfying most of the statehood criteria, including partial international recognition, but are denied admission to the United Nations. In international literature, such entities are referred to as de facto states, aspirant states, or contested states (Grzybowski 2019; Griffiths 2021; Ker-Lindsay 2012). So there is an intrinsic relationship between the path toward state recognition and the prospects for eventual recognition and derecognition. State creation often follows two significant paths, namely through consensual and nonconsensual separation from the base state or other dissolving units. Consensual state creation occurs when the state units, through a democratic, peaceful, and deliberative process, agree to the breakup. Ultimately, as this consensual path to state creation is not internally contested among the constitutive units, it enjoys external acceptance and results in collective recognition through admission to the UN or through other multilateral or bilateral means. However, nonconsensual state creation often results in contested statehood, which is expressed through limited domestic and international sovereignty, partial or no diplomatic recognition, limited access to international organizations, and, most important, exposure to different forms of contestation, among them, withdrawal of recognition by third countries or various forms of impositions by the former base state. When two UN member states decide to downgrade their diplomatic relations, such instances are referred to as a breakup of diplomatic relations. But when third countries decide to downgrade their diplomatic relations with contested, non-UN member states, this is commonly called derecognition or withdrawal of recognition.

These dynamics mainly affect the state-like entities that have secured partial diplomatic recognition, cases that have recognition by fewer than ten states, such as Abkhazia and South Ossetia, as well as those that have secured between fifty, one hundred, or more recognitions, such as Taiwan, Western Sahara, and Kosovo (see the appendix). In 1963, Taiwan was recognized by sixty-six states, of which only twelve continued to recognize it as of January 2024. Taiwan's derecognition process started when the People's China of China was allowed to take its seat at the UN. China claims it is the only sovereign authority over Taiwan, despite not having de facto control over the territory since its foundation. In the case of Western Sahara, fifty-three out of eighty-four UN member states have withdrawn their recognition of the SADR. The dispute over Western Sahara concerns Morocco's unilateral occupation of the territory and the prevention of a self-determination referendum to conclude the decolonization process in Africa. Kosovo has recently been added to the list of states that have encountered derecognition by other states. Of the 117 states that initially recognized Kosovo's independence, as of January 2024 there was evidence that 18 states had withdrawn recognition, of which at least five subsequently reinstated it, whereas 10 other states had either frozen or withdrawn recognition, but they were contested by the Kosovo side. Serbia continues to claim sovereignty over the territory of Kosovo despite not having had access to it since 1999, when the UN placed Kosovo under international administration; in 2008, the country declared independence after Serbia rejected an UN-mediated proposal for supervised independence for Kosovo. Finally, Georgia's breakaway territories, Abkhazia and South Ossetia, have been recognized by seven UN member states, two of which subsequently withdrew recognition. These figures are fluid, as the state derecognition process is dynamic and subject to change. While at first sight, the derecognition of these five states might represent an insignificant story in world politics, they play a far more significant symbolic role in explaining the reversal politics and dynamics of secession and state creation, as well as the diplomatic battles that shape regional peace, increase geopolitical rivalries, and endanger the existing international order.

Despite the presence of state derecognition in contemporary international affairs, our knowledge of it remains scattered and outdated. Derecognition has featured in a limited number of studies within the field of international law, diplomatic studies, conflict resolution, and area studies (Lauterpacht 1947; Grant 1999; Crawford 2007; Visoka, Doyle, and Newman 2020). Key textbooks and reference works on international law, diplomatic practice, and statecraft almost entirely ignore the subject (Shaw 2021; Roberts 2017; Constantinou, Kerr, and Sharp; McKercher 2022). We have much better understanding of the law, politics, and practices surrounding the recognition and nonrecognition of states than the withdrawal of recognition. State derecognition has been discussed only peripherally as part of other studies that have mainly focused on secession, self-determination, international law, and statehood norms in world politics (Pavković and Radan 2011; Vidmar, McGibbon, and Raible 2022). In theory, the revocation of recognition is seen as impossible unless recognition is reassigned or extended to another entity or the original conditions for recognition no longer exist (i.e., loss of statehood capacity). Another circumstance that may explain or justify the derecognition of states is when the claimant state emerges through aggression or loses the core attributes of statehood. However, as it will be discussed in Chapter 2, existing accounts provide conflicting and futile views on state derecognition, draw mainly from the American and British doctrine of recognition, and are informed by outdated and historical examples.

Most importantly, these perspectives—mainly legal—need more in-depth empirical analysis and examination in the context of contemporary world politics and transitional international order. They are primarily based on hypothetical situations, deriving mainly from the interpretation of broader international law, norms, and rules, including a narrow understanding of sovereignty, recognition, and the agency of state-like entities in world politics, or on old examples of state practice and discourse (Lauterpacht 1947; Grant 1999; Crawford 2007). Some of the contemporary examples of state derecognition—mainly Taiwan and Western Sahara—are so far studied in isolation—mostly as contextual investigations of foreign policy implementation and diplomatic conduct of states in conflict over territory, sovereignty, and resources (Taylor 2002; Van Fossen 2007; Smith 2015; Kingsbury 2015; Tudoroiu 2017; Abidde 2022). However, these case-specific studies cannot offer a broader understanding of this diplomatic practice, which ultimately requires engaging with comparative, globally existing examples of state derecognition and critically examining knowledge across different scholarly debates in broadly defined international studies.

This book offers the first comprehensive, global, and comparative outlook on this underexplored diplomatic practice. It aims to develop a general account of state derecognition that is both conceptually and empirically rich, critical of existing practices, and path-setting for future research. This book aims to inductively trace contemporary state practices, actors, justifications, and effects of this under-explored diplomatic practice to make sense of the complexities and controversies surrounding state derecognition. The book's focus is on states that have received some official recognition from UN member states, and it does not deal with cases of de facto states that have not received any official recognition. It also does not deal with cases of state death as a result of dissolution, annexation, or reincorporation within the former base state. It offers original insights from five partially recognized, contested, and de facto states currently experiencing withdrawal of recognition: Taiwan, Western Sahara, Abkhazia, South Ossetia, and Kosovo. By offering original analysis and tracing contemporary state practices, the book adds both conceptual and empirical nuances to the dominant legal views on the derecognition of states. Moreover, by disentangling the complex diplomatic, economic, and geopolitical linkages and trans-scalar agency that shape decisions of states to withdraw recognition, the book aims to enrich further existing accounts in diplomatic studies about the role of great power politics, normative institutions, international organizations, and foreign policy of contender states.

MAKING SENSE OF STATE DERECOGNTION

Making sense of state derecognition requires addressing a number of puzzling questions to which we have yet to learn the answers. How can we conceptualize the derecognition of states? Can states derecognize other states? Under what circumstances would the withdrawal of recognition be an acceptable and justifiable act? What drives states to withdraw the recognition of other states? What are the political, economic, normative, and geopolitical rationales for derecognition? What diplomatic strategies, actors, and approaches facilitate the derecognition of states? How does the withdrawal of recognition impact the claimant states and their international standing? Why is there no institutional and normative framework for regulating this diplomatic practice? Tackling these questions requires understanding holistically the derecognition of states in world politics, in particular, the diplomatic process, actors, justifications, and effects of this practice in the political existence and international standing of derecognized states and its broader impact on world order. Starting from the concept of derecognition, there are multiple semantical invocations and no clear definition in diplomatic theory and practice. While scholars and practitioners alike use interchangeably "derecognition" with "withdrawal," "retraction," "suspension," and "freezing of recognition," there is a need to examine the nuances this terminology carries. Conceptualizing this diplomatic practice requires shedding light on contemporary state discourse and scholarly debates. Offering a more concise account of state derecognition enriches existing scholarly debates on statehood and recognition and helps practitioners make sense of this evolving and underexplored diplomatic practice. State recognition and nonrecognition concepts are well established in literature and state practice. However, the concept of derecognition is only marginally examined and defined. Thus, it is essential to explore how derecognition is treated in scholarly literature, especially whether and under what conditions recognition is reversible.

Understanding state derecognition in practice, first and foremost, means examining which states are subject to the withdrawal of recognition and which are prone to withdrawing the recognition of other states—although this would not be sufficient without bringing in former base states and regional powers, which play a role in determining the positions of all the parties involved. Self-determination outside the decolonization process and state birth without the consent of the former base state reduce the prospects for collective recognition (Laoutides 2020). This has resulted in the creation of new contested states with different degrees of international recognition and a limited capacity to survive independently without external support (Visoka 2022). It is in this context that derecognition has primarily affected states that have declared their independence without the consent of their base state and have failed to secure collective recognition, namely states that are outside the UN system or have not been yet admitted as full members (Griffiths 2017). As I have already mentioned, they range from states that have secured recognition from fewer than ten others, such as Abkhazia and South Ossetia, to states that have achieved around one hundred or more recognitions, such as Taiwan, Western Sahara, and Kosovo. While Taiwan is a unique case, as it claims to be a continuing state rather than a new, independent state, it is crucial to examine it, as it has been the most prominent case affected by diplomatic derecognition (de Oliveira 2023). Without full membership in the UN and support from major international powers, aspiring states with partial international recognition risk losing their diplomatic allies and becoming subject to delegitimization. Therefore, the practice of derecognition remains a conceptual and empirical puzzle because contemporary examples of derecognition encompass different political entities or claimant states with distinct pathways to independent statehood, different degrees and forms of recognition, and varying statehood capacity.

Similarly, looking at which states are implicated in freezing, withdrawing, switching, and reinstating recognition of other states is crucial for holistically understanding derecognition. Evidence shows that derecognizing other states has emerged as a common practice mostly among postcolonial states in the global south that gained independent statehood as part of the decolonization process, who continue to struggle with chronic poverty and geopolitical vulnerabilities, or are ruled by semi-authoritarian regimes. Small Caribbean, Pacific, and African states are the main protagonists of derecognition and re-recognition practices, having made the business of recognition one of their foreign policy priorities and a solid source of much-needed economic development and humanitarian aid (Tudoroiu 2017: 204). Among the most prominent of those involved in withdrawing, "renting," or switching their recognition of other states are Burkina Faso, the Central African Republic, the Dominican Republic, Gambia, Lesotho, Liberia, Malawi, Nauru, Panama, the Solomon Islands, Suriname, Tuvalu, and Vanuatu. For these states, derecognition is one of the only available foreign policy assets to reduce their vulnerability, benefit from foreign aid, renew alliances, and influence the international system more generally (Thorhallsson and Bailes 2016: 297). Thus, by looking only at the foreign policy decisions of these states, especially their transactional understanding of state recognition and derecognition, we cannot uncover the entangled politics and nature of state derecognition in world politics.

In addition to the former base and claimant state, the regional and global powers, in their capacity as patron or kin states, must also be accounted for when discussing state derecognition. Support or opposition from the great powers plays a pivotal role in deepening and entrenching the contestation of claimant states (Coggins 2014). Great powers, unless they are themselves the base state, are mainly reactive actors who support the diplomatic agenda of former base states for geopolitical interests (Newman and Visoka 2023). In relation to Taiwan, China is obviously the main competing authority and has also utilized its global political and economic status to reduce the number of Taiwan's diplomatic allies. Despite being among the first countries to withdraw its recognition of Taiwan, the United States remains one of its vital global allies, seeking to use Taiwan as a geostrategic asset to advance its interests abroad. In the case of Western Sahara, the SADR is backed militarily and diplomatically by Algeria, while Morocco continues to benefit from French and US support in its campaign for derecognition (Huddleston 2021). Kosovo's main allies remain the United States and most EU member states, while Serbia is backed by Russia (and China to a certain point) in its pursuit of the derecognition of Kosovo (Visoka 2020b). Finally, Abkhazia and South Ossetia are backed by Russia, while Georgia enjoys strong support from the United States and all the EU and NATO member states (Ó Beacháin 2020). Thus, the involvement of regional and global powers is an important indicator of the significance of derecognition for making sense of contestation and rivalries among dominant powers.

Beyond protagonist states, another question that needs to be addressed is whether states can legitimately derecognize other states and, if so, under what conditions such a move is justifiable. International lawyers and foreign policy and diplomacy scholars are divided on this question. When assembling knowledge from various disciplinary fields—mostly from international law—we can trace two significant perspectives on state derecognition. The first group of scholars argues that once a state has been recognized as sovereign, it cannot be derecognized. The leading proponents of this view mostly subscribe to the declaratory theory of recognition, which holds that the existence of a state is independent of recognition as long as that state fulfills specific substantive criteria. They hold that once full and formal recognition has been granted and diplomatic relations have been established, derecognition cannot retrospectively undermine statehood, especially if recognition has been granted de jure and the claimant state satisfies the criteria of statehood (Lauterpacht 1947; Chen 1951). In this instance, derecognition means that the legal existence of the claimant state vanishes only in relation to this particular (derecognizing) state. In effect, derecognition is nothing but discontinuing diplomatic relations. In policy discourses as well, especially among the claimant states, the withdrawal of recognition is categorically denied. For example, in the case of Kosovo, both its national leaders and the United States as their primary international ally consider Kosovo's independence and sovereignty as "irreversible and inviolable" (US Department of State 2022) and assertively claim that "the independent, sovereign, free Kosovo is an irreversible reality" (President of Kosovo 2022). Similarly, the European Parliament through its nonbinding resolutions has affirmed on several occasions that "the independence of Kosovo is irreversible" (European Parliament 2022).

However, such a view is often refuted by former base states and their allies, who consider the withdrawal of recognition possible and utilize it to advance diplomatic and military goals against claimant states. This corresponds with the second view, which considers both recognition and derecognition to be essential elements of independent statehood. Scholars upholding this view—affiliated with the constitutive theory of recognition—take an affirmative stance regarding the possibility of reversing the recognition of states. For constitutive theorists, a state exists only when others recognize its sovereign status. In this regard, constitutive theorists consider derecognition a critical indicator undermining the claimant state's ability to perform sovereignty in international society (Talmon 1993; Raič 2002). The former base states and their international allies usually adopt this view, considering derecognition to be an international blessing of the return of symbolic sovereignty over the contested territory, including permission to extend the base state's authority and control over the derecognized state. They also maintain that as long as state recognition remains unregulated in international law, it will remain a discretionary state practice to decide on the conduct of their foreign policy (d'Aspremont 2012; Dugard 2013). This implies that diplomatic recognition could be withdrawn from an effective de jure government for political reasons (Tierney 2013).

Although these views on the permissibility of derecognition hold attractive argumentative grounds, they are not sufficiently investigated—either at the conceptual or empirical level. Is derecognition what states make of it, or do more objective criteria guide it? We need a much richer account of state derecognition to answer this query, including the clear presentation and categorization of competing perspectives. While there is some debate about the politics and ethics of using economic, political, and military incentives in the pursuit of derecognition, there is no sufficient research on and analysis of the instruments used by states to incentivize the derecognition of states. Similar to the case of recognition in the first instance, the derecognition of states is also embedded in legal, political, and situation arguments, which may vary from one case to another (Ker-Lindsay 2012; Visoka 2018). A proper and systematic analysis of public justifications and rationales used by third states is essential to understanding the discursive and strategic narrative that drives the decision to derecognize states. The wording of derecognition notes is crucial to deconstructing and tracing the normative and political language used and the influence of the former base states in framing such decisions. Similarly, we still have a limited understanding of the scale and scope of effects that the derecognition of states may have on the disputant parties and the prospects for conflict resolution, on the interference of third countries in the foreign policy conduct of derecognizing states, and on international peace and stability. Although state derecognition currently affects a small number of partially recognized states and remains widely contested by the international community, its impact on global order and the relationship between great powers and the existing international order is enormous.

Thus, examining the derecognition of states is also about significant questions concerning international transitional order and the politics of disassembling statehood, which ultimately raises questions about the changing nature of world order and the growing hostility between states over state creation and over the use and abuse of state recognition to promote sovereign inequality in world politics. Finally, as the derecognition of states tends to have far-reaching consequences for claimant states, it is essential to question what institutional and normative mechanisms exist to regulate or sanction the derecognition of states. Although the derecognition of states remains a highly polarized issue, it is essential to explore policy and institutional mechanisms that could be developed to regulate this controversial practice in world politics or set some consensual contours and normative considerations that may guide international policy thinking and practice.

THE ARGUMENT AND MAIN THEMES

The Meaning and Invocation of State Derecognition

The first theme of this book concerns the meaning and invocation of state derecognition. The book finds that the derecognition of states is invoked, applied, and interpreted differently and inconsistently by protagonist states. Empirically, the book finds that practices of derecognition are characterized by a mismatch between the original conditions for recognition and those invoked for derecognition; a mismatch in how derecognizing states respond to different cases; a mismatch between declared justifications and hidden motives for derecognition; and, finally, a mismatch between the desired and the actual effects of derecognition. Derecognition is what protagonist states decide to make of it. For the former base state and the claimant state, derecognition is a central feature of diplomatic warfare for defending self-determination versus resorting to territorial integrity; for derecognizing states, derecognition serves as a generator of foreign aid, personal profit, and military assistance; and finally, for regional powers, derecognition bolsters geopolitical rivalries.

These divergent views derive also from ambiguities among scholars and a need for more consensus among practitioners on whether diplomatic recognition can be withdrawn, making state derecognition a highly contested concept and unstable practice. The majority of legal scholars perceive state recognition as irreversible. According to this view, when a country is recognized as an independent and sovereign state, it cannot be derecognized as long as the conditions on which the recognition was offered have stayed the same (Lauterpacht 1945; Chen 1951). In other words, as long as the claimant state continues to satisfy the statehood criteria—namely, have an effective authority over a population, a specific territory, an effective and functioning government, and the ability to enter international relations—derecognition should not have any legal and political weight. This position is, however, complicated in cases such as Taiwan and the ambiguities surrounding claims over continuing or titular sovereignty. According to some scholars, even if the original conditions are altered, recognition cannot be revoked because the original act of recognition is declaratory and not a constitutive act of sovereign statehood (Vidmar 2013). Thus, derecognition, in effect, represents discontinuing bilateral relations between states, not the annulment of a claimant state's statehood (James 2016).

Moreover, legal and normative perspectives maintain that the withdrawal of recognition is permissible when a new state emerges through acts of aggression, thus requiring collective nonrecognition or derecognition if deemed necessary to restore the peremptory norms of international law (Raič 2002: 90). The main concern here is the external, illegal use of force, or another form of intervention, in a sovereign state to annex a part of the territory without the consent of the host state or without a justifiable and legitimate case for intervention to prevent a humanitarian crisis that would endanger international peace and stability (Grant 1999: 30). So these exceptions notwithstanding, the recognition of states, in general, is seen as a welcome development in world politics because it contributes to the global expansion of international law's jurisdiction, as well as the promotion of regional stability and conflict resolution (Lauterpacht 1945). In turn, the derecognition of claimant states that do fulfill the criteria for statehood and have a legitimate case for independent statehood is seen as an aggressive, irresponsible, and devastating attack on the rules-based international order, as it results in the expansion of ungoverned territories, regional instability, and fierce rivalry between contender states and global powers. However, another worldview holds that both recognition and derecognition are essential elements in the making and unmaking of independent statehood (Kelsen 1941). Only through recognition can a state-like entity become a sovereign state, and when recognition is withdrawn, it can bring into question the capacity of the claimant state to act as an independent subject in international affairs. In other words, when a country is massively derecognized, its changed status weakens the claimant's ability to engage in diplomatic relations with other states, undermines its interests, excludes its from international bodies, and complicates its ability to perform sovereign equality.

However, state practice does not follow theory regarding state derecognition. Since recognition, nonrecognition, and derecognition remain at the discretion of states, they have autonomy in deciding when to grant, withhold, or withdraw recognition regardless of the presence or absence of statehood criteria (d'Asprement 2012). Through an intertextual and comparative analysis of derecognition discourses, this book finds out that the norms and justifications invoked during the derecognition process are pretentious, two-faced, and inconsistent. There is a mismatch between the criteria and justification of derecognition and the original conditions for recognition. Namely, there is a normative conflict where derecognition becomes a counternorm to the original recognition, significantly when the target state has not changed in some fundamental way. One would expect that since derecognition is the reversal of a previous recognition decision, such a process should demonstrate normative consistency, namely, show that the original conditions for recognition have changed so as to render the process and act of derecognition possible.

In most cases, the original grounds for recognition combine normative, legal, and political conditions, such as the fulfillment of statehood criteria, a desire to establish friendly relations and bilateral cooperation, compliance with international law, and support for the principle of self-determination of peoples, as well as other context-specific circumstances leading to independent statehood. With few exceptions, the overwhelming number of derecognition cases tend to ignore the original conditions for recognition and sometimes invoke norms and rationales that contradict one another. The two dominant norms invoked by derecognizing states include conflict resolution among the contender states and compliance with international norms on statehood, such as the sovereignty and territorial integrity of the former base state. While these arguments carry significant weight, they do not correspond with the reality on the ground and contradict original decisions for recognition. They show that both recognition and derecognition are guided by competing and often incompatible norms, further complicating state derecognition's analytical, normative, and practical properties. Most importantly, these inconsistencies raise questions about derecognition's validity and normative rightness.

The book instead finds that economic benefits, domestic political dynamics, and geopolitical interests play a far more significant role in informing the decisions of third countries on withdrawing recognition than the presence or absence of the original conditions for recognition, such as the statehood capacity of claimant states, international norms, and other bilateral factors. Political systems, religion, collective identity, and geography have little or no effect on derecognition decisions. Thus, what contemporary examples show is that the derecognition of states is not entirely about asserting that a state does not fulfill the core criteria of statehood, nor is it merely an instrument for upholding international institutions and norms on sovereignty and territorial integrity. Instead, the derecognition of states has emerged as a foreign policy instrument for advancing the domestic and international self-interest of the derecognizing states and their international allies. The legal, political, economic, normative, and geopolitical justifications for state derecognition, rather than being based on facts and objective truths, tend to serve as legitimization frameworks to satisfy domestic audiences at home, sponsors, or buyers of derecognition (the former base state and their allies) and international audiences, primarily for reputational damage control and mitigation of potential consequences. These rationales and discourses behind derecognition demonstrate that the politics of recognition often have little to do with the proclaimed norms, principles, and legal rules governing the birth of new states in international society. Political self-interest rather than a principled stance across the board guides derecognition in contemporary state practice. Nonetheless, these justifications offer helpful hints about the patterns in derecognition. Derecognition grounded on outward-looking rationales tends to be more ambiguous and temporary, expressed as suspension or freezing of recognition rather than complete, formal, and definitive withdrawal of recognition. In inward-looking rationales, where derecognition is guided by economic interests, domestic political rivalry, and geopolitical considerations, derecognition tends to be more definitive. It takes the shape of either a complete withdrawal of recognition or a termination of diplomatic relations.

The predominantly inward-looking rationales for justifying the derecognition of states demonstrate the diplomatic hypocrisy of third countries implicated in transactional forms of trading recognition in exchange for material and political security goods without any regard for the damage caused to the derecognized state or geopolitical implications of such decisions. Derecognition, as much as it is a symptomatic feature of diplomatic warfare that undermines contested statehood, is also enabled by the inherent diplomatic cultures of third countries implicated in selling their recognitions or votes in exchange for aid or other specific goods (Thorhallsson and Bailes 2016). While powerful states mostly use recognition as a tool to advance their interests, derecognition is mostly pursued by weak states to compensate for their strategic vulnerabilities in world politics. As much as the former base states try to serve as masters and exploit third countries as their servants in their diplomatic warfare against the claimant state, the third countries often act as masters who turn other contender states into their servants. So state derecognition has effectively become a tool of statecraft for third countries implicated in transactional forms of recognition and derecognition of states. They use it to compensate for their national underdevelopment and perform their sovereignty abroad regardless of the implications for international norms and order. Paradoxically, the same states implicated in trading derecognition for self-interest, which tend to promote self-determination at home, are implicated in promoting anti-self-determination abroad by way of recognizing the sovereignty of the former base state over the claimant state.

The politics of inwardness underpinning most of the decisions for recognition help explain why derecognizing states trade the withdrawal of recognition for political, material, and security interests. First and foremost, third countries (mostly underdeveloped, postcolonial states) perceive their right to establish or break diplomatic relations and simultaneously withhold, grant, or/and withdraw recognition of other states, as a sovereign and exceptional right. They also consider the goods that derive from trading or renting recognition as essential for their socioeconomic development and geopolitical position. Moreover, disregarding diplomatic norms and conventions guiding state relations is also central to their desire to rejuvenate the revolutionary spirit, foregrounded in their historical struggle for independent statehood. In this regard, noncompliance with international norms on state recognition is a response to and rejection of Western-imposed norms on sovereignty and statehood. Third countries strengthen their foreign policy independence by performing the diplomatic ritual of recognition and derecognition, thus empowering themselves as sovereign actors. Finally, the overwhelming number of derecognizing states are semi-authoritarian or undemocratic, whose unprincipled, untransparent, and compromised foreign policy derives from their domestic political culture and governance. Thus, by denying recognition, third countries constitute themselves as international actors (Weber 1994).

In sum, state derecognition epitomizes three denials and discordances in world politics. First, it remains underexplored at the epistemic level and denied, mainly by legal scholars, as a viable and acceptable diplomatic practice. Second, at the political level, derecognition is denied by the claimant state as a possible and actual occurrence, which highlights various reasons why such a practice is dubious, especially when the original conditions for recognition are intact and there hasn't been a change in the effective functioning of the state. Moreover, derecognition doesn't dismantle independent statehood, as that would legitimize external denial of self-determination. Third, at the operational level and in denial of the first two denials, the former base state, through third countries pursues the derecognition of the claimant state to deny the latter self-determination, diplomatic equality, and normal access to international resources, events, and organizations and thus render its sovereign statehood dysfunctional. Third countries, through the political discretion of granting, withholding, or withdrawing recognition, perform their foreign policy self-determination at the expense of the claimant state's self-determination. So at the heart of derecognition as diplomatic hypocrisy, there are multiple denialisms and self-determinations: between reason and experience, between desirability and actuality of diplomatic relations, and between intentions and effects. This multiplicity of denialisms and incongruences doesn't support friendship among nations; on the contrary, it contributes to anti-diplomatic relations centered on estrangement and outrage.

The Process and Tactics of State Derecognition

The second theme of this book concerns the tactics and strategies contender states pursue to reverse the recognition of claimant states. Although the derecognition of states is not guided by clear rules and norms but by political expediency and arbitrary actions of states, there are patterned practices that help us make sense of it. Just as they can withhold or grant recognition to new states, third states can also withdraw it and reinstate it. We have examples of a claimant state that has been recognized, derecognized, and re-recognized at least three times. State derecognition resembles the steps undertaken in the struggle to secure diplomatic recognition, but in reverse order, demonstrating that statehood, sovereignty, and international legitimation are dynamic (Kyris 2022). The recognition process, in the first place, involves gradual lobbying and investment in shifting the position of third countries from complete estrangement and nonrecognition to informal interactions and institutional engagement until formal recognition is granted (Visoka 2018; Newman and Visoka 2018a). In the reversal of this order, the process of derecognition moves from formal recognition to ambivalent forms of diplomatic disengagement and gradual estrangement to the formal end of diplomatic relations. While the relationship between the claimant state and third countries can be located in any of these stages or trajectories of diplomatic relations, they are temporal and subject to change due to foreign policy frictions or external interventions by other contender states. In this sense, the process of recognition and derecognition shows patterns of advancement and reversal of diplomatic ties, making diplomatic recognition, nonrecognition, derecognition, and re-recognition a complex and intricate open-ended loop with multiple possibilities that underpin interstate relations. For instance, since many countries tend to reverse their derecognition decisions—sometimes in a matter of days if not months or years—it can be claimed that derecognition is a temporary political decision, more like a de facto act of derecognition than a permanent one. While the process of derecognition, especially the forward-backward nature of diplomatic relations, gives the sense of a path that can be traveled in two directions, the campaign for derecognition itself exposes how fluid the process of derecognition can be. It is a process that cannot be predefined but is determined in practice by combining multiple interplaying actors and factors.

The first phase in the process of derecognition is domestic and international contestation of the claimant state's sovereignty and independence. It involves a range of diplomatic actions that the former base states take to try to prevent the recognition, retain nonrecognition, or reverse the recognition of the new claimant state. The contestation starts at home, where the former base state seeks to undermine the empirical sovereignty of the claimant state by causing political, legal, economic, and security blockages to the normal functioning of the society (Ker-Lindsay 2012; Ojeda-Garcia et al. 2017). This effort involves delegitimizing and questioning the historical, legal, and factual grounds for statehood and misrecognizing the agency of the political leadership and the community at large seeking independent statehood. The domestic contestation of the claimant states varies from one case to another. However, it often involves maintaining an administrative and military presence in certain parts of the claimant's territory, manipulating kin ethnic minorities, or blocking free movement across the contested border, increasing pressure for democratic change by discriminating against the secessionist community and supporting a new community of settlers, who usually come from the territory of the former base state. The former host state also seeks to constrain the claimant state by blocking strategic economic routes, prosecuting the political leadership and pro-independence activists, and appropriating and exploiting resources. Internationally, the former base state frequently uses its diplomatic network, its presence within multilateral organizations, and its strategic relationships with influential states to prevent the claimant state from gaining diplomatic recognition, participating in or joining regional or international bodies, or strengthening its international standing by other means. State contestation also involves exploiting international legal instruments to prohibit the claimant state from accessing the international community. Thus, the first feature of the derecognition campaign is the maintenance of abnormal relations with the claimant state to ensure that the claimant state's sovereignty is contested and challenged at home and abroad. It involves deploying counter-secession measures (Griffiths and Muro 2020), which first and foremost combine diplomatic and anti-diplomatic methods for undermining the consolidation of the claimant state's domestic and international sovereignty to preserve the base state's territorial integrity, at least for symbolic and strategic purposes.

The second phase in the process of state derecognition involves persuading other states to rethink their position on the claimant state. An initial sign of derecognition is when third countries issue antagonistic statements on the claimant state, avoid diplomatic interactions, or flirt diplomatically with the former base state. In other words, the third countries refuse to establish diplomatic relations with the claimant state, ignoring the request for accreditation of ambassadors and abstaining from voting or voting against the claimant state in international organizations. The former host states use political, economic, and diplomatic methods to bargain for the derecognition of the claimant state. This campaign often entails providing economic and development assistance, deepening bilateral military and security cooperation, and defending mutual interests within multilateral organizations. Corruption, sabotage, and manipulation are also common anti-diplomatic tactics that the former base state uses to persuade third countries to reconsider their position on the claimant state. Consequently, the desire of the former base state to offer economic incentives in exchange for derecognition has encouraged several impoverished, postcolonial states to take advantage of this situation and bargain with the highest bidder for a reversal of recognition.

In most cases, state derecognition occurs through secret diplomacy, characterized by "the total isolation and exclusion of the media and the public from negotiations and related policy-making" (Gilboa 1998: 213). Corneliu Bjola (2014: 88–89) shows that beyond its benefits in limited instances, secret diplomacy can deepen the distrust between states, tarnish the reputation of diplomatic actors and states, and, most importantly, undermine fundamental norms and principles of democratic rules as well as norms governing diplomatic relations between states. Although the former base state is often behind the campaign for derecognition, third countries tend also to lead the process guided by their foreign policy of trading or renting recognition in exchange for personal, economic, and security goods. Despite such incentives, this phase in the derecognition process can be lengthy, costly, and unpredictable. It can take many years of political and economic investment and the involvement of significant powers to persuade countries to rethink their decision and consider the derecognition of another state. In some instances, although the lobbying campaign does not result in full and formal derecognition of the claimant state, it results in freezing recognition and downgrading bilateral relations, which can be manifested by reduced bilateral contacts and the absence of support in multilateral forums.

The third phase in the derecognition process involves reconsidering and taking actions regarding the recognition of the claimant states, which can take the shape of downgrading and severing diplomatic contacts, cutting off bilateral and multilateral cooperation, freezing recognition, or adopting a neutral position. Thus, the gradual suspension of diplomatic relations takes the shape of "recognition without engagement," which entails taking an ambiguous position of neither fully withdrawing recognition nor maintaining normal diplomatic contacts. Such an ambivalent position is often justified as a cooling-off period and a measure to encourage disputants to resolve the self-determination conflict through peaceful dialogue. In other instances, a similar anti-diplomatic discourse is invoked, labeled as freezing the recognition, which entails "abnormalization" of diplomatic relations for an undefined period. This entails reverting to a de facto nonrecognition and neutral position pending dispute resolution. Diplomatic systems are characterized by a repertoire of diplomatic languages designed to "minimize misunderstandings and miscalculations that give rise to conflict" (Oglesby 2016: 244). During this phase, the announcement of diplomatic disengagement contains a vague language of duplicity and often is filled with factually inaccurate details (supplied by the sponsors of derecognition), which ultimatelys tend to maximize misunderstandings and miscalculations and aggrieve rather than settle diplomatic disputes between the claimant entity and the former base state. While these intermediary variants of diplomatic disengagement lack clear policy and a legal basis, they nonetheless play in favor of the former base state and put pressure on the claimant state to downgrade its ambitions for integration in the international system and, in turn, give concessions in peace talks. In most cases, though, such intermediary disengagement prepares the grounds and boosts the cost of full withdrawal of recognition.

The fourth and final phase in the derecognition process involves formal and explicit withdrawal of recognition and the ending of official diplomatic relations. In most cases, derecognition is formalized by sending a note verbale to the former base state, either reaffirming the recognition of its sovereignty over the contested territory or taking a neutral stance pending the peaceful resolution of the sovereignty dispute. However, it is not uncommon for the derecognizing state to directly send the notice of the withdrawal of recognition to the claimant state. Countries involved in renting recognition, however, seem intentionally to frame their decision (to recognize or derecognize) in vague, ambiguous language to keep open the option of switching to the highest bidder. Often the power to recognize or derecognize states is not explicitly enshrined in domestic legislation, and this is used as a pretext for making uncoordinated decisions on sensitive foreign policy matters. In most cases, such a decision is taken by either the president or the government, depending on which has constitutional power in foreign affairs. Hence the derecognition of states tends to spark domestic political disputes within the derecognizing states. Following the withdrawal of recognition, claimant states usually face a dilemma about how to respond. Their retaliatory opportunities following derecognition are limited. Apart from expressing regret and cutting diplomatic ties, claimant states are often vulnerable and restricted in what they can do in return. However, the failure of the claimant state to have more sovereign agency is often turned into inspiration for democratization and development at home and contribution to common goods internationally (Epstein, Lindemann, and Sending 2018). In most cases, the international community remains silent, and an organized reaction or sanctions against the derecognizing states or their patron state are unlikely and unexpected. For claimant states, the struggle for recognition, as much as it brings collective anxiety to the claimant state, also becomes a constitutive feature of their identity and how they act internationally. To counter their derecognition, claimant states and their international allies use a wide range of foreign policy instruments, such as offering technical or economic assistance, as well as leveraging their special relations with influential states. However, formal withdrawal of recognition does not necessarily mean the end of diplomatic contacts between the protagonist states. The decision for derecognition can be revoked and the previous diplomatic relations retained, or afresh recognition could take place at a later stage. This is a common practice among third countries who consider state recognition to be a diplomatic transaction, a commodity that can be sold to the highest bidder.

In sum, these four phases show that state derecognition is a complex and intricate process that is not guided by clear rules and norms. It involves a range of diplomatic actions that the former base states take to prevent recognition, retain nonrecognition, or reverse the recognition of the new claimant state. The process can involve domestic contestation of the claimant state's sovereignty and independence and international lobbying and persuasion of third countries to rethink their position on the claimant state. This can mean the downgrading or of severing diplomatic contacts, cutting off bilateral and multilateral cooperation, freezing recognition, or adopting a neutral position. Ultimately, the process can involve the formal and explicit withdrawal of recognition and the ending of official diplomatic relations. While derecognition can have serious implications for the claimant state, the process is often reversible, and recognition can be reinstated later.

The Effects and Implications of State Derecognition

The third theme of this book concerns the effects of state derecognition on protagonist states and broader implications for international order. Mutual recognition of states is seen as a foundational principle of the rules-based international order. The book finds that derecognition is a norm-breaking practice that undermines the foundational norms and institutions of international diplomacy, statehood, and recognition. While international norms on diplomatic recognition have never enjoyed global acceptance, they have helped guide the state responses to state creation and have promoted a sense of common purpose by trying to base decisions for recognition on the criteria of effectiveness and legitimacy (Nicholson and Grant 2020). Whereas the function of state recognition is to declare that a political entity fulfills the conditions of statehood and contributes to the consolidation of statehood, the function of state derecognition is to deny and object that the said entity fulfills the conditions of statehood. It is part of the counter-secession strategy to make the new state unviable and failed (Oltramonti 2020). Like non-consensual secession, the reversibility of the recognition of states represents a fundamental challenge to the international order. The analyses in this book show that derecognition as a renegade counternorm and anti-diplomatic practice is prone to producing far-reaching political, legal, economic, and geopolitical consequences that affect the protagonist states and often implicates global powers. In the worst-case scenario, it can be a prelude to war.

State derecognition contributes to international disorder in five inter-linked ways. First, the process leading to derecognition disrupts normal diplomatic relations between states. It undermines the prospects of the claimant state for full integration into the international system. It inhibits its prospects for cultivating bilateral relations with other states, especially with those third states indicating or committing to the contestation, suspension, freezing, or full withdrawal of original decision for recognition. Second, derecognition contributes to international instability since the claimant state and its allies perceive it as an act of diplomatic aggression, which often results in deepening hostilities, undermining any effort toward conflict resolution and normalization of relations with the former base state. Such hostilities often implicate major powers and bolster regional rivalries, which in turn can threaten the protagonist states and the wide region. At least in the three out of five cases examined in this book, derecognition has been a prelude to the return of hostilities and hybrid warfare. Third, since derecognition is unregulated in the international system, it creates international legal and diplomatic uncertainty. It contributes to hollowing out diplomatic rules and relations among states. In other words, it weakens the application of international law, widens the estrangement and hostility between protagonist states, blurs the lines between friendly and enemy nations, and enhances the chances for diplomatic and military confrontation. Fourth, derecognition involves secret and dubious transactions, including corruption, deception, and manipulation. This contributes to breaching and disregarding the ethics, norms, and principles governing good and friendly relations between states. Finally, since derecognition is driven by political expediency and not principled stances, it undermines international institutions, laws, conventions, and authorities, which in turn promotes unilateralism at the expense of multilateralism. This in turn weakens the very institutions established to protect small states, especially those implicated in the derecognition of states, against the predatory actions of major powers.

In a narrow sense, state derecognition is an anti-diplomatic practice because it often involves abrupt and unannounced decisions to derecognize the claimant state and simultaneously involves secret negotiations and dubious dealings with the former base states without consultation with the government and diplomats of the derecognized state. The campaign for derecognition tends to ignore the official channels of communication, dialogue, and negotiation. It involves subversive and corruptive means to influence foreign policy decisions. Accordingly, the campaign for derecognition resembles diplomatic warfare, which entails perverting the original functions of diplomacy by using conflictual politics, deception, material incentives, and alliances to pursue political warfare. Derecognition as anti-diplomacy represents "war-by-other-means, practices that do violence" (Hall 2006: 150). In more moderate terms, the campaign for derecognition is subversive diplomacy that involves breaking diplomatic standards, using secret tactics and incentives, and co-opting the foreign policy of third countries so as to delegitimize the claimant state (Sharp 2009). The rationale for such a diplomatic war is evident. In the existing world order, former base states are strongly discouraged from taking back control over their lost territory through coercive methods. The norm of self-defense is not supported in the aftermath of losing territory. Exceptions, however, are re-emerging. Russia's violent occupation of Crimea, China's territorial claims over the South China Sea, and the United States' controversial recognition of Israel's claim over the Golan Heights and recognition of Morocco's occupation of Western Sahara are all examples involving extralegal territorial acquisitions (Paris 2020). However, such extralegal exceptionality is impossible for middle-range or small powers with territorial disputes or breakaway regions. Thus, they revert to the diplomacy of counter-recognition and derecognition as an optimal method to continue making claims over the claimant state's territory. It is a quest to maintain symbolic sovereignty over the claimant state. In this sense, derecognition is a type of externally infused state weakening, which is not entirely determined by the domestic lack of statehood capacity but is instead imposed from outside to prevent state consolidation.

In the broader sense, state derecognition is an anti-diplomatic practice because it undermines the entire spectrum of the conventional diplomatic system and contravenes legal and judicious conventions governing interstate relations. If recognition that precedes the establishment of "diplomatic relations is the key which opens the door to easy and straightforward interstate contact" (James 2016: 258), then the withdrawal of recognition that precedes the termination of diplomatic relations is the lock that closes the door to easy and straightforward interstate contact. In essence, derecognition undermines the core norms and standards of diplomatic recognition and the establishment of friendly relations among nations. It contributes to the emergence of multiple discontinued, disengaged, and pluriversal worlds. It deepens the estrangement between peoples and nations, and it promotes animus rather than friendly relations, which endangers international peace and security. It breaches the foundational norms of international relations, such as sovereign equality and noninterference in the internal affairs of sovereign states. It contravenes the principles of estoppel, which require states to respect international norms and rules consistently. State derecognition as a unilateral breach of a bilateral treaty (such as the agreement for establishing diplomatic relations) also undermines the principle of good faith in diplomatic relations. In this sense, derecognition, as an anti-diplomatic practice, represents desertion and insubordination from institutionalized and obligatory forms of conventional diplomatic conduct. By challenging these diplomatic norms, derecognizing states become complicit in breaching general international law and contribute to conflictual and unpredictable relations among states. Such anti-diplomatic and norm-breaking conduct with far-reaching and harmful consequences makes states that derecognize and their sponsors renegade-like regimes in the international system (Nincic 2005).

Even with these concerns, the withdrawal of recognition does not instantly result in the factual loss of sovereignty and the independent statehood of a claimant state. The derecognition of states that continue to satisfy both objective and subjective criteria of statehood supports the claims of the declaratory theory, which considers state existence to be independent of external recognition. However, derecognition by default can lead to diplomatic isolation, domestic political turmoil, limited access to international bodies, exposure to external interference, and collective insecurity. In this sense, derecognition can become a delegitimizing feature, undermining the claimant state's domestic and international sovereignty. The diplomatic isolation that may result from derecognition undermines claimant states' ontological security and national identity, reducing incumbent governments' authority and undermining both domestic and regional stability. Derecognition can sometimes prolong undemocratic rule and an ongoing state of emergency within claimant states, such as the Western Sahara. In other instances, derecognition tends to improve the democratic performance of the claimant state. In the cases of Taiwan and Kosovo, for example, it has positively affected the democratization process, forcing targeted states to seek international legitimation based on democratic performance (Caspersen 2012; Visoka 2018).

State derecognition can be seen as the extension of contestation of the claimant state by the former base state and other third countries. By default, the withdrawal of recognition signals that the derecognizing state does not consider the claimant state a subject of international law. Accordingly, it avoids acknowledging or supporting the claimant state's international legal personality in their encounters. Effectively, the derecognition of the claimant state keeps its statehood status unresolved and even more contested. It exposes it to uncertainties about the extent to which and terms under which it can survive, with a threat of extinction as an independent and sovereign state. Derecognition, a deliberate strategy instituted by the former base state and enabled by derecognizing states, tends to weaken the claimant state. Countries affected by derecognition tend to have certain aspects of statehood still under consolidation. Derecognition complicates the efforts of the claimant state to complete state consolidation—namely, the ability to directly govern its territory and represent its interests internationally. In particular, the act and process of derecognition undermine the prospects for the consolidation of international sovereignty, which requires, in the first instance, wide recognition of sovereignty and the ability to establish diplomatic relations and participate in international organizations, as well as become a legal subject and party to international legal, economic, political, security, and sociocultural treaty bodies. In turn, incomplete state consolidation becomes a source of domestic fragility by significantly reducing the ability of the claimant state to provide stability, development, and well-being to its citizens. Consequently, as Peter Radan (2019: 48) states, there is a risk that, without recognition, "the continued viability and survival of a territorial entity as a state is unlikely to be maintained." In this sense, derecognizing states play a direct role in weakening the sovereignty of other states.

State derecognition—motivated by self-interest and performed in disregard for historical and contemporary circumstances that claimant states must address in their quest for self-determination and recognition—contributes neither to international peace and stability nor to the advancement of justice and rights in world politics. On the contrary, such a controversial practice limits the international community's role in resolving statehood and self-determination disputes and gives the former base state greater scope for behaving aggressively toward the claimant state and its subjects. While former base states and their international allies tend to invest significant legal and political capital in the withdrawal of recognition, the claimant state and its international allies tend to downplay its significance and impact. However, contemporary state practice decisively shows that derecognition undermines the claimant state's international standing. It prevents the claimant state from having normal diplomatic and economic relations and impedes its participation and membership in international and regional organizations. In particular, state derecognition limits the claimant state's chances of establishing diplomatic contacts, building consular services abroad, concluding bilateral agreements, traveling abroad, and making trade deals. Contrary to references to peaceful resolution of disputes, derecognition deepens counter-peace dynamics and contributes to the re-escalation of hostilities because it legitimizes the interference of the former base state in the internal affairs of the claimant state. In this regard, derecognizing states become complicit in pushing for internalization rather than the internationalization of self-determination disputes, which reduces the ability of the international community to contribute to conflict resolution, protection of human rights, and provision of foreign aid and assistance to the affected population.

Derecognition has far-reaching consequences, not only for the derecognized states but also for those derecognizing them. In an attempt to either retain or withdraw recognition, foreign states tend to use domestic political rivalry between the derecognizing states to further their foreign policy interests. This can undermine democratic processes, nurture corruption, and promote the hostile conduct of foreign policy. As external actors incentivize derecognition, it can destabilize and undermine the sovereignty of the derecognizing state by allowing external countries to influence their domestic democratic processes and foreign policy. The struggle to retain or withdraw diplomatic recognition directly impacts the longevity of authoritarian leaders, promotes corruption and the misuse of foreign aid, and results in external interference in democratic processes (Tudoroiu 2017: 209). As leading states engaged in switching diplomatic recognition often endure chronic poverty by withdrawing their recognition of nascent states, they risk provoking a humanitarian crisis locally. When tracing the effects of derecognition, this practice neither resolves self-determination conflicts nor reduces the risk of creating new conditions of fragility inside claimant states and their wider region. On the contrary, derecognition can have a spillover effect that undermines efforts to normalize relations between the parties in conflict and deepens great power rivalries. It creates territorial zones ungoverned by international law and encourages predatory, clientelist, and illicit transnational practices. The derecognition of states poses challenges to the domestic stability of claimant states and tends to affect regional peace and broader international stability. It is also a contagious practice that expands not only among contested states but also among UN member states. For example, following Russia's aggression war against Ukraine, in 2022, Russian Duma discussed a draft bill on the derecognition of Lithuania (TASS 2022). In November 2022, Australia reversed its previous decision to recognize Jerusalem as Israel's capital (Slonim 2022).

Recognition is essential not only for the aspirant state but also for existing states because recognizing other states is the very act that constitutes international society—namely, the collective features that unite and differentiate sovereign states (Visoka 2018). However, when states withdraw the recognition of other states, they risk promoting international disorder and thus unmaking foundational principles of international society. The economic bribery and military interests involved in state derecognition significantly undermine the values, norms, and principles governing matters of statehood in the international community. Derecognizing states may constitute delinquency by emphasizing self-interest rather than shared interests such as peace, justice, and development and disassembling international norms, institutions, and rules governing diplomatic relations. While diplomatic recognition was invented by Western colonial powers keen to exert control over their former colonial subjects and determine which had the chance to become a sovereign state (Ringmar 2014; Anghie 2004), nowadays, derecognition has become a common practice among underdeveloped postcolonial states in Latin America, Africa, and the Pacific.

So checkbook diplomacy and rental recognition are not sustainable practices, as they turn international recognition into a tradable diplomatic commodity that can be shifted depending on self-interest, government change, or the highest bidder. Switching recognition is purely a product of domestic politics and economic incentives. The diplomacy that dictates retaining or switching recognition is highly unpredictable, corruptive, and prone to promoting domestic and international instability. The abuse of state derecognition risks reducing recognition from being an essential feature of external certification and the acceptance of new states in international society to be a politically and economically motivated foreign policy instrument of states. Derecognition promotes international disorder by emphasizing self-interest rather than shared interests such as peace, justice, and development, as well as by disassembling the international norms, institutions, and rules governing diplomatic relations, including by disregarding the rules of proper diplomatic behavior, exploiting vulnerabilities, and promoting unfair terms in relationships. Moreover, the derecognition of states for political self-interest amounts to unilateral interference in the normal functioning of fledgling states. It can amount to indirect participation in the conflict between the claimant and base states. States that constantly rent diplomatic recognition have become pariahs that constitute a source of disorder in international society. Therefore, it seems reasonable to suggest that the derecognition of states for domestic selfish, political, or economic interests, with no regard for the norms, values, or principles of statehood in world politics, may amount to international delinquency.

State derecognition can be considered an arbitrary practice that can have far-reaching political, economic, legal, and geopolitical consequences. Derecognition as an anti-diplomatic practice not only undermines the prospects of the claimant state for full integration in the international system but also limits its ability to establish diplomatic relations and participate in international organizations. Derecognition also contributes to the emergence of multiple discontinuous, disengaged world orders, deepening the estrangement between peoples and nations and promoting animus rather than friendly relations, thus endangering international peace and security. Moreover, derecognition can destabilize and undermine the sovereignty of derecognizing states by subsidizing government work through renting recognitions or derecognition. It can encourage predatory, clientelist, and illicit transnational practices and have a spillover effect that undermines efforts to normalize relations between the parties in conflict and triggers regional tensions. In this sense, derecognition has unwanted effects on the derecognized states and those implicated in derecognizing them.

The Way Forward

The final theme of this book explores the prospects for regulating the derecognition of states in the international system. Currently, both the recognition and derecognition of states remain at the discretion of existing sovereign states, and there needs to be a consensus on the conditions that should guide both practices (French 2013; Ninet 2024). The book argues that the lack of a legal and institutional regime that regulates which entities should be recognized or derecognized as a sovereign state has resulted in the emergence of a dysfunctional state expansion system forcing, first and foremost, many ethnic groups to use both violent and nonviolent methods to create their independent state, and also exposing existing states to the practice of derecognition (Naticchia 2016; White, Cunningham, and Beardsley 2018). At its core, state derecognition exposes and deepens the conflict between diplomatic norms on the irreversibility of statehood and recognition and the discretion of states to conduct their foreign affairs independently. It deepens the conflict between the norms of self-determination and territorial integrity. The derecognition of the claimant states has become a political battlefield for conflicting great power agendas and proxy wars. Powerful states—such as the United States, China, and Russia—often take opposing sides in self-determination conflicts, which contributes to the creation of stalemates and protracted conflicts (Coggins 2014; Chiang and Hwang 2008). The main protagonists of derecognition aren't great powers but small number of postcolonial and undeveloped states that exploit loopholes in the system to their advantage and turn their sovereign statehood into a tradable asset in exchange for economic and security goods. While diplomatic recognition emerged as part of the European state-making process and later as an instrument of colonial powers to exert control over their colonial subjects and determine which had the chance to become a sovereign state, nowadays derecognition has become a common practice among underdeveloped postcolonial states in Latin America, Africa, and the Pacific. The oppressed have become oppressors. While the international recognition regime has been mostly guided by discretionary conduct of states, the lack of clearer guidelines on derecognition has left room for third states to exploit such loopholes for their own benefit. Arbitrary conduct of states, such as the withdrawal of recognition, often serves as a gateway for identifying different pathways for regulating state recognition and derecognition in practice. Thus, this book examines three potential options for regulating derecognition in the international system: through existing UN multilateral mechanisms, an incremental and bottom-up process, and the sanctioning of unjustified derecognition.

The first option would be to regulate both the recognition and derecognition of states within existing UN multilateral mechanisms or through a parallel norm-building process. It would require a mandate from the UN General Assembly or the UN Security Council followed up with resolutions, periodic reports, and high-level policy debates, similar to other major topics such as the right to self-determination, peacebuilding, protection of civilians, and other international norms. Such a process would require wide international consensus on defining statehood, who is entitled to state recognition, and whether and under what conditions nonrecognition and derecognition would be permittable. While both the League of Nations and the United Nations have played an essential role in shaping the norms and politics of state recognition—through their legal opinions and responses to specific cases, including the criteria for admission and exclusion of member states—neither has been able to develop a normative and legal corpus and an institutional mechanism on legislating and adjudicating matters concerning the recognition and derecognition of states. So there is little hope that the international community will generate sufficient political will in the near future to regulate the recognition and derecognition of states in world politics. Nonetheless, such a process remains a possibility, especially if the recognition and derecognition of states become a major cause of the escalation of protracted self-determination conflicts, which are present but need to be acknowledged sufficiently.

While the chances for regulating state recognition through legal and institutional mechanisms remain slim, there should be a search for alternative solutions to reduce arbitrary derecognition by states and ensure that such anti-diplomatic practices do not remain a black hole in international law and an unpredictable, destabilizing foreign policy instrument. The second option is regulating state recognition and derecognition through an incremental and bottom-up process. Such an arrangement would seek to tame forces that want to approach state derecognition through the prism of hegemony or multilateralism (Bower 2017). Initially, such a process can take the shape of voluntary and normative guidelines adopted by like-minded states on the meaning and procedures of state recognition and derecognition. It could be attached to existing policy and institutional mechanisms or operate as a new stand-alone process. Numerous similar norm-building processes exist in peace, conflict, human rights, and democracy studies (Risse, Ropp, and Sikkink 1999). Such anti-derecognition norm would aim to raise international awareness of the impact of the practice in world politics and set standards by which to assess and examine individual cases.

The option of scraping entirely the practice of state recognition and derecognition in world politics is problematic despite its potential effect of minimizing the interference of other states in the sovereign matters of states. The third and minimalist option could take the shape of scrutinizing the justification of state derecognition and considering sanctioning the premature and unprincipled withdrawal of recognition. Although derecognition is likely to remain at the discretion of states and driven by political expediency, improving the justification, deliberation, and transparency of derecognition and offering informed and well-analyzed legal and political arguments would enhance clarity and reduce the hypocrisies surrounding the process of derecognition. It would also pressure third countries implicated in transactional recognition and derecognition of states to rethink their foreign policy conduct and avoid causing international harm.

However, as derecognition seems primarily driven by economic self-interest, with far-reaching consequences, another option would be to sanction the irresponsible derecognition of states by withdrawing recognition from those that abuse their discretionary right to recognize or derecognize other states. Grounds for derecognizing states can be found in the very practice of the collective nonrecognition of states, which sanctions aggressive acts perpetrated by them. As will be shown in the remainder of the book, the derecognition of states is destabilizing not only for the claimant state but also for the derecognizing states themselves and the wider international community. Hence, states that offer recognition for rent out of self-interest are unlikely to be peace-loving nations. Unjustified and unprincipled derecognition could be considered an act of aggression against the claimant state and international peace and stability. From this point of view, the derecognition of states that fulfill the criteria for statehood and can make a legitimate case for independent statehood represents an aggressive, irresponsible, and devastating attack on the international rules-based order, as it results in the expansion of ungoverned territories, regional instability, and increased rivalry between dominant powers. In other words, unjustifiable derecognition may breach the fundamental norms of international society—namely noninterference in other states' affairs, international peace and stability, justice, and order. While there is no policy debate on regulating both the regulation and the derecognition of states, the conceptual, normative, and empirical aspects discussed in the remainder of the book will help advance knowledge on and responses to this critical yet underexplored topic.

THE OUTLINE

This book comprises five substantial chapters organized around the key themes outlined above. Chapter 2 ("Conceptualizing State Derecognition") examines existing legal, normative, and political perspectives on the derecognition of states across disciplinary debates in international law and politics. Although derecognition features only a little in most legal or normative perspectives, a thorough reading of the existing literature shows no consensus on whether states can be derecognized or on the conditions under which a reversal of recognition would be permissible. The first section of the chapter surveys three significant perspectives on the derecognition of states, critically examining the competing views that are positioned on a continuum: (1) those that argue recognition cannot be withdrawn; (2) those that claim statehood can be reversed and recognition can be withdrawn; and (3) those that adopt a more neutral and indeterministic view, considering the practice a discretionary right of states. The second section of the chapter outlines the conceptual framework and the research approach adopted in this book for tracing derecognition in practice.

Chapter 3 ("The Process of State Derecognition") explores the core diplomatic efforts, tactics, and stages employed by the former base states, the powerful external actors, and the derecognizing states in revoking the recognition of states. The chapter first sets out the conceptual contours for exploring derecognition as a performative process that takes place simultaneously with and through similar mechanisms (but in reverse order) as the struggle of claimant states for international recognition. The analysis then focuses on four major phases of state recognition, mainly drawing on contemporary examples of derecognition. The chapter first examines the domestic and international contestation of the claimant state, which foregrounds the entire derecognition process and the responses of third countries. What follows is a discussion of legal, political, economic, and military efforts to persuade third states to rethink their position on the claimant state. The chapter then looks at the third phase in the derecognition process, which involves severing diplomatic contacts, cutting off bilateral cooperation, freezing recognition, and adopting a neutral position. The chapter then looks at the crucial phase in the process of derecognition of states: the formal and explicit withdrawal of recognition, which involves a formal announcement of the end of diplomatic relations between the derecognizing and the derecognized state. The chapter finally looks at the aftermath of derecognition, which can involve volatile reaction by or silence among the contender states, and examines the prospects for reinstating the original decision of recognition of the claimant state, thus restarting the entire diplomatic relations afresh.

Chapter 4 ("The Rationales for State Derecognition") surveys the public justifications invoked by former base states, derecognizing states, and third countries in the process of derecognition of claimant states. The chapter examines the five most common rationales that are invoked by states for the derecognition of states. The rationales are divided into two main categories, which capture the inward-looking and internal determinant of derecognition among the third countries implicated in the derecognition of other states. The chapter examines three main inward-looking rationales: economic benefits, domestic political dynamics, and geopolitical interests. The second section of the chapter examines the outward-looking rationales, which include framing derecognition as motivated by the desire for conflict resolution and compliance with international norms and laws on statehood. The chapter interrogates these rationales for derecognition by comparing the original rationales for recognition, those propagated by the former base states, and the facts on the ground to expose their validity and justifiability.

Chapter 5 ("The Effects of State Derecognition") examines the effects of the withdrawal of recognition for the claimant states, former base states, derecognizing states, and other involved regional powers. First and foremost, the chapter examines the spectrum of political, legal, economic, and human consequences of derecognition for the claimant state. It sheds light on the diplomatic constraints and domestic turmoil that the derecognition process poses for the claimant state's leaders and government. The chapter probes the correlation between the desired outcomes for derecognition (stipulated in the form of rationales and justifications for derecognition) and the actual effects, in particular the extent to which derecognition as diplomatic pressure contributes to resolving or escalating conflict. The practice of derecognition has domestic ramifications for the derecognizing state, too. So the second section of this chapter examines how derecognition can destabilize and undermine the sovereignty of the derecognizing state by allowing external countries to influence their domestic democratic processes and foreign policy. The third and final section of this chapter explores how derecognition is entangled with the existing rivalries of dominant and rising powers and how it bolsters tensions and competition among powerful states and feeds into their hegemonic tendencies.

Finally, Chapter 6 ("Conclusion: Rethinking State Derecognition") offers critical reflections on the politics and impact of derecognition in the existing international order and offers policy-relevant observations that may result in regulating state recognition in law and practice. This concluding chapter weighs different policy measures that could tackle the problem of derecognition, ranging from full institutional regulation to a collective and voluntary system. It looks at existing and new institutional and normative mechanisms that could play a role in regulating this anti-diplomatic practice. It does so by tracing legal and policy thinking on this matter and exploring various policy pathways that could reduce abuses of state derecognition.

2 ✦ Conceptualizing State Derecognition

One of the most underexplored issues in statehood and recognition studies is the revocability of diplomatic recognition of states. While there is extensive research on the politics, norms, legality, and ethics of state recognition, there is as yet no in-depth work exclusively dedicated to state derecognition. Over time, the practice of recognition has emerged in different varieties and modes, such as de facto or de jure recognition, express or implied, formal or premature, and bilateral or collective recognition. These different forms of recognition are widely studied in international law, political studies, and other associated disciplines and debates. Similarly, the concept of nonrecognition, that is, the decision of states not to extend recognition to another state for bilateral or collective reasons, has received wide attention. Emerging between the concepts of recognition and nonrecognition, the concept of engagement without recognition recently has signified situations wherein third countries build informal and pragmatic relations with the claimant state but stop short of extending formal diplomatic recognition.

In this pool of concepts and practices, the concept of state derecognition remains largely overlooked. State derecognition is an umbrella term that describes a spectrum of actions encompassing suspending, freezing, rescinding, or formally withdrawing the recognition of claimant states. However, we have limited knowledge about it both as a heuristic device and as a highly contested diplomatic practice. This chapter offers a conceptual scoping of derecognition. It first surveys existing scholarly perspectives on derecognition and outlines dominant views on the topic. The corpus of legal, doctrinal, and normative thinking on the irrevocability of state recognition provides valuable evidence and a starting point for laying out the diplomatic codes that states are expected to adhere to, as well as examining their breaches in retrospect. A thorough examination of the existing literature shows that there is no consensus on whether states can be derecognized. Nor is there a consensus on the conditions under which a reversal of recognition would be permissible. So far, international law has been the main intellectual domain for examining the derecognition of states. Diplomatic studies or international relations debates overlook the intellectual contours of state derecognition and primarily focus on specific case studies. A significant number of scholars, mostly legal scholars, argue against the revocability of state recognition. For them, neither recognition nor derecognition by third countries is the primary determinant of independent and sovereign statehood. Recognition is merely an acknowledgment and ritual in the process of establishing diplomatic relations. This scholarly camp highlights that the most stable norm governing the recognition of states since the nineteenth century has been the recognition of de facto statehood and the effectiveness of the exercise of sovereign authority over a specific territory and population.

While legal and normative perspectives on state derecognition remain underdeveloped and do not engage with contemporary examples and state practices, they highlight that what is proclaimed as withdrawal of recognition is, in fact, discontinuance of bilateral relations. Furthermore, this group of scholars highlights that derecognition would be in breach of norms and rules governing state relations. This includes the principle of good faith and estoppel, which puts the burden on the derecognizing state for failing to administer international law and for contributing to the deterioration of the well-ordered relations with other states. According to this view, once recognition is granted, it cannot be revoked as long as the factual conditions concerning the fulfillment of the core criteria of statehood remain the same. Another normative view holds that derecognition is permitted if the original conditions of recognition cease to exist. In other words, derecognition is permitted when the claimant state loses the attributes of statehood and there are no objective grounds for continuing to recognize it as a state. Adding to this view, the form of recognition can also dictate the prospects for withdrawal of recognition, highlighting that de facto, temporal, or premature recognition can be rescinded, whereas rescinding formal, express, and de jure recognition is unjustifiable.

Other alternative viewpoints highlight that as long as state recognition and derecognition remain unregulated in international law, they will remain discretionary practices that can be invoked for political and geostrategic reasons. In other words, the logic of state derecognition is governed by the legal maxim: that which is not prohibited is permitted. From this point of view, states are free to determine which other states they recognize and derecognize, and that is paradoxically one of the core features of independent statehood, namely the free conduct of foreign affairs. Yet scholars who argue that recognition is constitutive of independent statehood in certain instances also consider the withdrawal of recognition as unraveling or constraining the possibility of exercising independent and sovereign statehood.

These diverse perspectives on state derecognition provide a good starting point for understanding this diplomatic practice, but they are primarily doctrinal assertions, legal-normative opinions, and general political-theoretical observations. They lack an examination of contemporary examples and dynamics of derecognition, which can provide important grounds for expanding our knowledge on this underexplored topic. Thus, the task of the second section of this chapter is to outline a conceptual framework for tracing derecognition in practice and to generate, through a deductive and inductive process, the critical contours of a general theory of derecognition. In order to generate a general understanding of derecognition, a pluralist approach to foreign policy analysis will be deployed to study the actors, processes, rationales, and effects of derecognition. This comprehensive heuristic outlook enables research to move beyond simply questioning whether states can or cannot or should or should not derecognize another state, and instead focus on how derecognition has become a transgressive diplomatic practice. Undertaking a foreign policy analysis of derecognition requires exploring relevant case studies and countries implicated in this diplomatic practice. Thus, the final section of this chapter highlights the methodological and research approach taken in exploring the case-specific, comparative, and general patterns of derecognition in practice.

THE IRREVOCABILITY OF STATE RECOGNITION

The question of whether a state can be derecognized and what implications it has for the independent statehood of the affected state is central to unpacking the puzzling nature of this contested diplomatic practice. The overwhelming majority of scholars argue that once a state has been recognized as sovereign, that decision cannot be withdrawn. The main features of this view are derived from the declaratory theory of recognition. Declaratory theorists hold that the existence of a state is independent of recognition as long as that state fulfills certain substantive criteria. Vincent Lowe (2007: 161) argues: "The declaratory theory is correct . . . it is the most accurate description of what goes on in State practice in relation to the recognition of States." The only function of recognition is to acknowledge the existence of a new state as a subject of international law—not to determine its existence as an independent state. Proponents of this view find support in Articles 3 and 6 of the Montevideo Convention, which refers to the irrevocability of recognition:

> The political existence of the state is independent of recognition by the other states. Even before recognition the state has the right to defend its integrity and independence, to provide for its conservation and prosperity, and consequently to organize itself as it sees fit, to legislate upon its interests, administer its services, and to define the jurisdiction and competence of its courts. . . . The recognition of a state merely signifies that the state which recognizes it accepts the personality of the other with all the rights and duties determined by international law. Recognition is unconditional and irrevocable.

The declaratory view is also endorsed by judicial tribunals and authorities. The Arbitration Commission established by the International Conference on Yugoslavia in 1991 stated in its Opinion No. 1 that "the existence or disappearance of the state is a question of fact" and that "the effects of recognition by other states are purely declaratory." One of the leading scholars on this subject, Ti-Chiang Chen (1951: 259), holds that "existence once acknowledged is acknowledged; there is nothing to withdraw," adding that a state "continues to exist, independently of recognition or the 'withdrawal' of recognition." In other words, the "revocation of recognition does not affect the legal existence of the recognized entity" (Chen 1951: 8). Vincent Lowe (2007: 165) adds: "The road to Statehood is a one-way street. Once an entity has become a State it will remain one, no matter how useless and ineffectual its government might become." This view springs from the fact, as David Raič (2002: 84) maintains, that "recognition does not create the State or its international legal personality, but rather reflects a confirmation of the existence of statehood prior to the act of recognition." The commencement of full independent statehood often corresponds with the proclamation of independence. Similarly, Jure Vidmar (2013: 41) argues, "Once states have acquired statehood, the latter is difficult to lose, even when the Montevideo criteria are no longer met." Other leading international law scholars, such Antonio Cassese (2005: 73), argue that "the act of recognition has no legal effect on the international personality of the entity: it does not confer rights, nor does it impose obligations on it." However, he adds that recognition becomes relevant once granted because "it bars the recognizing State from altering its position and claiming that the new entity lacks statehood" (Cassese 2005: 74). Contemporary scholars such as James Ker-Lindsay (2012: 17) maintain that "recognition does not make a state. It simply represents a particular and formal procedure that allows states to enter into diplomatic relations with one another." To sum up with the influential scholar Hersch Lauterpacht (1945: 180): "Recognition is not a contract or grant. It is a declaration of capacity as determined by objective facts." Stefan Talmon (2005: 125) adds: "The creation of a State cannot be undone by non-recognition alone, and so non-recognition cannot have status-destroying effect either." This is also congruent with majority of political theories of the state, which center statehood attributes on the ability to perform and enforce centralized autonomous power over a specific population and territory (Mann 1984).

Most important, scholars subscribing to the declaratory theory of statehood argue that the derecognition of claimant states does not end their independent statehood. Derecognition, they argue, is a political act that does not presuppose the nonexistence of a state. For example, Lauterpacht (1945: 179) maintains that "the very idea that the legal personality of a State or the representative capacity of its government should be dependent on the continued good will of other States is deemed to be derogatory to the independence and the dignity of the State and inimical to the stability of international relations." Derecognition means that the legal existence of the claimant state vanishes only in relation to a particular derecognizing state. In turn, the claimant state will continue to exist legally concerning other states. This endurance notwithstanding, derecognition may become a contributing factor where the legal existence of the state concerned is questioned in relation to the derecognizing state or other states that endorse the act of derecognition. Unless it is a collective derecognition, which can impact a country's existence severely, a claimant state can endure and continue to benefit from the rights and meet the obligations assumed under international law.

Although there is no legal duty to recognize new states, Ian Brownlie (1982: 209) maintains that "if an entity bears the marks of statehood, other States put themselves legally at risk if they ignore the basic obligations of State relations." Similarly, Philip M. Brown (1942: 107) argues that "whether one likes the situation or not from the political or moral angle, a state is compelled diplomatically or judicially to take notice de facto or de jure of the existence of another state." This implies that states are expected to recognize one another as a prerequisite and foundational feature of international relations. Derecognition, in this instance, would imply setting up impediments to promoting and cultivating relations between states and societies. James Crawford (2007: 21–27) is of a similar view and maintains that "the test for statehood must be extrinsic to the act of recognition . . . [because] the denial of recognition to an entity otherwise qualifying as a State entitles the non-recognizing State to act as if it was not a State—to ignore its nationality, to intervene in its affairs, generally to deny the existence of State rights under international law . . . [which] is unacceptable." Brad Roth adds: "There is no duty to recognise states, but there is a duty to treat such entities as states with regard to their rights, obligations, powers and immunities. States cannot unilaterally change the terms of their legal obligations by refusing to recognize an entity that is generally understood to be a state" (Israel Law Review 2019: 377). The act of derecognition would also contradict the initial decision in favor of recognition. Lauterpacht (1944: 385) argues that "to recognize a community as a State is to declare that it fulfills the conditions of statehood as required by international law." In this regard, once full and formal recognition has been granted and diplomatic relations have been established, derecognition cannot retrospectively undermine statehood (see also Lauterpacht 1947; Grant and Barker 2009).

In particular, the derecognition of states is seen as a counterinitiative in circumstances where a country grants de jure recognition, proceeds to establish diplomatic relations, opens an embassy, and engages in joint political, economic, and sociocultural initiatives (Sharp 2009). According to scholarly views, whereas establishing diplomatic relations signifies recognition, this is different with derecognition. Ending diplomatic relations does not necessarily cast doubts on the state's existence or imply derecognition. As L. F. L. Oppenheim (1996: 177) argues: "Severance of diplomatic relations does not result in withdrawal of recognition." Chen's (1951: 8) perspective on this matter is also instructive:

> Recognition is both a declaration of fact and an expression of the intention to enter into political relations with the Power recognised. As a declaration of fact, it is both irrevocable and incapable of being subject to conditions; as an expression of the intention to enter into

political relations, it is both revocable and capable of being subject to conditions. But in the latter case, revocation of recognition does not affect the legal existence of the recognised entity.

Similarly, Alan James (2016: 257 claims that "a breach of diplomatic relations does not imply the withdrawal of recognition." In an earlier instance, he noted that "unlike recognition, diplomatic relations may be broken, either party having the unilateral right to take such a step" (James 1999: 467). From this perspective, one cannot talk about derecognition, but about a discontinuance of recognition, which is "at issue when a recognized government no longer fulfils the conditions of governmental status, i.e. when it no longer exercises effective control over the State's territory" (Talmon 1993: 262). Warbrick (1981: 569) shares a similar opinion that "unlike recognition, which may not be withdrawn or downgraded on account of the deterioration of the political climate between the two governments, diplomatic relations may be amended or withdrawn altogether in such circumstances." Chen (1951: 262), too, argues that "a State may decide to discontinue relations with another, without the slightest doubt of the latter's existence. Many cases described as 'withdrawals of recognition' in reality belong to this category." Yet it is widely maintained that "only actions unequivocally implying the intention to discontinue recognition, such as the formal or informal recognition of a new regime as the de jure government of the State, may be regarded as constituting informal discontinuance of recognition" (Talmon 1993: 263). Furthermore, even in such circumstances when parties sever diplomatic ties, the existence of the claimant state isn't affected, nor is the legal relationship between derecognizing and derecognized states as established by a treaty (see Wu and Liao 2021). This notwithstanding, the discontinuance of recognition loses its power when the derecognizing state already has diplomatic relations with the former base state. Suppose third countries do not offer dual recognition to the former base state and the new state. In that case, derecognition does retain some significance if it recognizes the authority and sovereignty of the base state over the claimant state. The derecognition of the claimant state would imply the re-recognition of the former base state that was derecognized in the first instance by the recognition of the claimant state.

This corpus of legal and normative thinking on the irreversibility of state recognition goes further to ascertain that the derecognition of states as an anti-diplomatic practice may breach the principle of estoppel in international law. The principle of estoppel disapproves of states' conduct in international relations, which adopt different positions on the same issue without regard to the truth and accuracy of circumstances. Consistency is required when approaching factual and legal situations. Estoppel is a principle of consistency in respecting norms and rules governing state recognition in the international system. Estoppel in the context of state recognition entails restraining from actions that may challenge that which was previously acknowledged (see MacGibbon 1958: 473). Dold (2012: 91–92) maintains that "in international law, if the legal status of an entity has been recognized by an existing state, the latter cannot anymore validly claim otherwise. Recognition therefore creates an estoppel." Corbett (1951: 61) adds that "recognition becomes a matter of evidence and, perhaps, estoppel. . . . If a number of important States had recognised a given community, either by explicit declaration or by the implication of their relations with it, this recognition created at least a rebuttable presumption of statehood and personality." Cassese (2005: 74) confirms this point when he argues that "recognition is legally relevant in that, once granted, it bars the recognizing State from altering its position and claiming that the new entity lacks statehoods. In other words, the granting of recognition creates an estoppel precluding the recognizing State from contesting the legal personality of the new State." Estoppel in this instance, as Cassese (2005: 74) explains, bars a party "from alleging or denying a fact or claiming a right, to detriment of another party entitled to reply upon such conduct in consequence of previous allegation, denial, or conduct, or admission by the former party." Similarly, Georg Schwarzenberger (1955: 316) argues that "irrespective of any other criterion, recognition estops the State which has recognized the title from contesting its validity at any future time." In other words, this doctrine, if and when applied to the practice of derecognition, would preclude derecognizing states from unprincipled, political, and selective withdrawal of recognition of other states. Recognition is binding and becomes a legal principle guiding the relations between states.

Derecognition undermines the need for predictability and the conduct of state relations in good faith and precludes the normal functioning of relations between states. Derecognition may be inconsistent with the principle of the sovereign equality of states (Cassese 2005: 74). Talmon (2005: 102) argues that the "idea of one State deciding upon another State's personality in international law is at odds with the sovereign equality of States." In essence, "Recognition by other existing states implies an acknowledgment that the entity has the capacity to fulfil its international duties and obligations as a state and that other states will deal with it as a sovereign equal" (Glahn and

Taulbee 2017: 199). Abhimanyu George Jain (2014) argues that "once an entity meets the criteria of statehood, and is recognised as such, the ability of individual states, or the international community, to revoke recognition and statehood would infringe the fundamental right of sovereign equality." Thus, it can be problematic for existing states to decide when a state no longer exhibits key hallmarks of statehood or to withdraw recognition of another equal member of the international community for political reasons. Accordingly, the principle of estoppel tends to be a mechanism against unilateral acts of states in international relations, which may amount to interference in the domestic affairs of the new state. By failing to consult or acquire the entire truth, states taking unilateral actions and suspending the recognition of other states may be in breach of customary international law, which requires good faith in the conduct of bilateral relations and the implementation of agreements governing the relations between states. In accordance with the principle of estoppel, a new government cannot take decisions that would reverse the decision of the previous government to grant recognition. The exclusion of evidence when deciding for derecognition may be found in breach of the principles of responsibility and consent in interstate relations. In customary international law, fraudulent conduct and the breach of good faith by derecognizing states may give rise to the duty of restitution for the moral, political, diplomatic, and economic damage inflicted on the aspirant state (MacGibbon 1958: 472). Moreover, as Dagmar Richter (2013) rightly points out, "An unfriendly act can turn out to be the starting point of an escalating conflict between States that disturb the peaceful relations among nations, particularly if it touches upon the vital interests or the status of any other State within the community of nations."

The derecognition of states is seen as problematic because it contradicts a number of well-established international norms and legal principles. Formal recognition is "binding on the recognizing State by virtue of the rule pacta sunt servanda" (Lauterpacht 1945: 179), which holds that every treaty is binding and must be performed in good faith. Joint communication for establishing diplomatic relations between states amounts to a bilateral treaty. Bilateral treaties are the primary source of international law. Withdrawal of recognition amounts to the breaking of diplomatic relations and thus the breaching a bilateral treaty. Such a breach violates the principle of good faith in fulfilling the obligations deriving from treaties. From this perspective, derecognition can be seen as a unilateral act that may not be accepted, especially when the core attributes of statehood continue to exist or when no fundamental change of circumstances has occurred (Eckart 2012: 257).

This has been clearly outlined in the Guiding Principles on Unilateral Acts of States, which prohibits arbitrary revocation of previous decisions. This is based on Article 62 of the Vienna Convention on the Law of Treaties, which highlights that even if circumstances change, states are bound by their treaty obligations. In the context of state recognition, the establishment of diplomatic relations amounts to a bilateral treaty, which should be respected by both signatory parties in good faith. As Eileen Denza (2016: 7–8) argues, "Establishment of formal diplomatic relations, if it does not actually constitute recognition of a new State, follows hard upon such recognition." Article 2 of the Vienna Convention on the Law of Treaties defines a treaty as "an international agreement concluded between States in written form and governed by international law, whether embodied in a single instrument or in two or more related instruments and whatever its particular designation." Ending diplomatic relations as termination from a bilateral treaty is expected to take place by the consent of both parties, not withdrawn unilaterally.

Often states grant recognition to other states on the condition that they commit or promise to fulfill an obligation. This may include the enhancement of bilateral economic, political, and sociocultural relations or the promises of assistance on various domestic issues. Lauterpacht (1945: 190) argues that nonfulfillment of such obligations should not result in withdrawal of recognition. According to this view, derecognition may not be permitted even when the affected states fail to implement an obligation deriving from a promise or bilateral agreement. Article 6 of the International Law Institute's resolution on state recognition holds:

> In the case of an obligation assumed by a State at the time of its recognition, failure to fulfil this obligation does not have the effect of annulling recognition or of authorizing its revocation, but involves the consequences of the violation of an international obligation. (Institut de Droit International 1936: 186)

Moreover, a significant question concerning state derecognition and its validity concerns the satisfaction of the mutuality and reciprocity. Concerning recognition, Kelsen (1941: 609) stipulated:

> In order that international law may become fully applicable to the relations between the recognizing and the recognized state the recognition has to be reciprocal. The recognized state, too, has to recognize the recognizing state. Both acts can take place at the same time only

44 • *The Derecognition of States*

if the community to be recognized as a state is, according to general international law, able to proclaim itself a state.

If the claimant state doesn't accept the derecognition decision, claims that it is a unilateral act, and does not reciprocate by suspending or ending diplomatic ties, then there are grounds to contest the validity and legality of derecognition.

Although this book doesn't deal with the derecognition of governments or belligerents, the above arguments apply to governments. Charles G. Fenwick (1948: 38) argues that a historical survey of principles and practical conditions of the recognition of new governments shows that "recognition once granted is irrevocable, so that in the event of the failure of a recognized government to carry out its obligations, it would be the right of third states to break relations with that government if they believed it desirable to do so; but such breaking of relations would not involve withdrawal of recognition." However, M. J. Peterson's (1997) seminal survey of legal doctrine and state practice of recognition of governments between 1815 and 1995 shows that traces of the derecognition of governments were present in both scholarly thinking and state practice. Peterson's analysis provides useful insights into the overlapping and ambiguous nature of withdrawing recognition of a particular government regime. At the same time, the state continues to exist as a legal personality in international affairs. Peterson (1997: 17) shows that derecognition was deemed problematic as it was perceived as a political tool to "exert additional pressure on governments by allowing anyone to threaten another with taking back recognition at any time." Regardless of governmental regime change, state continuation was seen as vital for the stability of the international state system. In nineteenth-century state practice, the only cases of revocation of government recognition "involved reversing a diplomat's error or exceeding of instructions" (Peterson 1997: 17). As Peterson (1997: 17) shows, " This problem seems to have been confined to the US government, which had to revoke recognitions of new governments in Sicily (1837), Nicaragua (1854), Mexico (1858), Venezuela (1862) and Mexico again (1913)." In the interwar period, derecognition of governments was discouraged even in the worst cases, such as the takeover of Germany by the Nazi regime. During the Cold War, however, there were more polemics on the necessity for the derecognition of governments for political reasons, or claims that "temporary or de facto recognitions were removable" (Peterson 1997: 18). Despite these occurrences, Peterson (1997: 18–19) shows that in the state practice there is a general agreement among governments to maintain "the view that recognition of another government is irrevocable except in cases of diplomatic error, making no distinction between de jure and de facto or 'permanent' and 'temporary' recognition."

The scholarly views examined in this section, predominantly from legal scholars, highlight that there is broad consensus on the irreversible character of state derecognition, which provides an important starting point for unpacking and making sense of this controversial diplomatic practice in world politics. However, this legal and normative corpus of knowledge assumes that statehood is linear and subject to a progressive trajectory. It relies on a positive view of state recognition as a welcome development that contributes to expanding the jurisdiction of international law in gray areas and promotes regional stability and conflict resolution. Despite its rational take on the subject, this perspective underestimates the fluidity and uneven politics of derecognition. It does not explain why countries continue to use the derecognition of other states as part of their diplomatic discourse and practice. Thus, it provides a valuable account but is partial, nonetheless. Moreover, the irreversibility of diplomatic recognition is challenged by alternative scholarly accounts that are closer to state practice and the messy reality of international diplomacy.

DISCRETIONARY CHARACTER AND QUALIFIED PERMISSIBILITY OF STATE DERECOGNITION

The second group of scholars takes a more flexible view on the derecognition of states, highlighting the discretionary character and specific circumstances under which withdrawal of recognition is plausible and even permissible. Hans Kelsen (1941: 610) argues that since there is no rule governing the recognition of states in international law, "the states would be free not only to determine whether in a given case a community is a state in an international law sense, but also free to determine what a state is and what conditions a community has to fulfill in order to become a state according to international law." Malcolm Shaw (2019: 407) adds, "Recognition may be withdrawn. This is essentially a political act. It is not usual but it does happen." Similarly, Stephen Tierney (2013: 376–77) argues that "the generally held view is that recognition is a uniquely political act, operating largely if not entirely at the discretion of states." Beat Dold (2012: 91) too argues that "no state can be compelled to grant recognition. In this sense, the act is of a discretionary, political nature. It is often used to demonstrate approval or disapproval." This implies that diplomatic recognition could be withdrawn even from an effective de jure government. Jean d'Aspremont (2012) maintains that "any subject of international law decides for itself how it interprets and construes the facts or the situation that is the object of recognition," adding that, "once granted, recognition can also be subsequently withdrawn if the author changes its interpretation (and policies) or wishes to make it known differently." The derecognition of states in practice is also supported by the Lotus principle, which permits states the discretionary space to conduct their foreign policy freely insofar as it does not infringe on the binding obligations. If derecognition resembled breaching of diplomatic relations, then as Eileen Denza (2016: 396) notes, "There are no legal limitations on the right of a State to break diplomatic relations with another."

The starting point for this group of scholars is that both recognition and derecognition of states remain primarily unregulated in international law and there is no institutional framework to oversee such practices. In the absence of such a regulatory regime, the derecognition of states remains at the discretion of individual states. John Dugard (2013: 6) maintains that as long as international law does not prohibit the withdrawal of recognition, it will be difficult to discipline state practice. Raič (2002: 83–84) adds that "because of the decentralized nature of international law and the absence of a centralized organ authorized to decisively and determinately decide upon the existence or non-existence of a State, existing States have to fulfil that function by granting or withholding recognition." This is particularly relevant for small states and microstates, which are often the most common protagonists in the state derecognition saga. Small states, J. C. Sharman (2017: 560) argues, "have taken a pick-and-choose approach to their sovereign prerogatives: energetically wielding some, delegating others in selectively forming hierarchical relationships, and commercialising still others." Sharman (2017: 559) blames the permissive international system (anarchical in nature), which "presents even the smallest and weakest states with a menu of choices to exercise, delegate or sell sovereign prerogatives." However, Chen (1951: 259–60) warned that "there is . . . no greater threat to international legal order than the unrestricted notion of the revocability of recognition." Similarly, Maziar Jamnejad and Michael Wood (2009: 373) argue that "a state's failure to recognize an entity that fulfils the criteria for statehood will not normally constitute intervention. International law does not generally impose an obligation to recognize. However, in certain exceptional circumstances, where non-recognition is intended to force a change of policy, there could be a breach of the non-intervention principle." Thus, short of an international regulatory mechanism, grounds for derecognition risk become hallowed in two specific circumstances. The first is when third states withdraw recognition for domestic and foreign policy interests. Second, when there is an internal contestation between different governmental organs and their procedures and competencies for granting or withdrawing recognition of other states, unauthorized actions on recognition of states by a governmental official may result in disavowing the action and annulling recognition.

The discretionary character of state recognition highlights the role of power politics and self-interest in the derecognition of states and the historical patterns underpinning this diplomatic practice in the first place. As Jens Bartelson (2013: 111) maintains, "The struggle for recognition takes place between unequal parties, in which the stronger party is in a position to grant or withhold recognition to the weaker one, and in which the stronger party is likely to perceive demands for recognition as challenges to its standing." Notably, state practices of recognition and nonrecognition are historically affiliated with the discriminatory and racist practices of European states to differentiate civilized nations from "uncivilized," "savage," and "barbarian" nations (Ringmar 2014: 450). For most of the modern history of states, "Recognition was granted by states not in accordance with any international principle, but according to the powerful and unpredictable expediencies of competition for colonies" (Anghie 2004: 78).

If we take its discretionary character and self-interest as the main determinants behind state derecognition, the meaning and significance of derecognition become apparent only when the effects are examined on a case-by-case basis. From this point of view, derecognition may have a constitutive effect since it undermines the claims to, and in some instances blocks the derecognized state's access to, essential and substantive political, economic, diplomatic, and security goods. Lora Viola (2020: 69) holds that "the first, most basic, good provided to members is the recognition of their right to exist as independent political units with self-ownership and control." When recognition is withheld or withdrawn, the process entails the denial of an essential good of the international system. Another set of goods provided by the international system comprises legal personhood, which "gives recognized states standing within the international system and makes them capable of being subjects of international law" (Viola 2020: 69). Similarly, Stephen Krasner (1999: 7) stipulates that "recognition facilitates treaty making, establishes diplomatic immunity, and offers a shield against legal actions taken in other states." The reversal of recognition could be interpreted as denial of legal personhood to claimant states, which makes it difficult for them to exercise the rights and obligations deriving from membership in the club of sovereign states, such as signing treaties, participating in international arrangements, and claiming the rights developed within the framework of international law. Finally, derecognition prevents the claimant state from enjoying substantive rights, which Viola (2020: 70) defines as "everything from peacekeeping, to loans, to disaster relief and more . . . that collective action within the system provides to its members to bring them benefits." Overall, Viola (2020: 70) argues that once a state is denied the spectrum of international goods, then derecognized states ensure negative effects, which come from "not having the life-protection that international law and institutions afford, putting survival at stake, and from not having access to the goods that can improve the quality of life."

Beyond these political views, a normative argument could permit derecognition in specific circumstances. Normative perspectives hold that withdrawal of recognition is permissible only when the claimant state has lost its core statehood conditions upon which recognition was granted in the first place. To Chen (1951: 263) it is obvious that, in practice, "the only legitimate consideration for the withdrawal of recognition is the disappearance of the requirements of statehood or governmental capacity." And even in this case "withdrawal of recognition is conceived as nothing more than the registering of the fact that these [statehood] requirements have ceased to exist" (Chen 1951: 160). Lauterpacht (1945: 180) argues that derecognition in general should be "exercised with a circumspection and restraint even more pronounced than the positive act of granting recognition," adding that "it cannot properly be used as an instrument of political pressure or disapproval." Similarly, Thomas D. Grant (1999: 30) shows that withdrawal of recognition from the state-like entity among international lawyers is considered only when one of the essential criteria of statehood disappears. Peter Radan (2020: 57) is of same view, arguing that "many territorial entities that do not meet one or other of these criteria have had their statehood confirmed by recognition. Conversely, territorial entities that satisfy the criteria for statehood are not recognized as states. Furthermore, it is arguable that recognized states that cease to meet the criteria for statehood should be derecognized." However, Kelsen (1941: 613) goes further and argues that "any state is entitled, according to general international law, at any time to establish the fact that a community which has been a state in an international law sense, has ceased to be such, because it no longer fulfills the condition prescribed by general international law." Kelsen (1941: 613) adds an important nuance here, arguing that "the establishment of such a fact is not a withdrawal of recognition. The establishment of a fact cannot be withdrawn, it can only be replaced by another establishment, namely, the establishment that the previously established fact no more exists." In this sense, the act of derecognition is, in essence, recognition of the authority of the former base state over the claimant state.

Article 5 of the Resolution Concerning the Recognition of New States and New Governments issued by the International Law Institute in 1936 holds that recognition "ceases to have effect only in case of the definite disappearance of one of the essential elements whose conjunction was established at the moment of recognition" (Institut de Droit International 1936: 186). Lauterpacht (1945: 179) maintains that "in principle there would seem to be no reason why recognition should not be liable to withdrawal so long as that act, like that of granting recognition, is conceived not as an arbitrary act of policy but as one of application of international law, namely, as a declaration that the objective requirements of recognition have ceased to exist." Chen (1951: 281) maintains that "the recognition is definitive and cannot be withdrawn as long as the requirements continue to be met." However, he adds, "The only legitimate consideration for the withdrawal of recognition is the disappearance of the requirements of statehood or governmental capacity" (Chen 1951: 262–63). Even then, Chen (1951: 259) submits, "Taking notice of the non-existence of the formerly existing entity by a foreign State is a fresh act of acknowledgment of a new fact, and not the withdrawal of the previous recognition." Oppenheim (1996: 176) adds, "A state may lose its independence . . . in all these cases recognition of the former state of affairs ceases to be appropriate and will usually be withdrawn or discontinued." Christian Tomuschat (2012: 36) is of the same opinion: "The recognition of a State must be considered as unlawful if the territorial entity concerned is unable, under any conceivable aspect, to meet the minimum requirements of statehood." This is the case when states dissolve or unify with another state. Derecognition may be permissible when a state becomes extinct as a result of dismemberment or when it merges with another state (Cassese 2005: 77). Denza (2016: 21) maintains that the "disappearance of a State implies the end of its diplomatic relations." For example, the reunification of Germany in 1990 ended East Germany's distinct diplomatic representations abroad, which the new federal government then took over. The dissolution of Yugoslavia resulted in the disappearance of its international legal personality, and the successor states became the newly recognized entities. In fact, even when a state "dies" or disappears, the termination of diplomatic relations is the ultimate action that indirectly implies derecognition (Chen 1951: 261). Warbrick (1981: 242) adds that "it has been suggested that not only is withdrawal of recognition not usual, but it is not necessary, since recognition automatically lapses with the incumbent government's loss of effective control."

From this normative and qualified standpoint, derecognition may also be permissible when the state ceases to exist. If this is applied to the derecognition process, one can assume that withdrawal of recognition represents a unilateral decision indicating that a particular state does not fulfill the conditions of statehood as required by international law and state practice. In other words, derecognition is permissible if it is governed by the same principles as recognition when the state (a) no longer has an independent government, (b) lacks effective authority and habitual obedience by the majority of the population, (c) no longer has clearly defined territory and frontiers and lacks jurisdiction over that territory; and most important, (d) has, according to clear factual evidence, earned independent statehood through aggression and the use of force. So, as long as the claimant state satisfies the core requirements of statehood, derecognition may not be taken seriously or be permissible under these general principles governing the recognition of states.

In addition to the discretionary and normative views on derecognition, some views highlight the form of recognition and procedural aspects that could influence the prospects for derecognition. In other words, how a state is recognized in the first place might have implications for the possibility of derecognition. When a state is only de facto recognized, such recognition may be provisional—for instance, until the criteria of state effectiveness and independence from other states are satisfied—and may thus be liable to withdrawal. This view is advocated by Lauterpacht (1945: 179), who maintains that "de facto recognition, it has been shown, is provisional in its nature and is, therefore, liable to be withdrawn as soon as it becomes clear that there is no prospect of the requisite conditions of recognition being fulfilled." However, Lauterpacht (1945: 185) stipulates that "recognition de jure can properly be withdrawn only if at the same time it is granted to another authority which combines more effectively the requisite conditions of statehood or governmental capacity." From this point of view, the withdrawal of recognition from one state should ultimately result in the transfer of such recognition to the new authority. The withdrawal of recognition would not make sense in cases of dual recognition, namely when the derecognizing state already recognizes the former base state from which the aspirant state has separated. Derecognition may also be permissible in cases of premature recognition, namely when the claimant state has not been able to establish effective statehood in a defined territory, over a particular population, and through a government capable of engaging with other states. However, if the claimant state has effective control over the territory, then withdrawal of recognition does not have solid political and normative grounds and, accordingly, may amount to premature derecognition (Peterson 1982).

Other scholars disagree with the permissibility of withdrawal of derecognition due to de facto recognition in the first place. For example, Chen (1951: 282) argues that "recognition, whether de facto or de jure, as evidence of the existence of the body recognized, is incapable of being withdrawn, while as a manifestation of friendly relations it is revocable at will in both cases." Even conditional recognition may not be subject to withdrawal, as Chen (1951: 266) argues, because "as evidence of the fact of the existence of a State or government, recognition is irrevocable" and "failure to discharge the obligations attached does not affect the recognition, which is an act accomplished beyond redemption." Moreover, M. J. Peterson (1997: 18–19) argues that recognition is "irrevocable except in cases of diplomatic error, making no distinction between de jure and de facto or 'permanent' and 'temporary' recognition," though Lowe (2017: 163) adds, "There is always a time during which it is unclear whether the attempt to establish the new State will succeed" (Lowe 2007: 163). According to James Ker-Lindsay (2019: 22), "Recognition is fundamentally and wholly about intent. A state cannot recognize a territory unless it clearly wishes to do so. There is no such thing as accidental recognition." In this regard, recognition cannot be accidental as it requires intent, especially when it is confirmed through an explicit diplomatic note. Thus, states can withhold recognition in the first instance until they are satisfied that the claimant state will succeed and effectively perform its sovereign statehood. There is an understanding that when a state is de jure recognized—where the act of recognition is intentional and reasons for recognition are clearly outlined in an official diplomatic document—it is considered nonrevocable.

Finally, a group of scholars argue for the withdrawal of recognition of existing states that lack statehood capacity and are implicated in severe human rights abuses. These views concern the use of recognition and derecognition as instruments for promoting statebuilding and political reforms. Stephen Krasner (2013: 174) argues that "poorly governed and states without autonomy are recognized; states that are autonomous and effectively governed have not been recognized." In this regard, Krasner (2013: 175) submits that "recognition does not, however, guarantee success as the existence of so many failed states demonstrates." In this context, derecognition is an instrument of the international community to punish and discipline states that are implicated in severe human rights abuses. George Schwarzenberger (1943: 105), as transmitted by Chen (1951: 260), proposed that "the simplest method of outlawing a state which persistently violated the principles of international law would be by a withdrawal of its recognition as a subject of International Law." He adds that "such a step could be taken collectively at an international conference, . . . or individually by the members of the international society" (Schwarzenberger 1943: 99–100). Recent work by Chris Naticchia (2017) also suggests that if existing sovereign states fail to fulfill the criteria of statehood set to recognize new states, they should also be derecognized:

> As we ask whether this or that future political entity ought to be recognized as a state, so too can we ask whether this or that current political entity ought to have been recognized as a state—that is to say, we can ask whether its standing, as a recognized member of the international community, ought to be *revoked*. (Naticchia 2017: 14)

Danny Auron (2013: 480) argues that since "recognition is granted based on the existence of certain elements of statehood or capacity . . . the definite disappearance of these can justify derecognition." Auron (2013: 443) further suggests that "states and international organizations should consider the derecognition of dictatorial regimes that face mass non-violent opposition from their population and that choose to meet this opposition with violence rather than reform." He adds that "international law presently withholds recognition from governments installed by force or illegal means, but not from governments that remain in power with the same techniques" (Auron 2013: 498). Jeffrey Herbst (2004: 312) proposes decertifying failed states, which entails acknowledging "officially that some states are simply not exercising formal control over parts of their country and should no longer be considered sovereign." According to him,

> Decertification would be a strong signal that something fundamental has gone wrong in a country, and that parts of the international community are no longer willing to continue the myth that every state is always exercising sovereign authority. . . . Decertification would also be a signal that a country should not be accorded the usual privileges of sovereignty. (Herbst 2004: 313)

By doing this, "The long-term aim would be to provide international recognition to the governmental units that are actually providing order to their citizens as opposed to relying on the fictions of the past" (Herbst 2004: 315). However, Cedric Ryngaert and Sven Sobrie (2011: 488) argue that "in the interest of international stability, it is desirable that a high threshold is set before a state loses its statehood—witness cases such as Sudan and Somalia, entities still recognized as states notwithstanding their continuing lack of effective governments." Robert J. Delahunty and John Yoo (2005: 155) make an important observation when they argue that "the Montevideo Convention's tests for statehood are framed in general terms, and could readily apply to both situations [recognition and derecognition]. Nevertheless, it is usually taken for granted that the tests for initial recognition of statehood do not carry over, or in any case should not carry over, into the context of state derecognition." There is also fear that "the derecognition of a particular failed state—i.e., the withdrawal of the recognition of its international legal sovereignty—risks 'domino' effects, leading to the derecognition of other states, and thus weakening the (fictitious, but arguably salutary) conception that the entire globe is and should be divided up into nation-states" (Delahunty and Yoo 2005: 149–50). Moreover, Ryngaert and Sobrie (2011: 488) submit that "imposing such criteria as human-rights protection or democratic institutions on existing states would probably be perceived as a flagrant violation of the well-established prohibition of intervention in internal affairs."

The discussion in this section has highlighted that scholarly perspectives on the derecognition of states are far more complex than often assumed. There is little consensus among legal, political, and normative scholars on whether state derecognition is permissible and under what qualified circumstances it could be. In the absence of governing rules and institutions on state recognition, nonrecognition, and derecognition, there is room for third states to use and abuse at their discretion their capacity to recognize or derecognize other states for political rather than principled reasons. Yet there is a general understanding that the derecognition of claimant states that do fulfill the criteria for statehood and have a legitimate case for independent statehood is unacceptable. More broadly, the discussion so far in this chapter highlights that while a corpus of scholarly views on derecognition exists, such knowledge and scholarly debates mostly remain doctrinal and lack empirical features. Most importantly, such views tend to theorize old and historical diplomatic practices and do not capture the contemporary state practice, which can offer valuable grounds for comprehensively understanding derecognition in theory and practice.

54 • *The Derecognition of States*

FROM THEORY TO REALITY: TRACING STATE DERECOGNITION IN PRACTICE

As discussed in this chapter, the existing theoretical knowledge on derecognition offers valuable normative and doctrinal observations with which we can examine the contemporary politics of derecognition. However, most existing accounts on derecognition are a product of outdated historical, normative, and legal thinking and do not correspond with contemporary state practice. They also operate on ideal-typical conceptions of statehood, recognition, and derecognition and often examine hypothetical situations. As outlined in the introduction, the derecognition of states is a political fact in world politics; what is lacking is a comprehensive and in-depth understanding of its contemporary manifestation. Specifically, we know very little about the meaning, politics, and effects of diplomatic derecognition in contemporary state policy and practice. Legal, normative, and political-theoretical views lack substantial empirical examination of why derecognition happens in practice, by whom, and at what cost or effect. Stephen Krasner (2013: 174) acknowledges as much: "Neither international legal theories nor international political sociology provide an accurate empirical description of the actual practices of states with regard to recognition." On the other hand, empirical knowledge on state derecognition is mostly case-specific. It tends to be absorbed by broader discussions of foreign policy, security, and geopolitics of specific regions where derecognition takes place.

Thus, to offer a complete account of derecognition in theory and enrich empirical investigation in practice, the remainder of this chapter and the proceeding chapters in this book will comprehensively look at the actors, processes, justifications, and effects of state derecognition (see Figure 2.1). In other words, a comprehensive analysis of derecognition requires the examination of agential, structural, institutional, and relational features that underline the formulation of specific policies as well as the decision-making process and procedures behind them. It also allows analyses of their implementation, the conduct of diplomatic relations, and the broader domestic and international effects of foreign policy. To do so, it is crucial to approach both the recognition and the derecognition of states as open-ended and polymorphic diplomatic practices comprising multiple actors, stages, tactics, discourses, and effects. Since derecognition is not regulated in international law, tracing various diplomatic practices is crucial to understanding how it is constituted, interpreted, and applied through diplomatic discourse and actions (Reymond 2019). In short, we should explore derecog-

Conceptualizing State Derecognition • 55

nition as an anti-diplomatic, but rule-making practice. Derecognition is an anti-diplomatic practice because it seeks to challenge, distort, and bypass conventional diplomatic practices concerning how diplomatic relations are established, maintained, downgraded, and discontinued. James Der Derian (1987) defines anti-diplomacy as a revolutionary type of diplomatic engagement that challenges and transcends conventional methods and approaches of mediating the estrangement among nations, namely drawing a balance between respecting sovereign equality and noninterference with building interstate relations that bridge differences and enhance joint interests. In other words, anti-diplomacy captures a broad spectrum of tactics, strategies, and discourses that tear down rather than cultivate good interstate relations, expand isolation, nationalism, and estrangement among nations, and promote archaic, unilateral, and hypocritical foreign policy (Murray 2018). The fact that it remains an unregulated practice allows state derecognition to be anti-diplomatic. Emmanuel Adler and Vincent Pouliot (2011: 4) define practices as "socially meaningful patterns of action which, in being performed more or less competently, simultaneously embody, act out and possibly reify background knowledge and discourse in and on the material world." So by approaching derecognition as an anti-diplomatic practice, we can explore the patterns and entanglements that constitute it as meaningful in practice.

State derecognition is an entangled practice that cannot be explained by looking only at singular cases, events, or acts. Entanglements are characterized by "complex intertwined networks, with no beginning and no end," and scholars have difficulty in trying to fix their "point of departure" (Duve 2014: 8). Derecognition is a complex and interactive process that requires tracing individual cases to show how they are entangled together to perform certain functions in world politics. It requires looking at how diplomatic agency, processuality, performativity, and seemingly isolated global ecology of events, interests, and encounters come together and shape the politics of statehood and derecognition. Moreover, to make sense of how derecognition is presented, justified, and legitimized to concerned publics, it is essential to analyze the text of derecognition letters, including the discourses, norms, rules, and principles invoked to make such decisions politically, legally, and socially apprehensible. Thus, the diplomatic discourse underpinning variants of derecognition will be examined to explore the rationales for withdrawing recognition of the claimant state. Finally, the true significance of derecognition can only be measured by looking at the effects it produces. Only by analyzing the implications of derecognition can we diagnose the entire complex tapestry of this practice in world politics, especially the con-

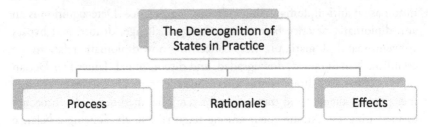

Figure 2.1. The Conceptual Framework

stitutive effects in making and unmaking the current international order. Thus, the framework presented below takes a comprehensive outlook on derecognition by linking various actors, processes, rationales, and effects as core features of this shady practice in contemporary world affairs.

The Process of State Derecognition

The optimal epistemological site for investigating derecognition as diplomatic practice is country case studies where such struggle occurs. Understanding the derecognition of states requires, first and foremost, identifying which states are exposed to the withdrawal of recognition and which are prone to withdrawing the recognition and the role that former base states and regional powers play in this process (Visoka 2020b). In general, as outlined in Figure 2.2, when we discuss cases of state derecognition, we are concerned with four actors: (1) the claimant state, which is subject to derecognition; (2) the former base state that lobbies for derecognition; (3) the third countries that withdraw the recognition; and (4) regional and global allies that support or oppose the derecognition of the claimant state. It is worth noting that the derecognition of independent statehood is particularly significant for claimant states that are outside the UN system and thus lack overwhelming international bilateral or multilateral support. In other words, derecognition primarily applies to claimant states that have secured partial international recognition. Expectedly, aspirant states not recognized by any other recognized state are not subject to derecognition, given that there is nothing to derecognize. Thus, derecognition concerns a narrow category of states that are neither entirely outside nor inside the club of sovereign states. In instances when two UN member states that enjoy universal recognition are implicated in a practice such as derecognition, it is widely referred to as a breakup or suspension of diplomatic relations. The category of former base

Conceptualizing State Derecognition • 57

states is determined by default due to their contestation and nonrecognition of the claimant state. The third countries implicated in the practice of derecognition are much more comprehensive and diverse in terms of their global status, economic status, and geographical location. However, what they may have in common is the use of derecognition and re-recognition as one of the few foreign policy assets available to them to reduce their vulnerability, benefit from foreign aid, renew alliances, and influence the international system more generally (Thorhallsson and Bailes 2016: 297). In addition to the base and claimant state, regional and global powers also need to be accounted for when discussing derecognition. Support or opposition from the great powers plays a pivotal role in deepening and entrenching the contestation of claimant states. Therefore, it is essential to include them in the pool of stakeholders in the process of derecognition.

When studying the actors or agents of state derecognition, it is worth noting that while they are primarily states, they shouldn't be treated as monolithic or rational and unitary agents. There should be a disaggregated examination of the stakeholders and institutions within each category of states to demonstrate the nexus between personal/individual and institutional and collective segments of foreign policy decision-making and implementation. In other words, by looking at various political subjectivities behind derecognition, the analysis will move beyond considering derecognition practices as being entirely guided by rational choice, unitary decision-making bodies (state representatives), or self-interest. By analyzing actor-centered discourses of derecognition, it is possible to identify various contextual rationales, beliefs, bureaucracies, and other situational inclinations that explain why countries are implicated in withdrawing the recognition of other states. Most important, it will be able to highlight mutually constitutive dynamics and the subjectivities among those involved on either the invoking or the receiving end of derecognition. Notably, the practice and process of derecognition is not regulated formally in the international system, but it is informed by a broad range of situational, transactional, and sociomaterial rules, which are informal yet procedural, in shaping the response and variety of outcomes of derecognition campaign. Like the lobbying process of state recognition in the first instance, the diplomatic practices and procedural rules underpinning derecognition consist of a constellation of persuasion, socialization, and strategic transactions (Griffiths 2021). Therefore, it is crucial to identify and explore the diplomatic craft behind derecognition.

Parallel to recognizing a multiplicity of actors involved in the derecognition of states, it is crucial to shift our understanding of state derecognition

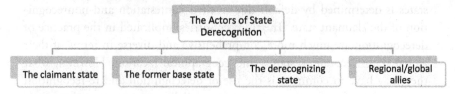

Figure 2.2. The Actors of State Derecognition

from a singular act and event into a multilayered and multistage process. Despite the well-known complexity of the dynamics of international diplomacy, early perspectives on state recognition have conceptualized recognition as a single act expressed in a specific time and space with explicit declarative intent. The recognition-seeking states are categorized in binary terms, either as recognized or unrecognized states. For instance, Ian Brownlie (2003: 89–90) conceives recognition as "a public act of state" that is "an optional and political act." David Raič (2002: 35) considers recognition to be "a legal act in the sense that it is intended to create legal consequences." Similarly, Mikulas Fabry (2010: 7) considers recognition to be "a single act with both legal and political aspects" similar to "an act of employing military force or an act of imposing economic sanctions or an act of expelling a foreign diplomat." Milena Sterio (2013: 48) also defines recognition as "a political act exercised by sitting governments of existing states vis-à-vis a newly created entity." Despite these prevailing views, mostly in legal theory, recent research exploring diplomacy as discursive and entangled performances shows that state recognition is more than a single act (Visoka 2018; Ker-Lindsay 2012; Huddleston 2020). It is a complex and multistage process, often started by sending a formal request for recognition, which justifies the proclamation of independence and outlines the benefits of mutual recognition. The next phase involves establishing direct contact and arranging an informal meeting in a bilateral or multilateral setting. This phase informs the basis of consideration of recognition and can signal eventual recognition. What proceeds next is often various political, diplomatic, and institutional engagements short of formal recognition. This phase can often be interpreted as fluid and de facto recognition. The final phase involves formalizing diplomatic recognition through an express and documented process, which often also involves establishing diplomatic relations. While the formalization of recognition frequently ends the recognition process, after which the two countries proceed with maintaining and cultivating bilateral relations, in some cases this process can reopen, leading to backsliding in the reverse direction (see Visoka 2018).

This book proposes to approach the withdrawal of recognition as a complex and multidirectional process comprising at least four major phases (see Figure 2.3). First, it is crucial to explore how the former base state contests the independence of the claimant state. In most cases, the origins of the state derecognition process are interwoven with the former base state's campaign to prevent or counter recognition of the claimant state. Derecognition should be seen as a continuation of such counter-secession campaigns and an attempt to undo what has been done in the past—it is an effort to correct failed diplomatic efforts of the past or to seize new geopolitical opportunities and entanglements in world politics. In short, it is essential to trace how the former base state seeks to deny the claimant state a political and diplomatic existence.

What comes next is to understand how third countries are targeted and incentivized to reconsider their recognition of the claimant state. It is essential to explore how diplomatic persuasions occur for third countries to either continue to recognize the claimant state or send signals for reconsidering it. While the process of reconsidering recognition is kept out of public attention, there can be instances where the derecognizing states indicate their potential change of position on the claimant state. The third phase, often definitive in the derecognition process, can involve suspension or freezing of recognition, which can take the shape of a de facto and temporal measure that can remain in an ambivalent state for an indeterminate period or lead to formal withdrawal of recognition. What follows then is the formal and official withdrawal of recognition whereby a third country directly or indirectly, publicly or through diplomatic channels, communicates the decision either to the former base state or to the derecognized state. Often this act attracts public and diplomatic attention and can become subject to domestic and international polemic in the affected states. It can bring to an end diplomatic relations and bilateral cooperation programs, or it can serve the situational interests of concerned states without significant diplomatic consequences. While this stage marks the end of diplomatic relations and engagement between the derecognizing and the derecognized state, it can be reversed. Thus, an additional stage in the recognition-derecognition saga that needs to be accounted for is the potential for re-recognition and re-establishment of diplomatic relations between the derecognizing and derecognized state.

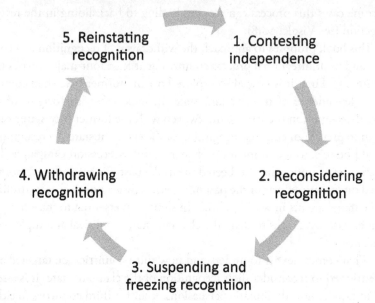

Figure 2.3. The Process of State Derecognition

When exploring the critical phases of state derecognition, it is also essential to identify the tactics and incentives that drive the derecognition process. Countries that possess power and status, economic and military strength, and access to multilateral bodies, diplomatic networks, and allies have a large toolbox of diplomatic means to realize their foreign policy goals (Barston 2014). Their diplomatic craft is rich and offers great scope to influence international affairs. Conversely, weaker actors in the international system, have much narrower foreign policy instruments and thus are forced to pursue a niche foreign policy that uses both the conventional and the non-conventional methods at their disposal (Cooper and Shaw 2009; Fry 2019). Yet it is vital to narrow down and explore the interplay of factors that shape the politics of derecognition in practice. This requires identifying, grouping, and labeling the key diplomatic instruments and rationales that are used by different actors involved in the different stages of the derecognition process.

The Justification of State Derecognition

Understanding the diplomatic justifications underpinning the discourse of derecognition is crucial for assessing the legitimization strategies and the arguments foregrounded in this practice. In foreign policy, justification tends to have two significant addresses: the first is directed toward domestic and internal audiences, which consist of government, the general public, and other interest groups; the second concerns external audiences, which can be directly and indirectly affected parties, actors, and institutions. In both instances, the purpose of justification of foreign policy actions and decisions is about legitimizing them to maximize their benefits and minimize their risks. As Helene Sjursen and Karen E. Smith (2004: 127) argue, the logic of legitimization in foreign policy is embedded in three criteria: utility, values, and rights (see also March and Olsen 1998). First, foreign policy decisions and actions can be justified around the logic of consequences, namely how such action or decision is an efficient solution to a problem. Second, they can be justified around specific values, which can be judgments of appropriateness embedded in normative, identity, or situational norms and values. Third, they can be justified around a set of legal and moral principles and frameworks of rights that are widely acceptable. When translated into the context of derecognition, these three logics of legitimation can be found within distinct or overlapping political, economic, normative, and geopolitical rationales that justify derecognition by third states.

Identifying the rationales of state derecognition requires examining official statements and public justifications of all concerned and affected parties. But it also requires triangulating the actors' interests, events, and circumstances that inform such decisions. Only by accounting for declared justifications and other implicit or related reasons can we provide a realistic and complete account of the rationales behind derecognition. Thus, tracing the justification of derecognition by third countries requires looking at official rationales and hidden motives that inform the decision for suspending, freezing, or entirely withdrawing recognition.. Since derecognition is highly contested, disentangling the motives behind it is essential to verify whether decisions for derecognition are grounded on principled and objective grounds or are motivated by self-interest and situational grounds. In other words, as analyzed earlier in this chapter, it is crucial to examine whether the decision for derecognition is about the satisfaction of the criteria for statehood or the original reasons for granting recognition or is motivated by reasons not directly related to the claimant (derecognized) state. So it is crucial when analyzing the derecognition statements or decisions to check for discursive compatibility between the recognition and derecognition rationales. Moreover, looking at the diplomatic intertextuality within and between case studies covered in this book is essential. In other words,

62 • *The Derecognition of States*

since derecognition is a diplomatic endeavor stimulated by the former base state, which justifies its counter-recognition and derecognition campaign in the first place, it is crucial to trace similarities of discourses and arguments across different derecognition cases.

The Effects of State Derecognition

Finally, an examination of derecognition in practice wouldn't be complete without studying the political and legal effects on the protagonist states. The starting point for studying the effects of derecognition is the assumption that, like the granting of recognition, the withdrawal of recognition tends to produce numerous political and legal effects, both intended and unintended (Delahunty and Yoo 2005: 149). Multiple factors and entanglements influence matters concerning diplomatic recognition and derecognition and are thus prone to disturb not only the hostile relations between the contender states but also implicate the wider international community. Practices of recognition, and subsequently of derecognition, represent significant forms of diplomatic constitution and assemblage, which entangle various entities and tie together remote issues. The derecognition of states is a diplomatic entanglement (resembling quantum diplomacy) undertaken in conditions of uncertainty (Der Derian and Wendt 2022). Moreover, exploring various direct and indirect effects of state derecognition helps us understand how salient this diplomatic practice is and how it shapes the international standing and statehood of the affected states as well as of the others implicated in the campaign to prevent or accomplish derecognition. Exploring what effects derecognition produces not only sheds light on the existence of this diplomatic practice but also highlights its constitutive features, which are crucial for understanding how derecognition impacts the legal, political, and practical existence and effectiveness of the claimant state. Nicolas Onuf (2013: 134) argues that "every such act is a constitutive event with effects that are simultaneously constitutive and regulative and quite likely at odds in their political implications." Since derecognition implicates domestic and international affairs, the empirical analysis will examine the internal and external effects on all involved parties, especially the derecognized and derecognizing states. The effects of derecognition will be traced by examining the reactions and responses to the process and by looking at the broader implications of the withdrawal of recognition or any of the associate stages of the derecognition process.

THE RESEARCH APPROACH

Since state derecognition remains a marginal subject of study in diplomacy and international relations, creating a consolidated knowledge on the subject requires a blended research approach that combines several epistemological and methodological perspectives. The book draws mainly on the methods of historical analysis and cross-case comparison, which are crucial for capturing both the contextual and general patterns underpinning the process, rationales, and effects of derecognition. Providing a rich account of derecognition in practice requires looking at how the different diplomatic discourses are invoked to influence states' decision to withdraw recognition, how different diplomatic performances are designed and implemented, and how entangled events, narratives, and assemblages of actors can play a role in the derecognition or re-recognition of states. It requires looking at the micropolitics of derecognition, encompassing contextual and differentiated discourses and performances invoked by former base states in their pursuit of diplomatic recognition and by the claimant state to prevent derecognition (Solomon and Steele 2017; Adler and Pouliot 2011; Visoka 2019). It also requires zooming out to explore the macropolitics of derecognition by tying together direct and indirect as well as intended and unintended effects across various states and regions (Mintz and Redd 2003).

Since derecognition is not a common diplomatic practice and only affects a small number of states outside the UN system, the case-specific and cross-case research approach is best suited for capturing the nuances of derecognition (Gerring 2017; George and Bennett 2005). While single case studies can trace historical events and provide rich descriptive analysis, they cannot offer a general outlook or capture varieties across different cases. Since this book aims to offer a general and comprehensive account of derecognition, the most suitable approach is to draw on representative case studies with different features, historical trajectories, and exposures to this phenomenon. Thus, studying more than one case ensures that a complex and unresearched diplomatic practice such as derecognition is not dominated by a specific case or particular set of circumstances, which offer rich but noncumulative knowledge. The book deals with typical and contemporary states that have exposed to both diplomatic recognition and derecognition. The book covers five contemporary representative cases of derecognition: Taiwan, Western Sahara, Kosovo, Abkhazia, and South Ossetia. As discussed briefly in the introduction, these states have received between five and one hundred recognitions and respectively have lost substantial number of recognitions (see the appendix for these data). These five claimant states that aspire to full membership in the club of sovereign states still exist as independent yet contested states. While there are other instances where entities have proclaimed independence and rule as de facto states, they are not the focus of this book's study because they haven't received any official recognition from UN member states and are instead subject to collective nonrecognition (Pavković and Radan 2011; Caspersen 2012; Griffiths 2021). The book also doesn't deal with cases of state death as a result of dissolution, annexation, or reincorporation within the former base state, such as East Germany or Manchuria or, most recently the Republic of Artsakh.

Each of the cases has distinct attributes, different levels of international recognition, and different levels of statehood capacity. However, what is common among them is exposure to derecognition by other states for different reasons and processes. Taiwan is not a straightforward secessionist case, because the main contestation is over who is the legitimate and representative government of China in the aftermath of the Second World War and the taking over of the mainland by Mao's communist forces, when nationalist factions were forced to move to the island of Taiwan. In the case of Taiwan, the issue of derecognition, prevalent since 1979, takes the shape of shifting or switching recognition to People's Republic of China as the legitimate government and representative of China at home and abroad (Somers 2023). The case of Western Sahara is also a complex one, as we are concerned with the derecognition of the Polisario Front and the self-proclaimed Sahrawi Arabic Democratic Republic (SADR), which operates as a government-in-exile and governs the population that is permanently displaced and in refugee camps in Algeria (Zunes and Mundy 2022). Western Sahara is a case of incomplete decolonization, and, pending the outcome of the UN-sanctioned referendum for self-determination, Morocco is widely seen as the occupying power. Morocco uses the derecognition of SADR in pursue of international legitimation of its control of Western Sahara. Two other cases examined in this book are Abkhazia and South Ossetia, two breakaway regions of Georgia, which declared independence in 2008 following a short war with Georgia and intervention of Russian troops (Ilyin 2011). With the support of the United States and EU, Georgia has lobbied against the international recognition of Abkhazia and South Ossetia and has succeeded in having recognition withdrawn in a number of instances (Ó Beacháin 2020). This book's fifth and final case is Kosovo, which declared independence in 2008 after Serbia rejected the UN's suggestion for a supervised independence (Weller

2009). After Kosovo received recognition from more than one hundred UN member states and was headed toward universal recognition, Serbia began the derecognition campaign (Visoka 2020a, 2020b). Thus, these five cases are representative because they enable us to capture both similar and diverse practices, discourses, and effects of derecognition. In turn, studying the process, rationales, and effects of derecognition in these five cases offers a considerable degree of generalizability of findings, which can form the basis for a general explanatory theory and lay out the grounds for further normative and empirical research on the subject.

Although the book focuses on these five cases, it also looks a broader range of protagonists: the former base states, derecognizing states, and other major global and international allies that have lobbied in favor or against the withdrawal of recognition. In the case of Taiwan, the analysis will include China's diplomatic efforts to reduce Taiwan's diplomatic allies (Van Fossen 2007). The book will also look at the United States, Australia, and other regional actors indirectly implicated in the case of Taiwan. In the case of Western Sahara, the analysis will focus on the diplomatic efforts of Morocco, the state with claims over the Western Sahara territory, often referred to as the occupying power (Boukhars and Roussellier 2014). In addition, Algeria, South Africa, and France will be included in the analysis as regional powers supporting different sides of the Sahara conflict (Ojeda-Garcia, Fernandez-Molina, and Veguilla 2014). In the case of Kosovo, Serbia's diplomatic efforts will be examined in its capacity as the former base state and successor of the dissolved state of Yugoslavia (Ker-Lindsay 2012). Finally, in the case of Abkhazia and South Ossetia, Georgia will be examined as the former base state, whereas Russia will be included as their patron state and the United States as their major global opponent (Yemelianova and Broers 2020).

The analysis of these protagonist states will take place through cross-case comparison analysis, which facilitates the identification of "useful generic knowledge of important foreign policy problems" that can be used both for theory building and testing (George and Bennett 2005: 67). When exploring these selected cases, the analysis will focus on both within-case and cross-case comparisons (Gerring 2016). Systematic comparison through a structured and controlled process (focusing on the actors, process, rationales, and effects of state derecognition) enhances the internal and external validity of observations made in the book. For this reason, the method of structured, focused comparison facilitates understanding of the process, discourses, and effects of derecognition across all cases under examination and helps organize the findings in a comparable manner to generate cumulative knowledge of the derecognition of states in practice. The book asks the same questions for each case study, ensuring a focused comparison and cumulation of observation that can inform our knowledge on derecognition in world politics. It seeks to understand who the actors have been and the stages of the derecognition process. This enables the categorization of the diplomatic actors as well as the development of a typology of different variants and steps of derecognition. By identifying and breaking down crucial stages and steps that guide the derecognition process and untangling diplomatic strategies and tactics used in performing derecognition, the book aims to construct a cohesive outlook on derecognition practices.

Next, to understand the rationales and justifications invoked by involved countries in the derecognition process, the book uses the method of discourse analysis (Titscher et al. 2000). Discourse analysis helps identify, categorize, and intertextually analyze, with facts and evidence, how the arguments for derecognition are presented and justified, as well as trace the discursive influence that the former base states (as contractors) have on derecognizing states (as executors). The legitimacy of a campaign to prevent or encourage or enact derecognition relies on the quality and justifiability of diplomatic narratives invoked by concerned parties (Morin and Paquin 2018). The battle for state derecognition, a performative process, is also textual. Interstate relations are, first and foremost, intertextual relations (Visoka 2018). Diplomatic narratives can be weaponized and become powerful tools in pursuing derecognition. They are socially constituted and, in turn, constitute social realities. Therefore, understanding derecognition requires tracing all concerned parties' diplomatic discourse and arguments (Oglesby 2016). Analyzing diplomatic discourses helps identify within- and cross-case dominant narratives and features that capture the essence of contemporary state practices and helps to critically interrogate the intertextual influence in world politics. So the book uses discourse-historical approach to scrutinize diplomatic texts and other textual content as well as explore the broader sociomaterial context and factors that have shaped derecognition arguments (Reisigl and Wodak 2009). This approach enables in-depth analysis of texts and discourses invoked in the context of derecognition. The book utilizes entry-level analysis to identify relevant texts and documents and categorize the content according to specific clusters of themes, which foreground the process, justification and effects of derecognition. The entry-level analysis helps categorize diplomatic text and justifications for derecognition into specific discourse topics. Then, an in-depth analysis proceeds by looking at the discursive strategies, the audiences of argumentation, and the inter-textuality, coherence, and inconsistencies of discourses invoked by the protagonist states. Moreover, the in-depth analysis enables exploring the relationship between the discourse and level or phase of derecognition. Thus, jointly through entry-level and in-depth analyses of derecognition discourses, we can problematize and critically interrogate the logics, claims of truth, normative coherence and rightness, and implications of arguments invoked for withdrawing the recognition of states. Finally, to understand the process, rationales, and effects of derecognition, the book draws on multiple data sources, including original interviews with diplomats and foreign policy experts from countries implicated in or affected by derecognition, diplomatic notes, reports, and statements, as well as media reports and public interview transcripts from protagonist states.

CONCLUSION

The derecognition of states is a niche topic and segment of diplomacy and foreign policy that, although it has only been studied marginally so far, is not without significance in world politics. The prospect of a state being derecognized or not is of great importance to the stability, continuation, and rise of reversal politics of statehood in world politics. This chapter has surveyed the existing legal and normative views on state derecognition and has offered a conceptual framework for updating and expanding our empirical knowledge on the topic. There is no consensus among legal scholars on whether states can withdraw the recognition of other states. The dominant view is that recognition is irreversible, and what we refer to here as derecognition is misleading since the focus should be on discontinuing bilateral diplomatic relations rather than decertifying statehood of a specific claimant entity. This view adheres to the doctrinal thinking that neither recognition nor derecognition is constitutive of statehood. Another view is that since matters concerning the recognition and derecognition of states are broadly unregulated and are left at the discretion of individual states, derecognition as a diplomatic practice is present and can produce political, economic, and legal effects. Other voices argue that derecognition is permissible if the original conditions of recognition are no longer present. Thus, derecognition is permitted when there is no state to recognize.

These viewpoints provide a helpful starting point but leave many questions unanswered. Evidently, derecognition is present in world politics and has become an essential diplomatic instrument for state contestation, shifting allegiances, and geopolitical rivalries. Thus, developing a general account of this diplomatic practice and exploring its salience and impact on world politics is crucial. For this purpose, a pluralist outlook of derecognition as a foreign policy instrument is proposed in this chapter as a suitable pathway for tracing contemporary state practices. The proposed analytical framework aims at disentangling the complex diplomatic, economic, and geopolitical linkages and trans-scalar agency that shape the decisions, processes, and outcomes of derecognition. The focus will be on exploring five case studies of states exposed to derecognition with unique sociohistorical trajectories, different geographical locations, statehood capacity, and great power support. The following chapters are organized thematically and examine the actors and process, the rationales, and the effects of state derecognition. Within each thematic chapter, the empirical and cross-case empirical findings will be clustered and organized along generalizable patterns and features.

3 ✦ The Process of State Derecognition

The derecognition of states is rare diplomatic practice. While many states may not get along well and have hostile relationships, they rarely question one another's existence. Even the breakup of diplomatic relations isn't portrayed as derecognition. So if there is a broad consensus that recognition is irreversible, why is derecognition present in contemporary state practice? This chapter examines how state derecognition unfolds in practice by looking at the actors and the process that underpins the severance, downgrading, suspension, and ending of diplomatic relations between states. The chapter approaches derecognition as a multistage and entangled process prone to uneven trajectories and unexpected twists, blockages, and ruptures.

This chapter identifies four significant phases or stages underpinning the state derecognition process. Although the process is complex and it is hard to delineate key stages, conceptualizing it into main phases helps break down its key features, tactics, strategies, outcomes, and broader implications. In other words, some of the stages or phases in the derecognition might be outcomes or extensions of preceding phases, but nonetheless are essential to be accounted for, as they have a formative role in later stages. The first phase of derecognition is contesting the sovereignty of the claimant state. During this phase, the former base state aims to undermine the domestic and international standing of the claimant state to weaken its sovereignty and capacity to act as a sovereign state at home and abroad. The second phase of the derecognition process consists of persuading third countries to reconsider their position on the claimant state, ranging from signaling the downgrade of its diplomatic relations to taking proactive measures to downgrade rela-

69

tions or take a neutral stance on the dispute. The third phase of the process entails instances when the lobbying campaign does not result in full and formal derecognition of the claimant state. However, it can result in freezing recognition, namely retaining recognition but ending diplomatic engagement. The fourth phase is the formal and explicit withdrawal of recognition of the claimant state by third countries. In certain instances, the formal withdrawal of recognition as a significant diplomatic act and the momentum it generates can go unnoticed. However, it can also cause significant diplomatic disputes among contender states. In some instances, regardless of the formal withdrawal of recognition, concerned states continue to have informal diplomatic relations that can last indefinitely or be a transitory phase for restoring diplomatic ties with the claimant state. There is a possibility of re-recognition, too, namely annulment of the derecognition decision and restoration of the original decision for recognition.

This chapter's discussion of each stage of state derecognition draws on a comparative examination of contemporary cases where new varieties and patterns of derecognition are analyzed by dissecting similarities and differences among the case studies. Yet tracing the derecognition of state is a complex process. Some claimant countries under examination in this book, such as Taiwan and Western Sahara, have been recognized, derecognized, and then re-recognized several times. Thus, the analysis of the process of derecognition focuses on the examples and cases that help inductively illustrate the politics and practices, as well as the pathways and variants, of derecognition in contemporary world politics. That said, each case has its unique trajectory and claims to self-determination and statehood, and has had different recognition and derecognition events. The key is to establish a balance between context-specific and contingent generalization when analyzing and exploring each stage and variant of derecognition.

The chapter is organized as follows. It first examines the domestic and international contestation of claimant states that foregrounds all cases of derecognition. The second section looks at the dynamics of shifting from contestation to reconsideration of recognition by third countries, namely looking at the features of anti-diplomatic campaigns that are characteristic across all cases. The third section looks at the intermediary and ambivalent actions that third countries take in neither fully withdrawing recognition nor fully endorsing the sovereignty and statehood of the claimant state. Next, the chapter looks at the formal and full withdrawal of recognition and its aftermath, especially how all protagonist states react and cope with such a decision and what actions are taken to sustain or reverse the new diplomatic reality.

CONTESTING THE INDEPENDENCE OF THE CLAIMANT STATE

The first stage in the derecognition process is contesting the independence and sovereignty of the claimant state. Former base states that contest a claimant state usually target two categories of third states. The first category is countries that have not yet recognized the claimant state. The focus of diplomatic efforts is to persuade these states not to change their position on the claimant state. The aim is to retain the position of nonrecognition. This phase is a response to the recognition quest of the claimant state, aiming to prevent and limit its success in consolidating international legal sovereignty through diplomatic recognition and membership in international organizations. Second, contesting the sovereignty of the claimant state aims to change the position of countries that have already recognized the claimant state or have established extensive institutional cooperation short of formal diplomatic relations. Thus, the process of derecognition often goes hand in hand with the process of preventing further recognition of claimant states. At its core, it aims to delegitimize the claimant state and ensure that its statehood remains contested and gradually unravels (Huddleston 2020).

First and foremost, state contestation starts by contesting the historical, legal, and factual grounds for statehood and attacking the claimant state's pro-independence leadership. Domestically, the former base state seeks to undermine the empirical sovereignty of the claimant state by creating political, legal, economic, and security blockages that hinder the normal functioning of the society (Ker-Lindsay 2012; Ojeda-Garcia et al. 2017). It can also involve maintaining administrative and military presence in certain parts of the contested territory, pressuring domestic changes by discriminating against the secessionist community, and favoring the ethnic and political communities loyal to the base state. Internationally, the former base state uses its diplomatic network, status within multilateral organizations, and strategic alliances with influential states to prevent the claimant state from gaining diplomatic recognition, participating in or joining regional and international bodies, and from strengthening its relations with other states (Weill 2020). Although contesting statehood and preventing recognition is about creating the conditions for a particular outcome, sometimes it is simply a part of a general strategy of the former base state to buy time in the hope that new and better options will become available for imposing a settlement (such as partition on ethnic lines) or reincorporating the territory through the use of force. In some instances, this may be because there is no clear consensus on the type of settlement people want. At other times, it may be that the solution on offer is generally unacceptable, and there is hope that the passage of time may create the conditions for a more favorable settlement (Ker-Lindsay 2012: 74). Ultimately, contesting the sovereignty of the claimant state by the former base state serves as a political weapon used to maintain enmity, politically and economically isolate and deviate the claimant state, diminish its prestige, lower its morale, and, most destructively, incite domestic and international instability (Berridge 1994: 6; Berg and Pegg 2020).

These domestic and international contestation features of the claimant states are prevalent in all case studies examined in this book. For example, mainland China claims Taiwan as part of its territory and wants the island to unite with the mainland, from which it split during the civil war in 1949. China uses the "One China Principle" as the core argument against the recognition of Taiwan, and respectively, as a normative basis for its derecognition. The One China Principle states that there is one China, but two political systems, and the sole representative abroad is Beijing. From the perspective of mainland China, Taiwan (or the Republic of China) ceased to exist in 1949, and the sole successor state is the People's Republic of China (MFA of PRC 2019). China uses UN General Assembly Resolution 2758 (1971) to support the claim that Taiwan is part of its territory and that there is one China regardless of the de facto lack of control over the island of Taiwan. Resolution 2758 considers the People's Republic of China to be "the only lawful representatives of China to the United Nations," and notes that Taiwan's representatives must be expelled from the positions they "unlawfully occupy at the United Nations and in all organizations related to it."

China perceives "the secessionist activities of the 'Taiwan Independence' forces [as] the biggest immediate threat to China's sovereignty and territorial integrity as well as peace and stability on both sides of the Taiwan Straits and the Asia-Pacific region as a whole" (Embassy of the People's Republic of China in Australia 2005: 18). For example, China's 2005 Anti-Secession Law states that if Taiwan formally declares independence, China will not rule out employing "non-peaceful means and other necessary measures to protect China's sovereignty and territorial integrity" (Ji 2006: 240). While cross-strait relations have remained relatively peaceful for a long time, in 2021 the situation deteriorated to the point that mainland China has increased its military provocations and warned of potential takeover of the island of Taiwan. For instance, in October 2021, "Chinese air force sent around 150 jets into Taiwan's air-defence identification zone" (Financial Times 2021). Around the same time, Chinese president Xi Jinping warned that "the historical task of the complete reunification of the motherland must be fulfilled, and will definitely be fulfilled." While China has pledged that reunification with Taiwan will take place in a peaceful manner and in line with the principle of one country and two systems, Taiwan has objected to such an arrangement, fearing that China would strip the island of its democratic and autonomous institutions and employ restrictive and authoritarian measures similar to those applied in Hong Kong (BBC 2021). On the domestic front, to retain Taiwan's contestation and partial isolation, China could deploy hybrid warfare relying on naval blockades, covert attacks against Taiwan's critical infrastructure, disinformation warfare, and political campaigns for undermining democratic institutions in Taipei (Easton 2022).

On the other hand, even as Taiwan considers itself a separate and independent state, it has never declared independence. While Taiwan enjoys economic and political stability domestically, it has relied on diplomatic allies and external bilateral recognition to maintain claims to separate and state-like subjectivity internationally. For Taiwan, the function of diplomatic recognition is to maintain a sense of sovereign statehood, expand international sovereignty, and use allies to represent its interests at international bodies that it cannot access. As Stringer (2006: 551) argues: "Diplomatic recognition provides the Taiwanese government with some legitimacy in pressing its claims in the international community, and some proof that it is a sovereign entity." The existing states that recognize Taiwan are small and weak states in the international plane, but, nonetheless, they formally enjoy sovereign equality and are subjects under international law (Chiang and Hwang 2008: 72). Hence, Taiwan is well aware of the significance of diplomatic allies for retaining at least symbolic claims to independent statehood. Taiwan's president, Tsai Ing-wen, admitted in 2021 that "Taiwan's exclusion from the United Nations and most other international institutions could have led to isolation, but Taiwan instead tapped into the tremendous creativity and capacity of its people, allowing us to establish global connections by other means—through small businesses, nongovernmental organizations, and various semi-official groupings" (Ing-wen 2021).

However, since mainland communist China was allowed to claim a permanent seat at the UN Security Council, Taiwan has gradually lost its diplomatic allies. The change in UN representation constituted a dramatic tipping point in the diplomatic competition between Taiwan and China since it was followed by a collapse of the ROC's formal diplomatic ties with other countries. In 1970, Taipei led Beijing in diplomatic recognition by a margin of 68 to 53. Just three years later, the PRC had a more than two-to-one advantage of 86 to 39; and by 1977 this had become an overwhelming margin of 111 to 23 (Clark 2008: 87). Over the years, Chinese diplomats have argued that countries that recognize Taiwan not only breach the sovereignty and territorial integrity of China but also undermine cross-strait relations and political dialogue. And to a large extent, China has succeeded in keeping the territorial claim over Taiwan alive and central to its foreign policy of switching diplomatic recognition from Taiwan to China. As of January 2024, only twelve countries had official ties with Taiwan—seven in Central America and the Caribbean, one in Africa, three small island states in the Pacific, and the Vatican. As this book went to press, Nauru withdrew the recognition of Taiwan in January 2024, which took place days after Taiwan elected the pro-independence president Lai Ching-te (Government of the Republic of Nauru 2024). Clark (2008: 87) shows, "The loss of the ROC's seat in the United Nations was devastating in terms of its international status because Beijing used the reversal of UN membership to solidify its claim to sovereignty over all of China, including Taiwan."

Consequently, over the years, China has contested the statehood claims of Taiwan by blocking its membership om international organizations and undermining its ability to participate in international forums. Most important and relevant for this study, China considers its campaign for the derecognition of Taiwan as crucial foreign policy instrument to keep alive its territorial claim over the island. China has forced several multinational corporations to erase any trace of digital or symbolic recognition of Taiwan's separate economic and trade subjectivity. Most recently, China has shifted its discourse and threatened the United States, EU, and Australia for encouraging Taiwan's independence and taking measures to undermine "China's sovereignty, territorial integrity and other core interests." Such actions, it warned, would force it to take measures "to defend . . . national sovereignty and territorial integrity" (MFA of PRC 2021). So the dynamics of mutual contestation are significant in the case of mainland China and Taiwan to the point that there is a risk of conflict escalation and breach of the status quo (Heath, Lilly, and Han 2023).

The dynamics of contestation as the first stage of state derecognition play out differently in Africa, as the dispute between Morocco and Western Sahara shows. Although Western Sahara has not formally undergone the decolonization process, Morocco, as the occupying power, continues to make claims over the territory and challenge the legitimacy of the Sahrawi Arabic Democratic Republic (SADR). The Polisario Front represents the SADR, the governance structures and population primarily based in exile or camps in Algeria (Wilson 2016). The main dispute over Western Sahara is the delayed referendum on self-determination. The UN has deployed a mission there but has been unsuccessful in completing the decolonization process. There is a dispute between Morocco and the Polisario Front on the electorate deemed eligible to vote in a self-determination referendum (Zunes and Mundy 2010). While Morocco seeks to expand the vote to all Saharan tribes linked to the colonial-period Spanish Sahara, the Polisario Front insists on limiting the count to those who were in the Spanish census of 1974 (Jensen 2005: 13). Over time, Morocco has expanded its settlements in the Western Sahara and has actively exploited natural and sea resources in a way deemed problematic under international law of occupation (Riegl and Doboš 2017a: 101). On the domestic front, Morocco has pursued a policy of isolation toward the Polisario Front and one of hardship for its supporters while simultaneously incentivizing defections among the Saharawi people to weaken the internal legitimacy and unity of the SADR authorities in refugee camps and exile.

As Morocco's occupation has expanded since the 1970s, the Moroccan authorities have prevented the Sahrawi people, represented by the Polisario Front, from consolidating state capacities and forcing them to operate in exile. It has maintained control in significant parts of Western Sahara's territory. Central to Morocco's policy on Western Sahara is the nonrecognition or derecognition of the SADR and the expansion of international acceptance to Morocco's control over the territory (Besenyő, Huddleston, and Zoubir 2023). Morocco has simultaneously taken a wide range of diplomatic steps as part of its efforts to undermine the SADR's international standing. The most important is the 2007 autonomy plan, which secured UN attention and allowed readmission to the African Union in 2017. Through these multilateral and regional platforms, Morocco seeks to strengthen its bilateral diplomatic efforts centered around economic and military cooperation with countries that have not recognized or have derecognized the SADR (Fakir 2017).

Moreover, Morocco has tried to solidify its claim over Western Sahara by encouraging other states to open consular offices in the occupied territories or by organizing international events, such as the Crans Montana Forum in the city of Dakhla (Morocco World News 2015). Such strategies, similar to Israeli's attempt to make Jerusalem its diplomatic capital, aim to secure wider international recognition of Morocco's territorial claims over Western Sahara. For example, African countries such as Senegal, the Ivory Coast, Gambia, Liberia, the Union of Comoros, Cape Verde, and Togo, among others, have also opened their honorary consulates in Laâyoune and Dakhla and have openly portrayed such gestures as recognition of Morocco's sovereignty over Western Sahara (Morocco World News 2020). Of significance importance has been the United States' recognition of Morocco's sovereignty over the entire Western Sahara territory in December 2020 and its pledge to open a consulate in the Western Sahara (White House 2020a). This proclamation, which US president Donald Trump signed, not only recognized Morocco's sovereignty over the territory but stated that "an independent Sahrawi State is not a realistic option for resolving the conflict and that genuine autonomy under Moroccan sovereignty is the only feasible solution" (White House 2020b). By doing so, the United States took a stance on this self-determination conflict whereby it rejected recognizing SADR as an independent state and expressed its preference for the outcome of the eventual referendum. Thus, these are examples of direct measures to contest the symbolic sovereignty of SADR over certain parts of Western Sahara, and they show how third countries are implicated in legitimizing Morocco's control over the contested territory.

Internationally, the struggle to claim control and sovereignty over Western Sahara occurs through the battle for recognition and derecognition. In the absence of control over the Western Sahara territory and de facto government on the ground, the Polisario Front, as founders of the SADR, has tried to retain the claims to independent statehood through bilateral recognition as well as participation and membership in regional bodies, such as the African Union. As of 2023, SADR was recognized by around 31 out of 193 UN member states. However, Morocco's decade-long campaign for international contestation of SADR has resulted in withdrawing or freezing recognition by 53 states. These figures fluctuate as several third countries have recognized, derecognized, and re-recognized SADR several times, as will be discussed later in the chapter. Thus, Morocco's main focus internationally has been to delegitimize the Polisario Front and persuade third countries to join its political strategy of denying the existence of any Sahrawi independent state in Western Sahara. Both sides have exploited the UN and international courts in this struggle to seek legal confirmation of their right to rule over the Western Sahara. As early as 1975, the International Court of Justice, through an advisory opinion, rejected Morocco's claim over the territory and reconfirmed the right of Sahrawi people to self-determination (Wooldridge 1979). Equally, the European Court of Justice contested a trade agreement the European Commission signed with Morocco to access fish and other resources from occupied territories. So, internationally, SADR has maintained a moral and legal upper hand, but when it comes to exercising sovereign statehood on the ground, it has been unable to do so.

Most important, Morocco's campaign for derecognition has been chiefly based on economic deals, and geopolitical and security pacts have significantly narrowed SADR's international space. Within the UN system, Morocco has enjoyed broad support from Western states represented at the UN Security Council for its autonomy plan and for curtailing the ability of the UN Mission for Referendum in Western Sahara to accomplish its mandate on the ground. So Morocco has successfully contested SADR's sovereignty at home and abroad, thus enhancing its chances for significant control over the Western Sahara (Besenyő, Huddleston, and Zoubir 2023).

In Europe, Serbia contests Kosovo's independence because it was declared without its consent and in breach of its sovereignty and territorial integrity. However, Kosovo has shown steady progress in the completion of international recognition since it declared independence in 2008 (Newman and Visoka 2018a). Over one hundred UN member states have recognized it. But, contesting Kosovo's statehood remains one of Serbia's most critical foreign policy goals. Serbia claims that it defends international law, the UN Charter, and the Security Council's supreme authority to preserve international peace by defending its sovereignty and territorial integrity. To solidify its territorial claims over Kosovo and justify its continued interference in Kosovo's domestic affairs, Serbia decided to change its constitution and incorporate Kosovo into its preambular clauses while in the middle of UN-led talks in 2006 on the territory's future status (Weller 2009). Serbia created parallel structures during the UN's transitional administration to protect the remaining Serb population in Kosovo, to prevent claims to independence, and, if necessary, to prepare grounds for the internal partition of Kosovo. These structures consist of a chain of entities within sectors such as security, education, health, and public services, which the Serbian government maintains politically and financially (Visoka 2016). Although formally, these parallel structures were dismantled after 2011 as part of the EU-led talks for the normalization of relations, in practice, they continued to operate over a decade later as informal structures under the political tutelage and financial support of the Serbian government (Balkan Insight 2021).

In the immediate aftermath of Kosovo's independence in 2008, Serbia tried to contest it by seeking an advisory opinion from the International Court of Justice (ICJ) on the accordance of Kosovo's independence with international law. Serbia argued that Kosovo's declaration of independence was unilateral, illegal, without the host state's consent, and against international law and the international system of states based on inalienability of sovereignty and territorial integrity. Despite the ICJ's advisory opinion in favor of Kosovo—stating that the declaration of independence did not contradict international law—Serbia continued to argue that Kosovo's independence breached international norms and laws on sovereignty, territorial integrity, and statehood (Ker-Lindsay 2012; Visoka 2018). Disregarding this crucial judicious ruling, Serbia claimed that Kosovo remains under international administration and that the ICJ "did not affirm the right of the province of Kosovo to secession from the Republic of Serbia" (UN Secretary-General 2010: 2).

Since 2008, Serbia has actively worked to prevent recognition of Kosovo, but with little success. Since the declaration of independence, 117 sovereign states have recognized Kosovo, and the country has established diplomatic relations with over 80 states, has opened around forty diplomatic missions, and has joined over fifty regional and international organizations (Visoka 2018; 2019). Central to Serbia's diplomatic warfare against Kosovo has been the prevention and reversal of Kosovo's recognition. Serbia considers recognition of Kosovo a threat to its national interests as well as a source of internal and regional instability (Ministry of Defence of Serbia 2017: 7). In 2017, Serbia launched a campaign to undermine Kosovo's international standing by offering economic and military assistance to freeze or withdraw the recognition of Kosovo. Between 2008 and 2014, when Kosovo received over one hundred recognitions, Serbia's diplomatic campaign was mainly focused on preventing the recognition of Kosovo and obstructing its membership in international organizations, such as the UN, Organization for Security and Co-operation in Europe, and the Council of Europe (Newman and Visoka 2018b). The campaign was possible mainly due to powerful support from Russia and other major regional powers in wider Europe.

Over time, Serbia realized that by getting recognition from over one hundred states, Kosovo had secured two-thirds of the votes needed to join UN specialized agencies and other regional organizations. As noted by Serbian foreign minister Ivica Dačić: "In 2015 we had an attempt to get Kosovo into UNESCO and then we faced the difficult task of preventing this, given that at that moment, in 2014, 113 countries had recognized Kosovo." Thus, by pursuing the derecognition of Kosovo, Serbia is seeking to block Kosovo's international access, namely, reduce the number of states that interact with or vote for Kosovo in multilateral bodies. Most international and regional organizations require two-thirds of votes or qualified majorities, which means Serbia would have a much broader support base to block Kosovo's participation and membership in those international bodies. The calculation of this campaign is straightforward: the more states withdraw the recognition of Kosovo, the smaller the chance of Kosovo joining international organizations. Therefore, Serbia's goal became to reduce the number of countries that have recognized Kosovo to under one hundred so that Kosovo would not have sufficient votes to join any major international or regional organization.

Moreover, by blocking Kosovo's advancement in the international arena, Serbia has exploited the international contestation of Kosovo to enhance its bargaining power in the EU-led dialogue for normalization of relations with Kosovo. In this context, derecognition has served as an instrument of sabotage and diplomatic duress to force Kosovo to make concessions in favor of Serbia (Novosti 2019a). Finally, Serbia's pursuit of the derecognition of Kosovo is seen both as a victory and as a restoration of its international influence after decades of humiliation and defeat and as a strategic move against Kosovo's international partners, demonstrating Serbia's ability to reverse Kosovo's international standing (B92 2018d).

Finally, in the South Caucasus, since Abkhazia and South Ossetia proclaimed their independent statehood in the early 1990s and were finally recognized by the Russian Federation in 2008, the main foreign policy goal of Georgia as the former base state has been contestation and international isolation of these breakaway territories. Both territories proclaimed independence after a short war involving Russia as their main ally. Since there is a de facto border between Georgia and these breakaway territories and the stakes are high for military confrontation due to Russia's military presence and the EU's monitoring mission, Georgia contests the independence of Abkhazia and South Ossetia mainly through legal, political, and administrative measures (de Waal and von Twickel 2020). Over the years, Georgia has condemned all traces of independent statehood for Abkhazia and South Ossetia. In 2008 the government of Georgia even approved a special law on occupied territories to "define the status of the territories occupied as a result of the military aggression by the Russian Federation and to establish a special legal regime in the above territories." In the international sphere, Abkhazia and South Ossetia have not managed to receive broad international recognition—primarily due to Western condemnation of Russia's intervention and the collective nonrecognition policy of the EU. As of 2024, Abkhazia and South Ossetia had been recognized by the Russian Federation and nine other countries closely allied with Russia. The United States, the EU, and the majority of UN member states remain committed to the territorial integrity of Georgia, advocate for the peaceful resolution of disputes, and support gradually reincorporating these breakaway regions into Georgia. Under these circumstances, Georgian diplomacy exerts pressure on third countries to thwart any public rallies by representatives of Abkhazia, whatever their focus may be—cultural, humanitarian, educational, musical, or other. The Georgian Foreign Ministry actively seeks out those planning to decide on the recognition of Abkhazia to apply diplomatic pressures (Ó Beacháin 2020).

Therefore, the domestic and international contestation of the claimant state foregrounds all anti-diplomatic actions of the former base states and represents the first significant hallmark in the derecognition process. The contestation of the independence and sovereignty of the claimant state— through nonrecognition and persuasion of third countries not to extend recognition—is the baseline and foundational feature of all state derecognition campaigns. Across all cases, it is clear that domestic and international contestation of the claimant states by the former base state and its allies is a crucial method for not only symbolically undermining the sovereignty and state consolidation of the claimant state but also for subversively continuing war by other means in the international arena by preventing recognition and eventually reversing international recognition of the claimant state. In other words, without the active contestation by the former base state, the third countries are more likely to continue recognizing the effective authority of the claimant state and accept it into the club of sovereign states. While contestation of statehood is ever present in policy discourse and state practice, it does not often lead to the derecognition of the claimant state. It is a necessary condition but insufficient in influencing third countries' decisions to withdraw recognition of the claimant state. Claimant states often launch their counter-campaigns to try to retain their diplomatic allies and prevent the prospects for derecognition. Thus, the other side of state contestation is the capacity and creativity of the claimant state to survive and adapt to the international system. It can be noted that, across all the cases examined here, the stronger the efforts of former base states to contest the statehood of claimant states, the more resilient the latter appear in defending themselves and building alternative alliances. Such dynamics of contestation are a significant source of instability and block normalization of relations and peaceful coexistence between contender states.

RECONSIDERING RECOGNITION OF THE CLAIMANT STATE

The second strategic step in the state derecognition process involves identifying third countries that have already recognized the claimant state but, for various reasons, would be open to reconsidering their position. Frequently, such reconsideration is a direct product of diplomatic lobbying by the former base state and its international allies during the state contestation phase. However, it can also be driven by other factors, such as the extortionist foreign policy of third countries that reach out to contested states and offer to trade or rent recognition for individual or state profit. Such a step in the derecognition process can be triggered by other international entanglements, such as rivalry among global and regional powers that use contested states as proxies to advance their own interests. As this section shows, lobbying for reconsidering, suspending, and freezing the recognition of the claimant state can take place in two forms: directly by the former base state that utilizes economic, political, and diplomatic means, and indirectly by its diplomatic allies, who exert their geopolitical and economic influence.

While the struggle between the claimant and former base state over recognition tends to reach out to all other sovereign states (UN members), only a limited number of states tend to be open to reconsidering their recognition of the claimant state and engaging in the derecognition saga. It is unusual and uncommon for established and powerful states to engage in the derecognition of other states. In fact, both democratic and undemocratic states with long-standing diplomatic traditions are wary of this anti-diplomatic practice. They either withhold the recognition first or proactively promote nonrecognition of a specific claimant state. For an overwhelming number of sovereign states, once recognition is granted, it is tough to withdraw. This is partially a result of the sustainability of foreign policy and the desire to project political and normative consistency as much as circumstances permit. There is also peer pressure among like-minded countries to hold on to the previous synchronous, joint, or collective decision for recognition.

However, evidence shows that derecognizing other states has emerged as a common practice among a small group of states—primarily located in the global south—that gained independent statehood as part of the decolonization process—who continue to struggle with chronic poverty and geopolitical vulnerabilities or are ruled by semi-authoritarian regimes. In particular, several African, Latin American, and Caribbean nations with weak economies and (semi)authoritarian regimes are keen to exploit their status as sovereign states and UN members and engage in trading their right to recognition and diplomatic allegiances in exchange for economic, political, and military favors. Among the most prominent of those involved in withdrawing, renting, or switching their recognition of other states are Burkina Faso, the Central African Republic, the Dominican Republic, Gambia, Lesotho, Liberia, Malawi, Nauru, Panama, the Solomon Islands, Suriname, Tuvalu, and Vanuatu (see the appendix). Notably, postcolonial states have a long-standing tradition of taking advantage of great power politics and rivalry to obtain concessions and favors in exchange for their political allegiance and security cooperation (Taylor 2002). As Stringer (2006: 548) notes, for small states, "Diplomacy is often their only effective instrument of statecraft for making an impact within the international system on issues critical to their national interests." So they are well positioned "to leverage the prerogatives of their sovereignty, specifically their ability to confer recognition on another state, in exchange for economic aid and private investment" (Stringer 2006: 564). For these postcolonial extortionist states, state derecognition is one of the only available foreign policy assets they can use to reduce their vulnerability, benefit from foreign aid, renew alliances, and influence the international system more generally.

In general, persuading other states to reconsider recognizing the claimant state requires extensive diplomatic investment by the former base state and its international allies. As the consideration for derecognition is often grounded on incentives of some sort, third states engage in bargaining games with both parties to maximize their gains. While such diplomatic bargaining is not very different from other bilateral diplomatic transactions, its impact on the claimant state is much more significant than normal diplomatic transactions. The campaign for state derecognition involves personal diplomacy, which requires knowing with whom to interact and lobby, which amounts to knowing where the power lies. In some places, presidents are more powerful than prime ministers, whereas in other cases, lobbying through the foreign minister or other designated ministers or advisers to the government can deliver better results.

Most important, knowing how to relate the campaign for derecognition to the historical, cultural, and economic features of the interlocutor is essential to acquiring the desired outcome. The diplomatic efforts to prevent or push for derecognition at this stage often entail providing economic and development assistance, deepening bilateral military and security cooperation, and defending mutual interests within multilateral organizations. Economic diplomacy, so-called checkbook and dollar diplomacy, has been at the heart of Taiwan's and China's struggle for international recognition. Notably, the checkbook diplomacy of Taiwan and China is partially determined by their status as strong economies that can afford to use economic levers to advance their interests and partially by the self-perpetuating culture of checkbook diplomacy, whereby derecognizing states themselves condition the retention or withdrawal of recognition in exchange of financial and economic goods. Checkbook diplomacy is not very common in other cases, such as Serbia and Kosovo, Morocco and Western Sahara, and Abkhazia–South Ossetia and Georgia. They tend to use other diplomatic and military means to encourage third countries to consider the derecognition of the claimant state.

As part of diplomatic efforts for or against derecognition, visit diplomacy and other diplomatic incentives are often at play. Since the third countries implicated in the derecognition saga are often ignored and marginalized, they benefit from visit and hospitality diplomacy by the contender states because such events boost national pride and increase international attention (Yang 2011). Visit diplomacy involves large delegations from third countries who receive luxury treatment, financial payments, and treatment as world leaders (Brady and Henderson 2010: 212). The payoffs of visit diplomacy can range from establishing and maintaining personal relationships to negotiating deals for retaining, reconsidering, or shifting diplomatic recognition. In this context, visit diplomacy by the claimant state often indicates that bilateral relations are threatened and that additional financial incentives must be injected to prevent derecognition. For example, in 2006 Taiwan's president and foreign minister visited Chad to prevent derecognition, but they could not stop it. In another case, the Taiwanese government invited the leadership of the Solomon Islands to visit Taiwan as part of its efforts to prevent derecognition. Before losing Burkina Faso, Gambia, Malawi, and São Tomé and Príncipe as diplomatic allies, Taiwan tried to strengthen personal relationships with their leaders by organizing joint events such as the Africa-Taiwan Summit and injecting further socioeconomic assistance. However, there are instances when visit diplomacy results in defusing or delaying derecognition. For example, in 2019, the Taiwanese president visited Palau, Nauru, and the Marshall Islands to cultivate diplomatic ties with them. Similarly, increased diplomatic interaction between specific third countries and former base states could indicate their attempt to lobby for derecognition. However, such a process is often channeled through secret diplomacy and out of public eyes to avoid potential backlash and international condemnation.

The derecognition saga forces both the former base state and the claimant state to expand their diplomatic networks and open embassies in countries and regions that otherwise would not be considered strategic from the perspective of economic and social ties. In exchange for the derecognition of Taiwan, China tends to open embassies and deepen economic ties. China now has the most significant diplomatic network in the world, surpassing that of the United States and other global powers. Taiwan also has opened embassies in countries that recognized its sovereign statehood even if no Taiwanese citizen or businessperson resided in those countries (such as Nauru before 2024). As part of its efforts to derecognize Kosovo, Serbia added seven new embassies and consulates to its existing network of sixty-nine embassies and twenty-four consulates. The new embassies were in locations where Serbia had promised to open them as part of a deal to withdraw the recognition of Kosovo. Serbia's foreign minister admitted that "in selecting the location of new diplomatic missions, we took into account one of the most important foreign policy goals of Serbia—preserving the sovereignty and territorial integrity of the state and strengthening our position on the unilaterally proclaimed independence of Kosovo" (Novosti 2019b). In an attempt to mitigate unwanted effects, in 2018, Kosovo's Ministry of Foreign Affairs proactively worked to expand diplomatic relations and accredited its diplomats as nonresident ambassadors in different parts of Africa, Latin America, and Asia. In February 2018, Kosovo established diplomatic relations with Bangladesh and Oman (MFA of Kosovo 2018b, 2018c). The embassy in Panama, serving as Kosovo's hub in Latin America, has gained diplomatic accreditation and representation in four other countries in this region: Barbados, Belize, Costa Rica, and Saint Kitts and Nevis. Similarly, to prevent the recognition of Abkhazia and South Ossetia, Georgia rushed to establish diplomatic relations with all UN member states and expand its diplomatic network in all parts of the world.

A change of government in many countries can signal a change in foreign policy orientation, especially as the contenders have different ideological and personal motivations. Electoral processes and changes of government open up the opportunity for the former base states to approach third countries to reconsider their recognition of claimant states. Contender countries try to work with different political parties, hoping that once in power, the party will formulate a foreign policy in their interest. The approach of both China and Taiwan is to influence targeted states even without diplomatic ties through trade relations and other informal assistance to opposition parties, media, and interest groups. For example, China worked with several

Latin American nations for many years before they derecognized Taiwan and established diplomatic relations with China. Thus, elections are essential to measure how the long-term investment pays off. For example, Taiwan's deputy minister rushed to visit Tuvalu, one of its few remaining allies in the Pacific region, following the 2019 elections in the small island nation, fearing that a change of government could impact their diplomatic relations (Taiwan News 2019a). In preventing derecognition, Taiwan even granted airplanes and helicopters to Latin American presidents and statemen for personal use (Atkinson 2014: 426). In another context, Morocco utilized the rise of post-left governments in Latin America to persuade them to revise their decision on recognizing SADR (Masiky 2017). Within weeks of government change in El Salvador, the country decided to withdraw the recognition of SADR (Morocco World News 2019a, 2019b). In another case, when the pro-SADR president of Bolivia was forced to step down in 2019, the new interim government in power suspended the recognition of SADR. It adopted "constructive neutrality" until "a just, lasting and mutually acceptable political solution is reached . . . in accordance with the principles and objectives set out in the Charter of the United Nations" (Government of Bolivia 2020). Thus, electoral cycles offer opportunities to third countries and the contender states to exploit domestic openings to retain or reconsider the recognition of the claimant state. However, they also prove how unstable is the institution of diplomatic recognition, which requires constant incentives to maintain relations with third countries and exposes how indecent and damaging such extortionist diplomatic relations are.

In addition to checkbook diplomacy, former base states use personality politics, history, and symbolic relations to leverage third countries into reconsidering their recognition of the claimant state. For example, Serbia has used the diplomatic legacy and heritage of Tito's Yugoslavia as a leader of the nonalignment movement during the Cold War to persuade countries in the global south to reconsider their position on Kosovo. Yugoslavia played an essential role in decolonization and supported new postcolonial states in their early quest for national development. While Serbian nationalism has been one of the key reasons for the dissolution of Yugoslavia and for diminishing its heritage and legacy, this has not stopped the Serbian government or third countries in the global south from considering Serbia the successor of Yugoslavia and inherent its international heritage. During the campaign for the derecognition of Kosovo, Serbian foreign minister Dačić argued that "Africa is very important for us. There are fifty-four members of the United Nations from Africa. Also, these are our traditionally friendly countries from the time of Tito and Yugoslavia where no one has been for ten, twenty, and in some thirty years" (RTS 2019b). Dačić added: "Most of them have never been to our region, and the only thing they know about our region is probably Tito and Yugoslavia." As will be shown later in this chapter, several African countries, such as Ghana and Comoros, have acknowledged Yugoslavia's legacy as part of their consideration of the derecognition of Kosovo's independence. It takes more than such symbolic leverage to persuade other states to withdraw the recognition of claimant states. Nonetheless, it provides an important entry point for negotiating the terms of derecognition.

Concerning European states, Serbia has deployed a different strategy for the derecognition of Kosovo. It has exploited chiefly the diaspora community and local interest groups to lobby from the bottom up. So far, Kosovo has been recognized by twenty-two out of twenty-seven EU member states. Five countries, namely Cyprus, Greece, Romania, Slovakia, and Spain, continue to withhold the recognition of Kosovo pending a settlement with Serbia. In addition to ensuring these five EU member states do not recognize Kosovo, Serbia reached out to other European countries, such as the Czech Republic, Slovenia, France, Italy, and neighboring Montenegro, to try to initiate a domestic debate to rethink their positions on Kosovo and eventually either suspend or withdraw recognition. In the Czech Republic, Serbia initially worked with opposition parties and interest groups sympathetic to Serbia. Since 2001, groups such as Civil Society Friends of Serbs in Kosovo and Metohija have regularly pressed the Czech government to consider withdrawal of Kosovo's recognition by labeling the declaration of independence in 2008 and NATO's intervention in 1999 as a violation of international law (Civil Society Friends of Serbs in Kosovo and Metohija 2018). The campaign for the derecognition of Kosovo became serious in September 2019 when Milos Zeman, the Czech Republic's president, publicly stated that "if more countries withdraw that recognition, the Czech Republic could be among them." He added, "We support the Western Balkans region's gradual approaching to the EU, but I always say—without Kosovo" (N1 2019e). In France, Serbia lobbied for the derecognition of Kosovo through a petition initiated by Serb-French groups. The petition intended to pressure the French National Assembly to withdraw recognition of Kosovo and push for autonomy status as a region of Serbia (B92 2019). A similar petition was organized in Italy on the anniversary of Kosovo's independence, where Italian and Serbian lobby groups requested the government review its decision to recognize Kosovo (Telegraf 2019). In supporting these petitions, pro-

Serbian groups have invoked the derecognition of Kosovo by more than ten countries as a precedent that European states should follow. While these petitions did not have an immediate impact, their aim was to shape public opinion and prepare the grounds for contesting European support for Kosovo both from the bottom up and through bilateral diplomatic pressure.

While the process of state derecognition is predominantly a matter of diplomatic agency—namely the deployment of material resources, security arrangements, and diplomatic networks—evidence shows that the support of other states, especially that of regional and global powers, can play a significant role in shifting the balance of forces among the contenders. As part of the diplomatic efforts to pursue or prevent derecognition, the former base state and the claimant state tend to mobilize their diplomatic allies, especially the great powers, whenever possible. For example, Serbia pursued its derecognition campaign by itself, though it benefited from Russia and other non-Western states. Although Serbia denied Russia's support for its derecognition of Kosovo campaign, Russia's connection became obvious (Ni 2019b, 2009d). Russia signed bilateral agreements with Suriname, Burundi, the Commonwealth of Dominica, Grenada, and Madagascar only days after they decided to withdraw their recognition of Kosovo (Radio Slobodna Evropa 2019). Russia abolished visa requirements with some of these countries, while it signed military cooperation agreements with others. Russia played a direct role in persuading Suriname to derecognize Kosovo in 2018. Suriname announced the decision to revoke Kosovo's independence while Suriname's foreign minister was visiting Russia, demonstrating Russia's support for Serbia's campaign for the derecognition of Kosovo (MFA of Russia 2017).

Meanwhile, the United States tries to indirectly support Taiwan internationally by discouraging existing allies from switching allegiance to Beijing and warning them of the potential consequences of such action. For instance, a group of US congressmen proposed the Taiwan Allies International Protection and Enhancement Initiative (TAIPEI) Act to "strengthen Taiwan's standing around the world." The proposal, said the group, was "in response to several nations breaking official diplomatic ties with Taiwan due to Chinese pressure and bullying tactics" (Sunshine State News 2018). US senator Ed Markey declared in 2018 that "without a coherent U.S. strategy to push back, Taiwan's official partners might drop from 17 to zero. We must stand up for our friends in Taiwan" (Sunshine State News 2018). Most importantly, the locus of this initiative was, as the act says, "to downgrade U.S. relations with any government that takes adverse actions about Taiwan,

88 • *The Derecognition of States*

and to suspend or alter U.S. foreign assistance, including foreign military financing, to governments that take adverse actions with regard to Taiwan" (Sunshine State News 2018).

Backed by Russia, Abkhazia was close to securing recognition from the Dominican Republic, but the development never materialized once the United States summoned President Fernández for an urgent meeting in New York (Ó Beacháin 2020: 435). Prior to the visit of Serbian MFA to Grenada to lobby for the derecognition of Kosovo, the US Department of State sent a demarche to the government of Grenada to prevent such a move. In this demarche, which was leaked to Serbian diplomatic channels, the United States encouraged Grenada to strongly confirm the recognition of Kosovo as a full member of the international community. The demarche also highlighted that derecognition would run contra the decision taken by over one hundred UN members, undermining democracy and stability in the region. Most importantly, the United States portrayed the derecognition of Kosovo as helping "backward elements in the region, working to undermine normalization efforts between Kosovo and Serbia and oppose the integration of the entire region into Euro-Atlantic institutions" (Novosti 2018b). It is also underlined that it would "act against the key efforts of the United States and the EU to tackle the fragility of the region" (Novosti 2018b).

The outcome of these diplomatic efforts to persuade third countries to reconsider the recognition of the claimant states is hard to predict as it depends on several factors, which are discussed later in this chapter. However, we can ascertain with confidence that efforts lead to three potential outcomes: (a) rejecting the request for derecognition, (b) suspending or freezing the recognition, or (c) proceeding with formal withdrawal of recognition and ending of diplomatic ties. When it comes to the first possible outcome, this could be determined by several context-specific but also cross-case factors, such as the excessive price and high transactional and reputational cost, demands on time due to other pressing national and regional issues, and the tendency to raise the bid for derecognition. A case in point is Lesotho's reconsidering its position in Western Sahara. In 2019, Lesotho caused diplomatic drama when the foreign minister announced a reconsideration, only to have the government reject it just days later. On 4 October 2019, the Ministry of Foreign Affairs of Lesotho announced the suspension of diplomatic ties with SADR "pending the outcome of the United Nations process" (MFA of Lesotho 2019). Five days later, the government of Lesotho issued a statement clarifying "the unfortunate, irregular publication of a confidential, State-to-State diplomatic communication between Lesotho and the Kingdom of Morocco," and denied the suspension of recognition of SADR (Government of Lesotho 2019). According to this statement, the position of Lesotho advocated "Morocco's total withdrawal from the Saharawi territories it is currently occupying, and respect for the self-determination and territorial integrity of the SADR and its people" (Government of Lesotho 2019).

Another twist to this debacle emerged in December 2019, when Lesego Makgothi, minister of foreign affairs and international relations of the Kingdom of Lesotho, insisted on maintaining a neutral position on Western Sahara. Foreign Minister Makgothi added that Lesotho had "conducted a thorough evaluation of the effectiveness of the kingdom of Lesotho's position concerning this regional dispute," concluding that "promoting a just and peaceful solution of this regional conflict will best be served by a 'Neutral' yet strong support of the Kingdom of Lesotho to the ongoing UN-led process under the guidance of the United Nations Secretary General and supervision of the United Nations (UN) Security Council" (Lesotho Times 2018). The foreign minister insisted that the note verbale dated 4 October 2019 was Lesotho's "sovereign decision to suspend all its decisions and statements related to Western Sahara and 'SADR,' pending the outcome of the United Nations process" (Lesotho Times 2018). However, the Lesotho government spokesperson, Thesele Maseribane, soon denied for a second time the derecognition of Western Sahara, stating: "Lesotho has maintained its firm position of principles to support the struggle of the people of Western Sahara." The controversy was finally settled in June 2020, when Lesotho's new foreign minister, Matsepo Molise-Ramakoae, issued a statement on the country's position on Western Sahara. The statement reaffirmed its support for the self-determination of the people of Western Sahara and clarified that "any pronouncements made purporting to change Lesotho's position on this issue are of no force and effect"(Government of Lesotho 2020: 4).

In the case of Taiwan, despite China's diplomatic lobbying and economic incentives, Eswatini (formerly Swaziland) declared its relationship with Taiwan to be based on mutual interests, not money. "We're very happy with our relationship and intend to maintain it for a very long time because our friendship is based on our national interests and not on the size of Taiwan's wallet," a government spokesperson stated (Bloomberg 2017). Despite mixed messages sent by Czech politicians on reconsidering Kosovo's independence, ultimately the foreign minister of the Czech Republic, Tomas Petricek, stated: "The Czech Government, which is responsible for country's foreign policy, hasn't changed its stance towards Kosovo or any of the Western Balkans countries. We continue to support fully the dialogue between

Serbia and Kosovo and their path to the EU" (Zëri 2019e). The Czech Ministry of Foreign Affairs issued a statement recalling that the 2008 decision to recognize and establish diplomatic relations with Kosovo was "de jure recognition, ie full and final recognition of the state in terms of international law," adding that "the Czech Republic has also never revoked the recognition of any state in its practice" (MFA of Czech Republic 2019). In the case of neighboring Slovenia, Serbia worked with a small pro-Russian socialist party to rethink the recognition of Kosovo. However, soon after, Slovenian minister of foreign affairs Miro Cerar dismissed the possibility of Slovenia revoking recognition of Kosovo, stating, "I think there was sufficient basis for recognition of Kosovo as a country" (N1 2019a).

The reconsideration of recognition is a significant stage in the derecognition process, and the diplomatic battle that takes place during this stage between pro-recognition and counter-recognition forces influences the prospects for retaining recognition or pursuing derecognition. It is not a predetermined process but open to diplomatic bargaining, external and internal pressure, and calculation of costs and benefits of all possible outcomes. The multiplicity of these factors often results in settling for in-between arrangements that permit all competing forces to declare their ambivalent victories.

DIPLOMATIC AMBIVALENCE: FROM RECOGNITION WITHOUT ENGAGEMENT TO FROZEN RECOGNITION

The third stage in the derecognition process comprises instances when third countries unilaterally reconsider their position on the claimant state and take affirmative actions by either suspending or freezing recognition of the claimant state. This entails taking intermediary measures that in effect resemble severance of diplomatic relations, namely moving from some sort of diplomatic relationship to nonrelationship. According to normal diplomatic practice, severance of diplomatic relations can be done by mutual consent or unilaterally, and it is a culmination of several reciprocal and retaliatory actions undertaken by both sides (Denza 2016). Historically, "The severance of diplomatic relations was an act of extreme gravity, often a prelude to a declaration of war" (Giegerich 2018: 1110). In the case of derecognition, consideration of suspension of recognition is unilateral and doesn't involve hostile actions by the claimant state. Usually it starts by issuing antagonizing statements and flirting diplomatically with the other contender states. Meetings between diplomatic allies and the adversaries of the claimant state signal the possibility of switching or withdrawing recognition. This was the case with Panama and China prior to Panama's derecognition of Taiwan in 2007. The president of the Dominican Republic made two trips to China before it derecognized Taiwan, signaling the instability of their bilateral relations (MFA of Taiwan 2018a). Third countries also engage in secretive talks (anti-diplomatic actions) on switching diplomatic ties among the contenders. In 2017, Burkina Faso's foreign minister publicly admitted that people and companies with close links to China had offered millions of dollars in exchange for the derecognition of Taiwan. While this was a warning sign, Burkina Faso stated it had no reason to reconsider the relationship with Taiwan (Taiwan News 2017). Yet this warning resulted in boosting Taiwan's investment in Burkina Faso's education, agriculture, and defense sectors. However, in 2018, Burkina Faso snubbed Taiwan and established diplomatic ties with China. In justifying the sudden change of position, the same foreign minister who praised diplomatic ties with Taiwan stated that "the evolution of the world and the socio-economic challenges of our country and region push us to reconsider our position" (New York Times 2018). The reason behind this sudden change was apparently an additional request of $23 million from Burkina Faso that was rejected by Taiwan (Burcu and Bertrand 2019).

As part of the process of reconsidering ties with the claimant state, third countries can go halfway by suspending the recognition of the claimant state. This is especially observed when third countries frame derecognition decisions in vague language, leaving open the option of swinging back and forth according to changing circumstances. Suspending recognition is often framed as a strategic decision to encourage parties in conflict to resolve the disputes through peaceful dialogue. It amounts to some sort of formal recognition without diplomatic engagement. This form of derecognition resembles in reverse order features of "nonrecognition lite," or engagement without recognition—namely when third countries do not formally recognize the claimant state but in practice have active diplomatic interactions and support the claimant state's membership in international bodies (Coppieters 2020). In 2018, the Ministry of Foreign Affairs of Liberia informed its Serbian counterpart of the "reconsideration of its decision to recognize independence of Kosovo" in order to allow "for a sustainable solution for citizens of Serbia and Province of Kosovo, as is being done through current negotiations," adding that "this decision remains in effect until the discussion and negotiations are completed under the European Union" (MFA of Liberia 2018). Similarly, Grenada stated that "in the interim, the Government of Grenada suspends any previous decision or declaration on the question as to the status of Kosovo . . . once the two parties reach an agreement, the Government of Grenada will steadfastly support the position reached by the parties" (MFA of Grenada 2018). In 2012, Dominica recognized Kosovo as an independent and sovereign state. In the original recognition letter, Dominica commended "the commitment of the people of Kosovo to build an independent state based on the principles of freedom and democracy" (Dominica News Online 2012). Six years later, in 2018, Serbia persuaded Dominica to temporarily suspend Kosovo's recognition, indicating that when both sides came to an agreed settlement, Dominica would support the position they agreed on (Government of Serbia 2018a). On 5 July 2018, the Serbian foreign minister announced that Papua New Guinea had suspended the recognition of Kosovo. In a letter dated 27 June 2018, the minister of foreign affairs, Rimbink Pato, retracted the 2012 decision to recognize Kosovo's independence, considering it "most appropriate to adopt a neutral stance . . . allowing both parties to find a peaceful and lasting solution" (MFAT of Papua New Guinea 2018). The derecognition letter concluded that "as a result of this position, any letters/communications issued by PNG in October 2012 recognizing Kosovo's independence are to be terminated forthwith until both parties complete the negotiations process and agree on the final status of Kosovo under the auspices of the EU and the UN pursuant to the UNSC Resolution 1244 referred to above" (MFAT of Papua New Guinea 2018).

Similarly, in the case of Western Sahara, the majority of countries that have agreed to reconsider their recognition of SADR have in fact only suspended or terminated their recognition pending a settlement between Morocco and the Polisario Front. In 2000, Honduras suspended the recognition of SADR pending the outcome of a referendum. However, on that occasion, the Moroccan Foreign Affairs and Cooperation Ministry twisted the reasoning behind suspended recognition and attributed this success to "the growing awareness that the Polisario entity is artificial, ephemeral and doomed to disappear" (Arabic News 2000). In 2007 Kenya decided to freeze the recognition of SADR "until the conflict is resolved, within the framework of the United Nations where progress is currently being made" (Maghess 2007). Soon after, Morocco restored diplomatic relations with Kenya. Yet in 2022 Kenya called "for the self-determination of Western Sahara through a free and fair referendum administered by the U.N. and the A.U." (MFA of Kenya 2022).

There are instances when third countries claim they are taking a neutral position on the status of the claimant state. Serbia managed to convince several states to take a neutral stance on Kosovo's independence, thus neither officially rescinding recognition nor continuing normal diplomatic relations. This is labeled "frozen recognition." Freezing recognition involves less severe forms of diplomatic friction, which can entail suspending institutional contacts, not appointing an ambassador or opening an embassy, or avoiding supporting or voting in favor for membership in international organizations. Egypt is a case in point. Egypt originally recognized Kosovo in 2013 during a period of democratic transition, which was interrupted by the military takeover of the country by General el-Sisi. The recognition of Kosovo by Egypt was never communicated to the Kosovo government directly. Instead, Egypt's letter on Kosovo recognition was sent to Germany and communicated to the public through a brief press statement. Subsequently, Serbia targeted Egypt, arguing that Kosovo was recognized during the Muslim Brotherhood's brief period of governance and thus, given the organization's late outlaw status and expulsion from the political scene, the decision could be contested (B92 2018a). However, this argument doesn't stand because Kosovo was recognized by the MFA of Egypt, which was under the control of the military during Morsi's short-lived rule. This partially explains why Egypt did not formally withdraw the recognition of Kosovo. Moreover, the Egyptian ambassador in Serbia, Ezzedine Fahmy, stated: "International law does not allow the withdrawal of state recognition of another state, this is an irreversible obligation. Thus, withdrawing Egypt's recognition of Kosovo became impossible according to the law" (Al-Ahram 2016). Under these circumstances, Serbia claimed that Egypt had frozen the recognition of Kosovo, which, according to the Egyptian foreign minister, meant "there is no implementation of this decision until the negotiations confirm that this status is in accordance with international law" (RTS 2018). In the words of the Egyptian ambassador in Serbia, Egypt "will not develop our relations with Kosovo. There will be no exchange of embassies between the two countries. Our position will remain constant. There will be no kind of diplomatic representation until things become clear in Serbia and there is a referendum on this issue" (Al-Ahram 2016). With President el-Sisi, Egypt has not advanced any further in economic or diplomatic ties with Kosovo and has often abstained when Kosovo has aspired to membership in international organizations (B92 2018b).

However, frozen recognition is often an intermediary and prolonged phase, frequently ending with the withdrawal of recognition. For example, Barbados froze the recognition of SADR in 2013 until it decided to withdraw the recognition in 2019. Having recognized Western Sahara on 6

March 2014, Malawi derecognized it in 2017, stating the wish to maintain a neutral position vis-à-vis "the regional conflict over the Sahara" (New Times 2017). For Morocco, a neutral stance by third countries on Western Sahara amounted to support for Morocco's sovereignty and territorial integrity as taking the position in effect legitimized the status quo of Morocco's control over the occupied parts of Sahara. Despite claiming to take a neutral stance, in the derecognition letter to SADR, Bolivia affirmed commitment to "the principles of mutual respect, sovereignty and territorial integrity, non-aggression, non-interference in the internal affairs of Morocco" (Government of Bolivia 2020).

In the case of Kosovo, in May 2018 Ghana signaled it would reconsider its position. During a visit to Belgrade, Aaron Mike Oquaye, speaker of Ghana's parliament, stated that he would "suggest to the president and foreign minister of Ghana to re-examine the decision on the status of Kosovo" in exchange for Serbia's economic and military assistance (N1 2018b). However, in June 2018, President Hashim Thaçi of Kosovo accepted the credential letters from Ghana's nonresident ambassador to Kosovo, Salma Frances Mancell (President of Kosovo 2018). On that occasion the Ghanian diplomat expressed her desire to deepen the bilateral ties between the two countries. But in a sudden turn of events, Serbian foreign minister Ivica Dačić and Ghanaian foreign minister Shirley Ayorkor Botchwey met later in 2018 in Belgrade to "reconsider the decision to recognize an independent Kosovo made by the previous administration, adding that it was the chief obstacle to the development of relations with Serbia" (Beta 2018). The Ghanaian foreign minister stated: "It's true the decision was made (to recognize Kosovo's independence), but what matters is our presence here, today. The decision has been the main obstacle to the development of relations. Yet, we are here now. No one from the Ghanaian government has visited Kosovo" (Beta 2018). In May 2019, Dačić visited Ghana, where he requested that Ghana revoke its decision to recognize Kosovo and revert to "a status-neutral position pending the conclusion of the dialogue and to honor the outcome of the dialogue which would be presented in the United Nations" (MFA of Serbia 2019b). Finally, in November 2019, Ghana took the decision to derecognize Kosovo, stating that its previous decision was premature and contravened international norms and laws. Dačić hailed the decision as "the result of a state policy pursued by Serbia for many years, adding that such a decision by that African state required a year and a half of talks and meetings and a lot of work" (Novinar 2019). Dačić affirmed that "the talks with Ghana had been going on for a long time, that all levels had been discussed, that Serbian President Aleksandar Vucic, Parliament Speaker Maja Gojkovic and he as Foreign Minister had also talked with the representatives of that country" (Blic 2019). Serbia's foreign minister stated that Ghana's decision to withdraw recognition could influence other countries, especially African countries, to derecognize Kosovo.

The suspension and freezing of recognition are misleading practices that don't correspond to the provisions of diplomatic law on the suspension of diplomatic relations. As shown in this section, third states that reconsider the recognition of the claimant state tend to settle temporarily for a variant that can be labeled "recognition without engagement," which entails suspending bilateral contacts without formally announcing the withdrawal of recognition. Another intermediary and ambivalent variant is labeled "frozen recognition," a pragmatic move to reduce criticism and backlash from domestic and international forces and avoid the question of the legality of derecognition. Regardless of the terminology, both of these intermediary variants appear to be tactics to maximize the potential profits from either reversing the original position or going full scale and formally withdrawing recognition of the claimant state. Moreover, these intermediary variants seem to be more prevalent when the claimant state doesn't have either formal diplomatic relations or close bilateral ties with the derecognizing state.

THE FULL WITHDRAWAL OF RECOGNITION

The final stage in the derecognition process is the full withdrawal of recognition of the claimant state. In most cases, derecognition is formalized through a note verbale sent to the former base state conforming to the derecognition of the claimant state and subsequently reaffirming the sovereignty and territorial integrity of the former base state over the derecognized state. Like the recognition note, the express intent is crucial to ascertain whether the decision entails withdrawal of recognition and whether the issuing authority has legal powers. In other words, the derecognition note needs to explicitly state that country X withdraws or revokes the recognition of country Y. An example of a clear expression of withdrawal of recognition is Vanuatu's derecognition of Abkhazia in 2011. The letter stated, "The prime minister of Vanuatu, the Honorouble Nipake Edward Natapei, has today cancelled and withdrew [*sic*] Vanuatu's recognition of the, so called, [*sic*] independent state of the Republic of Abkhazia" (Government of Vanuatu 2011). In addition, the letter acknowledged that Abkhazia is "a break-away autonomous province of the Republic of Georgia." In this iteration, withdrawal of recognition takes the shape of re-recognition of the other contender entity or state. Similarly, when Peru withdrew recognition of SADR in 2022, it issued a statement stating that "taking into account that there is no effective bilateral relationship to date, the Government of the Republic of Peru decides to withdraw its recognition of SADR and break all relations with this entity" (MFA of Peru 2022). In the same letter, Peru expressed its "respect for the territorial integrity of the Kingdom of Morocco, its national sovereignty, and the autonomy plan relating to this regional dispute."

Another relevant example is the case of China and Taiwan. What follows the announcement of derecognition is ending diplomatic ties with the claimant state and subsequently either re-establishing or deepening diplomatic relations with the other contender state. Withdrawal of recognition amounts to the unilateral termination of diplomatic relations. So, in this instance, state derecognition is particularly relevant in a situation where two states compete for recognition and where shifting recognition from one entity to the other requires first derecognizing the previously recognized entity. Mainland China refuses double recognition; that is, countries that recognize China cannot have diplomatic relations with Taiwan (Chiang and Hwang 2008: 65). For example, in 2017 the joint communication between China and Gambia was labeled a "resumption of diplomatic relations." What this entails is that Gambia "recognizes that there is only one China in the world, and that the Government of the People's Republic of China is the sole legal government representing the whole of China and that Taiwan is an inalienable part of China's territory," and that agreed "not to establish any official relations or engage in any official contacts with Taiwan" (MFA of China 2016).

Following another derecognition, the MFA of China declared that it "highly commends the decision of the Solomon Islands' government to recognize the one-China principle and sever the so-called 'diplomatic ties' with the Taiwan authorities" (MFA of China 2019). Soon after, China and Solomon Islands established diplomatic relations and agreed "to develop friendly relations on the basis of the principles of mutual respect for sovereignty and territorial integrity, mutual non-aggression, non-interference in each other's internal affairs, equality, mutual benefit and peaceful coexistence" (Xinhua Net 2019). Similarly, when Tuvalu in 2014 retracted its recognition of Abkhazia and South Ossetia, it established diplomatic relations with Georgia, committing to territorial integrity in its internationally recognized borders, including Abkhazia and South Ossetia (Radio Free Europe

2014). Georgia established diplomatic relations with Vanuatu following the derecognition of Abkhazia and South Ossetia.

While derecognition of a claimant state could mean re-recognition of the base state, this is not always true. In the case of Kosovo, Lesotho in 2018 issued a two-page decision outlining the reasons for derecognition and explicitly stated that "the Government of the Kingdom of Lesotho revokes all previous statements made with regards to the status of Kosovo, especially those that could be interpreted in a way as the recognition of Kosovo" (MFA of Lesotho 2018). However, this letter ambiguously revokes the recognition of Kosovo and doesn't make explicit reference to Serbia's sovereignty over Kosovo, but that is implied by other provisions of the letter, such as the addressing of the letter to the MFA of Serbia. Similarly, when Papua New Guinea derecognized Kosovo, it framed the decision as termination of its original recognition decision issued in 2012, pending the completion of negotiation and agreement on the final status of Kosovo (MFAT of Papua New Guinea 2018). While the notion of termination alludes to ending a diplomatic relationship, in this instance it is not clear whether the decision is definitive or interim, especially since other conditional clauses are attached to the termination of recognition. This is explained by the fact that Serbia tolerates double or dual recognition. In other words, when third countries recognized Kosovo, Serbia did not break diplomatic relations with those third countries. When Kosovo was recognized in the first instance, Serbia either sent a protest note, temporarily pulled its ambassador, or symbolically suspended bilateral cooperation, but it did not cut diplomatic ties. It is strategically convenient for Serbia to maintain relations with those states as it offers access to domestic actors to gain momentum to push for derecognition. Permanently cutting diplomatic ties would make the derecognition campaign much more difficult. So when the derecognition campaign comes to fruition and the claimant state is derecognized, the contender state usually re-establishes or deepens diplomatic relations with the derecognizing states by immediately signing political, economic, and military agreements. In other words, for the former base state, the derecognition of the claimant state represents an opportunity to restore and deepen bilateral ties with the derecognizing states, especially in implementing derecognition conditions. Thus, it remains questionable whether the derecognition letter should refer to the transfer of recognition and statehood entitlement to the former base state, which entails references to respecting the sovereignty and territorial integrity of the latter.

Most countries that derecognize the claimant state tend to cut off diplomatic correspondence with it and communicate the derecognition decision only to the government of the contender state. For example, in 2019 the Government of El Salvador "informed the Government of the Kingdom of Morocco of its decision to withdraw its recognition of SADR and to break all contact with this entity" (Morocco World News 2019b). However, it is also communicated to the derecognized state in certain instances. For example, the Ministry of Foreign Affairs of Suriname (2017) informed Kosovo authorities that "after careful consideration, the Government of the Republic of Suriname has decided to revoke the recognition of Kosovo as an independent and sovereign state." Similarly, the Solomon Islands' derecognition note was communicated to the Embassy of Kosovo in Canberra via the Solomon Islands High Commission in Australia. The note conveys "the decision the Government of Solomon Islands has taken on the recognition of the Republic of Kosovo, until negotiations under the auspices of the European Union is concluded" (Solomon Islands High Commission in Australia 2018). While there might be a period of international reaction and condemnation following such a decision, things tend to settle down quickly and disappear from the international agenda. In this instance, although the derecognition of the claimant state might appear to be a fresh recognition of the former base state, in essence it is nothing but a reaffirmation of the sovereignty of the former base state over the contested territory, given that both countries already have diplomatic relations and recognize one another.

Regarding the procedural formalities concerning the decision-making and the announcement of derecognition, practices vary across the board. As with many other foreign policy decisions, there is little public information on the political process and institutional deliberation when it comes to state derecognition. In legal doctrine and practice, establishing diplomatic relations is a bilateral, mutual, and reciprocal act (James 2016: 263). However, in the case of derecognition, both the withdrawal of recognition and the breach of diplomatic relations tend to be unilateral acts initiated and imposed by third countries under the tutelage and instructions of the former base state. Sometimes the derecognition decision is made public, but in other instances only a press release is issued, with few details. Notably, as discussed in the next chapter, the derecognition letter usually contains a brief normative and political justification. It tends to replicate the diplomatic narrative of the former base state, which bears the marks of the transactional nature of derecognition. In most cases, the decision to derecognize is exclusively taken by the executive branches of government with little public or political deliberation. The derecognition process and the ultimate decision are surrounded with secrecy and ambiguity, which is a testimony to how contested and anti-diplomatic this practice is but also a reflection of the diplomatic culture of derecognizing states characterized by solid power and authoritarian attitudes of state leaders, who make foreign policy decisions based on personal interests and ideological and relational ties with little regard for international norms and principles (Spies 2019).

While the derecognition process is often kept away from the public eye, the Solomon Islands' derecognition of Taiwan in 2019 is a unique case of a deliberative derecognition process, or at least one that resembles a policy-informed process. In June 2019, the Solomon Islands warned Taiwan that it was reconsidering transference of allegiance to China. Its foreign minister, Jeremiah Manele stated: "It is a sovereign decision, a matter for the Solomon Islands government to look at. On that note, the government is making a comprehensive assessment of the issue so that the government, the caucus, and the cabinet is well informed on the matter" (The Guardian 2019). He denied, however, that Taiwan's ties with the Solomon Islands were at risk. Taiwan initially disregarded this move and hoped it could count on soft pressure from Australia, which opposes China's expansionist policy in the Pacific region, and renewed support from the Solomon Islands cabinet and parliament (Taiwan News 2019b). One year earlier, as stated in the Framework Co-operation Agreement, the Solomon Islands reiterated "the inalienable right of the Government and people of the Republic of China (Taiwan) to be a member of international and regional organizations, and to participate fully and fairly in the affairs of the international community" (Government of Taiwan 2017). To review its diplomatic ties with Taiwan, the Solomon Islands government established a task force, which sent officials to China to weigh the benefits of an eventual switch.

Parallel to this, the Foreign Relations Committee of the National Parliament of Solomon Islands launched an inquiry into severing existing ties with Taiwan (National Parliament of Solomon Islands 2019). The government's bipartisan task force was established "to assess the gains of the current bilateral relations with ROC and to provide a strategy for the government to counter any positive and negative impacts of a potential switch" (Government of Solomon Islands 2019: 5). In carrying out this review of diplomatic relations with Taiwan, the task force committee, which lawmakers in favor of a diplomatic shift dominated, visited China and neighboring Fiji, Papua New Guinea, Samoa, Tonga, and Vanuatu (Government of Solomon Islands 2019: 9). Taking into account the economic and geopolitical benefits, on 13 September 2019 this task force recommended the establishment of new diplomatic relations with China and the severance of the thirty-six-year-old diplomatic ties with Taiwan (Government of Solomon Islands 2019: 5). During the period of reassessing diplomatic ties with Taiwan, Solomon Islands prime minister Manasseh Sogavare sent mixed messages. In August 2019, he praised Taiwan's assistance to the country and called them the two countries friends. In contrast, a month later, prior to announcing derecognition, he called Taiwan "completely useless to us," suggesting that "China could be a better diplomatic partner for the Pacific nation because it could stand up to Australia" (The Australian 2019).

Opposition parties in the Solomon Islands were against switching the country's diplomatic allegiance to China. The Foreign Relations Committee in parliament formulated its report in November 2019, recommending that, instead of severing its existing ties, "the Solomon Islands Government should deepen its relationship with the Republic of China (Taiwan)" (National Parliament of Solomon Islands 2019: 11). The report criticized the government's decision as "carried out in a hasty manner and strongly condemn[ed] the manner in which the decision was reached" (National Parliament of Solomon Islands 2019: 24). The committee noted that the Solomon Islands government failed to respect the constitutional rules governing the establishment and severance of diplomatic ties with other states. The committee stated that "it is deeply troubling that . . . the sovereignty of parliament and the sovereignty of Solomon Islands [and] that legislative processes are usurped by external considerations [and] pressured by foreign actors with little regard for Solomon Islands' internal processes" (National Parliament of Solomon Islands 2019: 34). In the meantime, Taiwan tried to prevent derecognition by promoting a discourse that called out China's empty promises of aid that trapped small nations in debt they were unable to pay, thus forcing them to share national assets and sovereignty with China (Malay Mail 2019). The Taiwanese MFA described the report of the task force as biased and distorted and called "all sectors of Solomon Islands to reject the predetermined conclusions of the report and the debt trap they may lead to" (MFA of Taiwan 2019a).

Claimant states also utilize their allies to lobby to prevent derecognition. For example, in 2019, a member of the US National Security Council visited the Solomon Islands to discuss issues with government leaders, and a Taiwan deputy foreign minister also attended the meeting (Taiwan News 2019b). Similarly, Australian prime minister Scott Morrison also visited the country to maintain the status quo and counterbalance China's increased influence in the Pacific region. While such a position is de facto derecognition, in practice it can take the shape of a neutral stance or the temporary suspension of recognition and the freezing of diplomatic ties. Suspending and freezing recognition in practice has taken the shape of severing diplomatic contacts with the claimant state and deepening political and economic relations with the former host state despite pledging to take a neutral position (Middle East Monitor 2018). It is expected that once recognition is suspended, official relations and exchanges will no longer take place between the two countries. Thus, unclear boundaries among these indicative forms of derecognition create conceptual and practical confusion in interpreting their meaning and significance.

THE AFTERMATH OF STATE DERECOGNITION

In the aftermath of derecognition, the claimant state faces serious dilemmas in responding. In all iterations, derecognition is a significant diplomatic move, signifying an end to diplomatic relations. Derecognition not only has a symbolic effect; it also directly impacts the ability of a derecognized state to protect its citizens abroad, cooperate with foreign governments on legal and judicial matters, and have diplomatic access to specialized international bodies. The retaliatory opportunities of claimant states following their derecognition are limited. Apart from expressing regret and cutting diplomatic ties, they are often vulnerable and limited in what they can do in return. Nonetheless, derecognized states have two significant ways to respond. The first option is to condemn derecognition and end the bilateral relations with the derecognizing state, including the closing of embassies, ending economic, political, and technical cooperation, and withdrawal of citizens, as appropriate. The second option is to contest the legal and political grounds of derecognition process and act. While in the first instance the claimant state accepts the derecognition decision and reciprocates by discontinuing bilateral relations, in the second instance the claimant state questions the unilateral character of recognition and thus rejects it since the principle of mutual consensual and reciprocal derecognition isn't fulfilled.

Taiwan's diplomatic approach resembles the first mode of response to derecognition. Although Taiwan considers derecognition a "unilateral termination of diplomatic relations" by the derecognizing state (MFA of Taiwan 2018c), it tends to respond to the humiliating withdrawal of recognition by certain states with mutual derecognition, which has entailed ending diplomatic relations as well as cutting all bilateral political and economic cooperation. Mutual derecognition seems to hurt the emerging state; for example, Taiwan may have only domestic or strategic costs in the derecognizing states. However, the fact that derecognizing states are UN members protects them from the effects of mutual derecognition.

In most cases, when Taiwan was derecognized, it expressed regret and discontent with the derecognizing state's decision. It also strongly protested against and condemned China and its efforts to diminish Taiwan's international space. For instance, following derecognition by Panama, the Taiwanese government expressed "indignation and deep regret over Panama's unilateral decision to sever diplomatic relations" (MFA of Taiwan 2017). Likewise, Taiwan expressed "profound disappointment, regret, and outrage that the government of Burkina Faso has succumbed to the enticements of dollar diplomacy" (MFA of Taiwan 2018b). In response to El Salvador's derecognition, Taiwan immediately terminated diplomatic relations, to uphold its national dignity. This involved ending all cooperation and assistance projects, closing its embassy, and recalling its diplomatic and civilian staff.

Similarly, when the Dominican Republic switched to China after seventy-seven years of diplomatic relations with Taiwan, the Taiwanese government announced "the termination of relations with the Dominican Republic, effective immediately . . . to protect both the nation's dignity and sovereignty" (MFA of Taiwan 2018a). Taiwan also tends to express official feelings and pass judgment on the character of countries that withdraw their recognition. For instance, when Malawi derecognized Taiwan, its criticism was explicit. Taiwan regretted, it said, that "the leaders and government of Malawi have forsaken their national dignity, turned their back on commitments made to Taiwan and sold their soul to China" (MFA of Taiwan 2008). In the aftermath of derecognition, Taiwan has a tradition of immediately ending diplomatic relations with the derecognizing state and terminating bilateral assistance projects and technical missions. "Without concern for long-established ties, the wishes of the Dominican people, or the years of developmental assistance provided the nation by Taiwan, the administration has accepted over-blown promises of investment and aid by China" (MFA of Taiwan 2018a). When the Solomon Islands and Kiribati switched allegiance to China in 2019, the Taiwanese government demanded that both countries "immediately recall its government personnel from Taiwan" (MFA of Taiwan 2019b). In the case of Taiwan, other remaining diplomatic allies often send reassuring messages that they will continue their diplomatic allegiance with Taipei. For example, when Nauru abruptly derecognized Taiwan in January 2024, the Marshall Islands and Tuvalu reaffirmed their diplomatic recognition and solidarity with Taiwan (Radio New Zealand 2024).

In contrast, there are instances when the claimant state continues informal and unofficial relations with the derecognizing state. Therefore, the end of diplomatic relations does not necessarily mean the end of diplomatic interactions between the derecognized and derecognizing states. As Barston (2013: 27–28) argues, "In these cases involving non-recognition, derecognition or exiled entities, several different mechanisms have evolved for transacting official and other business. These include the honorary representative, liaison office, representative office and trade mission." In a number of cases, after derecognition Taiwan has tried to retain a presence in countries it once had diplomatic ties with in the hope of a future rerecognition. Although Papua New Guinea derecognized Taiwan in 1999, it continued to maintain informal contacts and, on certain occasions, voted in favor of Taiwan at international forums (Yang 2011: 62). After severing diplomatic relations with Taiwan, the Solomon Islands government claimed that the "people-to-people relationship, cultural exchanges, trade relations and investment . . . will continue as long as Taiwan and Solomon Islands continue to exist on planet earth" (Solomon Times 2019b). Taiwan, however, characterized derecognition a diplomatic tactic aimed to "diminish Taiwan's international presence, hurt the Taiwanese people, and gradually suppress and eliminate Taiwan's sovereignty" (MFA of Taiwan 2019b). Taiwan expressed regret at "the São Tomé and Príncipe government's abrupt and unfriendly decision and condemns this action" (MFA of Taiwan 2016). Following derecognition by the Solomon Islands and Kiribati in 2019, Taiwan's foreign minister warned the Pacific nations that "from the long-term strategic perspective, like-minded friends and partners should really be worried whether the Pacific will remain free and open, and whether the key actors follow the rules-based international order" (Reuters 2019c).

The second option involves ignoring and disregarding the decision to derecognize in the hope that the decision turns out to be premature, temporal, and reversible. This mode of response is also conditioned on how visible and explicit the derecognition process and decision are. The more ambiguous the derecognition decision, the higher the likelihood that the derecognized state will challenge it. This form of response to derecognition intends to minimize and mitigate the broad negative impact and spillover effect on other countries that follow a similar derecognition trajectory. Kosovo's experience resembles the second form of response. Kosovo has denied that most countries that have derecognized it have actually done so given that the MFA of Kosovo has not received any formal notification of the decisions for freezing, suspending, or withdrawing recognition. As the texts in most of the derecognition notes are almost identical and use the same rationales, Kosovo has alleged that Serbian diplomats drafted these derecognition notes and then had them signed or sealed by particular parties within the derecognizing states (Assembly of Kosovo 2018). Kosovo's foreign minister Behgjet Pacolli stated, "I assure you that Kosovo as an entity, as the main address of these verbal notes, has not received any verbal note from these states where it is said that our state has withdrawn its recognition, respectively has ceased relations with your state" (Assembly of Kosovo 2018). The Kosovo MFA refuted the derecognition by Lesotho, describing it as fake news. "As in previous cases this 'document' has been produced in Belgrade to produce a fake news, at the time Kosovo is working intensively to become a factor in powerful international organisation, whereas Serbia's diplomacy has no tools to prevent this process" (MFA of Kosovo 2018c). After the Union of Comoros derecognized Kosovo, the MFA of Kosovo issued a statement asserting that "all of the countries Serbia is referring to have confirmed that it is about fake news and their recognitions, pursuant to the international relations practice, are irreversible acts" (MFA of Kosovo 2018a). Kosovo denied the derecognition decision of Ghana on the same basis, maintaining that "Ghana has an accredited ambassador in Kosovo. Ghana also has an honorary consul in Kosovo that represents them. Minister Pacolli has recently met with Ghana's Foreign Minister at the United Nations in New York" (Koha 2019b).

To downplay the significance of derecognition, Kosovo's foreign ministry intentionally refused to update the list of countries that have recognized the country, which nurtured domestic and international confusion on the exact number of states that have recognized Kosovo. In a number of other instances Kosovo has argued against the possibility of states' withdrawing recognition. On the occasion of Suriname's derecognition of Kosovo in October 2017, the Ministry of Foreign Affairs of Kosovo reacted by pointing out that "first, in the international law there is no concept of withdrawing a recognition, there is the freezing of diplomatic relations or the withdrawal of diplomatic staff; second, there is no state called 'Kosovo and Metohija' as in the letter presented in Belgrade, but in international relations exists a sovereign and independent country called the Republic of Kosovo" (Balkan Insight 2017). In an interview with the press in 2018, the prime minister of Kosovo, Ramush Haradinaj, admitted, "We are not protected from revocations of recognitions, this possibility exists. I don't know how the revocation from Burundi came about, but we are interested that nobody damages Kosovo's interests and its strategic plan" (Prishtina Insight 2018). Only in 2020 did Kosovo come to terms with the ramifications of Serbia's derecognition campaign. For example, when the new government led by Albin Kurti came to power in February 2020, it pledged to formulate a new foreign policy strategy targeted at "countries who have not yet declared about the independence of Kosovo; for countries who have not recognized Kosovo, and for those who have declared for the withdrawal of recognition" (Government of Kosovo 2021). Kosovo's foreign minister at that time, Glauk Konjufca, stated, "Our government started operations on 4 February. Foreign policy has been in a serious crisis in recent years. There is an aggressive Serbian campaign to get countries to withdraw recognition of Kosovo. Twelve to fifteen countries are affected, most of them in the Pacific region and Africa" (Stuttgarter Zeitung 2020).

In response to all the derecognition decisions announced by Serbia, Kosovo admitted that the Solomon Islands was the only country that notified it about the decision to withdraw recognition. In a note verbale sent on November 2018, soon after the announcement of derecognition, Kosovo's MFA reminded the Solomon Islands authorities that "Kosovo is and remains an independent and sovereign state recognized by 116 countries, including by the Solomon Islands" and that "under international law de-jure recognition, like that of the government of the Solomon Islands, is definitive" (MFA of Kosovo 2018b). The letter went on to remind the Solomon Islands that the two countries "established diplomatic relations based on the principles of the UN Charter and the provisions of the Vienna Convention on Diplomatic Relations of 1961" and that both had "enjoyed cordial relations and had no bilateral or multilateral dispute, but contrary, shared similar values and principles" (MFA of Kosovo 2018b). Thus, for Kosovo, "Once full and formal recognition has been granted, and diplomatic relations have been established, withdrawal of recognition is not permitted nor cannot retrospectively undermine sovereign statehood." It backed up the statement with Article 6 of the Montevideo Convention, which stipulates that "recognition is unconditional and irrevocable." Moreover, the MFA of Kosovo (2018b) noted that

> any attempt to withdraw the recognition for political, economic, or personal interests would contradict the initial decision in favour of recognition and constitute a breach of fundamental norms of the international law, such as requirement for promoting peaceful and

friendly relations between nations, it would undermine the principle of sovereign equality, and may work against the commitment of states for non-interference in internal affairs.

The Kosovo MFA note insisted that "in the view of the government of Kosovo, Kosovo and the Solomon Islands have diplomatic relations established fully under international law as two independent and sovereign states, and as such, these diplomatic relations are valid" (MFA of Kosovo 2018b). Finally, the MFA of Kosovo (2018b) expressed the wish "to continue the cordial relations established with the Solomon Islands" and stated the commitment "to dispatch a Special Envoy to the Solomon Islands to discuss with your esteemed government all raised issues and clarify the misunderstanding created in the bilateral relations between Kosovo and the Solomon Islands."

Abkhazia and South Ossetia tend to take an approach similar to Kosovo's. For instance, they have exploited the confusion over institutional and constitutional responsibility for recognizing Abkhazia, which has been caused by Pacific island states such as Vanuatu and Tuvalu, to deny their derecognition. Originally, when Vanuatu recognized Abkhazia in 2011, conflicting reports came from three governmental instances: while allegedly Vanuatu's prime minister signed the agreement to establish diplomatic relations, a senior adviser to Vanuatu's government sent confusing messages, along with the country's ambassador to the UN, who "strongly denied Abkhazia's claims that Vanuatu had recognized it" (Civil Georgia 2011c). The Vanuatuan ambassador further stated, "We don't know who is responsible for declaring that this is true. As far as we are concerned, we are dealing with Georgia, not Abkhazia" (Civil Georgia 2011b). Vanuatu signaled the recognition of Abkhazia in May 2011 by signing a memorandum enhancing bilateral relations and mutual interests. However, the Supreme Court of Vanuatu declared that the government of Prime Minister Sato Kilman was unconstitutional and invalid. Soon after the new interim government came to power, the new prime minister, Nipake Edward Natapei, "cancelled and withdrew Vanuatu's recognition of the, so called, independent state of the Republic of Abkhazia, which is a break-away autonomous province of the Republic of Georgia" (Government of Vanuatu 2011). Soon after, the overthrown government returned to power and sent mixed messages regarding the recognition of Abkhazia. The foreign minister of Vanuatu, Alfred Carlot, sent a letter to the MFA of Abkhazia conveying the message that "the Council of Minister of Vanuatu has voted in favour of supporting the Republic of Abkhazia in establishing diplomatic and financial ties between our respective nations" (MFA of Vanuatu 2011). In this letter Vanuatu stated that it "would like to re-assure that the memorandum dated 23 May 2011 is valid and remains in force despite earlier announcement" (MFA of Vanuatu 2011). Finally, in 2013 Georgia and Vanuatu signed an agreement on establishing diplomatic and consular relations, putting an end to the confusion and uncertainty over recognition of Abkhazia by this Pacific Island state. The Georgian foreign minister stated that the decision of Vanuatu put an "end to the previously existing confusion in this regard and represents an unambiguous support to Georgia's sovereignty and territorial integrity as well as unequivocal respect for fundamental principles of international law" (Civil Georgia 2013).

Similarly, in 2011 Tuvalu recognized Abkhazia and both governments signed a joint statement on establishing diplomatic relations. However, in 2014, Tuvalu established diplomatic ties with Georgia, indicating severing diplomatic relations and withdrawal of recognition of Abkhazia. The reaction of the Ministry of Foreign Affairs of Abkhazia was a statement asserting that the Abkhazia had not received official notification from the authorities of Tuvalu about the severance of diplomatic relations; therefore, these relations continued. On that occasion, it appears that the Government of Abkhazia decided to do nothing and ignore this anti-diplomatic move and avoid becoming implicated in the game of demanding money for recognition/derecognition every time a government changed. Similarly, when Tuvalu derecognized South Ossetia, the foreign minister of South Ossetia stated it had "not received notifications from Tuvalu about changes in positions. It is not possible to comment on the statements of the Georgian Foreign Ministry and the information circulated in the media until we receive any legally relevant documents" (State News Agency RES 2014). Former foreign minister of Abkhazia Viacheslav Chirikba (2013: 11) stated: "There is no doubt that the most important source of the legitimacy of a State is the recognition of its legitimacy first of all by its people, and not some external factors, including the diplomatic recognition by other states or the declarations made by some governments or international organizations."

For the SADR, however, both recognition and withdrawal or suspension of recognition are political decisions states make in their bilateral relations with other states. In this sense, as a matter of policy, it admits that states can, at will, recognize, withdraw, or suspend their recognition of other states. However, the SADR takes the position that recognition is unconditional and irrevocable as stipulated by the rules of international law of recognition of states contained in the 1933 Montevideo Convention. Once other states have recognized the SADR as a sovereign state, they cannot revoke their recognition, unless the SADR or the recognizing states no longer exist.

In most cases, the international community is silent on state derecognition. In particular, organized reactions or sanctions are not expected against derecognizing states and their patron state. However, the interests of global and regional powers are affected by the derecognition of the claimant state. In that case, they tend to react and undertake retaliatory measures against the derecognizing states in certain instances. Although the United States does not formally recognize Taiwan, it remains one of its main international allies. In reaction to the derecognition of Taiwan by Dominican Republic and El Salvador, the United States temporarily recalled its top diplomats in protest. In a swift response to the US criticism, Chinese diplomats stated that "as a sovereign country, the Dominican Republic had the absolute right to decide its own foreign policy and that no other nation had the right to interfere" (Reuters 2018a). Following the derecognition of Taiwan by El Salvador, there were rumors that Guatemala was considering switching to China as well. US senator Marco Rubio warned Guatemala that if it derecognized Taiwan, the United States might withdraw foreign aid (Taiwan News 2018). In response to the Solomon Islands' and Kiribati's derecognition in September 2019, the United States and Taiwan organized a joint event with Taiwan's remaining four partners in the Pacific region to increase cooperation and "to meet the development needs of Taiwan's diplomatic partners in the Pacific." Highlighting China's aggressive and military intentions in the Pacific, Taiwanese foreign minister Joseph Wu called on "all responsible stakeholders in the region to realize the value of Taiwan's presence in the Pacific, and push back strongly against China's efforts to erode that presence" (South China Morning Post 2019a). In an attempt to prevent further loss of diplomatic allies, the US deputy assistant secretary of state responsible for the region, Sandra Oudkirk, stated that "Taiwan is a force for good in the Pacific, and in the world. That is why we firmly support Taiwan's relationships with Pacific Island nations" (South China Morning Post 2019a).

The derecognition saga, however, does not end with the formal withdrawal of recognition because there are many examples when third countries have resumed full diplomatic relations and thus re-recognized the claimant state afresh. This also partially resembles the diplomatic practice of states after cutting bilateral ties (Constantinou, Kerr, and Sharp 2016). The prospects for re-recognition are predominantly influenced by the level of political, economic, and cultural ties the claimant state has with the re-

recognizing state. Especially if there are linkages between derecognized states and a political faction that comes to power, chances for retrieving recognition are high. Though such domestic polarization has turned diplomatic derecognition into a fluid foreign policy instrument, what evolves depends on which political faction comes to power. Re-recognition is often branded as restoration and resumption of diplomatic relations, which signifies that derecognition in the first instance did not bring into question the factual existence of the derecognized state. An example is Taiwan's resumption of diplomatic relations with Saint Lucia in 2007 after a decade of derecognition. This was formalized by signing a Joint Communiqué on the Reestablishment of Diplomatic Relations. What led to re-recognition is a better deal offered by Taiwan and disappointment among the local population with China's limited investment in the country. Taiwan promised to "help St. Lucia diversify agriculture, help tourism, develop livestock and create information technology learning centers" (New York Times 2007). Similarly, Nauru re-recognized Taiwan in 2005 after claiming that Chinese assistance pledges were not fulfilled as promised, restoring diplomatic relations after unilaterally severing ties in 2002 (Rich and Dahmer 2018). Nauru expressed regret about past mistakes. Restoring full diplomatic ties resumed Taiwan's education, agriculture, fisheries, tourism, healthcare, and aquaculture assistance. In turn, Nauru offered its position as a UN member to lobby for and represent Taiwan's interests within multilateral organizations. Similarly, Vanuatu for a while served as a strong supporter of Taiwan in international organizations. In the face of this rotating recognition, Taiwan over the years has become "disinclined to fight to maintain diplomatic recognition with states who swap sides to recognize the PRC for increased economic aid" (Brady and Henderson 2010: 195).

In another part of the world, Zambia, Malawi, and Mauritius have derecognized and re-recognized SADR several times over the years, as did Burkina Faso. Saint Lucia first recognized Taiwan in 1984, then derecognized it in 1997 only to restore ties with Taiwan in 2007 and, finally, switch back to China in 2011. The diplomatic logic was to grant recognition to the highest bidder (BBC 2017). In 2015, Mauritius agreed to recognize "anew the Saharawi Arab Democratic Republic (SADR) as a sovereign State, in line with the aim of the Government to forge new relationships across the world as enunciated in the Government Programme 2015–2019" (All Africa 2015). Similarly, Zambian authorities derecognized and re-recognized Western Sahara in months (Zambian Watchdog 2017). In 2018, Guinea-Bissau re-recognized Kosovo, reversing the decision in late 2017 to derecognize, stating that it "continue[s] to recognize Kosovo as an independent and sovereign state." This back-and-forth foreign policy of small states has led to the emergence of rental of diplomatic recognition. Burundi froze the recognition of Western Sahara in 2006. In 2008, it decided to restore the recognition because "this decision stems from the will of the Government of the Republic of Burundi to better integrate the country into the East African Community, the Member States of which together have opted for a harmonization of the external policy for the sake of synergy in order to create a truly integrated space" (MFA of Burundi 2008). However, in 2010, Burundi again decided to withdraw its recognition of the SADR "to encourage, like many other countries, the UN process and the momentum brought about by the Moroccan autonomy initiative" (Agence Maghreb Arabe Presse 2010). In 2020, Bolivia announced suspension of its ties with the SADR in exchange for Morocco's recognition of the interim president, Jeanine Añez Chávez, who came to power after a chaotic election. However, as soon as she left office and leftist parties came to power, the decision was reversed. In September 2021, Bolivia issued a press statement announcing the strengthening of diplomatic relations with the SADR. It noted that "diplomatic relations were interrupted by a misguided press release issued on January 2, 2020, during the de facto government of Jeanine Áñez, which does not reflect the universal commitment to fight against colonialism and preservation of peace, traditionally upheld by the Bolivian government" (MFA of Bolivia 2021). While the Bolivian MFA reduced the previous decision to derecognize SADR to an interruption of diplomatic relations, Sahrawi diplomats considered the move a restoration of diplomatic relations with the Sahrawi Republic.

In Kosovo's case, a dozen countries announced by Serbia as withdrawing recognition of Kosovo re-established diplomatic contacts with it and implicitly continued their bilateral ties, which can be seen as restoring the original recognition. An instance is Guinea-Bissau, which originally recognized Kosovo in 2011 but announced in 2017 that it had withdrawn recognition. However, with the lobbying support of the United States, the president of Guinea-Bissau reversed the decision to rescind the recognition of Kosovo. As part of the restoration of recognition, a delegation from Guinea-Bissau attended the celebration of Kosovo's tenth anniversary of independence in Prishtina. Soon after, in June 2018, Kosovo's ambassador in Senegal was accredited as the nonresident ambassador to Guinea-Bissau for the first time. On 28 July 2021, Kosovo's foreign minister, Donika Gërvalla, held a virtual meeting with her homologue from Guinea-Bissau, Suzi Carla Barbosa. A statement issued by the MFA of Kosovo stated that the two foreign ministers "discussed opportunities for bilateral cooperation with the aim of creating bilateral relations in the spheres of common interest." They highlighted cultural and economic cooperation. Although Suriname withdrew the recognition of Kosovo in 2017 and voted against its consideration for membership in Interpol in 2018, Kosovo's foreign minister met with Suriname's homologue on the margins of the Summit of the Americas in Los Angeles in June 2022, showing that both sides agreed to enhance cooperation. In the case of Dominica, Kosovo tried to formalize the establishment of diplomatic relations in an effort to overcome uncertainty over the alleged derecognition, whereas in the case of Palau and Grenada, high-level bilateral meetings and visits were used as evidence of stable bilateral relations (Office of the Prime Minister of Grenada 2023).

Diplomatic relations after derecognition continue in a somewhat ambiguous format, driven mainly by interpersonal relations between diplomats of derecognizing and derecognized countries. For example, Kosovo diplomats stationed in Japan continued holding public and bilateral meetings with Palau diplomats in Japan even after derecognition. An example is the April 2021 visit of the ambassador of the Republic of Palau to Japan, Francis Mariur Matsutaro, to the Embassy of Kosovo in Tokyo, where it was reported in social media that "the meeting was a good opportunity to discuss the excellent bilateral relations between our two countries, Palau and Kosovo." The Embassy of Kosovo in Japan (2021) publicly shared the news on Facebook. It highlighted that the diplomats discussed "the need to have a non-resident ambassador of the Republic of Kosovo in Palau in the near future" and the "need to continue the close and friendly cooperation between the two embassies." Kosovo has also arranged meetings with Papua New Guinea, Dominica, and Grenada for the 2022 UN General Assembly annual session. Examples such as these highlight that formal derecognition and its aftermath aren't the end of the story but only another stage in an ongoing struggle between contender states, which remains largely an open-ended process until a final settlement centered on mutual recognition is achieved.

CONCLUSION

This chapter examined the process of state derecognition, looking at key stages, tactics, and outcomes. As the illustrative examples and evidence show, derecognition is present in world politics and has become a major diplomatic battlefield for contender states. While the act of derecognition is only a declaratory and textual endeavor, the fact that it implicates multiple states and touches various interests is actualized as a significant diplomatic encounter with potential and probable legal and political effects. Thus, what gives derecognition reality-making character is that it operates as an anti-diplomatic assemblage of multiple actors, tactics, and practices that occur in several stages and tend to produce not only microscaled effects but also much broader systemic effects. The diplomatic campaign of the former base state, blended with a strong diplomatic narrative and assisted by foreign allies, plays a significant role in identifying countries willing to trade their capacity to recognize or derecognize other states in exchange for economic and political goods. As shown in this chapter, contender states combine various diplomatic tools and link their foreign policy of state derecognition with the specific context and needs of third countries to render them more receptive to the derecognition goal. The blended campaign for derecognition, in most cases, consists of using economic diplomacy (checkbook diplomacy), exploiting electoral cycles and government change in third countries, opening embassies in exchange for derecognition, using historical, societal, and ideological ties, and lobbying through powerful global/regional allies.

The diplomatic dynamics underpinning the derecognition of states are like the process of state recognition in the first instance, but in the reverse order. The process of recognition undergoes several stages, from estrangement and disengagement to acceptance, institutional engagement, and then formal recognition. In turn, derecognition as a process can take multiple shapes, such as retaining formal recognition but suspending institutional engagement or freezing recognition and taking a neutral stance pending a settlement between contender states. Jointly, these variants reveal a multiplicity of diplomatic relations that countries can maintain, ranging from full and solid diplomatic relations to disengaged relations and formal withdrawal of recognition. They show that countries can and do have diplomatic contacts and interact with one another regardless of the formal diplomatic status of their relations, whether they do or do not recognize one another on paper. In this sense, static and dogmatic views of recognition, nonrecognition, and derecognition do not correspond with real-world developments. Even with such a multiplicity of diplomatic relations, as much as it enables all protagonist states to count their international allies, this diplomatic ambivalence does not contribute to stable and predictable bilateral relations.

Ultimately, what gives global relevance to the struggle for recognition and derecognition is the buy-in of third countries who add weight and significance to this controversial practice. By tracing the process of state derecognition, the chapter exposed the category of states that were more willing to engage in trading recognition or derecognition in exchange for political, security, and material goods. Most countries implicated in the derecognition of other states are newly established as part of the decolonization process. They lack political stability, diplomatic tradition, and economic prosperity. These states, located in Africa, Latin America, and the Pacific region, have histories of shifting diplomatic allegiances to different dominant global powers. Because they are members of the UN, are universally recognized, and thus are expected to adhere to international norms and laws, they tend to exploit normative gray zones surrounding foreign policy conduct and state recognition to secure foreign aid, military support, and recognition of their government and their rulings. For these states, reconsidering the recognition of the claimant state or engaging in various in-between and hybrid forms of weakening, discontinuing, and breaking diplomatic relations appears to be normal and acceptable foreign policy. Since there are no organized and widely present instances of Western states engaging in derecognition games, derecognition is more of a characteristic of non-Western diplomatic culture. This indicates that the irreversibility of state recognition is more of a feature of Western diplomatic systems and cultures of interstate relations than a universal feature endorsed and practiced worldwide.

Thus, recognition and derecognition are not governed by rules, norms, and principles but are a by-product of regional diplomatic cultures and practices and the interests they nest and entangle. As the discussion in this chapter has shown, incremental downgrading, suspension, and withdrawal of recognition is an optimal solution for derecognizing states to balance competing pressures, enhance bargaining powers, and mitigate adverse effects. By reconsidering and withdrawing recognition incrementally, third states can retain some autonomy in running their foreign affairs and reduce domestic and international criticism of diplomatic overtures. It leaves the door open for restoring diplomatic ties with the claimant state and starting another round of bargaining with the competing states for recognition. Moreover, cases of derecognition guided by geopolitical and economic incentives are more likely to lead to full withdrawal of derecognition. In contrast, those driven by normative considerations are more likely to lead to freezing recognition and suspending official diplomatic ties. So the stronger the interests and higher the reward for derecognizing states, the clearer and more complete the derecognition variant. Therefore, it is essential to explore further the link between the variant or scale of severance of diplomatic relations and the rationale and justifications stimulating state derecognition.

4 ✦ The Rationales for State Derecognition

The derecognition of states remains a puzzling feature in world politics. Since there are no legal guidelines and policy blueprints on the derecognition of states, it remains at the discretion of states to selectively invoke legal, political, and normative arguments and criteria to justify their decisions. Since state derecognition is an unnatural process in diplomatic affairs and is initiated by contender states, it is interesting to evaluate the invocation and application of different discourses and justifications for reconsidering, suspending, freezing, and ultimately withdrawing the recognition of claimant states. This chapter surveys and examines the most common rationales and justifications for withdrawing the recognition of states. It argues that to sense the prevalence of this diplomatic practice in contemporary world politics, it is essential to examine jointly the inward-looking rationales and outward-looking justifications underpinning the derecognition of states. Foreign policy justifications are always entangled in multiple logistics of argumentation, which are shaped by domestic and international considerations. Understanding state derecognition as a two-level discursive game, the chapter finds that inward-looking rationales—such as economic, domestic, and geopolitical interests—are more persuasive in explaining the motives behind state derecognition than those camouflaged as outward-looking rationales—such as conflict resolution and compliance with international norms. This chapter looks across all the contemporary cases and interrogates their argumentative coherence and flaws, namely the compatibility between the factual and invoked justifications for derecognition and, most important, the compatibility between the original grounds for recognition and those for withdrawing it.

114

Since the act of derecognition signifies the withdrawal of the previous decision to recognize the claimant state as a sovereign state, it is crucial to examine the extent to which the justification of derecognition reflects on the original condition for recognition or other reconsiderations that have been overlooked in the first place. In other words, is state derecognition motivated by the absence or reversal of original conditions for recognition? In most cases, when new states are recognized, it is done because the claimant state satisfies the objective criteria of statehood: a stable population, territory, functioning government, and capacity to enter international relations. As Mikulas Fabry (2020: 39) shows, "Recognizing states have certainly sought to justify their decisions as reflecting, or at least not contravening, the prevailing criteria of statehood." However, third countries often invoke more nuanced criteria, such as the remedial right to self-determination, the decolonization process, the dissolution of the former base state, systematic human rights abuses by the former base state, and other historical, sociocultural, and economic considerations.

Contrary to the original justification for recognition, contemporary state practice shows that the derecognition of states is not entirely about asserting that a state does not fulfill the core criteria of statehood, nor is it merely an instrument for upholding international institutions and norms on sovereignty and territorial integrity. Third states' political system, religion, collective identity, and geography influence the derecognition of states. Inward-looking rationales, such as economic incentives, domestic political rivalries, and geopolitical self-interest, offer a better explanation of the determinant behind such diplomatic ventures. Such rationales reveal how state derecognition is a polymorphous instrument that entangles issues primarily relevant to derecognizing states and is less a response to the actual reality of the claimant state, namely the presence or absence of statehood criteria and other political considerations. In the predominant number of cases, the original conditions for recognition are either ignored or distorted with half-truths, one-sided diplomatic narratives, and contractions. The two main outward-looking narratives for state derecognition include promoting conflict resolution and compliance with international norms. Even though many derecognition cases are framed as being about conflict resolution and respecting international norms, they end up promoting hurting stalemates. Framing derecognition decisions as being about peaceful conflict resolution, in essence, serves as a means of putting pressure on the claimant state to engage in diplomatic talks and make concessions with the threat that the failure to do so will result in increased political pain for the claimant state and society. Derecognition inflicts political pressure and undermines the claimant state's ability to fully realize its national priorities and, most notably, exercise its sovereignty and act as a normal state. Moreover, ignoring that circumstances on the ground have not changed makes the justification of derecognition a diplomatic illusion detached from reality. This in turn, undermines the credibility of recognition and derecognition as an institution of diplomacy.

The shifting interlocutor and target audience can explain the incompatibility between the criteria for withdrawing recognition and the original criteria justifying the decision for recognition in the first place. In instances of recognition, the justification corresponds with the diplomatic narrative and affirms the needs and interests of the claimant state. In this instance, there is an intertextual connection between the arguments of the claimant state and the recognizing state. However, in instances of state derecognition, the interlocutor is not the claimant state but the former base state. Hence, the decision for derecognition corresponds with the prescribed discourse and interests of the former base state. So, in this instance, the logic shifts the other way around. The discourse of derecognition is intertextually connected with the discourse of the former base state and not with that of the claimant state. These discursive shifts show that the rationales for state derecognition are contingent on the target audience and can only be explained by looking at them as an intertextual relation between the derecognizing state and the client of such decisions, the former base state. The rationales for state derecognition are purely informed by self-interest despite occasionally being presented as congruent with international norms and principles. Normative references are not intended to uphold international norms and principles. However, they reflect the desire of the derecognizing state to avoid international condemnation and the political agenda of the former base state for conflict ripeness and statehood resettlement. In short, the mismatch between the genuine reasons for derecognition and those communicated in official documents exposes the hypocritical character of this diplomatic practice. Nonetheless, this indicates that derecognition as an emerging anti-diplomatic practice is normatively and politically unstable. Its argumentative foundations are not driven by solid norms and principles but by agential, relational, intertextual, and material factors.

This chapter is organized as follows. The first section examines the inward-looking rationales that tend to be the genuine reasons behind the derecognition of states, such as economic incentives, domestic political and ideological rivalries, and geopolitical and security interests. The second section examines the outward-looking justifications, such as conflict resolution and compliance with international norms, which also guide the derecognition of states in specific circumstances.

INWARD-LOOKING RATIONALES

Economic Incentives

The most significant determinant behind derecognition practices is economic benefits. The diplomatic battle for recognition between China and Taiwan has been predominantly fought through "checkbook" or "dollar" diplomacy, whereby each side has lured impoverished and small states to recognize it and derecognize the opponent in exchange for economic benefits, trade deals, and other gifts. Compared to other cases, the wealthy economies of China and Taiwan have enabled them to use economic incentives to buy diplomatic recognition and cut ties with the other side. He Li (2005: 77) maintains that Latin America and the Caribbean, in particular, "have become a very important battleground of the 'foreign policy war' between Beijing and Taipei over international legitimacy and recognition." The two contenders are the largest aid donors to some countries in this part of the world. For Taiwan, buying recognition became a vital element of its foreign policy strategy of surviving its ambivalent existence in the international system. As CzeslawTubilewicz (2004: 803) argues, "Taiwan has little to offer in exchange for diplomatic relations, except money. Thus, the candidates for Taiwan's diplomatic partners are by necessity small, impoverished and distressed." In turn, impoverished countries have utilized the instrument of state derecognition to overcome economic crises, strengthen regime security, and secure external aid (Van Fossen 2007: 138). Similarly, Timothy Rich and Andi Dahmer (2022: 360) conclude, "Taiwan's formal diplomatic relations remain precarious not only due to China's desire to isolate Taiwan diplomatically, but also due to the incentives of some recognizing states to consider using diplomatic recognition as a bargaining tool for more aid." Small states have eagerly traded and rented their sovereign right to recognize or derecognize other states in exchange for financial incentives (Stringer 2006: 552).

There is extensive evidence that Taiwan has used development aid and technical assistance for decades to maintain relations with a handful of diplomatic partners mainly located in impoverished parts of Latin America, Africa, and the Pacific region. The exact figures for the economic assistance and its use remain largely unknown, as such funds are kept secret from the public. But evidence does exist that shines some light on these economic incentives. For instance, Taiwanese deputy foreign minister Wu Chih-chung confirmed that in 2017 "Taiwan spent about NT$9 billion (US$293 million) a year in its economic cooperation programmes with its Latin American allies" (South China Morning Post 2018c). Earlier evidence shows that "Grenada in 1989 benefited $10 million, Liberia in 1989 benefited $20 million, Nicaragua in 1990 benefited $100 million, and Central African Republic in 1991 benefited $300 million" (Cheng 1994: 176–77). While the recipient countries could spend the money as they wished, they were expected to maintain formal diplomatic relations with Taiwan as well as support and represent its interests in international organizations (Alexander 2014: 30). Most notably, Taiwan's diplomatic allies tend to use high-profile events, such as the UN General Assembly annual session, to advocate for Taiwan's full admission into the international community. For many years, Taiwan supported the Rural Constituency Development Funds in the Solomon Islands, which involved paying millions of dollars to individual elected members of parliament to use discretionally for constituency development projects in exchange for continuing diplomatic recognition. Trade relations with China, including the significant presence of Chinese economic migrants in the Solomon Islands who run most of the commercial outlets across the country, played an essential role in the Islands switching sides from Taiwan to China in 2019 (Aqorau 2021: 337–38). To maintain diplomatic relations, Taiwan paid Nauru's members of parliament regularly without any apparent accountability process (Van Fossen 2007). It is alleged that, at some point, Nuaruan ministers earned stipends of $5,000 a month as part of switching recognition from Taiwan to China and vice versa. Reportedly, the Nauru politicians used this money to respond to the needs of the impoverished population, which was a key source of their local political legitimacy and electoral support (The Australian 2010). Nauru sees renting and trading state recognition and derecognition as an essential policy to generate external assistance in a country with almost 90 percent unemployment and poor social services. This small Pacific Island state followed the same logic when it derecognized Taiwan in 2024 for economic reasons (Global Times 2024; Focus Taiwan 2024a). Reports emerged in early 2022 that, to retain diplomatic ties with Guatemala, Taiwan agreed to pay $75,000 per month to a lobbying firm in the United States to provide strategic consultancy and advocacy services for the Guatemalan government. The action was taken when the Guatemalan government was scrutinized for corruption and undemocratic practices (Associated Press 2022).

While economic incentives have sustained Taiwan's diplomatic ties with a handful of countries, once the funds were drained, the decisions have backfired and led to the withdrawal of recognition. Between 2000 and 2008, the Taiwanese authorities tried to change their foreign policy by replacing economic incentives with a commitment to promoting human rights, democracy, and state capacity-building (Tudoroiu 2017: 206). As admitted by a Taiwanese official from the pro-independence party (DPP): "We advocated stopping the use of this money diplomacy and we advocated diversifying Taiwan's diplomatic practice using Taiwan's economic leverage and to bring more humanitarian emphasis to Taiwan's diplomacy" (cited in Alexander 2014: 30). However, the practice of buying diplomatic recognition had created a dependency among recipient states, which meant that when the money stopped, so did the support, undermining Taiwan's international position. Notably, in the case of Taiwan, a new wave of derecognition was partially triggered by the end of its checkbook diplomacy, which has stimulated relations with other small countries that have backed Taiwan internationally in exchange of economic aid. Li (2005: 88) argues that "when Taiwan cannot satisfy some countries' needs, diplomatic relations are likely to be broken." For example, in 2004, the Commonwealth of Dominica "asked Taipei for a $58 million aid, which is unrelated to public welfare . . . diplomatic relationship was soon broken after Taipei turned down the request" (Li 2005: 88). Gambia derecognized Taiwan in 2013 reportedly in response to Taipei's "rejection of President Yahya Jammeh's demand for an extra US$10 million in financial assistance for unspecified security projects" (Tubilewicz 2015: 15). In the case of El Salvador, derecognition came after Taiwan declined a request by the government of El Salvador "to develop a port in the eastern part of the country as well as a request by the Salvadorian ruling party for more Taiwanese help in raising campaign funds" (MFA of Taiwan 2018). This was not the only reason. China's global rise and its aggressive foreign policy certainly played an important role in undermining Taiwan's international standing (Van Fossen 2007). China has supplemented aid with additional "diplomatic support in international forums, arms sales, free trade agreements or large investment projects" (Tubilewicz and Guilloux 2011: 334). For instance, the Solomon Islands admitted that "the reason for choosing ROC or PRC, was never based solely on the attributes of democracy but rather the choice of diplomatic partners was premised on economic gain" (National Parliament of Solomon Islands 2019: 35).

Until 2018, Burkina Faso was Taiwan's "largest and probably most important partner in Africa" (Cabestan 2017). It is estimated that, between 1994 and 2018, Taiwan has released a total of US$707 million in grants and loans to Burkina Faso (Sydney Morning Herald 2018; see also Cabestan 2016: 500). However, in 2018, Burkina Faso broke diplomatic relations with Taiwan for the second time. China has lured this African country with promises of development assistance. On this occasion, Burkina Faso's foreign minister admitted that "the evolution of the world and the defined socio-economic challenges of our region required us to reconsider our position" (New York Times 2018). As China has become Africa's leading trading partner in the first two decades of twenty-first century with massive investments in all sectors, it has managed to pressure all countries in the region to derecognize Taiwan. The exception, so far, is Swaziland, may not be able to resist Chinese pressure for too long. The Marshall Islands also switched from one side to the other, offering Taiwan recognition in 1970, then derecognizing and recognizing again in the 1990s (Chien, Yang, and Wu 2010: 1195). Similarly, in April 2018, the Dominican Republic decided to derecognize Taiwan and establish diplomatic relations with China instead in exchange for loans and investments worth $3.1 billion. On this occasion, the Dominican Republic recognized that "there is only one China in the world and Taiwan is an inalienable part of Chinese territory" (CDN 2018). The Dominican Republic said it believed the switch would be "extraordinarily positive for the future of our country" (BBC 2018). A Dominican official explained that "history and the socioeconomic reality force us now to change direction" (BBC 2018). In exchange for derecognizing Taiwan, China helped Grenada rebuild and expand its national stadium, "constructed 2,000 housing units and new hospital facilities," and provided agricultural support, compensatory grants, and scholarships (Yang 2011: 54). Following the derecognition of Taiwan, China stated that it was "willing to provide assistance for the economic and social development of El Salvador as its capacity allows" (Reuters 2018b). It also offered support to El Salvador in education, medical care, water supply, disaster prevention, scholarships, and tourism. Soon after the switch, the Salvadoran president visited Beijing, where he received signals that China was willing to give El Salvador $150 million to spur the development of social and technological projects as a sign of deepening ties between the countries (Reuters 2018b).

While both Taiwan and China have written the saga of state derecognition in exchange of economic incentives, economic rationales have also been present in the case of the recognition and derecognition of Abkhazia and South Ossetia. In 2009, Russia allegedly paid Nauru $50 million in aid to diplomatically recognize Abkhazia and South Ossetia (New Republic

2014). Nauru has long been known as a money-laundering center for the Russian mafia, hosting over four hundred offshore banks with suspicious activities (New York Times 2001). Similarly, Vanuatu recognized Abkhazia in 2011, allegedly after Russia offered $50 million for the country's signature (Radio New Zealand 2013). In 2013, Vanuatu switched back to recognizing Georgia as the sole sovereign authority over the breakaway regions. According to an Abkhaz diplomat, "Vanuatu was constantly asking for money and the problem is that Vanuatu's instability is systemic. Abkhazia simply cannot afford to support such governments. If we support them, it will only last until the next government comes in" (New Republic 2014). Similarly, Nauru's reasons for derecognition of Abkhazia were as economic as the original reasons for recognition. Nauru had to withdraw the recognition of Abkhazia after signals from Western states that they would cut assistance by international financial institutions and UN development agencies to this impoverished Pacific island (Wyeth 2017). The United States legislated in 2017 that none of its foreign aid should be made available to countries that recognized or established diplomatic relations with Abkhazia and South Ossetia or those that supported Russian occupation of these breakaway regions (US Congress 2017: 572). Similarly, Tuvalu's minister of foreign affairs, Taukelina Finikaso, admitted that since it recognized Abkhazia and South Ossetia, it experienced "a drop in our assistance from the EU for this coming cycle and we sincerely hope that once we get back to where we were before that we would hopefully get some more assistance from the EU" (Radio New Zealand 2014).

Similarly, there are allegations that Moroccan diplomacy has also used material and economic incentives to persuade third countries to derecognize the SADR. Western Sahara, with its rich natural resources, has attracted several states and companies that benefit from Moroccan exploitation of Western Sahara's fishery and minerals despite it being prohibited under international humanitarian law and the law of non-self-governing people. Morocco has exploited natural resources through fishery and mines in the occupied territories in Western Sahara not only for its economic development, but also for making them available to third countries in exchange for the derecognition of the SADR. Exploiting natural resources in Western Sahara also serves Morocco's strategy for demographic change, whereby it uses these revenues to allow the settlement of Moroccan nationals in the occupied territories, who, in an eventual self-determination referendum, would vote favorably for unification with Morocco. As Jeffrey Smith (2015: 269) maintains, "An increasing Moroccan population coupled with a denial of self-determination, founded in part on the exploitation of natural resources, is clearly a valuable result for Morocco." For example, Smith (2015: 272) calculates that the value of natural resources extracted from Western Sahara between 1976 and 2016 amounts to $5.65 billion. As a case in point, India derecognized the SADR the same year it formalized industrial trade with Morocco (White 2015: 52). Similarly, Barbados froze the recognition of the SADR in 2013 after a visit of Moroccan diplomats and businesspeople to the impoverished Caribbean country, alluding to a strong link between economic incentives and the derecognition decision (African Bulletin 2013). Yet the formal justification by Barbados for recognition of the SADR has been "pending the outcome of the negotiation process" on Morocco's proposal for autonomy (African Bulletin 2013). Afghanistan derecognized the SADR in exchange for humanitarian assistance provided by Morocco (Arabic News 2002). El Salvador derecognized the SADR in 2019 in exchange for deepening economic and trade ties with Morocco (Article 19 2019). In 2015, Morocco prevented the recognition of the SADR by Sweden by using its economic and trade leverage. It threatened to boycott and block Swedish businesses like IKEA from operating in its territory (Lamb 2015).

Contrary to China and Morocco, there isn't enough concrete evidence to support the claim that Serbia used economic pressure or corruption to get other countries to derecognize Kosovo. Serbia's foreign minister claimed that "we did not achieve this with money—there's no money; we didn't do it with pressure—we have nothing to pressure with, but we must persevere" (B92 2017). Yet, in lobbying for the derecognition of Kosovo, Serbia has promised African and Latin American nations special deals in the areas of trade, education, science, and sports. In particular, Serbia has successfully lured a number of individual non-European states to withdraw recognition of Kosovo in exchange for waving visas to Serbia, which might be an attractive route for many countries in the global south to emigrate illegally to the EU (B92 2018c). In most of the countries that derecognized Kosovo, Serbia signed agreements on friendship, cooperation in economy, culture, and education, removal of visa requirements, and military assistance. In exchange for derecognizing Kosovo, Serbia pledged to deepen the strategic partnership with Suriname and committed to signing agreements "on the abolition of visas, memorandum of cooperation between MPs and political consultations, agreement on the friendship between the two countries" (Caribbean News Now 2018). Serbia and Suriname agreed to help one another in multilateral affairs. Similarly, Serbia signed a memorandum of understanding with Comoros aimed at "enhancing cooperation in the fields of education, agriculture, defense and other areas" (Government of Serbia 2018c; 2018d).

However, in August 2019, allegations emerged that the Central African Republic's derecognition of Kosovo might have involved bribery (CNC 2019). *Koha Ditore* (2019c), the top newspaper in Kosovo, ran an article in 2019 alleging that senior Serbian government officials were involved in fabricating derecognition notes and paying foreign diplomats to sign and stamp them in exchange for a specific sum of money. Another Serbian newspaper wrote, "All the diplomatic notes shown in Belgrade which have been rejected were written by an adviser to Serbian Foreign Minister Ivica Dačić" (N1 2019d). In response to this, the MFA of Kosovo noted: "We are deeply concerned that the Serbian government has installed corruption and bribes as diplomatic means to obtain counterfeit documents that serve only to escalate relations between Kosovo and Serbia" (Gazeta Express 2019). Kosovo's foreign minister, Pacolli, added: "The Serbian campaign to use bribes, corruption, arms sales and other dirty means with the aim of making individuals issue fake diplomatic notes with so-called derecognition of Kosovo is shameful for a European country that has the status of a candidate member state for the European Union" (Gazeta Express 2019). In response, the minister of foreign affairs of the Central African Republic, Sylvie Baipo-Temon, ignored the allegations in October 2019 and focused on the purpose of derecognition: encouraging Kosovo and Serbia to find a solution that would benefit both countries. Yet it is alleged that Serbia has exploited the Covid-19 pandemic in Africa to trade in the derecognition of Kosovo with food (sugar), vaccines, and other essential supplies (Albanian Post 2022).

As shown in this section, economic realism drives most decisions for state derecognition. Although the economic rationales behind the derecognition of states show that this anti-diplomatic practice has little or nothing to do with the presence or absence of statehood attribute, there is a consistency in this inconsistency. Most third countries implicated in trading, rending, or selling the recognition or derecognition of states are economically underdeveloped and have turned their capacity to recognize other states into a diplomatic tool for personal and state economic gains. So they tend to use the same tactics and rationales both when recognizing and derecognizing other states. Equally true is the fact that the economic incentives are also a diplomatic instrument that the claimant state and the former base state tend to use to pursue their diplomatic goals. So the other protagonist states are also to be blamed for installing this anti-diplomatic practice, which undermines the normative value of recognition and puts into question the entire seriousness of derecognition.

124 • *The Derecognition of States*

Domestic Political and Ideological Rivalries

The second rationale and determinant that explains the derecognition of states concern the domestic political entanglements and ideological rivalries in third countries with a history of trading, renting, or selling recognitions to the contender states. Most third countries implicated in state derecognition tend to develop their domestic and foreign policy positions around the political, economic, and diplomatic exploitation of other countries seeking recognition or derecognition. As such, there is evidence that the derecognition of states has become a field of domestic rivalry and political interests for incumbent governments and opposition parties in derecognizing states. In specific African, Latin American, and Pacific countries, the question of recognition or derecognition of claimant states often features in the electoral debates, indicating how derecognition has become a foreign policy instrument and a matter that also shapes domestic politics (Casas-Zamora 2009). The decisions for derecognition of other states most often occur after elections or government changes. This is especially relevant when the new government has an ideological stance in favor of derecognition or has received funding and other support before the elections to adopt such a stance. This postelection practice of renewing diplomatic alliances and relations with recognition-seeking states resembles old policies of recognition of governments every time there is a change of state leadership, which was eventually scrapped as it was deemed unnecessary and troublesome.

The change of government in some countries results in changes in their foreign policy and diplomatic allegiances. For instance, Western Sahara and Taiwan are regular foreign policy subjects in a good number of protagonist states where the periodic changes in government are accompanied by the extension of recognition, derecognition, and re-recognition to these claimant states. Many countries that recognized the SADR during the Cold War years did so for ideological reasons. Western Sahara's allies in Africa and Latin America had left-leaning and communist governments that supported the Polisario Front and its struggle for self-determination. Following shifts in their ideological stances which mean they are no longer associated with communism, many of have since derecognized the SADR. As Stephen Zunes and Jacob Mundy (2010: 123) confirm, "The reasons for these cancellations and suspensions of recognition range from external diplomatic pressure from France and Spain, economic incentives offered by Morocco, and regime change resulting in ideological antipathy towards Polisario." The most prominent region where the SADR has lost its diplomatic allies is Latin America, where several countries, such as El Salvador, Guyana, and Bolivia, ousted the leftist government. The loss of power for leftist governments has subsequently caused the derecognition of the SADR in exchange for economic and political incentives. For example, Peru derecognized the SADR in August 2022, just eleven months after it re-established diplomatic relations under President Pedro Castillo, who is now under investigation for abuse of power (Al Mayadeen 2022). While during the Cold War Peru sided with the Polisario Front, as most of the left-leaning governments in Latin America did, in 1996 it withdrew recognition of the SADR. The relations between Peru and the SADR were restored in 2021, reaffirming "their respect for international law and the principle of self-determination of peoples, under the principle of legal equality of States as a basis for respect for national sovereignty, peace, security and cooperation in international relations" (Atalayar 2021). However, contrary to these norms and principles, Peru revoked recognition of the SADR in 2022, noting that "in the absence of an effective bilateral relationship to date, the Government of the Republic of Peru decides to withdraw the recognition of the Sahrawi Arab Democratic Republic and to break all relations with this entity" (Cancilleria Peru 2022). In contradiction with the rationale promoted a year earlier, Peru's derecognition letter underscored the decision to withdraw recognition in line with international law and respect for Morocco's territorial integrity and sovereignty (MFA of Peru 2022). Yet what ties together these incompatible normative grounds for derecognition are economic and domestic interests, where both Peru and Morocco agreed to sign "a multisectoral roadmap covering regular political consultations, effective cooperation in economic, commercial, educational, energy, agriculture and fertilizer matters" (Cancilleria Peru 2022).

Predictably, most of Taiwan's derecognitions have occurred when there is a change of government among its diplomatic allies. Switching of recognition has often occurred after either China or Taiwan has agreed to increase "the rent of recognition," namely increased financial assistance or response to specific financial and material requests from diplomatic allies. Countries such as Burkina Faso, the Central African Republic, Gambia, Liberia, Saint Lucia, and the Solomon Islands have recognized, derecognized, and re-recognized Taiwan at least two to three times since its exclusion from the UN in 1970s (Alexander 2014). For example, regime change in Saint Lucia was the main reason for withdrawing recognition of Taiwan in 1997 after initially extending diplomatic recognition in 1984 (MFA of Taiwan 2007). However, in 2007, Saint Lucia re-recognized Taiwan by re-establishing full diplomatic relations, a decision stimulated by economic incentives. There are also exceptional cases that demonstrate the opposite behavior. Paraguay resisted the derecognition of Taiwan primarily because its political elite is highly insulated from domestic and foreign pressure and is committed to relational status-seeking. As Tom Long and Francisco Urdinez (2021: 7) maintain, "Relations with Taiwan offer a rare chance to be the proverbial big fish in a small pond in international relations, benefiting from attention, travel delegations, and discretionary donations." In other words, Taiwan's long-term investment and support across all sectors of society and government and its attention to the Paraguayan social, cultural, and political bonds could not be challenged by domestic electoral processes and external pressure.

Nevertheless, there are also instances where the depth of domestication of interference among the contender states determined the dynamics of derecognition, for example, among Latin American countries, where the decision has been taken to switch recognition for fear of either China or Taiwan interfering too much in internal affairs, thus endangering the political authority of incumbent governments and undermining their local democracy. As Colin Alexander (2014: 56) reveals, "Taiwan began to train the armed forces of Central America in political warfare, counterinsurgency, and information extraction techniques shortly after their diplomatic isolation was confirmed by their rejection from the UN." In Saint Lucia, the government was alerted whenever Taiwanese diplomats disbursed "funds directly to St Lucian village and town councils, rather than through the newly established and independently audited central government Consolidated Fund" (Alexander 2014: 31). For example, when Saint Lucia resumed diplomatic ties with Taiwan, a nationalistic discourse emerged in the country, saying, "St. Lucia did not win its sovereignty from one power to be now dictated to by another as to who its friends should be" (New York Times 2007).

In another part of the world, domestic institutional rivalries shaped the dynamics of derecognition. Tuvalu recognized Abkhazia and South Ossetia under the government of Prime Minister Willy Telavi. However, when he lost the elections in 2013, the new prime minister, Enele Sopoaga, decided in 2014 to retract the recognition of Georgia's two breakaway regions. His justification for the change was that the original decision was taken without consulting parliament (Civil Georgia 2014). Tuvalu initially recognized Abkhazia and South Ossetia after Russia's economic incentives and the establishment of diplomatic relations (Civil Georgia 2011a). Similarly, Vanuatu derecognized these two breakaway regions in 2013 when a new government came to power (Civil Georgia 2013). On both occasions, after derecognition,

Georgia established diplomatic relations and undertook commitments to deepen bilateral relations with the Pacific islands.

São Tomé and Príncipe recognized Kosovo in 2012 and retracted a year later for domestic political reasons. Allegedly São Tomé and Príncipe's prime minister recognized Kosovo without consulting the president of the country and the national parliament. On 13 March 2012, the minister of justice and state reform of issued a resolution stating that "the Council of Ministers, meeting under the chairmanship of His Excellency Prime Minister and Head of Government Dr Patrice Emery Trovoada, and with his members present, decided unanimously to recognize the Republic of Kosovo as a sovereign State and full member of the international community, and submit subsequent rectification and promulgation by the competent authorities" (Government of São Tomé and Príncipe). However, once the government changed, São Tomé and Príncipe revoked the recognition of Kosovo and strengthened ties with Serbia. Kosovo has since denied this derecognition, claiming that the recognition remains valid and "the verbal note received by Sao Tome and Principe on Kosovo's recognition proves the country has been recognized as an independent state" (Balkan Insight 2013). Recognition of Kosovo in the first place was allegedly connected to a major investment by a Kosovar private company in the oil industry of São Tomé and Príncipe (Prishtina Insight 2012: 2). However, President Manuel Pinto da Costa—who led the country to independence under an all-powerful communist regime—said he was never consulted about the decision to recognize Kosovo and, since the parliament has not ratified it, the previous government's decision was not valid. The derecognition letter signed by president's office stressed that "at no moment of the alleged recognition process" was the president of the republic "asked to pronounce, although referred to in the text of the resolution" (Jornal de Angola 2013). This confusion arises from requiring the president's approval for the recognition decision to become law. The parliament did not debate the matter either, the consent of which is not necessary for the foreign policy decision. São Tomé and Príncipe's policy change on Kosovo had nothing to do with the merits of statehood; it was solely about an internal political rivalry between political parties. A letter signed by President Manuel Pinto da Costa on 11 January 2013 stated that "with regard to the recognition of the Republic of Kosovo carried out by the government of Mr Patrice Trovoada, it must be said that the problem does not lie in the recognition itself, which many countries have already done, but in the biased and unilateral way in which the previous government proceeded" (Tela Non 2013b).

128 • *The Derecognition of States*

In a letter dated 9 January 2013 sent to the international community, Prime Minister and Chief of Government Patrice Emery Trovoada accused President Manuel Pinto da Costa of a "parliamentary coup d'etat" in which he took the powers of the national assembly and the government to consolidate the president's all-powerful position. Among other things, Prime Minister Trovoada claimed that "under my leadership we have been very conscious to play our role in defending internationally the principles and values of democracy and self-determination . . . therefore we recognized the Republic of Kosovo" (Tela Non 2013a).

In essence, São Tomé and Príncipe's derecognition of Kosovo was not about Kosovo's statehood, as it seems to have no objection to the independence, but one of the excuses for delegitimizing the former government (Tela Non 2013b). While Kosovo's government initially denied the withdrawal of recognition, it later wrote to President da Costa requesting that he correct the decision to recognize Kosovo in line with the country's constitutional procedures. This, in turn, allowed President da Costa to legitimize his objection to the work of the former government, which had boycotted institutions because of alleged irregularities in the transition of power. Although the situation is still confusing, as Kosovo continues to point to the original recognition by São Tomé and Príncipe, its foreign minister in 2017 stated that "Minister Botelho underscored that his country would continue to firmly uphold the position of non-recognition of the unilateral declaration of independence of Kosovo, non-acceptance of any form of relations, while advocating reaching of a peaceful solution, and respect of international law and the United Nations Charter" (MFA of Serbia 2017).

Some countries that have derecognized Kosovo have problems with breakaway regions or unresolved territorial disputes and legacies dating back to the end of colonialism (De Vries, Englebert, and Schomerus 2019). Serbia has intentionally targeted countries with which it shares similar problems to generate empathy for its campaign. Countries such as the Union of Comoros have justified their derecognition of Kosovo after realizing that their previous decision was contrary to their foreign policy principles of respecting the territorial integrity of other countries and noninterference in their domestic affairs. The Comoros Islands gained independence in 1975 from France through an independence referendum. However, among the three islands making up the Comoros, the predominantly Christian population of the island of Mayotte voted against independence. Since then, Comoros has contested French sovereignty over Mayotte Island, which remains an overseas territory of France. The situation is legally ambiguous, given that the

UN General Assembly recognized the Comoros' right to self-determination as part of the decolonization process. Utilizing this historical dispute, Serbian foreign minister Dačić, during his visit to the Comoro Islands in 2018, said that "the two countries shared similar problems in terms of territorial integrity, caused by unilateral separatism and the secession of a part of their territory, who are supported by some Western states, which used dual standards where your region is concerned" (Government of Serbia 2018b). Dačić stressed that "Serbia is a friend of the Comoros and that Serbia supports the territorial integrity of the Comoros. We also voted for all resolutions in the UN General Assembly concerning the territorial integrity of the Comoros and we will continue to do so." In turn, Comoros foreign minister Mohamed El-Amine Souef stated, "We are facing a similar problem. There is the Mayotte problem. If Mayotte declared independence tomorrow, we will follow Serbia's steps and we will do everything we can to restore territorial integrity in our country. So, taking that into consideration, of course we should observe international law, and we follow closely the situation, and we will continue to do so" (El-Amine Souef 2018).

Notably, the derecognition of the claimant state tends to boost the political legitimacy of the incumbent government of the former base state. Serbia utilized the derecognition of Kosovo to silence its domestic political opponents and boost its electoral support. It is becoming clear that one of the reasons Serbia pursued and justified the derecognition of Kosovo was domestic politics, namely, to silence the political opposition. The government tried to silence opposition parties by showing that they failed to prevent or withdraw recognition of Kosovo when they were in power. In contrast, the current government had successfully done so, thus showing it to be better suited to govern, including dealing with the Kosovo issue. Foreign minister Ivica Dačić argued that the previous government led by Boris Tadić and Vuk Jeremić sent the ICJ question to the UN General Assembly, which confirmed that Kosovo's declaration of independence did not contradict international law. Dačić recalled that during the government Boris Tadic and Vuk Jeremić eighty-four countries recognized Kosovo. Since he became the foreign minister, nine countries had recognized Kosovo, while thirteen had withdrawn recognition (RTS 2019). Similarly, China has used the derecognition of Taiwan to bolder the political legitimacy of its leadership and the coercive vision for reunification, and simultaneously, it has tried to weaken the legitimacy of pro-independence forces in Taipei.

The discussion in this section reveals how the derecognition of states has become part of the political and diplomatic ecology of third countries implicated in trading, renting, and transactionally granting, withholding, or withdrawing the claimant states. The decision to retain or switch diplomatic allies, as in the lucrative cases of Taiwan and China, reveals that for third countries, the derecognition of claimant states is no longer simply a foreign policy issue but also a deeply enshrined domestic political issue. Political cleavages are not only about domestic governance but are also based on leaders' position on the recognition or derecognition of contender states. The domestication and politicization of state recognition and derecognition thus add another layer of complexity and uncertainty to all cases under examination in this book. Most important, they reveal that rationales for derecognition have little to do with international laws, norms, and principles, the presence or absence of statehood capacity, or changes in the original conditions of recognition. Rather, domestic ideological divides, electoral politics, and the quest for sovereignty tend to be important rationales guiding the derecognition of claimant states. Such dynamics of policy demystification of state derecognition thus open opportunities for former base states to deploy predatory practices, including economic and geopolitical instruments, to exploit polarization in third countries to advance their diplomatic agenda.

Geopolitical and Security Interests

In addition to economic incentives and domestic political considerations, many countries have guided the derecognition of other states based on geopolitical and security rationales. This strand of rationales overlaps the domestic and foreign policy interests of derecognizing states and is part of the inward-looking logic of state derecognition. Decisions for the derecognition of other states, like those concerning recognition in the first instance, are often motivated by geopolitical considerations and vulnerable to pressure from dominant regional or global powers. Particularly as the international system is experiencing a transition from a Western-dominated order to a new fragmented order with multiple regional hegemons, smaller states with histories of swinging allegiances to dominant powers of the time tend to respond to external pressure and withdraw the recognition of states for geopolitical and security reasons. The contender states' global political and economic strength tends to play a significant role when third countries decide to continue or discontinue the recognition of the claimant state.

Several states that have switched recognition from Taiwan to mainland China have invoked geopolitical and security considerations in their public justification. For example, Costa Rica's derecognition of Taiwan in 2007 was openly a geopolitical move, admitting that the decision was "not the consequence of an ideological turnaround, or of geopolitical reasons or short term interests," but "an act of elemental realism, an awakening to the global context we are forced to deal with" (Casas-Zamora 2009). In addition to geoeconomic interests, Alexander (2014: 67) argues, "Costa Rica was motivated by the allure of temporary membership of the UN Security Council. A veto from the PRC, a permanent member of the council, would have prevented the Arias government from taking its place at the 2008–2009 session." This is congruent with broader trends showing that China proactively uses its veto power in the UN Security Council to make the derecognition of Taiwan a condition of its support for peacekeeping and humanitarian assistance in war-affected states. Countries affected by violent conflict and in need of UN peacekeepers are more likely to derecognize other states in return for support from powerful states. This has been the case with Macedonia, Chad, Burkina Faso, and other conflict-affected states. In 2006, Chad derecognized Taiwan after China threatened to veto a resolution to send UN peacekeepers to Sudan's region of Darfur, which threatened the country's stability, its ability to cope with Sudanese rebel groups and handle over two hundred thousand refugees who already had fled to Chad (Cooper 2016: 163). Similarly, due to security concerns, Burkina Faso decided to end two-decades-old diplomatic ties with Taiwan in 2018. The country is affected by political violence in the Sahel region, for which it needs the support of the UN and other regional bodies to finance peacekeeping and security arrangements. In particular, China offered to support the G5 Sahel group of states to tackle regional insecurity (Burcu and Bertrand 2019). Senegal derecognized Taiwan to achieve its ambition to be the center of the francophone world in Africa, for which it needed China's backing.

In 2019, the Solomon Islands derecognized Taiwan and allied with mainland China primarily in recognition of China's global economic, military, and political rise. In the rationale guiding the derecognition of Taiwan, the Solomon Islands argued that "the circumstances surrounding the decision to formally establish diplomatic relations with Taiwan no longer exist . . . the World then has changed. We must also change" (Government of Solomon Islands 2019: 10). "The involvement of the US is more on diplomatic and security issues. The US has not shown interest in addressing Solomon Islands' underdevelopment and poverty" (Government of Solomon Islands 2019: 13). As opposed to the United States' interests in the Indo-Pacific region, the Solomon Islands argued that "China does not pursue military expansion, per se. It's security involvement therefore is limited, compared to its diplomatic and economic engagements" (Government of Solomon Islands 2019: 10–11). However, for the United States, China's campaign for international derecognition of Taiwan in the Pacific Islands aims "to establish military access to the region, gain the benefit of these countries' voting power in the UN, undermine regional diplomatic support for Taiwan, and gain access to natural resources, among other goals" (U.S.-China Economic and Security Review Commission 2019: 401). It eventually aims "to achieve regional dominance and replace the United States as a vital economic partner and preeminent regional security guarantor" (U.S.-China Economic and Security Review Commission 2019: 401).

Another set of reasons is the stimulation of state sovereignty through the derecognition of other states, namely, using derecognition as a balancing act to demonstrate autonomy on foreign affairs and the ability to avoid reliance foreign allies. The government of the Solomon Islands portrayed the decision to switch from Taiwan to China as an opportunity to uphold its sovereign statehood and demonstrate its ability to decide freely on its foreign policy based on "mutual respect and trust, without third party interference" (Government of Solomon Islands 2019: 35–36). Taking Fiji as an example, the prime minister of the Solomon Islands argued that aligning with China would be a better way to assert more sovereign capacity in its relationship with Australia (The Australian 2019). In justifying the switch from Taiwan to China, the government of the Solomon Islands (2019: 36) argued that "as a sovereign independent nation, China respects non-interference and fundamental principles of international relations . . . China has never interfered in the affairs of countries." Thus, transactional exploitation of diplomacy recognition has enabled small, postcolonial states to generate alternatives for gaining assistance from more than one regional power without strings attached and conditionality. In other words, derecognition has enabled third countries to regenerate their sovereign agency manifested in the form of greater maneuverability in the conduct of domestic and foreign affairs.

While economic reasons were critical drivers of the Pacific islands' decision to rent recognition to other states, threats emanating from climate change also played an important role. With the United States and Western allies sending mixed messages on global climate governance, small Pacific islands looked toward China for resources and support in building resilience in the face of rapid climate change (NPR 2019). China claims to propagate its policy toward the Pacific island countries on grounds of mutual respect, equality, and mutual benefit, yet it has insisted that countries that have "diplomatic relations with China . . . should not participate in the dialogue with Taiwan" (Parliament of Australia 2006: 180). Chinese discourse mainly focused on respecting the sovereignty of their diplomatic allies. However, experience shows that once countries derecognize Taiwan and align with China, constraints on their foreign policy emerge, as was the case with Costa Rica's decision to refuse entry to the Dalai Lama in 2008 (Alexander 2014: 75). For a long time, both China and Taiwan expanded their influence among local and regional political leaders and lawmakers in the Solomon Islands and, through them, put pressure on state leaders to defend Chinese interests (Solomon Times 2019a). Following a similar logic, Suriname derecognized Kosovo as part of a strategic deal with Russia to counterbalance the United States' interference in its internal affairs following the isolation of the Venezuelan regime (Caribbean News Now 2017). In exchange for Russian weapons, missiles, and tanks, Venezuela recognized Abkhazia and South Ossetia in 2011 (Felgenhauer 2009). Similarly, Nicaragua recognized South Ossetia and Abkhazia to rebuild close ties with Russia. Its official justification was different: it argued that the recognition of these breakaway regions was based on historical similarities of their revolutionary struggles for freedom, the desire to reduce bloodshed and conflict, and the need to recognize the suffering of people in conflict.

Pacific island countries, in particular, have depended on Australia's one-sided terms for an extended period, which limited their capacity to influence bilateral cooperation and aid (Fowdy 2019). Over the years, Australia has often labeled the Pacific islands as "fragile tiny states," highlighting how they suffer from "poor governance, crime and corruption" and how they "pose a real threat to both economic development and to regional security" (Parliament of Australia 2006: 172). The Pacific islands found particularly problematic Australia's opposition to checkbook diplomacy and the critique of Canberra that such practices work "against regional countries' efforts to improve living standards, governance and political stability" (Parliament of Australia 2006: 174). For this reason, leveraging the capacity to recognize and derecognize other states has enhanced the capacity of the Pacific islands to reduce Australia's regional dominance by counterbalancing it with another powerful regional alliance. Thus, the derecognition of states, when motivated by economic interests, tends to change the dynamics of foreign aid. Often development assistance from wealthy Western countries or international financial institutions tends to have strings attached, such as structural adjustments of economy, governance, and human rights. "The provision of funds with no conditions attached allows particular elements in these countries to evade . . . the fiscal responsibility imposed on them by

134 • *The Derecognition of States*

our bilateral aid programs" (Senate Foreign Affairs 2005). As Stringer (2006: 565) maintains, "Pacific microstates become more willing to accept Taiwanese and Chinese money rather than Western money because there are fewer perceived strings attached, such as demands for good governance." Accordingly, this move tends to "strengthen their position towards Western nations since it gives the Pacific microstates alternatives in choosing foreign cooperation partners" (Stringer 2006: 565). In this regard, derecognition changes the power dynamics by offering greater bargaining power to the derecognizing states, allowing them to determine the terms of foreign aid and surpass any conditionality or accountability attached to such assistance.

The small Pacific island of Nauru has also been active in the business of switching state recognition not only for economic reasons but also for geopolitical balance. Nauru is located between Australia and Hawaii, with a population of about eleven thousand people and twenty-one square kilometers in space. Its close geographical location to Australia resulted in dependency and unequal sovereign relations. In an attempt to balance the country's reliance on Australia, Nauru attracted the attention and support of China and Russia by recognizing and then withdrawing the recognition of Taiwan and, later, Abkhazia and South Ossetia (Wyeth 2017). In 2011, Nauru recognized Georgia's breakaway regions in exchange for Russia building a seaport worth $10 million (The Australian 2011). However, pressure from the United States and Australia forced Nauru to derecognize Abkhazia and South Ossetia in 2014, fearing it would lose aid and assistance from Western states (Ó Beacháin 2020). Nauru's flirtation with Russia has raised concerns in Australia that this tiny island is expanding its illicit activity of hosting Russian offshore money laundering. Australia sees Nauru as significant for its national interests, serving as one of the offshore refugee processing sites in return for aid and assistance.

Moreover, countries with historical rivalry and chronic enmity tend to side with opposing sides in regional self-determination disputes. For example, Algeria, Iran, and South Africa support the SADR in a strategic rivalry with Morocco and its Western allies. On the other hand, Yemen's rivalry with Iran is reflected by siding with Moroccan authorities in this dispute. These dynamics are evident for several other countries. White (2015: 53) argues that "Morocco's trade relations, ideological orientation towards the West and the military support it has received from the US and France" seem to be strong points for leveraging its campaign for derecognition of the SADR and legitimizing the occupation of Western Sahara. The United States and Morocco have strong political, economic, and military ties. NATO and European powers view Morocco as a crucial security partner in North Africa and the Mediterranean. In the present international security environment, movements for self-determination are blended with transnational terrorist groups to legitimize state violence and foreground the derecognition campaign. Morocco uses counterterrorism momentum to deepen ties with Western allies and delegitimize the Polisario Front and its regional backer, Algeria, while expanding territorial annexation and crushing Sahrawi human rights groups.

Regarding Western Sahara, the EU member states are once again divided, highlighting the salience of strong advocate states in shaping the recognition policy (Benabdullah 2009). While Spain, a former colonial power over Western Sahara, appears to support the right of the Sahrawi people to self-determination, France tends to side more with Morocco for geopolitical and cultural reasons. Unable to generate a common affirmative position, the EU's position so far has been that it "supports the UN Secretary-General's efforts to achieve a just, lasting and mutually acceptable political solution, which will provide for the self-determination of the people of Western Sahara in the context of arrangements consistent with the principles and purposes of the Charter of the UN" (European Parliament 2015). Yet as part of its efforts to secure its southern borders and deepen political and economic influence in North Africa, including the benefits from the fisheries industry, the EU has signed an association agreement with Morocco, which entails enhanced political and economic relations. This implies, because of its geopolitical needs, that the EU, especially Spain, has come to gradually accept Morocco's de facto control of Western Sahara, despite its violating UN resolutions, international law, and a ruling by the European Court of Justice, which was appealed by the European Commission and subsequently turned down. In 2022, Spain sided with Morocco's autonomy plan for Western Sahara in an effort to curtail the uncontrolled flow of migration using Morocco as a transit country toward the EU (New York Times 2022). Another signal of the EU's siding with Morocco came from the EU high representative Borrell i Fontelles, who stated that "the EU supports United Nations' efforts in view of reaching a just, lasting and mutually acceptable political solution to the question of Western Sahara, in accordance with the United Nations Security Council resolutions, and in particular Resolution 2602 (2021)" (European Parliament 2022). The EU and other major international powers siding with Morocco have over time removed any reference to the right of the Sahrawi people to self-determination and the decolonization process. Again, this demonstrates the tension between the EU's normative self-image and

136 • *The Derecognition of States*

its material interests, exposed as a consequence of a more active external engagement (Newman and Visoka 2018a).

Finally, there are instances where recognition is reversed due to its high diplomatic and geopolitical cost. In justifying the derecognition of Abkhazia and South Ossetia, Tuvalu's minister of foreign affairs, Taukelina Finikaso, admitted that the country risked isolating itself when the previous government set up diplomatic ties with those breakaway territories. "Georgia is working towards becoming one of the EU members, and we have very strong bonds with the EU" (Radio New Zealand 2014a). Finikaso said assistance from the European Union had decreased for the forthcoming cycle and expressed the hope that the agreement with Georgia would rectify that in the future (Radio New Zealand 2014a). Foreign Minister Finikaso added that "we were heading towards isolation and it is not something that we want to face up with, as we have always been with the like-minded states, as in the EU and being a Commonwealth member also, we would like to keep with all the traditional friends and the members of organizations that we have been with since we started" (Radio New Zealand 2014b). As the *Baltic Times* reports, "Tuvalu sought to establish diplomatic relations with Lithuania in 2011 and 2012, but Lithuania declined on both occasions because in 2011 Tuvalu recognized the independence of Abkhazia and South Ossetia, which have seceded from Georgia, supported by Russia" (Baltic Times 2014). Soon after Tuvalu derecognized Abkhazia and South Ossetia, the Lithuanian government established diplomatic relations with Tuvalu.

Since 2008, the EU has pursued an explicit position of collective nonrecognition, as was the case with Abkhazia and South Ossetia, two breakaway regions of Georgia. This policy took a threefold position involving explicitly and unanimously stating that no EU members would recognize the breakaway territories, calling on other states not to recognize the independence proclamations, and condemning "Russia's unilateral decision to recognise the independence of Abkhazia and South Ossetia" (European Parliament 2008). In implementing this policy, the EU issued instructions in June 2011 to its delegations and diplomatic networks to send a demarche to countries worldwide. The purpose of this demarche was "to remind relevant EU partners about the importance that the EU attaches to the sovereignty and territorial integrity of Georgia" (European Union 2011). The demarche encouraged partner countries to maintain their policy of nonrecognition, highlighting the detrimental effect of secession "to the stability and security of the region," including "the ongoing international efforts to find a solution to the conflicts" (European Union 2011). Finally, the demarche threatened that "any recognition would hurt the core interests of the EU and would not be without consequences to the quality and depth of your relations with the EU" (European Union 2011).

In sum, geopolitical and security considerations behind the withdrawal of state recognition vary from one case to another. However, like economic interests, they highlight the complex and double-edged entanglement of domestic concerns of states with developments abroad. While invoking security and geopolitical concerns might be crucial for derecognizing states, it can also provide a suitable shield from international criticism and potential retaliatory measures. Yet the discussion in this section highlighted how volatile and risky can be the discontinuance of diplomatic relations and shifting strategic alliances, which can antagonize regional hegemons and thus deepen rivalry and conflict among other contender states.

OUTWARD-LOOKING JUSTIFICATIONS

Conflict Resolution and Status (Re)settlement

One of the dominant outward-looking justifications for state derecognition is facilitating the peaceful resolution of self-determination disputes. Contestation over the right of the claimant state to external self-determination and existence as an independent state tends to create frozen conflicts and stalemates (Weller and Metzger 2008). This involves the unwillingness of parties to engage in conflict resolution talks, or, if third parties mediate ongoing talks, they tend to stall (Pogodda, Richmond, and Visoka 2022). The quest for recognition and derecognition is a diplomatic battlefield between the claimant and former base states. Often third countries and international organizations utilize granting or withholding recognition as a conflict resolution instrument. However, the record is mixed regarding the effect of such acts in promoting stability and conflict resolution (Caplan 2005; Newman and Visoka 2018b). For example, a significant number of countries who have recognized Kosovo, have framed such decisions as contributing to regional peace and stability in the Western Balkans (Bolton and Visoka 2010). There are also rare occasions when the revocation of recognition is justified to "avoid broader international conflict that could arise by extending recognition," as with South Africa's Bantustans (Rich and Dahmer 2022: 356). Regardless of what rationales are invoked in the first place, the more countries recognize the claimant state, the greater their chances are to shape

138 • *The Derecognition of States*

the conflict resolution dynamics in their favor and to refuse concessions or renegotiations of their political status with the former base state. In this context, for the former base state and their allies, the derecognition of the claimant state is perceived as a necessary effort to unlock enduring hostilities and transform the dynamics of intractability in conflict resolution talks. It is a method of indirect diplomatic pressure and subversion without the need to resort to covert or open war (Lee 2020). Such indirect diplomatic method is less expensive than the aggressive and coercive method. It is an effective method to degrade the claimant state's sovereignty while reducing the risk of losing international legitimacy for such actions.

Thus, for the protagonists (former base state and derecognizing states), framing the campaign for derecognition as part of conflict resolution efforts is a sophisticated approach that enhances the legitimacy and credibility of such decisions and successfully disguises other covert and subversive functions of this anti-diplomatic practice. It is challenging to refute derecognition when it is presented as part of efforts for peaceful resolution of disputes. However, there is another side to the story that it is essential to highlight. Although derecognition tends to serve as a pressure mechanism for conflict resolution and resettlement of the political status of the claimant state, it is utilized as a conflict ripeness instrument where the burden for engaging in peace talks falls on the claimant state. In contrast, the bargaining power of the former base state is significantly enhanced. The logic of conflict ripeness is to pressure conflict parties into a hurting stalemate and an impasse where they will be forced to make concessions and engage in conflict resolution talks (Zartman 2003). But in this instance, derecognition effectively performs the function of coercive diplomacy directed to one conflict party to force it to make undesirable concessions.

In the case of Western Sahara, a good number of states have justified their derecognition decision because they are supporting the UN-led process for conflict resolution between the Polisario Front and Morocco. The UN's MINURSO mission was mandated to facilitate a referendum in Western Sahara to enable its people to realize their right to self-determination. However, the situation remains deadlocked on the disagreement between Morocco and the Polisario Front on the demographic eligibility for a referendum. The Polisario insists that the vote should be limited to the local Sahrawi population identified by Spain shortly before the official end of Spanish colonial rule in 1976. They mainly reside in the refugee camps in Algeria. Meanwhile, Morocco insists on including the wider Sahrawi population living in Morocco and Moroccan settlers residing in Western Sahara. While many countries consider Western Sahara the last colony in Africa, Morocco's autonomy proposal has received comprehensive international support as a realistic, practicable, and enduring political solution (Pham 2010: 11). The United States, for instance, views Morocco's autonomy plan as "serious, credible, and realistic, and it represents one potential approach to satisfy the aspirations of the people in Western Sahara to run their own affairs with peace and dignity" (US Mission to the United Nations 2020). Similarly, France openly considers the 2007 Moroccan autonomy plan to be "a serious and credible basis for discussions" (UN Security Council 2019b: 3). The autonomy proposal is seen as a viable option because of fears that an independent Western Sahara would end up becoming a failed state and an extension of Algerian and anti-Western block in North Africa and the Middle East (Bolton 2007: 368–69). It is also seen as a solution to end this conflict and discourage other secessionist African movements from seeking external self-determination. For example, UN Security Council Resolution 2412 (2018) called for a "realistic, practicable and enduring" political solution to end the decades-old conflict between Morocco and the Western Sahara. In putting pressure on the Polisario Front and its international allies, Morocco's allies, including the United States and France, pushed for renewing the MINURSO's mandate for six months instead of one year, hoping that parties in the conflict would return to the negotiation table and resolve the prolonged self-determination dispute over the Western Sahara during that time (US Mission to the United Nations 2020).

Morocco has lobbied for the derecognition of the SADR because the Polisario Front, which has represented the Sahrawi people, allegedly is unwilling to resolve the self-determination conflict through peaceful talks. This diplomatic narrative has been successful and accepted by many countries that have suspended or withdrawn recognition of the SADR. For instance, Guinea-Bissau in 2010 justified derecognition of the SADR as supporting Morocco's initiative for autonomy for the territory of Western Sahara as part of the UN-led talks. Panama committed to suspending diplomatic relations with the SADR "until the peace process is completed, initiated and mediated by the United Nations, without prejudice to the support that will be given in future to the initiatives adopted at the multilateral level in this matter" (MFA of Panama 2013). In 2013, Haiti withdrew the recognition of the SADR, originally granted in 2006, "to promote the settlement process of this matter by the United Nations Security Council and to support the efforts of the Secretary-General of the United Nations Organization and his Special Envoy to achieve a definitive political and mutually acceptable solution between the parties" (MFA of Haiti 2013).

Similarly, Haiti's justification for derecognition of the SADR was framed as an attempt to encourage "the parties to continue negotiations in good faith to maintain the momentum generated by the Moroccan proposal to grant a Statute of wide autonomy to the Sahara region and to reach a solution based on realism and the spirit of compromise in accordance with the relevant resolutions of the Security Council of the United Nations" (MFA of Haiti 2013). Similarly, Suriname withdrew recognition of the SADR in 2016, claiming that such a decision was "in the interest of promoting a just and peaceful solution of said conflict, through the good offices and efforts of the UN Security Council, and to encourage the efforts of the United Nations Secretary General and his Personal Envoy to reach a political, definitive and mutually acceptable solution" (Government of Suriname 2016). The Commonwealth of Dominica and Burundi justified derecognition of the SADR, encouraged by UN-led momentum and the Moroccan territorial and functional autonomy initiative, claiming that this process might lead to a mutually acceptable solution to this protracted disputed (Agence Maghreb Arabe Presse 2010). Malawi has recognized and de-recognized the SADR four times since 1996. In the 2017 reiteration, Malawi withdrew its recognition of the SADR to maintain "a neutral position vis-à-vis the regional Sahara conflict" and "to make a positive contribution to the UN process by maintaining a neutral position without pre-judging its outcome." Malawi further claimed that "this position of neutrality and support for the UN process will send a strong signal to all the parties concerned in favour of a solution to this long-standing regional conflict."

Although these examples show that derecognition has served as a strategy to pressure Polisario representatives to come to the negotiation table, they were not precisely designed to resolve the conflict or respect the will of Sahrawi people for self-determination. Rather, Morocco used them to undermine the SADR's prospects for recognizable statehood by successfully luring a significant number of states to withdraw recognition and suspend diplomatic relations with SADR authorities. The Polisario Front considers holding a referendum to be the only legitimate solution for democratically determining the fate of the Western Sahara. Critics also argue that the Moroccan autonomy plan is "impossible because of many constitutional, legal, economical, historical, ethnic and geographical factors," including fears that such an arrangement would not last in a monarchical and centralist political system

(Lakhal, Khalil, and San Martin 2006: 336). When the UN proposed a settlement plan in 1991, the Moroccan government argued that maintaining the recognition of the SADR predetermined the process in favor of the independence option and, consequently, states should derecognize the Sahrawi state and wait for the referendum outcome. The same argument was used to discourage other states from recognizing the SADR. The view that the recognition of the SADR should be withheld pending the ongoing UN-led negotiations is seen as untenable because Morocco has blocked and prevented the people of Western Sahara from exercising their right to self-determination. As early as 2004 South Africa noted that Morocco's autonomy plan and the UN-led conflict resolution process were to deny the people of Western Sahara the right to self-determination by insisting that in future talks Morocco would not negotiate over its sovereignty and territorial integrity (President of South Africa 2004). In response to this move, South Africa recognized the SADR, stating that it was left with no choice because of the slow progress of the UN peace process (BBC 2004). Similarly, Mozambique described Morocco's approach as "dilatory manoeuvres that delays [*sic*] the achievement of the inalienable right of the Saharawi people to self-determination and independence" (President of Mozambique 2004). Thus, the experience of Western Sahara shows that framing derecognition as a reason for conflict settlement was not entirely a genuine effort toward a peaceful and just resolution of the self-determination dispute. Rather, it was also a policy to pressure the SADR to make concessions and reverse the independence project. According to this logic, the weaker Polisario's international position is, the more likely it is to accept compromises in eventual talks or encounters with Morocco.

In another part of the world, Serbia has exploited the EU-facilitated dialogue with Kosovo to encourage states that haven't yet recognized Kosovo to delay the decision or to pressure those states that have already recognized Kosovo to backtrack. Following Kosovo's independence in 2008 and the 2010 ICJ advisory opinion on Kosovo, the UN General Assembly authorized the EU to facilitate a dialogue to normalize relations between Kosovo and Serbia. In 2013, Kosovo and Serbia signed the first agreement governing the principles for normalizing relations (Beha 2015; Visoka and Doyle 2016). The essence of this agreement was to find a mutually agreeable solution for removing Serbia's parallel institutions in Kosovo and de facto accept Kosovo's sovereignty as sole legal and political authority in Kosovo's territory and as an independent state in the regional instance. Equally, the agreement also contained provisions for expanding the autonomous self-governance for the Serb community in Kosovo, which has been widely contested in

Kosovo. However, since Serbia refuses to recognize Kosovo's independence, the normalization process has stalled, and both sides have refused to uphold their commitments fully. While Kosovo, backed by the United States, has set mutual recognition as the end goal of the dialogue, the EU remains more open to an implicit and de facto form of recognition branded as a full and comprehensive settlement in the form of a legally binding agreement. Undoubtedly, the most controversial issues underpinning the incoming phase of the political dialogue between Kosovo and Serbia are the controversial proposals for an expanded autonomy for local Serbs in Kosovo, the issue of partition and border adjustment between Kosovo and Serbia, and the prospects for recognition and the admission of Kosovo to the UN.

Serbia intensified its derecognition campaign once it realized that Kosovo was reluctant to discuss autonomy for the Serb population on Kosovo or accept the partition of Kosovo along ethnic lines as a basis for an agreed settlement. In this context, Serbia persuaded the derecognition campaign to force Kosovo to return to the negotiation table and make painful compromises on its sovereignty and statehood. As Serbian foreign minister Ivica Dačić, stated: "In ten years Kosovo has not managed to round off its independence and will not do so in the coming decades if it does not sit at the negotiating table with Serbia" (N1 2018a). Thus, Serbia's primary rationale has been that recognition of Kosovo undermines the conflict resolution process and discourages Kosovo Albanians from reaching a mutually consensual agreement in line with international norms and law, which would contribute to international peace and stability. Serbia's discourse on the derecognition of Kosovo was framed around the importance of suspending recognition of Kosovo. Serbia's diplomatic discourse and practice show that derecognition is an instrument to enhance its bargaining power in the EU-led talks with Kosovo, aimed at either gaining a better deal for Serbs living in Kosovo or creating a situation of ripeness where Kosovo would eventually agree to ethnic-based territorial adjustment. Hence, Serbia has framed the derecognition of Kosovo as a peace-making gesture, encouraging third countries to "wait for the dialogue to be finished, to remain status neutral until then and respect the outcomes of the dialogue which will be presented at the United Nations" (MFA of Serbia 2019a; 2019b).

For Serbia, the derecognition of Kosovo became a means to prolong Kosovo's contested statehood. In this instance, derecognition serves as a diplomatic instrument intended to establish a status quo and derail Kosovo's and its allies' quest for international recognition and membership in multilateral bodies. Serbia has argued that it will end the derecognition campaign when Kosovo and its allies end their recognition campaign. In this regard, Serbia wanted to neutralize and eventually debilitate Kosovo's foreign policy and its international legal sovereignty. A former Serbian diplomat admitted that "the withdrawal of recognition of Kosovo is a moral victory for Serbia, which gives her an infusion of confidence in the negotiations with Pristina" (Novosti 2018a). Suppose Kosovo does not settle the outstanding disputes with Serbia. In that case, it will be obliged either to continue its current approach of seeking incremental integration into the international system or to seek a radical change to its status by looking for functional and gradual reunification with the kin state of Albania. Such an unlikely move could result in redrawing political borders and the return of troubles in the Balkans. From this perspective, the question of Kosovo's sovereign status is not yet entirely closed, and the next stage will be definitive in either making or breaking the country's desire to become a fully fledged sovereign state.

This diplomatic discourse has formed the bedrock of Serbia's campaign for the derecognition of Kosovo, which received small yet not insignificant international traction. Between 2017 and 2020, it is alleged that eighteen countries withdrew or suspended the recognition of Kosovo using arguments identical to those made by Serbia, which often contradict the original justification for recognizing Kosovo. In 2023, it was alleged that about nine countries had withdrawn the recognition of Kosovo, but the MFA of Kosovo has refuted such claims and provided counterevidence of continued diplomatic interaction with some of those states (Balkan Insight 2023). In 2018, Burundi revoked unilaterally the recognition of Kosovo. In the derecognition letter, Burundi stated that Kosovo's declaration of independence was in contradiction with the Helsinki Final Act provisions on territorial integrity and with UN Security Council Resolution 1244 (1999), which placed Kosovo under UN transitional administration (MFA of Burundi 2018). Furthermore, Burundi's derecognition letter explained that Kosovo and Serbia are in a dialogue for a peaceful settlement, and Serbia has not yet recognized Kosovo as an independent state. Burundi initially recognized Kosovo in 2012 based on the 2010 advisory opinion of ICJ, which concluded that Kosovo's declaration of independence was in accordance with international law (MFA of Burundi 2018). Five years after establishing diplomatic relations, in 2018, Grenada imposed an interim suspension on the recognition of Kosovo in order to support a "solution to the future status of Kosovo to be reached through the dialogue between Belgrade and Pristina, and that it is the desired mechanism for achieving a just, lasting and sustainable solution" (MFA of Grenada 2018). Similarly, the MFA of Madagascar stated that having thoroughly considered the situation and wished for each to encourage dialogue continuing between the Republic of Serbia and the organs of Kosovo with the application of Resolution 1244 (1999) and also to allow both sides to come to a fair, just and lasting political solution to the question of Kosovo's status, the Ministry of Foreign Affairs of the Republic of Madagascar made the decision to withdraw the recognition of Kosovo as an independent state until the negotiations under the auspices of the international community are concluded. (MFA of Madagascar 2018)

When Nauru derecognized Kosovo in 2019, it stated that "the decision to recognize Kosovo as an independent state was premature and viewed as contradicting the principles of the UN Security Council Resolution 1244 (1999)" (Republic of Nauru 2019). It also stated that it would "terminate any communication documents issued by the Republic of Nauru until both parties complete the negotiation process and finalize the status of Kosovo as per the UN Security Council Resolution 1244 (1999)" (Republic of Nauru 2019).

Similarly, the government of the Kingdom of Lesotho maintained that "its only contribution to the solution of the future status of Kosovo should be the support of the dialogue between Belgrade and Pristina, rather than defining the status before the dialogue is over, so the issue of the statehood in Kosovo is premature." Accordingly, the government decided to "neither declared itself on this issue, nor will it do so until the dialogue between the two sides has been completed," adding that "when the parties reach an agreement, the Government of the Kingdom of Lesotho will firmly support it" (B92 2018e). Following Serbia's lobbying campaign, Sierra Leone issued a diplomatic note in March 2020 communicating to Serbia that "the Government of the Republic of Sierra Leone has noted with concern the continuing impasse between the Republic of Serbia and Kosovo on the question of the Independence of Kosovo, and that both parties are currently engaged in dialogue on the matter" (MFA of Sierra Leone 2020). The letter further stated that Sierra Leone "is of the considered view that any recognition it has conferred (expressed or by necessary implication) on the Independence of Kosovo, may have been premature, bearing in mind the ongoing dialogue." Consequently, Sierra Leone "has decided to withdraw any such recognition of the Independence of Kosovo, out of respect for the said ongoing dialogue, whilst looking forward to a mutually acceptable outcome" (MFA of Sierra Leone 2020). Sierra Leone initially recognized Kosovo in 2008, and in 2009 it lodged a statement in favor of Kosovo during the ICJ proceedings, adding that "Kosovo's independence itself (in addition to the act of declaring independence) was in accordance with International Law, as well as with the consistence provisions of the United Nations Security Resolution 1244" (MFA of Sierra Leone 2008, 2009).

The references made to premature recognition are interesting but, at the same time, also problematic. There is wide consensus among legal scholars that in premature recognition an entity proclaims independence without consent and in defiance of the base state's resistance, and the latter prevents the new state from consolidating the attributes of statehood, including territorial sovereignty and international subjectivity (Peterson 1997; Grant and Nicholson 2020: 27). In other words, third countries are encouraged to wait until the dispute calms down and that the nascent state has effective control over the claimed territory, and the independent statehood matures and becomes irreversible (Roth 2020: 195). However, there is no consensus on when the right moment is to grant recognition, especially pending the recognition by the former base state, nor on resolving outstanding issues with the former base state or ongoing diplomatic disputes with other states. It is left to the discretion of states to make that judgment. Additionally, there is no consensus on whether premature recognition is a regrettable or unlawful act in international affairs (Tomuschat 2012). Most important, in general literature, premature recognition doesn't necessarily entail the phase before recognition by the former base state, but the interim period leading to consolidation of effective statehood.

For example, most countries that have derecognized Kosovo did not recognize Kosovo in the immediate aftermath of the declaration of independence. Some did so years after Kosovo demonstrated that it fulfills the objective and subjective criteria of statehood: its distinct population, territory, government, and capacity to enter into relations with other states. Especially concerning the capacity to enter into diplomatic relations with other states, Kosovo was already recognized by over fifty countries when most of the now derecognizing states conferred recognition on Kosovo. When it comes to premature recognition, timing is considered crucial. Namely, recognition can be considered premature "before the entity truly fulfils the criteria of statehood" (Lowe 2007: 164). Accordingly, the only circumstance that may explain or justify derecognition of states is when the conditions attached to the original recognition are not fulfilled. Thus, the argument for premature recognition invoked in several instances of derecognition is hard to justify. In truth, most of the cases of derecognition examined in this book amount to premature derecognition, since the original conditions of recognition have not changed, and the justificatory rationales for derecognition have nothing to do with the effectiveness and legitimacy of the claimant state. Following on from this point, since the decision to derecognize a state does not correspond with unfulfillment of the original conditions of recognition, the practice of derecognition falls into declarativism, namely a declaration that in the eye of the derecognizing state the claimant state is not independent and bilateral relations are discontinued (Nicholson and Grant 2020: 30). Accordingly, the practice of revoking diplomatic recognition seems to indicate that we have to deal with premature derecognitions, which represent foreign policy adventures intending to gain politically and financially in full disregard of the fulfillment of statehood conditions and broader adverse effects.

Although Kosovo initially denied the withdrawal of recognition by several states, it eventually came to terms with the reality. The MFA of Kosovo saw Serbia's utilization of the EU-facilitated dialogue for normalizing relations with Kosovo as a justification for the derecognition of Kosovo and considered it a manipulative act of aggression aimed at undermining Kosovo's sovereignty and international image. Concerning Serbia's usage of the EU-facilitated dialogue as a rationale for derecognizing Kosovo, in 2019 the prime minister of Kosovo, Ramush Haradinaj, sent a letter to each country in the world pointing out that the dialogue was not about the future status of Kosovo, which had already been decided by the ICJ advisory opinion when it found Kosovo's declaration of independence to be in accordance with international law. Prime Minister Haradinaj added that Kosovo engaged in the normalization dialogue as a sovereign independent state aiming to achieve a comprehensive and legally binding agreement between the two countries leading to mutual recognition and Kosovo's membership in the United Nations (MFA of Kosovo 2019c). Furthermore, the MFA of Kosovo sent diplomatic notes to countries that recognized Kosovo clarifying that the "dialogue process with Serbia is not about Kosovo's political status as it is resolved already, but on establishing a relationship with Serbia that will address the historical outstanding issues that our two countries have" (MFA of Kosovo 2019a). The note stated, "Kosovo is an independent and sovereign country recognized broadly by the international community and does not negotiate its independence with anyone" (MFA of Kosovo 2019a). The EU has never issued a denial of the claim that the dialogue between Kosovo and Serbia is about the status of Kosovo, which has offered Serbia room to exploit the process for withdrawing the recognition of Kosovo. One of the leading opposition parties in Kosovo, LDK, argued that "Serbia's strong commitment in international diplomacy against the state of Kosovo, in particular its efforts for withdrawing the recognition of Kosovo, is a sign that it is not interested in reaching an agreement on the recognition of the state of Kosovo but works for the dissolution of the state of Kosovo" (Zëri 2019c). Through its campaign for derecognizing Kosovo, Serbia tried to establish a new status quo on the question of Kosovo where Serbia maintained the upper hand in future talks. Serbian foreign minister Dačić argued that the derecognition of Kosovo showed that the only way to resolve this issue was through negotiations with Serbia. It has said that it will end the derecognition campaign when Kosovo or its allies end their recognition campaign. It seems that as part of the resumption of the EU-mediated dialogue, Serbia and Kosovo have agreed to cease actions that may seem detrimental to the normalization of interstate relations. However, it appears to have been more of a verbal promise than a written agreement.

In sum, the justification of state derecognition on the grounds of facilitating conflict resolution represents a sophisticated way of framing the decisions for reconsidering, freezing, suspending, and formally withdrawing the recognition of claimant states. Although this discourse for state derecognition originates from and is manufactured by the former base state, it is convincing, resonating with broader international norms and efforts to settle disputes peacefully. Yet, since it is becoming clear that state derecognition is one of the many instruments that the former base state uses as part of its diplomatic strategy to contest and undermine the independence of the claimant state, it is very problematic to consider the argument for state derecognition a genuine and persuasive way to facilitate the resolution of statehood conflicts. Similar to other discursive framings deployed to justify state derecognition, this outward-looking justification aims to reduce the external contestation and implications of such a controversial decision. State derecognition as coercive diplomacy minimizes the probability of claimant states' ability to attain their goals for full international recognition and admission into international society. At the same time, it enhances the domestic and international standing of the former base state and can undoubtedly increase its leverage in an eventual settlement with the claimant state. Thus, derecognition has become an instrument that pressures the claimant state to make concessions against making refusal too costly, which suits the former base state and its allies.

Compliance with International Norms

Another set of arguments third countries use to justify the derecognition of claimant states is compliance with international norms on statehood. In all derecognition cases, third countries tend to invoke two sets of international norms: (1) failure of the claimant state to fulfill all the core objective criteria of statehood (Montevideo criteria) as prescribed in the customary international law; and (2) failure to comply with international norms on sovereignty and territorial integrity of the former base state. While referring to these international norms and legal sources is essential to clarify the rationales for derecognition, they only partially cover each claimant state's normative and legal merits. These invoked norms are the same arguments used by the former base states and their allies to oppose the creation and recognition of claimant states, which exposes the lack of independent judgment and assessment on the side of derecognizing states. Moreover, invoking compliance with international norms tends to disregard other norms that have become important in granting or withholding recognition, such as the remedial right to external self-determination, democratic legitimacy, protection of human rights, and democratic governance.

One of the most valid and interesting arguments raised by third countries to justify their derecognition decisions is the absence of objective criteria of statehood. The absence in this context can entail both the failure and inability of the claimant state to consolidate sovereign statehood and the disappearance of the attributes of statehood over time. The most acceptable criteria for statehood are laid down in Article 1 of the Montevideo Convention on the Rights and Duties of States of 1933, which holds that "the State as a person of international law should possess the following qualifications: (a) a permanent population; (b) a defined territory; (c) government; and (d) capacity to enter into relations with other States." While most states tend to meet these criteria, there is no consensus whether a state is a state if it doesn't entirely meet all the attributes of statehood. As Jure Vidmar (2013: 241) argues, "The fact that states grant recognition even where the statehood criteria are not met and withhold it where they are met indicates that state practice does not accept that statehood would depend on the Montevideo criteria." There is also vast evidence that established and emerging states have problems with territorial sovereignty, government functionality, and constrained foreign relations due to shared sovereignty. In legal theory and practice, as Georges Abi-Saab (2006: 475) explains, "A State may come into being and exist before its borders are totally defined, and even if some parts of its territory are subject to claims by other States." However, he maintains that "the crucial element in evaluating the effectiveness of the State is ... the existence of an effective government which rules the people within the territory, and which embodies the sovereignty of the State" (Abi-Saab 206: 475). Conversely, as Peter Radan (2020: 57) maintains, "Recognized states that cease to meet the criteria for statehood should be derecognized." Regardless of these scholarly views, in practice, the invocation of the absence of statehood criteria appears as a strategic narrative to make the decision for derecognition acceptable while at the same time discrediting the sovereignty of the claimant state and, most importantly, enabling the contender state to retain territorial claims over the contested state.

A case in point here is Morocco's diplomatic campaign to derecognize the SADR. Since the SADR largely operates as a government-in-exile, with most of the Sahrawi population displaced in refugee camps in Algeria, Morocco has argued for the derecognition of the SADR on the grounds it lacks the basic elements of statehood, considering it a "ghostly entity" (Arabic News 2000). Morocco has argued that the SADR does not have a state's attributes; it lacks effective governmental control over a given population living in a clearly defined territory. As a matter of fact, a state without territory is unable to exercise its territorial sovereignty over a particular population. These arguments are, however, challenged by pro-SADR voices arguing that it cannot exercise effective control over the whole of Western Sahara and half of its population precisely because of Morocco's forcible occupation and annexation of parts of the territory. The claim that the SADR does not exercise effective control over the main part of its territory or the population living there is untenable, as no treaty or principle of customary law stipulates that recognizing states should be conditioned on their effective control of the "main part" of their territories. Moreover, the lack of effective control of territory did not obstruct the SADR's admission to the Organisation of the African Unity in 1982.

Yet Morocco's rationale for the derecognition of the SADR on the grounds of lack of statehood capacity has gained international traction. In 2013, Panama justified the derecognition of the SADR because it has not managed to consolidate the fundamental elements of statehood (territory, population, government, and independence) since its proclamation of independent statehood. The Panamanian declaration stated that "as a result of this situation, in accordance with the principles of International Law and the exercise of its sovereignty, the Panamanian State decides to suspend diplomatic relations with the Sahrawi Arab Democratic Republic" (MFA of

Panama 2013). The note held that "this decision will continue until the end of the peace process, initiated and mediated by the United Nations, without prejudice to the support that will be given in the future to the initiatives that are adopted at the multilateral level in this matter" (MFA of Panama 2013). Similarly, in June 2019, when El Salvador decided to derecognize the SADR, President Nayib Bukele stated: "We stop recognizing a country that does not exist, we strengthen our ties with the Kingdom of Morocco and we open the doors of the Arab world" (Wise Afri 2019). "I don't know why the recognition was made, I imagine it was because of ideological positions but not because of real issues," he said, adding that El Salvador "had recognized a republic that does not exist, that has no territory and no people" (Telesure 2019). Morocco has effectively used the argument that the SADR and Polisario Front are not truly independent as they serve as geopolitical proxies of Algeria, which has hostile relations with the countries in the region. The Union of Serbia and Montenegro derecognized the SADR in 2004, claiming opposition to "the establishment of a so-called state on the territory of another sovereign and independent state" (Arabic News 2004). In this instance, the rationale for derecognition is that the original decision contravened international law and norms; it might look like a correction of previous errors in judgment and thus restoration of enforcement of international law. However, in essence, the decision of derecognition undermines the institution of diplomatic recognition in itself and the entire goodwill, trust, and friendship among nations that equivocally recognize one another's independent statehood and commit not to question one another's sovereignty (in line with the provisions of Vienna Conventions on Diplomatic Relations). Many states (often pejoratively referred to as quasi-states, or failed states) lack objective elements of modern statehood, including empirical and domestic sovereignty. Still, their sovereign statehood is not scrutinized or subject to derecognition.

Compared to the SADR, countries that have allegedly withdrawn recognition of Kosovo have never justified their decision by referring to the lack of statehood capacity. Kosovo has not lost any of the core attributes of statehood that would justify the withdrawal of recognition on those grounds. However, they have endorsed the rationales and arguments that Serbia and its international allies have offered. Serbia, backed by Russia, framed its derecognition discourse around universalistic claims that would appeal to many states, such as state sovereignty, territorial integrity, dangerous precedents, regional instability, and breaches of international law (Visoka 2018). In framing its quest for Kosovo's derecognition, Serbia has argued that the actions of states that have recognized Kosovo constitute an intervention into its internal affairs because the act of recognition imports the right of the claimant state to govern the contested territory, which would breach the principle of territorial integrity of states. As Serbia put it during the ICJ proceedings on Kosovo, "It is a duty placed on all States and relevant non-state actors to recognise that the very territorial structure and configuration of a State must be respected" (Government of Serbia 2009: 152). Such a duty is engrained in the foundational principles governing relations between states, such as the UN Charter and other declarations and resolutions. Alexander Chepurin, the Russian ambassador in Serbia, argued that "it is important to rely on international law. The solution to the problem is possible on the basis of UN Security Council Resolution 1244. Russia is in favor of both dialogue and agreements" (B92 2018g).

Similar to other cases and framings of derecognition, the diplomatic rationale for the derecognition of Kosovo appeared almost identical to those propagated by Serbia since 2017. In late 2017, Serbia, with Russia's help, persuaded Suriname to withdraw its recognition of Kosovo independence. Suriname originally recognized Kosovo in July 2016 after a sustained lobbying campaign through the Organization of Islamic Cooperation and other Kosovo allies. Back then Suriname not only "decided to recognise the Republic of Kosovo as an independent and sovereign state," but also offered to further the establishment of diplomatic relations (MFA of Suriname 2016). However, in 2017 Suriname sent a letter to the Ministry of Foreign Affairs of Kosovo stating that "after careful consideration, the Government of the Republic of Suriname has decided to revoke the recognition of Kosovo as an independent and sovereign state" (MFA of Suriname 2017). In an immediate visit to Belgrade, Suriname's minister of the interior, Mohamed Neorsalim, justified derecognition with an allegedly principled stance on noninterference in the internal affairs of friendly countries. In response, Serbia's foreign minister, Ivica Dačić, considered this "a historic event for us—we haven't achieved this with money since we don't have it, nor by exerting pressure since we are not able to do so—but through our dedication instead" (MFA of Serbia 2017). Yet despite claims by Serbia that there was no economic incentive involved, Suriname openly admitted that the decision "represents a good basis for the development of bilateral cooperation between Serbia and Suriname, especially in the field of the economy" (Government of Serbia 2017). So, in this instance there seems to be a selective invocation of the discourse of noninterference on internal affairs, and only about the former base state and not about the claimant state, whose sovereign titles are

152 • *The Derecognition of States*

questioned. The withdrawal of recognition as an act of interference in the internal affairs of the claimant state, especially when the original conditions of recognition are intact, highlights the paradox and uneven application of international norms and principles governing the derecognition of states.

Several states implicated in the derecognition of other states have invoked international law, and different norms provide the basis for changing their position on the claimant states. The policy of state nonrecognition is often justified on the grounds that the claimant state has acquired statehood and territory through illegal means and in breach of fundamental international norms, such as forceful annexation or occupation of foreign territories. The contemporary countries examined in this book have not acquired or annexed new territories. They tend to be regarded as titular people of said territories. There is scope to debate, for instance, the assistance provided by third parties to achieve their desire for self-determination and independent statehood. In the example of Kosovo, NATO intervened in 1999 after diplomacy failed to prevent further escalation of conflict and created conditions to determine the status of the territory through a UN-led process, which in the end failed due to Serbia's rejection of the UN mediator's proposal for supervised independence and subsequently rejected the ICJ's advisory opinion, which found that Kosovo's declaration of independence did not contravene the international law or UN Security Council Resolution 1244 (1999), which has governed the territory since 1999. In the case of Western Sahara, the SADR was established on the territory where the Sahrawi people historically resided, and the assistance provided by Algeria by hosting two refugee camps and supporting the government in exile has emerged as part of the survival process and efforts for facilitating the decolonization and self-determination process. The quest of Sahrawi people for self-determination is established in the context of decolonization norms. Accordingly, the UN and third states have opposed Morocco's illegal expansion in Western Sahara (Zunes and Mundy 2022).

There are other instances when third countries have referred to UN documents and resolutions as a basis for justifying their decisions to withdraw recognition. Since UN documents constitute part of general international law, justifying derecognition on such grounds tends to add normative legitimacy to the findings, although other interests may lie beneath such diplomatic moves. Although most of the countries that derecognize Taiwan tend to invoke economic and domestic political rationales, there are instances when the one-China policy and its legitimization by UN documents is the guiding normative and policy framework for the withdrawal of recognition.

Beijing insists that the process of establishing diplomatic relations with third countries must involve the one-China policy, which maintains that there is only one China and that Taiwan is part of it despite having a separate political system. For example, the government of the Solomon Islands (2019: 38) justified the decision to end diplomatic ties with Taiwan as necessary to respect "UN Resolution 2758 on Taiwan" and act "in compliance with international law, consensus, and norms upheld by all nations." UN Resolution 2758 recognizes the representatives of People's Republic of China "as the only legitimate representatives of China to the United Nations" and expels "the representatives of Chiang Kai-shek [Taiwan] from the place which they unlawfully occupy at the United Nations and in all the organizations related to it."

Similarly, when Nauru broke diplomatic relations with Taiwan in January 2024, they noted that "in the best interests of the Republic and people of Nauru, we will be moving to the One-China Principle that is in line with UN Resolution 2758 which recognises the People's Republic of China (PRC) as the sole legal Government representing the whole of China and seeking resumption of full diplomatic relations with the People's Republic of China (PRC)" (Government of the Republic of Nauru 2024). While most of the countries that have diplomatic ties with China entirely adhere to the one-China policy and thus do not have any relationship with Taiwan, the situation is complicated, as there is more than one interpretation of the one-China policy, as pushed by Taiwan and the United States, which has enabled third countries to switch recognition from one side to the other several times while still claiming adherence to the one-country, two-systems policy (Lin, Wu, and Yeh 2022: 44–46). For instance, Taiwan has refuted the one-China principle as manipulation by mainland China, adding that "the fact that the Republic of China (Taiwan) is an independent, sovereign nation cannot be denied by the so-called 'one China principle'" (MFA Taiwan 2016). As the U.S.-China relations have worsened over the years, the U.S. policymakers have argued that China is distorting the 1971 UN resolution to justify Taiwan's international isolation. Following the derecognition of Taiwan by Nauru, the American Institute in Taiwan, which acts as an informal U.S. embassy in Taiwan, argued that the U.N. resolution 2758 "did not make a determination on the status of Taiwan; does not preclude countries from having diplomatic relationships with Taiwan; and does not preclude Taiwan's meaningful participation in the U.N. system" (Focus Taiwan 2024b).

In the case of Kosovo, several countries that reconsidered, suspended, or withdrew their recognition selectively invoked international norms and

UN documents without sufficiently clarifying and justifying with counter-evidence. Lesotho's derecognition of Kosovo shows discordance between original justifications for recognition and those subsequently invoked to withdraw it. In 2014, Lesotho recognized Kosovo, stating that "after a clearer understanding of these positive developments and achievements . . . the Government of the Kingdom of Lesotho has reached a decision to officially recognize the Republic of Kosovo as a sovereign, independent State." What Lesotho refers to as achievements and positive developments include, as acknowledged in the same latter, "the latest impressive developments and progress towards Kosovo's sovereignty" as well as "the steady emergence of peaceful coexistence for mutual benefit between Kosovo and Serbia" (MFA of Lesotho 2014). Lesotho's original decision reveals that its decision for recognition neither was premature nor raised concerns about the legality of Kosovo's independence. By contrast, it was a recognition of Kosovo's effective statehood and peace-loving character. Obliviously, while these arguments reflect Kosovo's narrative for international recognition, they also reflect the factual reality on the ground, namely irrefutable evidence of Kosovo's state-building progress and its commitment to normalizing relations with Serbia (Visoka 2018). However, when Lesotho decided to withdraw recognition of Kosovo in 2018, it invoked different justifications that were not related to the original ones. Lesotho pointed out that "the unilateral declaration of independence of Kosovo from February 2008 is in contradiction with the Helsinki Final Act, inter alia, with its principles 3 and 4 and is even more in contradiction with UN Security Resolution 1244 (1999) that was adopted in accordance with Chapter VII of the UN Charter" (B92 2018e; MFA of Lesotho 2018). Principles 3 and 4 of the Helsinki Final Act of 1975 cover the inviolability of frontiers and the territorial integrity of states.

Invoking the territorial integrity argument in the case of Kosovo is problematic as Serbia did not have a claim over the territory when it emerged as a new state following the dissolution of Yugoslavia and applied for membership in the UN. Most importantly, UN Security Council Resolution 1244 (1999) effectively suspended Serbia's territorial sovereignty over Kosovo and facilitated the path to independent statehood, which as stipulated by the ICJ advisory opinion of 2010 wasn't in contradiction with international law (Weller 2008; Vidmar 2013). Moreover, as Christian Tomuschat (2013: 37) maintains, "The territory of Kosovo had been defined by virtue of the Yugoslav constitutional legislation" and "What in territorial terms amounts to Kosovo has never been contested, not even after the disintegration of the Socialist Federal Republic of Yugoslavia." Most of the countries that have derecognized Kosovo and based their justification on the Helsinki Final Act are not participating states of this normative document, nor have they been part of the implementing mechanisms. Although UN Security Council Resolution 1244 (1999) did not deny Kosovo the right to self-determination or prevent the proclamation of independence, derecognizing states selectively refer to outdated and preambular provisions that reaffirm the commitment of the UN "to the sovereignty and territorial integrity of the Federal Republic of Yugoslavia and the other States of the region, as set out in the Helsinki Final Act and annex 2" (UN Security Council 1999). As Tomuschat (2013: 41) maintains, "The recognition of Kosovo constitutes . . . a special case which cannot be measured by the usual, traditional yardsticks." However, these norms and legal documents are rhetorically used (following Serbia's suggested diplomatic lines) to make derecognition decisions more compatible with internationally accepted norms and thus avoid criticism from other states. For example, Russian foreign minister Lavrov said Russia welcomed Comoros' derecognition of Kosovo, adding that "the decisions of some countries to revise their positions on Kosovo's recognition, to withdraw it or abstain from taking a decision on it, testified to their responsible approach while relying on the standards of international law" (MFA of Russia 2018).

Similarly, Ghana's derecognition of Kosovo invokes selective passages from general international documents and specific UN resolutions, which contradicts rationales for recognition in the first place. Ghana withdrew the recognition of Kosovo in 2019, claiming that although the "decision of the Government of Ghana at the time must have been inspired by the quest for peace and harmony," it nonetheless was "in contravention of the Helsinki Final Act, and more fundamentally, in contravention of the UN Security Council Resolution 1244 (1999)" (MFA of Ghana 2019). The derecognition note also maintained that "the decision to recognize Kosovo turned out to be premature in view of paragraph 10 of the UNSC Resolution 1244 (1999) which authorized the Secretary General to establish an international civil presence in Kosovo in order to provide an interim administration for Kosovo under which the people of Kosovo can enjoy substantial autonomy within enjoy substantial autonomy within the Federal Republic of Yugoslavia, and which will provide transitional administration while establishing and overseeing the development of provisional democratic self-governing institutions to ensure conditions for a peaceful and normal life for all inhabitants of Kosovo" (MFA of Ghana 2019). Ghana's reference to the international civilian presence and the provisional character of Kosovo's self-governing institutions fails to note that such provisions, contrary to what is claimed in the derecognition note, have played a vital role in the consolidation of Kosovo's independent statehood before and after independence. As acknowledged by the debates around the ICJ advisory opinion of 2010 on Kosovo, the UN Security Council, General Assembly, the United Nations Interim Administration Mission in Kosovo, and other international organizations have not condemned Kosovo's declaration of independence. The provisional character of Kosovo's institutions wasn't an impediment for the representatives of Kosovo people to declare independence in 2008 (ICJ 2010).

The continued presence of the international community after Kosovo's independence with minimal executive powers hasn't prevented Kosovo from consolidating its empirical, domestic, and international legal sovereignty (Weller 2010; Perritt 2010; Visoka 2018). Moreover, none of Ghana's invoked provisions or documents hold Kosovo's independence in suspension or require Kosovo and Serbia to negotiate the final status. The statehood status was closed with the failed efforts of the UN special envoy for Kosovo status negotiations, who recommended supervised independence for Kosovo after two years of negotiations between Serbia and Kosovo. The subsequent UN General Assembly Resolution 64/298 (2010) has two purposes. First, it "acknowledges the content of the advisory opinion of the International Court of Justice on the Accordance with International Law of the Unilateral Declaration of Independence in respect of Kosovo, rendered in response to the request of the General Assembly." Second, it "welcomes the readiness of the European Union to facilitate a process of dialogue between the parties; the process of dialogue in itself would be a factor for peace, security and stability in the region, and that dialogue would be to promote cooperation, achieve progress on the path to the European Union and improve the lives of the people." Neither of these provisions talks about the statehood status of Kosovo. On the contrary, the provision on the ICJ advisory opinion indirectly acknowledges the Court's verdict that Kosovo's declaration of independence was in compliance with international law.

While Serbia's rulebook ultimately influenced Ghana's discourse on the derecognition of Kosovo, it deserves further elaboration since it may contradict Ghana's earlier rationales and grounds for recognizing Kosovo. Contrary to what is stated in the derecognition note, the process and the formulation of Ghana's recognition of Kosovo shows that the decision was mature and took into consideration international norms and diplomatic conventions. As early as 2009, there was evidence of communication between Ghana and Kosovo, which was capitalized with formal recognition granted in 2012. In May 2009, for example, the president of Ghana, John Evans Atta Mills, responded to a correspondence sent by the president of Kosovo in March 2009 on the occasion of the anniversary of Ghana's independence, stating, "As you are aware, Ghana subscribes to the principle of the sovereignty and the rights of all people and entities for self-determination. Ghana is therefore following with keen interest the international discourse on Kosovo's declaration of independence" (Republic of Ghana 2009). On this point, Ghana clearly showed an implicit yet positive approval of Kosovo's self-determination through the declaration of independence and was open to consider recognition of Kosovo's independence depending on the response by the international community, which ultimately was supportive of independence (evident with recognition by over fifty UN member states at the time). Mills also noted that Ghana was "encouraged by the UN General Assembly's adaptation on 8 October 2008, of a resolution to seek an advisory opinion from the International Court of Justice on the matter" (Republic of Ghana 2009). He added, "As we await the outcome of the future consultations on the matter[,] I wish to assure Your Excellence, that Ghana will convey its position on the matter as soon as the advisory opinion is conveyed to the General Assembly" (Republic of Ghana 2009). On this point, Ghana committed to decide on the recognition of Kosovo based on the outcome of the ICJ advisory opinion, which in the subsequent year, in July 2020, concluded that Kosovo's declaration of independence did not contradict international law. It took Ghana another two years to make a decision on Kosovo's recognition, but finally in January 2012 the MFA of Ghana issued a letter to the MFA of Kosovo "to convey the Government's decision to recognize Kosovo as an independent and sovereign state" (MFA of Ghana 2012). In granting Kosovo its recognition, Ghana did not attach any condition or justification, except that "it is hoped that diplomatic relations shall be established between the two states in due course" (MFA of Ghana 2012). What this entails is that Ghana's recognition was not premature, as it took place four years after Kosovo had established effective control over its territory and an international presence was in charge of running the domestic and international affairs of the country. It can be also inferred that it took place after the ICJ advisory opinion, which confirmed that Kosovo's independence was congruent with international law. And finally, it expressed readiness to establish diplomatic relations with Kosovo, which implies considering the country mature enough to be treated as an equal state in the international diplomatic order.

Similarly, the government of the Commonwealth of Dominica suspended the recognition of Kosovo in 2018 using as justification the 2010 UN General Assembly Resolution 64/298, which encouraged the EU to facilitate a dialogue for normalization of relations between Serbia and Kosovo, following the 2010 ICJ advisory opinion on Kosovo. In its communication, Dominica held that "after appropriate consideration and deliberation and in light of the recommendation of the UN General Assembly and the International Court of Justice and in the interest of comity, we have agreed to review the position taken earlier by the Government of the Commonwealth of Dominica to accord recognition to Kosovo as an independent State" (MFA of Dominica 2018). Following the similar fallacies discussed above in the case of Ghana and Lesotho, Dominica's reference to the UN General Assembly resolution and ICJ verdict contradicts what these documents are about and how they are invoked to justify the suspension of recognition. The decision for derecognition certainly contradicts the original justification for recognition provided on 10 December 2012, whereby Dominica commended "the efforts and determination of the people of Kosovo in their struggle to establish and develop and independent state built on the principles of freedom and democracy" (Prime Minister of Dominica 2012). And most important, Dominica explicitly stated that "since its declaration of independence, Kosovo has demonstrated its commitment to cooperate with the international community, especially the United Nations, to resolve all conflicts with its neighours." Finally, to confirm its steadfast recognition of Kosovo's independence and sovereign statehood immediately after recognition, on 11 December 2012 Dominica and Kosovo signed a joint communiqué on the establishment of diplomatic relations "in accordance with the purpose and principles of the Charter of the United Nations, the norms of international law, and in accordance with the Vienna Convention on Diplomatic Relations of 18 April 1961 and the Vienna Convention on Consular Relations of 24 April 1963." Notably, the documents that Dominica refers to in the derecognition note concern the events of 2010, whereas the decision for recognition was taken two years later, in 2012, which means that Dominica had sufficient time to deliberate and come to an informed conclusion for recognition. Certainly, Kosovo's cooperation with the international community hasn't changed, nor has its commitment to normalization of relations with Serbia and resolving outstanding issues in the region, as well documented in UN secretary-general periodical reports on Kosovo. Therefore, Dominica's rationale for derecognition is unclear and not congruent with its original recognition rationales and the facts on the ground. Despite claiming that they took their derecognition decision based on appropriate deliberation, the Dominican authorities have not provided any public justification for changing their position on Kosovo.

Across all the cases that invoke international norms as the basis for withdrawing the recognition of the claimant state, there is a contradiction between the original rationales for recognition and the subsequent justification for rescinding these decisions. There is also selective and misplaced reference to the relevant international norms and documents. As illustrated in this section, such misguided and contradictory references, mirroring the diplomatic discourse of the former base states, show that third countries make such decisions without independently verifying or undergoing their assessment of the factual circumstances in the affected states. It is worth noting that international norms invoked by derecognizing states, such as noninterference in internal affairs, are primarily those promoted by non-Western states, often to reflect their colonial and postcolonial histories but also to justify their suppressive policies and authoritarian rule. Hence, in the diplomatic discourse of derecognition, there is no discussion of democratic legitimacy and protection of human rights, particularly minority rights, which have emerged as new criteria upon which the international community conditions the recognition of new states (Frank 1992). In other words, contemporary practices of state derecognition entirely disregard democratic legitimacy as a norm governing the decision to withhold, extend, or retract the recognition of new states. Taiwan and Kosovo, which have experienced different degrees of derecognition, are broadly considered democratic countries with broad support among other democracies. Perhaps the disregard for democratic legitimacy is symptomatic of the fact that postcolonial undemocratic or semidemocratic regimes rule most derecognizing states. While in most cases, democracies tend to refrain from derecognizing other states, undemocratic or semidemocratic countries seem to be more prone to derecognize other states.

CONCLUSION

This chapter has identified, categorized, and examined the dominant rationales and arguments for derecognizing states as they are presented in contemporary state practice. By showing five significant strands of arguments put forward by derecognizing states, the chapter has illustrated that the politics of state derecognition are overwhelmingly a by-product of domestic politics and economic and security incentives rather than an articulation of the desire to uphold international norms or laws. The actual diplomatic dealings behind derecognition—whether through personal or collective material and political favors or other incentives—often remains secret and out of public reach. Claims about corruption or other means of influence remain primarily speculative and difficult to authenticate unless there is a legal investigation. Yet the congruence of the arguments for derecognition among the derecognizing states and the former base states exposes the politics behind such decisions. Different rationales and justifications for state derecognition examined in this chapter reveal a particular intertextuality of diplomatic narratives among the former base state and the derecognizing states. Namely, the arguments and reasons for derecognizing states are not original and genuine formulations of the derecognizing states but have their origin in the diplomatic discourse formulated and transmitted by the former base state. This reveals the diplomatic influence of the former base state, which literarily dictates to third countries the rationales for justifying the withdrawal of recognition of the claimant state, demonstrating the presence of hidden motives and agenda behind the publicly announced rationales. As the discussion in this chapter showed, there is an intrinsic relationship between the chosen form of derecognition and the diplomatic reasoning to support it. Countries that have used the conflict (re)settlement as a rationale tend to suspend and freeze the recognition of claimant states. In contrast, countries driven primarily by economic and geopolitical rationales tend to cut off diplomatic ties with the claimant states and fully withdraw their recognition.

In most cases, the decision for recognition and the subsequent decision for derecognition are embedded in different rationales and normative grounds. There is a discrepancy between the original arguments for recognition and the justifications to reverse such a decision. In principle, derecognition should be justifiable and thus permissible if the original conditions of recognition have changed or the claimant state ceases to exist. That is one of the arguments various legal and political scholars put forward, as examined in Chapter 2. Most derecognition decisions that tend to reproduce arguments about conflict settlement are incongruent with the original justifications for recognition. Malcolm Shaw (2017: 164) argues that recognition is "a method of accepting certain factual situations and endowing them with legal significance." Gerhard von Glahn and James L. Taulbee (2017: 199) add: "While international law specifies the requisite facts that define a state, each existing state has the right to determine for itself if the set of facts, as reflected in each situation, merits the judgment that a new state exists." While recognition is perceived as "providing strong evidential demonstration of satisfaction of the relevant criteria" of statehood (Shaw 2017: 164), the same cannot be said about the derecognition of states. On the contrary, the contemporary diplomatic discourse underpinning the derecognition of states seems not to rely entirely on the factual situation. Rather, the rationales for state derecognition are written and prepared by the former base state and then adopted and presented by derecognizing states as their judgment. Since such narratives are one-sided and often not based on the factual situation, they have little resemblance to reality and are thus discreditable.

Despite all discrepancies, countries that frame the decision for derecognition with economic and geopolitical rationales demonstrate a degree of diplomatic honesty regardless of how destabilizing such moves could be for claimant states and broader international relations. They openly admit that they trade their capacity to recognize or derecognize other states with economic and trade benefits and, through such moves, they meet some of the pressing socioeconomic needs in the countries. However, normative justifications, particularly those referring to international law and norms and the desire for conflict resolution, tend to expose diplomatic hypocrisy, as they are inconsistent with previous decisions for recognition and the hidden motives for derecognition. Thus, most of the cases of derecognition examined in this book amount to premature derecognition, as the original conditions for recognition have not changed, and the justificatory rationales for derecognition have nothing to do with the effectiveness and legitimacy of the claimant state. Similarly problematic are instances when third countries justify the derecognition of the claimant state on the grounds of correcting the previous decision, which they consider to breach the territorial integrity and the principle of noninterference in the internal affairs of the former base state. While this argument might enjoy certain credibility, it is highly problematic and consequentialist. The attempt to correct the original act of recognition tends to undermine the consolidated sovereign statehood of the claimant state and its sovereign equality and the right to noninterference in its internal affairs. If countries in the present can revise their past foreign policy decisions, the entire cartography of states can be redrawn without considering historical circumstances. Such historical revisionism isn't possible and viable. Although derecognizing states tend to base their rationales for derecognition on international norms and conflict resolution, the wide-reaching and deleterious effects discussed in the next chapter show that state derecognition contributes to conflictual international politics and the destabilization of the international system.

5 ✦ The Effects of State Derecognition

Parallel to shedding light on the process, actors, and rationales of state derecognition, exploring the effects of this diplomatic practice is essential for developing a comprehensive picture of this anti-diplomatic practice in world politics. The chapter argues that the practice of state derecognition has far-reaching consequences not only for the contender states but also for the derecognizing states as well as regional and global powers. While the former base state's derecognition of the claimant state enhances its domestic legitimacy and international standing, it tends to produce adverse effects for the affected state. For the claimant state, derecognition tends to undermine its claims to domestic and external sovereignty, manifesting as domestic political instability, international isolation, and conflict with the former base state. It risks discouraging the claimant state from pursuing actions for validation of statehood through peaceful and diplomatic means and can disincentivize it to act consistently with international law. Scholars who support recognition as constitutive of sovereign statehood tend to highlight the ability of recognition to expand the claimant state's scope to exercise sovereignty and benefit from the goods that international structures provide. Seen from such a perspective, the derecognition of states tends to revoke certain features of the international legal sovereignty of the claimant state, for example, the ability to exercise sovereignty in bilateral and multilateral spaces and being widely accepted as an equal member of the international community. In particular, derecognition as a method of diplomatic subversion tends to deepen hostilities between the former base state and the claimant state. Thus, contrary to justifications for derecognition discussed in

162

the previous chapter, the evidence presented here shows that derecognition produces destabilizing effects in the short run.

State derecognition reveals how third countries, through reconsidering, suspending, or fully withdrawing the recognition of the claimant state, not only perform unfriendly acts toward the claimant state but also tend to become a constitutive part of a prolonged self-determination dispute. Derecognizing states shape the nature of internationalized conflicts and are shaped by such conflicts. Thus, derecognition also tends to produce destabilizing effects on the derecognizing states. Especially when recognition is granted for inward-looking rationales, it tends to have more a negative impact on the derecognizing states than on the contender states. For the derecognizing state, derecognition can similarly result in domestic instability, undermining its geopolitical interests and exposing it to international pressure and stigmatization, though this often depends on how much support the claimant state enjoys among competing global powers and how prominent the case is within the multilateral organizations. Inevitably, the struggle for recognition and derecognition pushes contender parties to interfere in the domestic affairs of third states, shaping their foreign policy and influencing electoral politics, democratic processes, and political relations between groups. Thus, practices of derecognition tend to de-democratize third countries implicated in such diplomatic games.

Finally, state derecognition becomes part of rivalries among existing and rising powers, with far-reaching implications for international peace, stability, and order. While great powers have different interests in the derecognition process, they often use it to advance their agendas and weaken their rivals. The self-determination disputes, including secessionist movements and de facto states, and their degree of recognition or derecognition tend to reshuffle the political geography of states and the power relations and interests of great powers. Historically, diplomatic recognition by great powers is considered the most significant determinant for the successful secession and admission of new fledging states in the club of sovereign states (Coggins 2011). Equally, the involvement of regional and global powers in the derecognition process plays a crucial role in persuading third countries to withdraw recognition. In this regard, state derecognition can change the balance of power or provide an opening for strategic rivals to interfere in the sphere of interests of a rival power. Thus, derecognition tends to trigger hostilities much wider than often assumed.

This chapter is organized as follows. The first section examines the extent to which state derecognition undermines the stability of the claimant state and weakens its sovereignty. The second section discusses how state derecognition adversely impacts the prospects for conflict resolution between the contender states. The third section looks at the adverse impacts of state derecognition on third countries implicated in transactional practices of withdrawing recognition in exchange for economic, political, and security goods. The fourth and final section examines how state derecognition bolsters great power rivalries and can contribute to the escalation of international hostilities.

UNDERMINING THE STABILITY AND SOVEREIGNTY OF THE CLAIMANT STATE

As discussed so far, derecognition has emerged as a crucial anti-diplomatic tool part of former base states' repertoire of nonviolent and subversive measures to undermine the claimant state's domestic stability and disrupt its exercise of international sovereignty. Contrary to the dominant views that stability is a driving force behind the decision for recognition (Paquin 2020; Huddleston 2021), the decision for derecognition appears to disregard the destabilizing effects it can have on all implicated parties. First and foremost, similar to the condition of nonrecognition, the withdrawal of recognition has a direct impact on the ability of the claimant state to exercise its sovereignty at home, but most obviously abroad (Sterio 2019: 83). The practice of derecognition thus risks denying claimant states the right to self-determination and prevents them from fully actualizing independent statehood. It also decreases their ability to conduct bilateral relations with other countries, especially those that discontinue recognition of the claimant's statehood. Fundamentally, beyond doctrinal thinking, the derecognition of states by third countries in practice amounts to an act of refusal to acknowledge the factual existence of another state. For example, when Nauru derecognized Taiwan in 2024, it meant "that the Republic of Nauru will no longer recognise the Republic of China (Taiwan) as a separate country but rather as an inalienable part of China's territory, and will sever "diplomatic relations" with Taiwan as of this day and no longer develop any official relations or official exchanges with Taiwan" (Government of the Republic of Nauru 2024). Refusal and withdrawal of recognition is considered an unfriendly act, which "inflicts a disadvantage, disregard or discourtesy on another subject of international law without violating any legal norm" (Richter 2013). Moreover, as Vaughan Lowe (2011: 164) argues,

"Denial of recognition might amount to the impeding of the right of a people to self-determination. There can be no real doubt, however, that an entity which meets the factual criteria of Statehood—population, territory, government, and independence—is entitled to the basic rights of a State, such as the right not to be attacked, and to be free from foreign intervention." From this point of view, ruining the claimant state's sovereignty is the principal effect of derecognition, which is against the norms of noninterference, loyalty, and comity. For instance, the 1981 Declaration on the Inadmissibility of Intervention and Interference in the Internal Affairs of States holds that it is "the duty of a State to refrain from any action or attempt in whatever form of under whatever pretext to destabilize or to undermine the stability of another State or of any of its institutions" (UN General Assembly 1981). Since the act of derecognition is often accompanied by agreeing to bilateral relations between the derecognizing state and the former base state, such acts could be considered forms of interference, especially if they have implications for the territory of the claimant state. The Declaration calls on states "to refrain from concluding agreements with other States designed to intervene or interfere in the internal and external affairs of third States" (UN General Assembly 1981).

In general, derecognition contributes to reversing the claimant state's ability to consolidate international legal sovereignty, namely the ability to represent itself freely in the international arena. It can affect the claimant state's ability to establish diplomatic relationships and conclude treaties, especially in a multilateral context. It impacts the claimant state's ability to represent its subjects before courts in the derecognizing states, especially if citizens and businesses reside there. In particular, it can undermine the claimant state's ability to access international organizations directly and indirectly. Derecognition tends to have more constitutive and performative effects on the international legal sovereignty of the claimant state than on its empirical or domestic sovereignty. The more countries derecognize the claimant state, the less votes and support it has when seeking access to multilateral organizations and bodies. The lack of sufficient votes and the fading away of diplomatic support undermines its claims for equal access to the international community. Such limited global access is not uncommon for fully recognized states once they are excluded or isolated by sanctioning measures taken by the international community, in a significant breach of fundamental norms and rules of international law. However, since "The international law of statehood does not impose an obligation upon states to enter into relations with other states if they do not wish to do so" (Vidmar

2013: 41), the effect of derecognition in diminishing the statehood of the claimant state is facultative. If the claimant state aspires to broad access to the international system—which most do—then derecognition has a constraining effect. However, if it is satisfied with a niche diplomatic network and access to international mechanisms, then the impact of derecognition is much smaller than often assumed.

The process and the act of derecognition thus might not unmake the factual existence of the claimant state but, as Lowe (2011: 164) argues, it diminishes "the possibility of participating fully in the international community." Mikulas Fabry (2012: 662) adds, "Non-recognized existence has historically led to a wide range of adverse repercussions . . . [including] the inability to carry out normal diplomatic and economic relations, to join international institutions, and to sign international treaties and agreements." The more countries derecognize the claimant state, the higher the chance it will lose support for membership in international organizations. In those organizations where the claimant state is not a member, the loss of diplomatic allies means the loss of indirect influence and the voice it had through partners. It is worth noting that while withdrawal of recognition tends to narrow down the international space for claimant states, it does not often affect their membership or participation in intergovernmental organizations. For instance, although Taiwan had only thirteen diplomatic recognitions (as of October 2023), it remained a member of over twenty international and recognitional organizations, including the World Trade Organization. Similarly, the derecognition of Kosovo has not undermined its existing membership in over fifty intergovernmental organizations. Derecognition does not mean that the claimant state no longer has the right to seek recognition from other states, nor does it mean that it cannot establish formal diplomatic relations with states that have already recognized it. Between 2017 and 2023, Kosovo was recognized by the Bahamas and Israel. During this period, the government of Kosovo formalized diplomatic ties with several states that had already recognized it and opened new embassies to expand its diplomatic network. Similarly, Taiwan established diplomatic relations with Somaliland in 2019 despite losing two important Pacific allies, the Solomon Islands and Kiribati. It also upgraded the status of its economic cooperation office in Lithuania, which triggered harsh reactions in mainland China and exposed Lithuania to an economic boycott.

What the act of derecognition can do, however, is undermine the prospects of the claimant state's membership in new international organizations. One of the adverse effects of derecognition for the claimant state is abstention or hostile votes by third countries that no longer recognize the claimant state. For example, the essential function of Taiwan's international diplomatic allies was to lobby for its participation and membership in international organizations. When third countries derecognize Taiwan, they no longer participate in such lobbying, thus undermining the prospects of Taiwan's joining multilateral bodies. As Xiaoxue Martin (2020) argues, Taiwan's government "relies on diplomatic recognition to legitimise its claim to sovereignty, contradicting the mainland Chinese claim that Taiwan is but a renegade province of mainland China." More so, as Matthew Southerland (2017: 2) argues, "Diplomatic relations are an important component of Taiwan's toolbox for maintaining a presence on the international stage." Similarly, Rich and Dahmer (2022: 4) maintain that "the lack of formal recognition undermines Taiwan's claims of sovereignty." The exclusion of claimant states from multilateral organizations tends to have high economic costs. This means they cannot exchange goods and services with other countries. They do not have open access to international markets or the freedom to establish normal trade relations with other countries and transnational companies. Being outside the UN system without access to multilateral treaties, claimant states cannot benefit from the legal, financial, and administrative services these treaty bodies and organizations provide. For example, Jieun Choi (2017) finds that while nonrecognition does not directly impact Kosovo's economy, it is indirectly affected by the country's inability to join multilateral bodies. Such economic isolation can expose the population of a claimant state to poverty, leading them to seek refuge in other countries. In its first decade of contested statehood and partial international recognition, Kosovo lost about 10 percent of its people to migration (GAP Institute 2023).

Derecognition can also push claimant states into suspending their ambitions for full diplomatic recognition and membership in international bodies. For instance, in 2008, China and Taiwan agreed to an unofficial truce to retain existing diplomatic allies and avoid changing the status quo. It was an unofficial agreement to refrain from pursuing more recognition or derecognition (Alexander 2014: 59). The truce took place when the China-friendly Ma Ying-jeou was elected as president of Taiwan in 2008, and both sides in the Taiwan Strait agreed to deepen economic and trade relations and avoid diplomatic and political antagonism (Shattuck 2020). As Matthew Southerland (2017: 1) shows, during Ma's presidential term, China allegedly "rejected overtures from several of Taiwan's diplomatic partners to establish formal ties with China." Similarly, J. Michael Cole (2013), confirms that "the truce has held for five years, and Beijing has kept its part of the bargain, refusing advances by countries such as El Salvador, and possibly Honduras, that have expressed the desire to abandon Taiwan, the world's 20th-largest economy, and establish ties with the increasingly attractive PRC." However, this official diplomatic truce broke in 2016 when Taiwan elected Democratic Progressive Party leader Tsai Ing-wen, who pushed for more independence and refused to endorse the "one China" policy agreed in 1992 (Grossman 2021). The truce ended when Gambia derecognized Taiwan and decided to establish diplomatic ties with China. On that occasion, Taiwanese authorities objected to the targeted diplomatic competition that mainland China relaunched: "We call on the mainland to face the reality that the Republic of China is a sovereign state and not carry out negative actions," adding that "otherwise, it must take full responsibility for the possible consequences" (Reuters 2016).

In response to the continuous instances of derecognition of Taiwan, Derek Grossman (2021) has suggested that since "Beijing's successful poaching of Taiwan's allies is harming the island's morale and tarnishing its image as a sovereign nation . . . Taiwan should further consider unilaterally shedding all remaining partners to strengthen its hand long-term against China." Grossman (2021) anticipates that the other remaining diplomatic allies will eventually derecognize Taiwan, and "by unilaterally turning down all official diplomatic relationships, Taiwan would shore up precious time and resources to further its diversification of economic relationships away from China to reduce Beijing's influence over the island." Ditching the existing unreliable diplomatic partners, Grossman (2021) argues, "could allow Taiwan to convert its Ministry of Foreign Affairs into a center for Track 1.5 or Track 2.0 diplomacy to focus on cooperation with powers of major consequence." Such a move would enable Taiwan to escape the recognition-derecognition saga and focus on securing its domestic sovereignty and security through informal diplomatic ties with like-minded states.

Similarly, in 2020, Kosovo agreed to a one-year mortarium to apply for membership in international organizations in exchange for Serbian suspension of its derecognition campaign. Before the move, Serbia's foreign minister argued that if the international community was requesting that "we stop campaigning for the revocation of recognitions, would it not make perfect sense for them to stop lobbying in favour of Kosovo unilateral declaration of independence first, while asking the so-called Kosovo authorities to do the same?" (UN Security Council 2020: 26). Such a pledge was made on 4 September 2020, when Kosovo and Serbia signed separate letters of intent on economic normalization. US president Donald Trump brokered the deal. In the letter of intentions on economic normalization, Kosovo agreed to "implement a one-year moratorium on seeking new membership into International Organizations," while Serbia agreed "to a one-year moratorium of its de-recognition campaign, and will refrain from formally or informally requesting any nation of International Organization not to recognize Kosovo as an independent state" (Exit Albania 2020). During this period, while it continued with low-intensity lobbying for diplomatic recognition, Kosovo did not formally apply for membership in international organizations. It took Kosovo two years to recover from this moratorium and proceed with the application for membership in the Council of Europe and file the intention for consideration for EU candidate state status (Balkan Policy Research Group 2023).

However, the letters of intent did not contain the necessary elements of an international agreement. It quickly became apparent that it would be difficult to assess, monitor, and evaluate their implementation and effects. During the one-year truce period, both sides blamed the other for not respecting the moratorium. Serbia proactively and openly lobbied to prevent or rescind the recognition of Kosovo by third countries, especially during the pandemic period. Its foreign minister paid numerous visits to African, Asian, and Latin American nations, lobbying against Kosovo's recognition, which contradicted its commitments in Washington in September 2020. Moreover, Serbia has used multilateral events, such as the Non-Aligned Movement meeting in Belgrade held in 2021, to lobby a wide range of nations against recognition of Kosovo and its participation and membership in international bodies. While there has been no formal announcement of derecognition, Serbian state leaders in media appearances have constantly signaled that several other countries are ready to reconsider their position on Kosovo. For instance, in July 2021, Serbian president Vučić warned that Serbia would retaliate against any country that recognized Kosovo and relaunch its derecognition campaign (Evropa e Lirë 2021). Such a warning not only was for domestic political consumption in Serbia but also pressured Kosovo to make concessions as part of the EU-led dialogue for normalization of relations. The Ministry of Foreign Affairs and Diaspora of Kosovo, while not giving details of when and where, has indicated it is preparing the application process for membership in a number of international organizations (Evropa e Lirë 2021). President Osmani-Sadriu, during an official visit to Portugal, indicated that Kosovo's primary focus remains membership in NATO, the EU, Interpol, and other international organizations (Telegrafi 2021).

In principle, this moratorium allowed Serbia to have a say on Kosovo's foreign affairs, thus weakening Kosovo's international sovereignty. It was also an admission by Kosovo that the derecognition problem exists and has influenced Kosovo's state behavior, causing its submission to Serbia in future applications for membership in international organizations. Moreover, the moratorium signaled to Serbia that if continued pressuring Kosovo with the withdrawal of recognitions and limitations on its international actions, Kosovo would eventually make concessions in the peace talks. Kosovo's president, Vjosa Osmani-Sadriu, admitted in December 2021, "Unfortunately by accepting the moratorium that violated our constitutional order and our right to consolidate our international subjectivity, our strategic interests were not only damaged but also the lights of our foreign policy were off" (Gazeta Express 2021). There are indications that after September 2021, the United States pressed both Kosovo and Serbia to informally extend the 2020 mortarium and avoid diplomatic provocations. While Kosovo has not formally agreed to such an arrangement, it has remained cautious and has been silently suspending its diplomatic actions to prevent retaliation from Serbia, which claims several countries are ready to announce their derecognition of Kosovo upon its request. Such instances of foreign policy self-suspension were reported in Kosovo media in late 2021 and early 2022. This includes the report that the Ministry of Foreign Affairs (MFA) of Kosovo hesitated to engage in talks with an African country for formal recognition (EuroNews Albania 2021), and that it avoided signing an agreement that would have established diplomatic relations with Timor-Leste (Gazeta Metro 2022). In response, the MFA of Kosovo argued it was in communication with the African country and did not want to prematurely discuss the details in public in case it compromised the recognition process (RTK Dukagjini 2021). Fearing retaliation by Serbia, since 2020 Kosovo has moved to conduct its foreign affairs discretely without much transparency or strategic clarity. For example, the MFA of Kosovo has shown signs of hesitation to lobby for new recognitions or to formalize the establishment of diplomatic relations with countries that have already recognized Kosovo, fearing that Serbia will make public alleged withdrawal of recognition notes from third countries (Demokracia 2022).

Diplomatic isolation as a result of derecognition makes it more difficult for the claimant state to comply with international norms and rules enforced by multilateral organizations and various treaty bodies. Accordingly, it can affect the international community's ability to enforce global rules and norms governing international relations. Before Serbia's derecognition campaign, Kosovo's aspiration was to gradually build up a critical mass of international recognition by securing diplomatic ties and recognition by two-thirds of the UN member states. This would have enabled Kosovo to gain the status of a nonmember observer state, similar to Switzerland prior to 2004 or Palestine after 2012. It would have also given Kosovo access to UN agencies and programs, providing a strong case to seek full membership when the conditions became ripe and Russian and Chinese vetoes were no longer viable. Once the number of countries continuing to recognize and support Kosovo in multilateral organizations dropped under one hundred, securing sufficient votes for membership in international organizations has become more difficult. When Serbia launched its derecognition campaign, its impact on Kosovo's ability to perform its international sovereignty was immediately apparent. In November 2018, Kosovo blamed Serbia's "wild campaign against Kosovo" (Radio Free Europe 2018) for its failure to secure membership in Interpol. The MFA of Kosovo (2018d) expressed "its deep concern over the non-membership in Interpol and the blackmailing approach of the Serbian state towards the officials of Interpol and some delegations of African countries, and condemns the attack of the officials of the Serbian delegation in their attempt to corrupt through bribes some of the participating officials of the Interpol member countries."

Moreover, the process and act of derecognition can undermine the independence of the claimant state in another perverse way. The derecognition of claimant states pushes them to develop new vassal relationships with other countries, especially those that for strategic or historical reasons serve as patron states. The more the claimant state depends on foreign assistance, the more it loses its independence and ability to exercise sovereign statehood. Derecognition tends to push the claimant states to change, forced to switch from seeking full sovereign statehood to accepting an obscured version of statehood without full international recognition, which can be described as a state of dependency on a more powerful state that serves as a protector (Igarashi 2002). As the claimant state runs the risk of becoming a vassal state with fractured internal sovereignty and weak external sovereignty, its status is more complicated than partially independent territories or non-self-governing territories under international trusteeship. Such a state of affairs brews more isolation and contestation and risks gradually unmaking the state. For instance, Russia continues to be a major source of economic and military support for Abkhazia. Following Russia's invasion of Ukraine in 2022 and Azerbaijan's reintegration of Nagorno-Karabagh in 2023, the likelihood of Abkhazia and South Ossetia being eventually united with Russia has increased. It is estimated that Russia provides 60 percent of the state budget and that Russian troops stationed in the territory act as national armed forces (Lambert 2020). Most importantly, such a dependency on third states may affect the ability of the claimant state to independently perform its domestic and foreign affairs without the interference of the patron state. The ability to have an independent foreign policy is in itself a core criterion of independent statehood. In fact, scholars such as Tanisha Fazal (2007: 17) define state death as "the formal loss of control over foreign policy to another state." Seen from this perspective, derecognition might contribute to the slow death of claimant states in that they have to delegate foreign policy autonomy to another state that utilizes it for strategic reasons.

The limited recognition of Abkhazia and South Ossetia and the subsequent derecognition by Vanuatu and Tuvalu have played a significant role in deepening the dependency of these claimant states on the Russian Federation as their main ally. Patron states frequently use both recognition and derecognition as weapons in their foreign policy arsenals to deepen ties and dependencies with the affected states, whether they are involved in defending the claimant state against derecognition or, in other cases, supporting the former base state in its efforts to pursue the derecognition of the claimant state. In the case of Abkhazia and South Ossetia, the Russian Federation takes advantage of these two claimant states' vulnerability and uses them as geopolitical leverage (Gerrits and Bader 2016). As Thomas De Waal (2018: 2) argues, "Russia's recognition of Abkhazia (and South Ossetia) in 2008 following its war with Georgia gave the territory more security and resources but has also led to its de facto integration with Russia and reduced international engagement." De Waal (2010: 2015) argues that "the paradox of Russian recognition was that it actually weakened the would-be sovereignty of both territories." In other words, "Abkhazia has effectively earned Russia's recognition in exchange for greater international isolation and de facto integration with Russia" (De Waal 2019: 20). It is estimated that "Russia is responsible for most of Abkhazia and South Ossetia's trade. Moreover, it subsidises about half of Abkhazia's annual budget and 90% of South Ossetia's" (Ó Beacháin 2020: 432). Limited recognition, including the process of derecognition of Abkhazia and South Ossetia, has pushed these two entities to consider closer association with, and eventual incorporation into, the Russian Federation. There have been increasing calls in Abkhazia and South Ossetia to join Russia since the escalation of Russia's aggression war against Ukraine. The fact that the vast majority of the citizens of these two claimant states have obtained Russian citizenship demonstrates that, as a result of the passportization policy, the claimant states have cemented their dependence on Russia and lost their sovereignty (Ganohariti 2021).

Beyond undermining the external capacity of the claimant state to exercise sovereign statehood, derecognition tends to undermine the legitimacy of incumbent governments, resulting in domestic political instability and polarization. The diplomatic isolation that can follow derecognition undermines emerging states' ontological security and national identity. It can also increase the claimant state's resentment toward the outer world for lacking solidarity in its struggle for freedom, independence, and statehood after perceived injustices or oppression by the former base state. When it emerges bit by bit, derecognition inhibits the claimant state's sense of self-realization as an intersubjective necessity to exist and be appreciated as an equal and respected member of the community of sovereign states. China intensified efforts to derecognize Taiwan during the years in which the pro-independence party was in power, seeking to undermine its domestic legitimacy and force political change in favour of a status quo that suited Beijing (Stratfor 2019). When Kiribati derecognized Taiwan, the government in Taipei stated: "It is blatantly obvious that the Chinese government, by creating these diplomatic incidents, seeks to manipulate public opinion in Taiwan, influence Taiwan's . . . presidential and legislative elections, and undermine its democratic processes." The statement continued with the vow to "stand firm in upholding Taiwan's sovereignty, making no concessions with regard to its sovereignty in the face of China's diplomatic assaults" (Tiezzi 2020). In another case, the MFA of Taiwan considered the timing of Nauru's derecognition, lured by China's economic assistance, "as a repudiation of democratic values and an open challenge to the international order." (MFA of Taiwan 2024b).

Sometimes, the announcement of derecognition decisions results in the resignation of politicians and governments among the claimant and derecognizing states. For example, when Burkina Faso derecognized Taiwan in 2018 and the Solomon Islands followed in 2019, Taiwan's foreign minister, Joseph Wu, offered his resignation to the president and took responsibility for failing to prevent the loss of diplomatic allies. However, in both instances, the president of Taiwan asked him to continue, stating that the Taiwanese "had already done all they could to prevent the switch, and that Beijing was to blame rather than Wu" (South China Morning Post 2019a). Regardless of such expressed resilience, for the Taiwanese public, "The loss of those diplomatic allies feeds fears that Taiwan is slipping into vulnerable isolation and increasingly subject to Chinese intimidation. There is growing social and political anxiety that other countries will follow and switch to Beijing" (Bush 2016). In 2018, mass street demonstrations took place in Taiwan rejecting China's bullying campaign, military provocation, and the loss of diplomatic allies. They called for an eventual referendum on Taiwan's constitutional independence from China (Voice of America 2018).

Although limited compared to other cases, the derecognitions of Kosovo have negatively affected the country's domestic political stability and deepened polarization among dominant parties. Opposition parties blamed the government for the lack of international recognition for Kosovo, saying its mismanagement and poor performance caused it due to unconditional talks with Serbia (Kallxo 2018). Avdullah Hoti, from the Democratic League of Kosovo, who in 2020 became country's prime minister, argued in April 2019 that "Kosovo's foreign policy is non-existent, completely in defensive, trying to prevent the withdrawal of recognitions. There are almost no important visits to Kosovo, nor any foreign visits of the heads of institutions" (Zëri 2019b). The first foreign minister of Kosovo, Skënder Hyseni, stated: "This situation with the recognition or derecognition of Kosovo comes as a result of a total misalignment of Kosovo's foreign policy. This is a lack of work, lack of coordination, lack of strategy and the strategy does not mean a political statement, but it means a systematic action plan and work that unfortunately has been missing for years in Kosovo's diplomacy" (Zëri 2019b). Similarly, in the Assembly of Kosovo, members from the opposition party, Movement for Self-Determination, stated: "In any normal country, the minister should have resigned due to successive failures and not only because of the lack of recognitions, but [also] because of the withdrawal of recognition due to the failure of membership in international institutions such as Interpol, UNESCO, and others" (Zëri 2019a).

Across all cases, political opponents have used derecognition to delegitimize governments in power (Hickey 2007: 64). Similarly, public opinion polls, think tanks, and mass media also indirectly impact the legitimacy of governments affected by diplomatic derecognition. In a survey published by Prishtina Institute for Political Studies in 2019, 52 percent of respondents believed that Kosovo's position has been weakened by Serbia's financed campaign for derecognition (PIPS 2019: 15). The same poll revealed that 50 percent of respondents believed that Kosovo's statehood depends on international recognition (PIPS 2019: 15). Another poll conducted in 2019 shows that 27 percent of respondents believed that the derecognition of Kosovo revealed its negotiating position toward Serbia; 42 percent thought that it undermined Kosovo's ability to join international organizations and deepened the country's international isolation; and 31 percent believed that the derecognition of Kosovo demonstrates weakening international support.

Finally, derecognition could contribute to deepening the fragility of the claimant state and, in some cases, have the effect of prolonging undemocratic rule and a permanent state of emergency within the political community seeking statehood and recognition. Nina Caspersen (2015: 298) argues that "recognition remains an existential issue for de facto states and the pursuit of recognition also serves an important legitimating function internally: the promise of future recognition can be used to excuse current shortcomings." In the case of Western Sahara, J. Peter Pham (2010: 15) argues that the SADR has been governed by the same "chief of state," who has power over all governmental and parliamentary bodies in its controlled territories and the government-in-exile. Moreover, it is stipulated that political pluralism and free association among Sahrawi people are only allowed when the territory secures complete sovereignty and recognition (Pham 2010: 15). Since the right to self-determination has been denied for over forty years, the Polisario Front has effectively gained unending political power in the absence of a democratic system. According to Freedom House (2021), Western Sahara was "not free" in 2021 due to a number of issues, including the absence of free elections, corruption, and restrictions on the right to free speech and assembly. However, in another set of circumstances, as witnessed in the case of Taiwan, derecognition has positively affected the democratization process, forcing this contested country to seek international legitimation based on its democratic performance (Madsen 2011). Nina Caspersen (2012: 70) stipulates that "the process of derecognition and the accompanying crisis of international legitimacy provided an important impetus for Taiwan to replace decades of authoritarian rule with gradual democratization." Moreover, Pasha Hsieh (2019: 96) argues that "de-recognition of the Republic of China (ROC) in global politics and Taiwan's democratization movement have crystalized the Taiwanese identity, which has gradually departed from the Chinese identity." In turn, "The emerging Taiwanese identity has promoted Taipei to seek recognition of its sovereign state status" (Hsieh 2019: 98), though it has also polarized the political spectrum in Taiwan. Cal Clark (2008: 90) argues that Taiwan faces "a major threat to its sovereignty and statehood from the PRC. This threat, unfortunately, is exacerbated by the domestic dynamics of Taiwan's politics that have prevented the country from developing a unified and coherent strategy for responding to Beijing during this decade."

In sum, although the withdrawal of diplomatic recognition does not result in the extinction of statehood of claimant states, it can significantly

176 • *The Derecognition of States*

undermine their sovereignty, domestic stability, and international standing as equals among other nations. In other words, derecognition deepens the existential insecurity, prolongs instability, and expands the claimant state's frozen conflict and international contestation. Moreover, it forces the claimant state to scale back its international engagement and make unfavorable concessions to the former base state and third countries. The capacity of the claimant state to enjoy fundamental rights of states like independence, sovereign equality, noninterference, and peaceful coexistence is also diminished (Shaw 2017: 166–69).

DEEPENING DISPUTES BETWEEN THE CLAIMANT AND THE FORMER BASE STATE

As discussed in the previous chapter, a dominant rationale for derecognition is the willingness of third countries to contribute to resolving disputes through peaceful dialogue. Contrary to such claims, derecognition tends to exacerbate conflict rather than resolve disputes between the claimant and the former base state. The derecognition process has not, in any of the cases examined in this book, pushed the parties toward normalizing their relations or finding a solution to a statehood dispute. Seen as a form of diplomatic aggression and a zero-sum game, derecognition tends to deepen distrust, undermine confidence-building measures, and risk the return of violent conflict. The derecognition of states, like nonrecognition policies, tends to serve as a sanction imposed by the former base state and its allies on the claimant state. While in most cases the logic behind nonrecognition is to sanction (punish) the claimant state for creating itself through nonconsensual and revolutionary methods, in the case of derecognition the purpose is to pressure the claimant state to ensure it does not benefit from the fruits of independent statehood. This results in the alienation of the claimant state and damage to confidence-building and normalization measures undertaken by the international community. Seen from this perspective, practices of state derecognition tend to undermine the international community's role in resolving statehood and self-determination disputes and permit former host states to expand their aggressive behavior and crush secession without scrutiny. This serves the former host or occupying state's agenda to consider the self-determination dispute an internal matter of law and order that does not require international engagement. In other words, the derecognition of states risks internalization rather than internationalization of claims for self-determination.

Among other cases, the renewed tensions between China and Taiwan after 2021 reveal state derecognition's political and security effects. As part of China's global rise and its assertive foreign and security policy, Taiwan has become the test case for demonstrating its quest for recognition as a global power. In policy discourse, Chinese leadership has increased its threats to reunify with Taiwan, even forcefully if necessary, and has warned other countries that back Taiwan of severe diplomatic and military consequences. As Peter C. Y. Chow (2022: 4) argues, "China's tactics against Taiwan have included shows of military might, cyberattacks, disinformation campaigns, intimidation, united front activities designed to destabilize Taiwan from within, and use of its economic power to reward those countries and individuals that support China's claims in Taiwan while punishing those that do not." In addition to low-intensity military provocations, China has utilized the derecognition of Taiwan as a symbol of its diplomatic war, which could escalate into a fully-fledged and violent conflict. Taiwanese foreign minister Joseph Wu stated in September 2021 that "the silent diplomatic war has been going on for many years. The Chinese foreign ministry has a mission to take out our diplomatic allies and sabotage our relations with like-minded partners who do not have diplomatic relations with us. The Chinese also block us out of major international organizations" (Hoover Institution 2021).

As a result, there are more calls in Taiwan to pursue independence and thwart a Chinese invasion as a result of state derecognition becoming a weapon. In 2019, a Taiwan Public Opinion Foundation poll showed that "53 percent of Taiwanese do not worry about losing diplomatic allies, while 43 percent find it worrying" (Shattuck 2020: 336). Another poll showed that in Taiwan 46.6 percent support independence, whereas 11.1 percent support unification, and 26.4 percent support maintaining the status quo (Yinglung 2021: 8). This is a major change in Taiwan, as in 1991, only 12.5 percent supported independence (Yinglung 2021: 12). Moreover, Taiwan has increased its military spending and has aligned more closely with the United States and other democracies to deter eventual Chinese occupation. Following the Dominican Republic's derecognition in 2018, Taiwan condemned "China's contemptible decision to use dollar diplomacy to wrest away Taiwan's diplomatic allies, and its heavy-handed methods of suppressing Taiwan's international participation" (President of Taiwan 2008). It further stated that "Beijing's crude attempts at foreign policy can only drive a wedge between

178 • *The Derecognition of States*

the two sides of the Taiwan Strait, erode mutual trust, and antagonize the people of Taiwan" (President of Taiwan 2008). This isolation of Taiwan, as Chiang and Hwang (2008: 72) warn, "is a great disservice to the common interests in international peace and security since it leaves open the possible Chinese use of force against Taiwan based on its claimed sovereignty over the island." Yet, as they argue, "the most significant legal implication arising from regarding Taiwan as an independent State would be that China would be under an obligation not to try to "reunify" with Taiwan by nonpeaceful means" (Chiang and Hwang 2008: 73). They add that "recognition of the independent Statehood of Taiwan only renders unification through non-peaceful means illegal but does not make unification impossible" (Chiang and Hwang 2008: 73). So the more countries that derecognize Taiwan, the easier they make it for China to justify the use of force for unification. In this regard, derecognition of Taiwan only complicates the dispute and changes the status quo in favor of escalatory and violent actions.

Since 2020, Taiwan has intensified its diplomatic contacts with high-ranking officials in the US administration and Congress and among the EU member states and institutions to compensate for the loss of many of its diplomatic allies. Taiwan has tried to pay for the loss of recognition by traditional non-Western partners with informal yet enhanced ties with Western allies, such as the United States, Lithuania, and the Czech Republic. It has also managed to secure recognition by Somaliland, another unrecognized African state. These actions have profoundly antagonized China, which has taken retaliatory measures against Lithuania, symbolic actions against the United States, and direct threats to Taiwan by rehearsing military intervention and crossing into its territorial waters and airspace. A significant event was the August 2022 visit to Taiwan by the Speaker of the US House of Representatives, Nancy Pelosi, whose visit served as a pretext and drastically increased chances for an armed conflict between China and Taiwan (Associated Press 2022). In this regard, third countries have taken sides in the China-Taiwan dispute and their acts of derecognition have amplified tensions and been used by both sides in the conflict to pursue their strategic goals. For example, Somalia, in retaliation for Taiwan's recognition of Somaliland in 2020, publicly supported Chinese escalatory and military actions by expressing full "solidarity while the People's Republic of China in defending its sovereignty and territorial integrity" (MFA of Somalia 2022). Such statements tend to serve as external legitimization of China's violent reunification with Taiwan. On the other hand, Taiwan has used its existing diplomatic allies, such as in the visit by the Saint Vincent and the Grenadines prime minister to Taipei soon after Chinese provocative drills in the cross-strait space, to demonstrate international support for its struggle and push back against mainland China.

In another part of the world, the derecognition of Western Sahara has directly contributed to the worsening of the security situation in the region, which has moved from rhetorical and diplomatic warfare to low-intensity conflict. In 2020, the twenty-nine-year ceasefire arrangement between Morocco and Western Sahara ended after the Moroccan army used force against Sahrawi protesters who blocked the southern route through the territory connected with the rest of Africa. During this long ceasefire, Morocco expanded its military, economic, and demographic presence in the controlled territories. This included waging a diplomatic war for the derecognition of SADR and for the recognition of what it refers to as Moroccan Sahara. In particular, the UN's failure to resolve the conflict and Morocco's strategy of inviting other countries to open consulates in the occupied territory have pushed the Polisario Front to no longer tolerate the status quo. Since 2019, some ten African countries have opened consulates in Western Sahara (Dakhla and Layun), a step beyond declarative derecognition (Deutsche Welle 2020). It is a performative act showing derecognition is not a mere statements but has political and military effects. For instance, when Gambia opened its consulate in Dakhla in January 2020, Moroccan foreign minister Nasser Bourita stated that "the Kingdom of Morocco effectively exercises its sovereignty over its Sahara and The Gambia's decision to open a consular representation in this region of the Kingdom is in line with the positions expressed by this State at the UN General Assembly and other international fora backing Morocco's territorial integrity" (MFA of Morocco 2020). Countries that have opened consulates in the contested and occupied territories of Western Sahara and have recognized Morocco's sovereignty have done so in exchange for economic benefits such as the construction of government buildings, cancellation of foreign debt, and payment of membership fees to international organizations (Algeria Press Service 2020). These consulates are opened in cities and regions with no citizens of those countries to whom they can offer services. They seem to be concentrated in a single district and predominately remain empty with no regular consular activity. The Moroccan government allegedly covers the costs of running these consulates.

Ultimately, the opening of consulates in Western Sahara represents a form of derecognition and enables Morocco to expand its control and legitimizes its claims over the occupied territory. Moroccan diplomats certainly

180 • *The Derecognition of States*

see these diplomatic representations as confirming its "claim to sovereignty over the territory" (International Crisis Group 2021: 6). Following the same narrative, Morocco's foreign minister, Nasser Bourita, for instance, considered the opening of a Malawian consulate in Laayoune to be "part of the new dynamic of bilateral relations, after the decision of this country to withdraw in 2017 its recognition of the so-called 'SADR' and the will of the two States to further develop their cooperation" (Agence Marocaine de Presse 2021). Similarly, following the government's narrative, Morocco World News (2021) opined, for instance, that "Malawi's decision to open a consulate in Laayoune is the culmination of the country's shift from sympathizing with Polisario's self-determination claims to expressing support for Morocco's territorial integrity." Yet such a move is not only contrary to international norms on decolonization, self-determination, and illegal occupation but also contributes to conflict escalation and damages the prospects for long-term peace and reconciliation in the region. Other effects of opening consulates in contested territories of Western Sahara include pressure on the SADR and its international allies to accept Morocco's autonomy plan, thus denying the Sahrawi people their long-awaited right to self-determination and statehood. Human rights violations against Sahrawi activists residing in Morocco-controlled areas have been marginalized as a result of this legitimization of Morocco's control over Western Sahara (Human Rights Watch 2021). The secretary-general of the Polisario, Brahim Ghali, wrote several letters to the UN, calling the opening of consulates a "violation of international law and . . . breach of the international legal status of Western Sahara as a Non-Self-Governing Territory" (UN Secretary-General 2021: 19). Finally, countries that have established consulates in disputed areas run the risk of getting entangled in the conflict, undermining regional stability in a region of Africa that is already unstable.

In this situation, the Polisario Front's decision to return to active resistance, having lost faith in the UN's process for resolving conflicts, has been influenced by the SADR's derecognition. The International Crisis Group (2021: 2) held that "taking advantage of the diplomatic void left after [UN envoy] Köhler's departure, Morocco invited several African and Middle Eastern governments to open consulates inside Western Sahara. In response, Polisario officials and activists promptly labelled the move a return to war." In late 2021, the UN secretary-general admitted that "the security environment in the four security areas of MINURSO . . . remained unpredictable" (UN Secretary-General 2021: 19). It was also reported in 2020 that the Moroccan army had planted fresh landmines in the berm dividing areas of control (Sahara Press Service 2020). The derecognition process has deepened and escalated the conflict, despite the low level of hostilities and lack of many casualties. The loss of recognition and fruitless talks over a decade under UN auspices have damaged the Polisario Front's legitimacy among Sahrawi communities, especially those living in camps (IISS 2021). Thus, the end of the ceasefire has allowed the Polisario to restore internal legitimacy and prolong its political rule. As the International Crisis Group (2021: 9) shows, "The return to war has energised Sahrawi youth in the camps and abroad, and Polisario has reactivated its international solidarity networks to attract attention to the conflict." However, this escalation may "destabilise North Africa and the Sahel, with unforeseeable consequences for U.S. and European interests" (International Crisis Group 2021: 13).

Parallel to the opening of these controversial consulates, the US recognition of Moroccan sovereignty over Western Sahara has been the other significant trigger of low-intensity hostilities between Sahrawi and Moroccan forces. In December 2020, the Trump administration recognized Moroccan sovereignty over Western Sahara in exchange for Morocco's normalization of relations with Israel. In justifying this decision, President Trump stated that "the United States believes that Morocco's autonomy plan is the only realistic option to achieve a just, lasting, and mutually acceptable solution to the dispute over Western Sahara." While his hoped-for outcome is unlikely, Trump added that "this recognition leaves room for a negotiated solution and the United States remains committed to working with Morocco, the Polisario, and all involved regional and international actors to support the necessary work ahead and create a more peaceful and prosperous region." SADR diplomats strongly condemned Trump's decision as "a flagrant breach of international law in the case of Western Sahara" (Middle East Eye 2020). Algeria, Spain, and Russia similarly spurned the US recognition of Moroccan control, while France saw it as a positive step toward the autonomy arrangement, as proposed by Morocco in 2007.

To make matters worse, the United States opened a consulate in the city of Dakhla, referring to the occupied parts of Western Sahara as "Morocco's Southern Provinces" (US Embassy in Morocco 2021). This controversial and transactional decision could further "antagonise . . . pro-independence Sahrawis, especially Sahrawi youth, who have long been losing faith in a diplomatic solution to the conflict" (International Crisis Group 2021: 2). Damien Kingsbury's (2015: 256) research shows that young Saharawi who have grown up either in the refugee camps or under Moroccan occupation already "seem to believe that returning to war with Morocco to reclaim their land is now the only option." Moreover, the US recognition of Moroccan sovereignty over Western Sahara has opened the possibility of the United States selling modern arms to the Moroccan army with no restrictions on using them in Western Sahara. This can certainly change the dynamics of the conflict on the ground and risks dragging other regional contenders into it (Huddleston, Ghoorhoo, and Maquera Sardon 2021). It is reported that 2019 the United States has made an arms deal with Morocco worth $10.3 billion, which will mostly go to Royal Moroccan Air Force (Forbes 2019).

In Europe, Serbia's campaign for derecognition of Kosovo is also considered one of the main reasons why the EU-led dialogue for normalization of relations between the two countries halted for two years (2018–2019). Kosovo perceived the derecognition campaign as an attempt to damage its sovereignty and territorial integrity and described it as diplomatic aggression (Government of Kosovo 2018; Zëri i Amerikës 2018). The derecognition campaign has made the government of Kosovo doubt Serbia's willingness to normalize relations and enhance regional peace and stability. Thus, in response to Serbia's campaign, in November 2018 Kosovo imposed a 10 percent customs tariff on goods imported from Serbia and Bosnia and Herzegovina, the only countries in southeast Europe that refuse to recognize Kosovo's independence. Soon after, Kosovo increased the customs tariff to 100 percent, launching a trade war with Serbia. Justifying the retaliatory tax, Kosovo's deputy prime minister, Enver Hoxhaj, said: "When you are a young and small country and a neighbour like Serbia continuously strikes at Kosovo's external sovereignty with anti-recognition campaigns and blockades for membership in international organisations, we need to use what is at our disposal to exercise internal sovereignty by introducing economic measures and conveying clear message in relation to Serbia" (Koha 2019a). The MFA of Kosovo (2019c) justified the retaliatory tariffs as "a response to Serbia's aggressive campaign and destructive actions, which seeks to undermine Kosovo's sovereignty," listing among them the pressure put on countries to revoke recognition of Kosovo and sabotage its membership in international organizations. The MFA of Kosovo called upon "the international community in order to react immediately and warn the neighbouring country against such behaviours and actions which are in full contradiction of the expressed commitment to regional cooperation, commitment for integration to the EU, and the expressed declarative will for full normalization of relations with the two countries" (MFA of Kosovo 2019c). Serbia's foreign minister Dačić refuted the claims, stating: "Let me remind those who allege that our activities, and the withdrawal by 15 countries of their recognition of so-called Kosovo, are undermining the dialogue that after the negotiations began in 2012, 25 countries recognized the unilateral declaration of independence while all along Serbia participated in the dialogue, despite Pristina's refusal to fulfil its obligations under the Brussels Agreement" (UN Security Council 2019c: 5).

Through the derecognition campaign, Serbia not only managed to temporarily neutralize and limit the scope of Kosovo in the international arena, but also undermined Kosovo's special ties with the United States and major European countries that have since reduced international support for Kosovo and conditioned it on continued dialogue and abolition of the tariffs. As Kosovo did not adequately justify the tariffs as a measure in retaliation for Serbia's derecognition campaign, the United States and EU began putting pressure on Kosovo to rescind the tariffs while mostly remaining silent on Serbia's derecognition campaign. Consequently, the blame for the stalled dialogue suddenly shifted from Serbia and its campaign to Kosovo and its retaliatory tax. A Deputy Assistant Secretary and Special Representative for the Western Balkans Matthew Palmer (2019) stated: "With negotiations at a standstill, both countries risk squandering the best chance in a generation to normalize relations and move towards a more secure and prosperous future." The United States wanted Kosovo to "demonstrate its commitment to these shared goals by suspending the tariffs imposed on Serbian and Bosnian imports that have damaged Kosovo's international standing." With the withdrawal of US support, Kosovo's international isolation was inevitable. The United States also called on Serbia to "cease its campaign to delegitimize Kosovo in the international community," stating that "through its campaign to incentivize countries to withdraw recognition of Kosovo and block its membership in international organizations such as INTERPOL, Belgrade has undermined international law enforcement cooperation and soured the atmosphere for compromise" (Palmer 2019).

While the EU remained silent on Serbia's derecognition campaign and pressured Kosovo to lift the customs tariffs, leading EU member states such as Germany urged "the Serbian Government to refrain from actions that undermine an environment conducive to negotiations . . . for example, efforts to persuade other countries to withdraw their recognition of Kosovo" (UN Security Council 2019a: 18). Similarly, the UK called on both Serbia and Kosovo "to remove obstacles to [dialogue] resumption. Pristina must remove tariffs and Belgrade must stop its de-recognition campaign. For dialogue to succeed, both sides must refrain from provocative rhetoric and actions" (UN Security Council 2019c: 13). The EU only implicitly and indirectly tackled the issue when the Council of the EU in its conclusions of 18 June 2019 called on Serbia "to make further substantial efforts and contribute to the establishment of a conducive environment, as well as refrain from any act that can be perceived as provocation" (Council of the EU 2019). Using Serbia's success at derecognition as a pretext, French far-right parties in the European Parliament started to question Kosovo's independence. Dominique Bilde asked the EU high representative: "With the international community's growing reluctance to recognise Kosovo, which still has not been recognised by five EU Member States, does the High Representative consider it realistic to pursue negotiations with Kosovo on possible membership of the European Union, notably given the Stabilisation and Association Agreement signed on 27 October 2015?" (European Parliament 2018a). In response, the high representative, stated: "The issue of the recognition of Kosovo is a competence of EU Member States. The European Commission follows a status-neutral approach in relation to Kosovo" (European Parliament 2018b).

As the Kosovar side continued to resist US pressure to remove the retaliatory tariffs on Serbia, the US Embassy in Kosovo issued a statement maintaining that "some commentators and politicians have suggested that Kosovo's status as an independent, sovereign state, closely aligned with the United States, will shield it from all consequences of its decisions in the international arena. We caution against assuming that Kosovo or any other friend of the United States can take actions that run counter to our strategic interests without facing consequences to our bilateral relationship" (US Embassy Pristina 2019). The statement explicitly called on Kosovo to immediately suspend "the tariff on imports from Serbia and Bosnia [as] one necessary measure to restore momentum to the Dialogue process." The call to Serbia to suspend its derecognition campaign, meanwhile, was only implicit: "We expect other stakeholders to take constructive measures of their own" (US Embassy Pristina 2019). There was also talk of the United States imposing sanctions and taking other measures that would undermine bilateral relations (US Government 2019). In a letter sent to Kosovo leaders, senior officials i the US government stated that "after our requests to suspend the tariffs went unheeded, we have decided to take steps to show our concern, including with regard to our security partnership" (US Government 2019). In this regard, Serbia has managed to influence the preferences of Kosovo's allies and, through them, impose new conditions on Kosovo. In a letter sent to President Trump, Serbian counterpart Vučić stated that "regardless of Serbia's wish and faith, tariffs imposed by Pristina on the goods from Serbia represent a burden and an unpassable obstacle for the continuation of the dialogue," thus blaming Kosovo for obstructing a US-backed settlement, which would have represented an essential foreign policy win for Trump's already-shattered presidency (N1 2019c).

Eventually, in March 2020, the new prime minister of Kosovo, Albin Kurti, notified the EU that Kosovo was "committed to the dialogue process" and believed that "it is the only way to reach an agreement, the ultimate goal of which should be the mutual recognition of both states." Prime Minister Kurti announced that "in line with this commitment, effective as of March 15, we will begin to remove the tariffs on goods from Serbia and Bosnia and Herzegovina that the previous government imposed and commitment to restarting the dialogue with Serbia." Kurti added that "in return we expect Serbia to remove all remaining non-tariff barriers to trade with Kosovo, as well as ending its derecognition campaign against Kosovo." On this occasion, Kurti invited "the EU and the United States to create monitoring and sanctioning mechanisms to ensure that both sides abide by their commitments in existing and future agreements" (Office of the Prime Minister of Kosovo 2020). The United States and Serbia found the offer unacceptable, demanding Kosovo drop the tariffs entirely and engage unconditionally in the dialogue (US Embassy in Kosovo 2020). Serbia did not end its derecognition campaign. On the contrary, days after Kosovo partially lifted its tariffs, it announced that Sierra Leone was the eighteenth country to withdraw the recognition of Kosovo. By threatening to impose sanctions on Kosovo, the US officials indirectly played a role in ousting the Kurti government and replacing it with one led by a more obedient prime minister (Prishtina Insight 2020). Avdullah Hoti, from the Democratic League of Kosovo, dropped the tariffs and restarted the EU-facilitated dialogue within days of taking office (The Guardian 2020a). Overall, the politically motivated decision to withdraw recognition of Kosovo did not contribute to the normalization of relations between Kosovo and Serbia and indirectly produced more regional instability, prolonging disputes in the Western Balkans. In this regard, the derecognition campaign was an early warning that the Kosovo-Serbia dispute would worsen, as happened during 2022 and 2023 with the escalation of the conflict in the north of Kosovo (Visoka 2023; Visoka and Musliu 2023).

Moreover, Serbia's campaign for the derecognition of Kosovo played a negative role in reaching a legally binding agreement for full normalization of relations. It solidified the differences of both parties as well as the ambition of the EU and the United States. to achieve durable peace through mutual recognition. The 2023 Agreement on the Path to Normalization of

Relations was centered on de facto recognition, but its implementation has stagnated due to disagreements on the sequence of implementation of different provisions. Kosovo insists on prioritizing the implementation of articles which enhance Kosovo's sovereignty and de facto recognition, whereas Serbia insists on the implementation of articles that expand the autonomy of local Serbs and derail Kosovo's sovereignty at home and abroad. Aware that it has damaged Kosovo's international standing through the derecognition campaign, Serbia has gone as far as to argue that it accepts the EU-brokered agreements as long as they "do not pertain to the de facto and de jure recognition of Kosovo" (Government of Serbia 2023).

State derecognition tends to undermine the claimant's self-regard and further deepens the claimant state's adverse attitudes toward the former base state and the wider international community. As Thomas De Waal (2018) shows, most claimant states "were born out of conflict and sustain themselves with a narrative of injustice and the belief that they have won statehood amid adversity." Derecognition often facilitates an inward-looking nationalism and a deeper dependency on the external patron states that use the claimant states as vassals for their geopolitical interests. For example, in Kosovo, 50 percent of respondents in a public opinion poll declared that Kosovo's statehood depends on international recognition (Berisha 2019: 15). In the midst of Serbia's derecognition campaign, over 85 percent of respondents in a poll considered "Serbia as a very hostile country toward Kosovo" and the "biggest external security threat" to the country (Emini 2018: 15). One of the main reasons for such hostility appears to be Serbia's "diplomatic battles in international arena," considering that "the obstructive role of Serbia has had a major impact in the process of gaining international recognition, de-recognitions from mostly African countries and the lack of progress in membership in international organizations" (Emini 2018: 15). Another poll showed that 52 percent of Kosovo citizens believed that the country's international position has been weakened since Serbia launched its derecognition campaign (Berisha 2019: 15).

Contrary to the claims that derecognition can serve as a conflict resolution instrument, the evidence presented here shows that the process of derecognition has a negative effect on the stability and normalization of relations between the contender states. The former base state weaponizes derecognition to bring the claimant state to its knees, forcing it to make concessions as part of formal or informal talks. This in turn pushes the claimant state to take action in self-defense, which can undermine confidence-building efforts, entrench hostilities, and escalate the political conflict.

Beyond this real-world impact, claimant states' adverse reaction to acts of derecognition signifies that, like recognition, the diplomatic practice of state derecognition can have constitutive effects on the contender states, including the derecognizing states.

DESTABILIZING EFFECTS ON THE DERECOGNIZING STATES

Derecognition not only undermines the sovereignty of the affected states and deepens hostilities with contender states, but, in most cases, also backfires on the derecognizing states themselves. First and foremost, the diplomacy of state derecognition frequently promotes political corruption and conflict between the ruling party and the opposition in the derecognizing states. Corruption and issues with governance are particularly bad in the Pacific islands, Latin America, and Africa due to China and Taiwan's rivalry for diplomatic recognition. Election interference and the disruption of the nation's sustainable economic development are clear signs that it has had a destabilizing and de-democratizing effect. Taiwan allegedly offered cash payments in an effort to entice its diplomatic allies, whereas China preferred to offer loans and direct investments. While China tends to trap states in long-term debt and dependence, Taiwan's approach breeds corruption and official misconduct and keeps the recipient nation underdeveloped. For instance, China and Taiwan have used "dollar diplomacy" to compensate various factions in the Solomon Islands, sparking violent riots in 2006 and 2021. Taiwanese aid has been focused on strengthening patrimonial personal rule (against the rule of institutions), which is more consistent with the shadow state analysis, according to Braithwaite (2010: 143). Although Taiwan has promoted democratic norms and values as the standards by which it conducts its foreign relations, in many cases it has supported authoritarian regimes, fostered undemocratic and unaccountable practices, and "exacerbated the country's corruption challenges" (Cavanough 2023: 4). For instance, in 2019 Nicaragua's congress approved a $100 million loan from Taiwan, providing support to President Daniel Ortega's administration, which has grown increasingly isolated as a result of a brutal crackdown on protesters (Reuters 2019a). Condemning the Nicaraguan government in this sociopolitical crisis, however, "could also mean antagonizing a regime that has so far maintained formal diplomatic recognition of Taiwan, risking a diplomatic reversal to China," as one commentator put it (Peralta 2018). It's estimated that Taiwan once directly paid Solomon Island lawmakers $9 million a year to invest in projects for constituency development at their discretion. This vote-buying scheme that purported to be for development purposes ran the risk of fostering corruption and abuse of power by political figures (Reuters 2019b). However, similar behaviors are observed in "interactions with Chinese and other foreign nationals [which] have introduced a level of corrosion to good governance and the government machinery" (Aqorau 2021: 344).

The "electoralization" of state derecognition is certainly fueled by foreign governments whose recognition is threatened, but it also provides an opportunity for national leaders to leverage the diplomatic wars between contender states to their political benefit. Paradoxically, Taiwan in 2019 initiated an anti-infiltration bill that "prohibits political donations, lobbying and attempts to interfere with local elections under the instruction of or with the financial support of anyone affiliated with a hostile force" (Focus Taiwan 2019b). Taiwan uses the same methods when seeking to extend its influence and interfere in the domestic affairs of other states to retain or regain diplomatic recognition. As a result of this interference in the internal affairs of diplomatic allies, the question of continued recognition or derecognition of claimant states often features as the main electoral cleavage in third countries, to the detriment of other, more pressing domestic issues. In Pacific island states, foreign policy position toward China and Taiwan has often been the main determinant of election victory. In Kiribati, the government derecognized Taiwan in 2019, subsequently losing its majority in the parliament, leading to fresh elections (The Guardian 2020b). The elections in June 2020 were primarily about the Taiwan-China issue, overlooking other domestic matters. Opposition parties in the country considered the campaign the most "aggressive" they have seen (Reuters 2020). Over a decade earlier, in 2004 the prime minister of Vanuatu, Serge Vohor, tried to recognize Taiwan, ending diplomatic ties with China. Within days, China intervened by offering a package of US$32 million more, convincing Vohor's cabinet to topple him and have the new cabinet restore official ties with China (Shen 2015: 889–90).

In 1999, Papua New Guinea established formal diplomatic relations with Taiwan. However, this recognition lasted only for a week and was overturned along with the government. The attempt by the prime minister of Papua New Guinea in 1999 to switch recognition to Taiwan provoked a powerful domestic backlash in favor of ties with China. The move cost him his job (Rich and Dahmer 2018). Taiwan allegedly spent millions of dollars to resume diplomatic relations with Papua New Guinea in the proceeding years, but the efforts have been in vain. Taiwan allocated $30 million to an account in Singapore to secretly buy Papua New Guinea through intermediaries who took the money and ran (New York Times 2008). This failed effort and misuse of funds caused outrage in Taiwan, which forced its foreign minister and two other top officials to resign. Taiwan has constantly denied its involvement in dollar diplomacy. However, cases such as this one and other disclosed cases illustrate that the Taiwanese are implicated in the practice of buying recognitions. In 2014, former president of Guatemala Alfonso Portillo (2000–2014) was found guilty of money laundering in the United States. The source of the funds was "bribery payments from the Government of Taiwan" (US Attorney for the Southern District of New York 2014). Similarly, Francisco Flores, El Salvador's former president, admitted to a congressional panel that he "received cheques worth millions of U.S. dollars from Taiwan but denied the funds were for his personal use" (South China Morning Post 2014). Yet, regardless of the means and methods, the act of recognition or derecognition of states is the responsibility of states and, as such, retains their validity. The conduct of persons on behalf of the states is considered an act of the state under international law. The *Solomon Times* reported in 2011 that "Danny Philip had been unseated as Prime Minister and is being investigated for alleged misuse of funds provided by Taiwan." Soon after El Salvador switched from Taiwan to China, an investigation was launched into the use of funds donated by Taiwan for the presidential election campaign. It is alleged that some US$10 million donated by Taiwan was used for partisan campaigning (South China Morning Post 2018b, 2018c).

In its efforts to retain diplomatic relations, Taiwanese authorities have granted significant funds to the interlocutor state without questioning how they are used. Anthony Van Fossen (2007: 139) argues that "a major effect of the Taiwan-China conflict in the Pacific Islands has been to introduce large amounts of foreign money into domestic political activities, which are oriented away from grassroots concerns and the interests of ordinary citizens, whose voting rights are thereby depreciated. These foreign institutionalized interests may corrupt domestic political processes." In a similar vein, Joel Atkinson (2014: 409) points out that "Taiwan provides aid without stringent accountability conditions to countries in Africa, the Americas, and the South Pacific in order to maintain official diplomatic relations in the face of Chinese opposition." The strategy of legitimizing incumbent government and creating patronage networks in third countries in exchange for continued recognition risks antagonizing opposition leaders in those countries who, once they come to power, retaliate by shifting diplomatic recognition to the other contender state. In countries such as Gambia, Liberia, and Nicaragua Taiwan's support for corrupt and authoritarian leaders has backfired (Taylor 2002: 129–30). Yet there are also cases where third countries try to avoid the never-ending derecognition saga by committing to their chosen diplomatic allies regardless of who comes to power. There were fears that the country would switch back to China following the 2012 elections in Saint Lucia. However, the new government stated: "Saint Lucia cannot look as if it is just prepared to jump from one side to another, after every general election, just for more largesse. We cannot behave as if our sovereignty is for sale to the highest bidder" (Edmonds 2012).

While most domestic political dramas in derecognizing states tend to be about the recognition and derecognition of Taiwan and China, similar patterns are also present in other cases. The recognition of Kosovo's independence by the Maldives is an interesting example of how lobbying from the base state can undermine domestic political stability in third countries. In 2009, the Maldives recognized Kosovo, following intensive lobbying efforts by Kosovo and its two major international allies, the United States and UK. In the recognition letter, Maldives foreign minister Ahmed Shaheed stated that "after carefully reviewing the special circumstances relating to Kosovo, and mindful of the fact that a large number of countries have extended diplomatic recognition to the Republic of Kosovo, the Republic of Maldives, with immediate effect, recognizes the Republic of Kosovo as an independent and sovereign state," wishing "the Government and the people of the Republic of Kosovo peace, prosperity and happiness" (Republic of Maldives 2009). Serbia lobbied Maldives to reverse the recognition of Kosovo through unofficial diplomatic channels, using influential personalities and activists with direct connections to the government (Wikileaks 2019). It is recorded that at some point in 2009, a twenty-one-member delegation from Serbia visited the Maldives and lobbied opposition groups to cancel the recognition of Kosovo. As the flow of events shows, it seems that the most effective method to question the recognition of Kosovo was to infuse tension between the government and opposition in Maldives by speculating that the government had been bribed. Serbia used its close ties with a minor opposition party (Islamic Democratic Party), which accused Foreign Minister Ahmed Shaheed of receiving a US$2 million bribe from Behgjet Pacolli, who later served as president and foreign minister of Kosovo (Minivan News 2009a). This controversy ended with an investigation by police and a parliamentary committee that found no evidence of bribery. The police investigation concluded "there was no evidence of corruption and the diplomatic process was conducted according to international standards" (Minivan News 2009b). To boost the political legitimacy of Foreign Minister Shaheed, the US secretary of state, Hillary Clinton, sent a personal letter thanking him and the Maldives for recognizing Kosovo and praising them for greatly contributing "to efforts to promote a stable and prosperous future for Kosovo and the Western Balkans" (Musliu and Gashi 2009). The issue of Kosovo's recognition resurfaced again in the Maldives in 2019 when Serbian diplomats encouraged an opposition member to seek another investigation.

Besides encouraging local corruption and undemocratic practices, this dependency on foreign assistance normalizes the practice of state derecognition as a foreign policy instrument and part of state identity in the international arena. It also creates a shadow state that lacks democratic grounds and falls in line with agendas of foreign governments. The politics of derecognition tends to become a priority for small and postcolonial states that mutilate their foreign policy to represent the interests of their allies outside the UN. Small Pacific island countries often represent Taiwan's interests and policy agenda at the UN General Assembly annual session. They even try to infiltrate Taiwanese diplomats as their delegates at various international events. Thus, the dynamics and politics of state derecognition reduce the foreign policy autonomy of existing recognized states. For example, the Solomon Islands was criticized for losing its autonomy when it had to back China at the UN and other international bodies, while the rest of the world was criticizing the Chinese government for its widely reported inhumane treatment of Uighurs and for revoking the autonomy of Hong Kong and installing a police state in its place. Thus, while derecognition signals the foreign policy autonomy and agency of derecognizing states, it can also become a diplomatic curse that undermines domestic and international sovereignty.

The checkbook diplomacy implicated in the practices of state recognition and derecognition has caused damage to the genuine diplomatic efforts of other claimant states that have been unable to meet the expectation of securing recognition in exchange for financial bribery and economic aid. It has also created a diplomatic subculture among small states to trade diplomatic recognition without regard to the far-reaching impact on the norms and rights of people for self-determination. Compared to Taiwan, Kosovo has a weak economy to fund its diplomatic campaign for recognition. Most of the recognitions can be credited to Kosovo's proactive diplomacy and extensive support from powerful and prestigious states. However, Kosovo's weak economy and the lack of trade with many regions meant that recognition was granted on intangible prospects for future political and economic cooperation. Kosovo received recognition from these countries but failed to continue establishing diplomatic relations and deepening bilateral relations. Kosovo's lack of resources to deepen bilateral relations with many countries represented a constant threat that, with the growing economic incentives of Russia and Serbia, they could reverse Kosovo's independence. Serbian and Russian diplomats have consistently tried to use their political and economic leverages to prevent, delay, or reverse the decision to recognize Kosovo. Particularly since the conflict in Ukraine, Serbia and Russia have developed closer ties, and they have agreed to undermine Kosovo's sovereignty both domestically and internationally (MFA of Russia 2023).

Diplomatic recognition and friendship based on economic stimulus are highly unstable and risk affecting wider beneficiary communities once they discontinue their diplomatic ties. In 2007, Malawi decided to end forty years of diplomatic relations with Taiwan. This controversial move had a strong impact on domestic socioeconomic affairs and risked producing a local humanitarian crisis. Taiwan in retaliation for Malawi's disloyal switch canceled all bilateral cooperation projects. The effects of this move were felt deeply in the impoverished African country. Taiwanese contractors abandoned road construction projects and dismantled healthcare services and hospital operations (Atkinson 2014: 417). When Kiribati derecognized Taiwan in 2019, the American charity Pacific Islands Medical Aid cut medical assistance and closed its mission in the country. This charity considered Kiribati's siding with anti-democratic China harmful to Taiwan's freedom. The Kiribati government lamented the decision and labeled it interference with its sovereign decisions (ABC News 2019).

In parallel to aid traps, third countries implicated in the derecognition of other states may also be exposed to various vulnerabilities, financial debts, and insecurities. China's approach to ensuring that third countries will not be lured into recognizing Taiwan involves long-term economic and trade relations often labeled debt trap diplomacy. The debt trap refers to "the consequences for a government, or an individual, of borrowing at an interest rate which exceeds the rate of growth of its income, causing its current expenditure on items other than debt servicing to be increasingly reduced" (Shaomin and Jiang 2020: 70). China is widely criticized for taking "the opportunity to acquire strategic assets or rights and interests should these countries not be able to repay, in order to achieve its strategic goals" (Shaomin and Jiang 2020: 70). One of the critical luring aspects of Chinese diplomacy is to identify states that are strategic to its military and trade interests and offer them loans to build seaports or other infrastructural projects in exchange for switching allegiances. It pursues this strategy with existing allies such as Sri Lanka and those that were until recently Taiwan's partners, such as El Salvador. In 2018, Vanuatu came under pressure to allow China to establish a permanent military base in the country. Vanuatu was also the first country to support China's claim over the South Chiba Sea (Swarajya 2018). Around the time when the Solomon Islands government decided to switch from Taiwan to China, the Central Bank of Solomon Islands concluded that "the country will not be able to absorb any additional borrowing from China should it decide to switch" (Solomon Times 2019a). Soon after it was revealed that, in November 2019, the Solomon Islands government was in contact with Chinese investors, exploring concessional grants and loans as high as US$100 billion, seventy-seven times greater than country's GDP (ABC News 2020a). The letter of offer by the Chinese investors highlighted that the loan would be unrestricted and could be used for poverty reduction, economic development, and other social investment, would have to be repaid within twenty years. A US State Department official warned that "allies of Taiwan who switch recognition to Beijing could be imperiling their sovereignty, citing risks such as debt and Chinese influence in domestic policymaking" (Focus Taiwan 2009a).

Soon after the Solomon Islands switched from Taiwan to China, a Chinese company attempted to lease an entire island in the Solomons (Tugali) for seventy-five years and hold exclusive rights over the island. The local government of Tulagi signed a strategic cooperation agreement with the Chinese company only a day after the Solomon Islands established diplomatic relations with Beijing, without seeking permission from the central government (The Guardian 2019). For the local population this raised fears that the purpose of the lease was not just commercial but also military and strategic (Smith 2019). However, the Solomon Islands government considered the deal signed by one of its provinces to lease the entire island "unlawful" and demanded it be "terminated with immediate effect." US Secretary of Defense Mark Esper applauded the veto, calling it "an important decision to reinforce sovereignty, transparency, and the rule of law." "Many nations in the Pacific have discovered far too late that Chinese use of economic and military levers to expand their influence often is detrimental to them and their people," Esper said in a statement (The Guardian 2019).

In rare instances, the derecognition of other states can result in social unrest. Following the derecognition of Taiwan in September 2019, the leadership and residents of the province of Malaita expressed deep dissatisfaction with the switch and threatened to mobilize forces for independence from the Solomon Islands (South China Morning Post 2019b). The Malaita leader declared that "the process through which the government has [made] the decision has not been transparent and could be undemocratic" (Solomon Star 2019), arguing that China "is no ordinary country like many other countries of the world" and has "a global ambition to dominate the world." Malaitans expressed the fear that the Solomon Islands would lose its economic sovereignty through debt traps and loss of access to natural resources (Solomon Star 2019). The Malaita province is one of the most underdeveloped regions of the Solomon Islands, with secessionist tendencies dating back to independence in 1978. Taiwan's assistance to the province has been vital in coping with the chronic vulnerabilities and has compensated for the absence of central government investments. Following the region's opposition to the derecognition of Taiwan, ex-militants sent on behalf of the central government appeared in the province, allegedly "to intimidate the province into supporting the switch" (South China Morning Post 2019b). Tensions heightened when the central government opposed the province's acceptance of Covid-19 donations from Taiwan, a move that was seen as an act of defiance and a violation of central government laws. Chinese authorities protested the presence of pro-Taiwanese voices and symbols in the province, which raised concerns among the local community about interference in domestic affairs. Drawing on these dynamics and embedded grievances, the province's leaders have called for a self-determination referendum, seeking to make Malaita an independent state. The local community in Malaita also grew impatient with Chinese residents on the island, requesting their immediate evacuation and suspension of business activities (ABC News 2020b). In response, the Ministry of Provincial Government and Institutional Strengthening issued a statement clarifying that "the Provincial Government Act 1997 does not provide any power to Malaita Province Premier, Daniel Suidani, to undertake a referendum of any sort" (Solomon Islands Government 2020).

As a result of this internal political disagreement, in November 2021 around a thousand protesters set fire to the Chinese business district, the parliament building, banks, and several police stations in the capital city of Honiara. The leader of Malaita province, Daniel Suidani, said: "The protests happened as a result of the government not listening to the people or engaging with their concerns on a range of issues, including infrastructure projects and the China-Taiwan switch" (The Guardian 2021). Chinese officials in Beijing expressed "grave concern" and called on the government of the Solomon Islands "to take all necessary measures to protect the safety of Chinese citizens and organisations" (SBS News 2022). Subsequently, Australia, New Zealand, and PNG were invited to deploy a small peacekeeping force to the Solomon Islands. While the discontent between provincial communities and the central government relates to long-standing disputes about corruption, lack of public services, and development assistance to local communities, the diplomatic switch in 2019 became the critical contention that led to the social unrest. Despite calls for the prime minister's resignation, Manasseh Sogavare survived a vote of no confidence. He remained in office amid deep social and political divisions caused by the row over socioeconomic underdevelopment and foreign policy. He blamed foreign powers who opposed his 2019 decision to switch the Solomons' diplomatic allegiance from Taiwan to China for fomenting the disturbances. Prime Minister Sogavare added: "These very countries that are now influencing Malaita are the countries that don't want ties with the People's Republic of China and they are discouraging Solomon Islands to enter into diplomatic relations and to comply with international law and the United Nations resolution" (ABC News 2021). In response, opposition leader, Matthew Wales, while categorically rejecting allegation that he incited unrest, stated that "the people in this country feel that the democratic processes are not working for them, that their own government is the puppet of China" (ABC News 2021).

Countries implicated in the derecognition of other states have also been exposed to unintended security consequences. An illustrative example of the security effects of state derecognition is Macedonia. In the late 1990s, Macedonia decided to enhance economic ties with Taiwan. In retaliation, China vetoed the extension of the UN Preventive Deployment Force (UNPREDEP) in 1999 (Taylor 2002: 128). Two years later, Macedonia relapsed into civil war, which the UN peacekeepers could have prevented. China warned Macedonia of its "determination to sever diplomatic relations and reconsider support for the extension of the UNPREDEP's mandate, had Macedonia not immediately reversed its decision" (Tubilewicz 2004: 786). However, "Macedonian leadership played down the prospects of China's possible UN veto, hoping that China as a major power would not block the extension of the UN peacekeeping forces' mandate . . . in a retaliatory move against the Taiwan policy of a small and impoverished Balkan state" (Tubilewicz 2004: 787). China did not admit that its veto of UNPREDEP was related to Macedonia's alignment with Taiwan, insisting that there was no need to extend the mandate further because "the situation in the former Yugoslav Republic of Macedonia has apparently stabilized in the past few years, its relations with neighbouring countries have been improved, and peace and stability there have not been adversely affected by developments in that region" (UN Security Council 1999a: 6–7). Canada, which at that time was sitting on the UN Security Council, stated that

> arguments that conditions no longer warrant the presence of UNPRE-DEP simply cannot be sustained by an examination of the facts. We believe that China's decision, seemingly compelled by bilateral concerns unrelated to UNPREDEP, constitutes an unfortunate and inappropriate use of the veto. In this same light, we deeply regret that actions taken by the Government of the former Yugoslav Republic of Macedonia precipitated the bilateral dispute leading to the present situation. (UN Security Council 1999a: 7)

The eleven-hundred-member conflict prevention force was key to facilitating Macedonia's transition after independence and mitigating ethnic tensions. Soon after the UNPREDEP departed Macedonia, ethnic tensions erupted in the country, resulting in a short civil war between the Macedonian government and ethnic Albanians who demanded equal rights and an end to discrimination (Neofotistos 2012).

One of the main reasons why China has become among the top ten UN troop and policy contributors is pragmatic. China has used peacekeeping to influence host countries, such as Haiti's relations with Taiwan, and to protect its economic investments in conflict-affected countries, located mostly in Africa (Gowan 2020). As Erikson and Chen (2014: 85) point out, "Since 2004, the UN peacekeeping mission in Haiti has come to the brink of losing its mandate each time the renewal date approaches, because China seeks to use its troop contribution and UN Security Council veto as an instrument to pry Haiti away from Taiwan's grasp." Similarly, when Haiti recognized the SADR, Morocco withdrew its peacekeepers from this war-shattered country and refused to send peacekeepers again. In 2003, fears that China would veto the deployment of UN peacekeepers in the Solomon Islands, which had diplomatic relations with Taiwan at that time, forced regional actors to back the Australian-led Regional Assistance Mission to the Solomon Islands (Ponzio 2005: 186).

Thus, as illustrated in this section, the derecognition of states tends to have double effects on those countries implicated in selling, renting, or trading diplomatic recognitions. Parallel to the economic and geopolitical benefits, the act of derecognition risks producing a spectrum of political effects that tend to undermine the stability of derecognizing states, ranging from promotion of corruptive and undemocratic practices to resignation of political leaders, election manipulation, disruption of socioeconomic developments, and deepening of domestic insecurity, including violent unrests. As much as it can be used to overcome national vulnerabilities, derecognizing other states can backfire and come at cost that outweighs the benefits.

BOLSTERING BIG-POWER RIVALRY

The process and the act of derecognition pose challenges for the contender states and regional and global powers. It disturbs the equilibrium among regional and international power interests in strategic regions. Accordingly, state derecognition has become part of big-power rivalry by default. It is well established that big powers compete "over largely unresolved, distinctive goal incompatibilities," where "both sides want things that the other side denies them and they have not devised a way to compromise" (Colaresi, Rasler, and Thompson 2007: 4). Yet, as Thompson (1999: 14, 16) argues, "Rivalries can begin abruptly" and "can begin over a real or imagined conflict." As with state recognition or nonrecognition practices (Coggins 2014), global powers tend to support the derecognition of states in regions and situations that would preserve or expand their influence and status (Murray 2019). If it runs against their geopolitical interests, they oppose it. Thus, state derecognition mostly plays out as a field of normative contestation among great powers. As argued elsewhere, "Normative contestation entails disagreement among states over the meaning and application of international norms—standards of behaviour reflected in general practice—to specific situations" (Newman and Visoka 2023: 366). While normative contestation in itself might result in an actual military confrontation, it is nonetheless a warning of escalation of political conflict with broader security implications. The politics of derecognition risk being implicated in the growing tendencies among great powers to pursue their self-proclaimed right to dominate other regions and rivals through extralegal methods, in breach of the legal equality of states and the principle of noninterference in domestic affairs (Paris 2020). The derecognition of states can become a pretext to deepen the polarization and disagreement among dominant powers on rules and institutions governing diplomatic affairs as well as on matters concerning statehood, self-determination, and territorial integrity.

Across all cases examined in this book, there is evidence to support that the derecognition of claimant states has mobilized global powers and deep-

198 • *The Derecognition of States*

ened their rivalries and hostilities. For instance, the derecognition of Taiwan strengthens China's claims over this contested territory and helps Beijing develop overseas strategic sites for economic and military purposes. In this context, the United States is prone to oppose the derecognition of Taiwan, as such a move empowers Chinese strategic interests and weakens the United States' influence in different parts of the world. Senior US diplomats have expressed concerns over "China's actions to bully Taiwan through economic coercion, squeezing Taiwan's international space, and poaching diplomatic partners" (Stilwell 2019). Preserving Taiwan's international allies is seen by the United States as being in the service of maintaining the status quo and de facto independence of Taiwan, which is seen as crucial to obstruct "China's projection of power into the Pacific and Indian Oceans and safeguards the vital sea lanes of communication for Japan and South Korea" (Loo 2014: 168). In particular, the United States fears that if China takes over the island of Taiwan, it will threaten the security of the entire region, exposing the Philippines, undermining the United States' access to Vietnam, Thailand, and Malaysia via the South China Sea, and endangering Japan (Colby 2021). In turn, Beijing has viewed the United States' support for Taiwan as an effort to "weaken and divide China" (Blanchette and Hass 2023).

In Latin America, the derecognition of Taiwan and the subsequent expansion of Chinese influence in countries such as Panama represent a threat to the United States' geopolitical interests. Panama utilized the sovereignty conflict between China and Taiwan to trade recognition for financial inducement to expand the Panama Canal. The switching of recognition from Taiwan to China raised geopolitical concerns for the United States, which feared China's eventual control of the Canal and strategic sea trade. The United States perceived the derecognition of Taiwan by Panama, Haiti, and El Salvador as a Chinese attempt to encircle US strategic interests in the Western Hemisphere. It undermines the long-standing US goal to keep any adversary out of its surrounding regions. Many US lawmakers have raised concerns that China's campaign for the derecognition of Taiwan is disrupting the world order and creating the conditions for another war (Washington Examiner 2018). The United States feared that China would use these states to entrap them into loans and other economic investments and turn them into bases for Chinese military and trade interests. For example, in 2018, the United States worried that El Salvador's derecognition of Taiwan could give China access to one of its ports that could be used for military purposes. As a result, the White House (2018) issued a statement: "The El Salvadoran government's receptiveness to China's apparent interference in the domestic politics of a Western Hemisphere country is of grave concern to the United States, and will result in a re-evaluation of our relationship with El Salvador." El Salvador's derecognition of Taiwan allegedly came after Taiwanese authorities rejected its request for harbor development funding and for additional resources to the ruling party for its electoral campaign (South China Morning Post 2018b).

As the rivalries between China and the West have deepened, the derecognition of Taiwan has contributed to the increased tensions in the Pacific region, and has provoked strong reactions from the United States and Australia. Evidence shows that since the early 2000s, "There have been increasing signs of a change in US interest in the region, partially in response to China's growing influence" (Brady and Henderson 2010: 204). Countries such as the Solomon Islands and other small surrounding states are caught in the crossfire between Australia and China over their political, economic, and military supremacy in the Pacific region. As Transform Aqorau (2021: 323) argues, "The Pacific Islands are important from a traditional security perspective because they provide a buffer against a forward attack on Australia and New Zealand, as well as because Chinese engagement in the Pacific Islands region is increasingly viewed as a threat to historical Western dominance." However, Australia took a passive approach to the Solomon Islands, allowing it to make its own decision. A spokesperson from Australia's Foreign Ministry said Australia respected the sovereign right of the Solomons government to make its own decision and that the decision would not alter the bilateral relationship between Canberra and Honiara. "Australia does not take a position on other countries' choices about their diplomatic relationships," the spokesperson said (Radio New Zealand 2019). Yet soon after the Solomon Islands derecognized Taiwan and established diplomatic ties with China, Australia complained that the Solomons government did not treat its mining companies fairly.

For the United States, China's assertive pursuit of the derecognition of Taiwan in the Pacific region threatens to undermine the rules-based international order (Epoch Times 2019). A US congresswoman stated in 2018 that "China's behavior toward Taiwan threatens regional stability and global democratic values." (US House of Representatives 2018). Following the decisions by the Solomon Islands and Kiribati to derecognize Taiwan in 2019, the US ambassador to the region declared that the United States was "disappointed by Beijing's continued campaign to shrink Taiwan's international space and change the cross-strait status quo through coercion, in violation of Beijing's commitments to engage peacefully with Taiwan" (South China

Morning Post 2019c). Soon after, the US House of Representatives passed the Taiwan Allies International Protection and Enhancement Initiative (TAIPEI) act to "support Taiwan in strengthening its official diplomatic relationships as well as unofficial partnerships with countries in the Indo-Pacific region and around the world" (US Congress 2019b). In particular, it called on the US government to "consider, in certain cases as appropriate and in alignment with United States interests, reducing its economic, security, and diplomatic engagement with nations that take serious or significant actions to undermine Taiwan" (US Congress 2019b). In response, the Chinese MFA urged "the US to respect other countries' sovereign rights in independently deciding their internal and foreign affairs, abide by the one-China principle and the three China-US joint communiques and prudently and properly handle Taiwan-related issues to avoid severe harms to China-US relations and cross-strait peace and stability" (MFA of China 2019). In retaliation, the United States has not only intensified its diplomatic interactions with Taiwan, including high-level visits to Taipei, but also has encouraged other European states to enhance diplomatic and political contacts with Taiwan. In an unexpected move, the former secretary of state Mike Pompeo called for US recognition of Taiwan as "a free and sovereign country" (Reuters 2022). Later, the Council on Foreign Relations (2023: 2) predicted that "a conflict between the United States and the People's Republic of China . . . over Taiwan is becoming increasingly imaginable."

Ahead of the presidential elections in Taiwan in January 2024, U S Congressman Mario Díaz-Balart (2024) went as far as to argue that "The robust relationship between the United States. and Taiwan is key to our national security, benefits the global community and is critical to prosperity in the region." Soon after, Nauru severed its diplomatic relationship with Taiwan, a move which is considered as China's retaliation after the victory of pro-independence forces (DPP) in Taiwan. While acknowledging that Nauru's move "is a sovereign decision" but "nonetheless a disappointing one," the US Department of State explicitly warned that "The PRC often makes promises in exchange for diplomatic relations that ultimately remain unfulfilled" (US Department of State 2024). Following the victory of pro-independence forces (DPP) and the US's pledge to deepen unofficial relations with Taiwan, several regional states, including Russia, publicly reiterated China's sovereignty over Taiwan (One-China principle) and spoke against an independent Taiwan. The MFA of Russia (2024) noted, "Attempts by certain countries to use the elections in Taiwan to pressure Beijing and destabilise the situation in the strait and across the region are counterproductive and must be condemned by the international community." Similarly, The Government of Maldives issued a statement on 14 January 2024 stating that it "opposes external interference in China's internal affairs under any pretext and supports all efforts made by China to achieve national reunification." (Government of Maldives 2024). The MFA of Taiwan responded to Russia's statement noting that:

> Russia has willingly become an accomplice of the Chinese Communist Party regime, deliberately echoing China's fallacious "one China principle" claims following Taiwan's elections. Not only does this do nothing to contribute to stability across the Taiwan Strait, it also proves once again that the collusion of authoritarian China and Russia jeopardizes international peace and stability and the rules-based international order. (MFA of Taiwan 2024a)

Some in the United States see the derecognition of Taiwan as a positive signal to dissociate the United States from Taiwan's sovereignty claims over the entire territory of China. For instance, Elbridge Colby, former deputy assistant secretary of defense for strategy and force development, argued that "having nobody recognise the Government in Taiwan as the Republic of China would seem to strengthen the idea that Taiwan is either what Beijing prefers, which is a province or that it has independence" (Global Taiwan Institute 2022). So derecognition removes the fiction that the government of Taiwan represents the government of China. Concerning US interests in the derecognition of Taiwan, Colby argued that "everything that Beijing does is provocative and we should respond not symmetrically like in a diplomatic context but by using this as an excuse to strengthen Taiwan's defense. So, if they switch Honduras . . . we should use the political capital that Beijing that has caused . . . the controversy . . . to sell them more weapons" (Global Taiwan Institute 2022). In this regard, the derecognition of Taiwan has served US interest in increasing arms sales. As reported in the media, "The United States has approved a $100m support contract with Taiwan aimed at boosting the island's missile defence systems amid heightened tensions with China" (Al Jazeera 2022). While Taiwan has welcomed this arms sale, Chinese authorities have strongly condemned it and warned of retaliatory measures. In this sense, the escalation of tension between Taiwan and China tends to benefit the US military industrial complex, regardless of the long-term implications of such arms sales.

In other cases, such as Abkhazia and South Ossetia, great power contestation roles are reversed. The United States actively opposes the independence of these de facto states and considers them to be Russian satellite states. While for Abkhazia recognition by Russia is a security guarantee, for Georgia and the United States recognition is a means to justify Russia's interference in its neighbors' internal affairs. According to an Abkhaz diplomat: "Recognition of independence from the largest state in the world, a nuclear power, and a permanent member of the UN Security Council significantly increased the security of Abkhazia and created the conditions for economic development. It is Russia that acts as the guarantor of the independence of the Republic of Abkhazia and, in fact, is the only real ally of Sukhum in the international arena." For Abkhazia, the recognition from Russia "neutralizes" the lack of recognition by other states. While South Ossetia is more prone to reintegration with the Russia, Abkhazia has signaled its willingness to retain its independent statehood and achieve wide international recognition. However, the United States and European powers have openly opposed Russia's close ties with these two breakaway countries and have turned them into a field of geopolitical rivalry. In 2019, the US Senate passed a special act in support of the independence, sovereignty, and territorial integrity of Georgia. The act reaffirmed that it is "the policy of the United States to not recognize territorial changes effected by force, including the illegal invasions and occupations of Georgian regions of Abkhazia and Tskhinvali Region/South Ossetia by the Russian Federation" (US Congress 2019a). Thus, the United States is also actively involved in the derecognition of Abkhazia and South Ossetia to directly challenge Russia's influence in the Caucasus region and around the world. The Western opposition to Abkhazia's and South Ossetia's special ties with Russia has shaped the discourse of international mediators in the Georgian-Abkhaz negotiation process, which have mainly supported Georgia's position and rejected the Abkhaz desire for self-determination (International Alert 2011: 7). In instances such as this one, the derecognition process can indirectly leverage the intervention by patron states to annex or take control of territory. For example, derecognition of Abkhazia and South Ossetia represents a diplomatic failure for Russia, which might consider incorporating the two breakaway territories as the only option left. It does so through neo-functional techniques such as offering Russian passports, establishing permanent military pacts, and removing economic and political bounties.

In retaliation, since 2017 Russia has encouraged and supported Serbia's campaign for the derecognition of Kosovo, as such a move weakens US influence in the Balkans and signals its fading effect among third countries implicated in the derecognition of Kosovo. Russia has openly taken Serbia's side, arguing that any eventual settlement should be a solution acceptable to Belgrade and must be approved by the UN Security Council (UNMIK Media Observer 2019). While Russia wants to appear as a constructive power, it prefers the status quo and protracted and frozen conflicts to undermine US and EU interests in the Western Balkans. It mainly wants to slow down the integration of the region into NATO. Some believe Russia is not committed to resolving the recognition saga between Serbia and Kosovo. As Maxim Samorukov (2019: 3) observes, "Russia has very little to gain and, potentially, everything to lose if the Kosovo conflict is resolved. Full recognition of Kosovo would end Serbia's dependence on Russia's continued international backing. If no longer constrained by the Kosovo issue, Serbia could accelerate its push for EU accession and deepen cooperation with NATO." Russia has actively labeled Kosovo a failed Western project. Derecognition is not seen as Russia's its own making but is presented as testimony to Kosovo's failure to consolidate its statehood. As stated by the Russian ambassador to the Organization for Security and Co-operation in Europe, "It is becoming increasingly clear that the quasi-State entity in Kosovo has failed. It is no coincidence that the number of countries that have withdrawn their recognition of its so-called independence is growing" (Permanent Mission of the Russian Federation to the OSCE 2019). Thus, seen from this vantage, the derecognition of Kosovo represents a method for Russia to undermine the US and EU position in the Balkans by prolonging the status quo and making a role for itself in shaping regional affairs. By rejecting the recognition of Kosovo, Russia has tried to weaken the United States' position in the Balkans, derail and delay NATO's enlargement, and turn the region into a political battlefield to advance its geopolitical and geoeconomic interests. According to Dimitar Bechev (2019: 7), "From Moscow's perspective, projecting power in the Balkans is tantamount to giving the West a taste of its own medicine. If the Europeans and the Americans are meddling in its backyard . . . Russia is entitled to do the same in theirs" (see also Grant 2015).

In the case of Western Sahara, the contestation among great and rising powers is primarily normative and takes place through multilateral diplomacy. The major rivalry is between, on one side, France and the United States—which back Morocco's de facto control of Western Sahara—and, on the other, Algeria, South Africa, and, to a certain extent, Russia, which support the SADR's and the Polisario's independence aspirations. The great power rivalry and geopolitical interests over Western Sahara are not new, dating back to the Cold War, dominated by the logic of spheres of influence pushed by the United States and the Soviet Union (Mundy 2017). Over the years, the Franco-American consensus on Western Sahara, which has effectively served Morocco's agenda to oppose the self-determination referendum, has played an essential role in entrenching the conflict and deepening hostilities (Zunes and Mundy 2022). In particular, France considers Morocco a crucial partner in North Africa and a strategic ally to counterbalance Algeria and other adversaries in the region. Similarly, the United States uses Morocco as a regional ally and supplies military assistance to advance its security interests in the Arab world (Darbouche and Zoubir 2008: 100). Each rival tends to use normative and institutional structures to its advantage. For example, Morocco's international allies try to keep the question of Western Sahara on the UN Security Council agenda, whereas South Africa and other regional partners are in favor of greater engagement by the African Union. France, the United States, and the EU are perceived as having hidden behind the UN-led process for resolving the Western Sahara self-determination conflict, which in practice enables Morocco to prolong its presence with impunity and advance its economic and geopolitical interests in the Western Sahara while neutralizing international opposition to the occupation (Noutcheva 2020). In this instance, the United Nations Mission for the Referendum in Western Sahara (MINURSO) is utilized to delay the four-decade-long quest to settle the future of the territory while still creating the impression that necessary efforts are in place for conflict resolution (Darbouche and Zoubir 2008: 92). France has threatened to use its veto power to block any arrangement that would not be congruent with Morocco's interests.

On the other hand, Algeria considers Morocco its main regional rival and has been for decades committed to supporting the SADR and the Polisario (Boukhars and Roussellier 2014). Morocco and Algeria have a history of conflict dating back to the War of Sands in 1963. In addition to hosting forcefully displaced Sahrawi people in refugee camps, Algeria provides the SADR military, economic, and diplomatic support (Mundy 2017). Morocco has insisted that Algeria be a part of the peace talks to undermine the diplomatic subjectivity of the SADR, since it is the patron state and main supporter. Algeria has refused to be a direct party to UN-led talks (Zoubir 2020). In response to the renewed hostilities between Morocco and the Polisario, Algeria raised its security alert levels and warned against adverse parties trying to destabilize the region. The renewed rivalry between

Russia and the United States indicates that the Kremlin is siding with the SADR and Algeria. For instance, in 2018 it successfully lobbied to shorten the renewal of MINURSO's mandate from twelve to six months as a form of pressure on Morocco to engage in conflict resolution talks (Roussellier 2018). In 2021, the Russian MFA in Moscow hosted for bilateral talks senior SADR diplomats seeking support within the UN Security Council (Sahara Press Service 2021).

In sum, the evidence provided in this section illustrates that derecognition has a far-reaching international impact beyond the directly implicated countries. It tends to increase geopolitical rivalries and mobilize regional and global powers to either leverage or try to control the damages arising from the derecognition of claimant states. Especially when contender states are strategic allies of global powers, any shift in the balance of influence caused by derecognition tends to mobilize great power rivalries and antagonism, initially in the form of normative contestation through diplomatic channels and then through other more militant methods. In this sense, state derecognition should be seen as not only a niche anti-diplomatic practice, but a window onto the unraveling of international order and the emergence of a new conception of sovereignty, power, and domination in world politics.

CONCLUSION

State derecognition produces a wide range of intended and unintended effects, which reveal its impact on the contender states and the broader dynamics of international politics. The analysis in this chapter examined the spectrum of political, legal, and security effects that the process and the act of derecognition have on implicated countries. Notably, the derecognition of the claimant state by third countries does not end the claimant state's political and legal existence. The claimant states tend to continue their existence as sovereign entities and, in some instances, without much disruption. Since the claimant states tend to value the recognition by big and regional powers more, when small and peripheral countries derecognize them, they are less concerned. For instance, Abkhazia and South Ossetia appear to be satisfied and confident that recognition by Russia is sufficient for their state survival. Similarly, Kosovo, as long as it enjoys support from the United States and most of the European countries, is not too concerned by the derecognition of faraway countries. The SADR also appears to be confident as long as it has the support of Algeria. Taiwan, while all diplomatic allies are important, seems to base its hope and reliance on informal security and economic ties with the United States and many other regional and global powers.

Yet the derecognition of the claimant state can be destabilizing if it occurs in bulk. It reaches a critical mass, producing a chain of adverse effects that can undermine both international legal sovereignty and the domestic stability of the claimant state. Derecognition results in shrinking bilateral relations with third countries, which then can have a narrowing effect on how much the claimant state can do in foreign affairs. It can also undermine the claimant state's ability to participate or seek membership in international organizations, due to the inability to secure enough votes to access multilateral bodies. So state derecognition tends to produce legal and political effects only when it reaches a particular critical mass of states required for the claimant state to exercise its external sovereignty and realize foreign policy goals. In other words, if the claimant state continues to enjoy broad international support and has sufficient votes to be admitted to different international organizations gradually, then derecognition by a handful of states is of little significance. However, if the claimant state, for example, Kosovo, is on the border of securing the critical mass for membership in prominent international organizations, then any withdrawal of recognition translates into fewer chances for membership. In other instances, when an insignificant number of states has recognized the claimant state, such as Abkhazia and South Ossetia, derecognition does not make a huge difference, as they already lacking in recognitions.

Ultimately, derecognition deepens the claimant states' dependency on international allies, and thus, in order to survive, they are forced to become vassals to another regional or global power that serves as the patron state. Dependency on the patron state brings further troubles to claimant states, as they tend to be pressured by the rivals of the patron state. Thus, such political associations become claimant states' perennial savior and curse. Furthermore, to survive as states they need to delegate their foreign policy allegiances, which provide reasons to other states to further alienate and exclude them from the common goods of the international system. Moreover, the cumulative effect of derecognition can result in the reduction of the strategic ambition of the claimant state to achieve full statehood and thus cause it to revert to the self-suspension of sovereignty, avoid further international humiliation, and, in turn, confront the former base or contender state. Furthermore, the process of derecognition undermines the domestic legitimacy of the government in the claimant state.

The evidence presented in this chapter shows that derecognition does not contribute to conflict resolution between the contender states. The former base state uses the derecognition to remind the claimant state that the former base state and its international allies hold the power to grant them access to the broader world. Consequently, the process of state derecognition is perceived by the claimant state as a form of diplomatic aggression and part of the political conflict, which in turn undermines efforts for conflict resolution by reducing confidence-building in third-party mediated talks. Seen as a diplomatic aggression, derecognition becomes a bellicose act that pushes both sides to heighten the dispute rhetorically and militarily. In all the cases studied here, the process of derecognition has become a key issue in the chain of provocative events, which has resulted in the deepening of hostilities and escalation of the conflict.

The derecognition of states tends to produce adverse effects beyond the contender states. In third countries that are implicated in selling or trading recognition for their self-interest, state derecognition tends to come with a cost to their domestic stability and quality of governance. The practice of state derecognition tends to polarize political parties in most of the derecognizing countries due to the lucrative benefits they might get from doling out their diplomatic allegiances. Moreover, practices of state derecognition in a number of cases show that corruption is part of lobbying efforts. In most cases, when third countries derecognize the claimant state, the latter pull out all bilateral cooperation projects and funding, which can negatively impact the socioeconomic development of local communities in third countries. In short, state derecognition mainly produces domestic consequences for third countries. There are few international implications in the form of sanctions or counteractions by the claimant state and its allies. This derives from the fact that without proper normative and policy mechanisms regulating the recognition or derecognition of states, third countries are allowed to change their foreign policy positions without any major cost or consequence. So the effects are bilateral and internal, not so much multilateral. Small states—mostly postcolonial ones—tend to engage in the derecognition of states without significant ramifications to their international standing and status. They generate influence only by engaging in controversial foreign policy adventures, where they tend to grab the attention of regional and global powers and maximize the benefits (Sharman 2017). This notwithstanding, it can't be ruled that derecognizing states might be subject to various international sanctions or countermeasures due to their conflict-infusing diplomatic actions.

Finally, state derecognition also has a broader destabilizing effect on the international order. Practices of derecognition are perceived by global emerging powers as antagonistic actions that deepen rivalry and confrontation. Consequently, the involvement of big powers results in paralyzing the ambitions of the claimant state for full international recognition and, in turn, deepens the logic of spheres of influence, forcing all sides in the conflict to group themselves around broader geopolitical causes that overshadow the normative and context-specific merits of claimant states for recognized statehood. In this regard, state derecognition tends to complicate the prospects for resolving self-determination and statehood disputes and encourages radical and militant solutions. In sum, the complex and far-reaching adverse effects of state derecognition show that this anti-diplomatic practice disorders diplomatic relations, the dynamics of conflict resolution, the ethics of foreign policy and aid, and the politics of global rivalries.

6 ✦ Conclusion

Rethinking State Derecognition

    This book provided a comprehensive examination of state derecognition in world politics by examining how the withdrawal of recognition is understood in scholarly debates and how protagonist states practice it. Drawing on the cases of Taiwan, Western Sahara, Abkhazia, South Ossetia, and Kosovo, the book approached state derecognition as a complex process based on multiple justifications and prone to producing a wide variety of effects. The derecognition of states is not widely practiced in international affairs and thus remains largely unexplored. However, as the analyses in this book have demonstrated, the withdrawal of recognition offers a window into the reversal politics of unbecoming a sovereign state and how the arbitrary beginning and the end of diplomatic relations between states take place. Derecognition is a scattered anti-diplomatic practice favored by three categories of states: (a) the handful of claimant states without universal recognition and thus outside the UN system; (b) those challenged by contender or former base states that reject the nonconsensual independence of the claimant state; and (c) states enabled by a limited number of third countries that are implicated in or have a tradition of renting or selling their capacity to recognize other states in exchange for personal goods or national geopolitical interests. Despite its relevance, existing knowledge on state derecognition is scattered and prone to scholarly and policy dissensus.

    This concluding chapter provides a reappraisal of the key arguments and findings of the book, their significance, and the prospects for regulating state recognition in the international system. At its core, the results of this book challenge linear, dogmatic, and monolithic views on the irreversible nature of statehood and recognition, exposing the norms and practices that underpin the reservable politics of diplomatic recognition. The process of state derecognition goes through steps and tactics similar to those of the recognition process but in reverse order and with different actors at the epicenter. Conceiving recognition and derecognition as on a spectrum reveals more than one form and variation, which requires rethinking the monolithic conceptualization of both recognition and derecognition as concepts and practices. Regarding the rationales and justifications for derecognition, a slight difference exists between state recognition and derecognition. Justifications for recognition tend to be encoded and furnished within the acceptable and dominant legal and normative discourses, whereas those concerning derecognition tend to be more straightforward and are centered around self-interest rather than global norms and order.

Finally, and most important, regarding the implications of both state recognition and derecognition, the former produces more stability and conflict resolution—though not always—whereas the latter produces more instability and conflict escalation. So recognition tends to promote equality, mutuality, and friendship among nations, whereas derecognition is implicated in promoting exclusion and estrangement. The recognition of sovereign equality of new states has resulted in the expansion of the international system. Withdrawal of recognition of sovereign equality results in either stagnation or narrowing the international system. Overall, there are overlapping similarities but also significant differences that, most importantly, lead to different implications. State derecognition is, ultimately, an anti-diplomatic practice arising in the absence of a consensual institutional regime governing the recognition of states. As long as derecognition remains at the discretion of individual states, we are likely to see situations where states use and abuse their status as members of the club of sovereign countries to exclude, and thus withdraw recognition from, other aspirant states. This creates room for using the recognition of other states as an instrument not guided by rules and principles but by self-interest and arbitrary considerations.

This chapter is organized as follows. The first section offers a summary of core findings on the meaning, process, justification, and effects of state derecognition. The second section provides a reflective and provocative discussion of different options and constraints for regulating state derecognition in the international system.

STATE DERECOGNITION: A REAPPRAISAL

The derecognition of states is a rare but significant anti-diplomatic practice. Derecognition has emerged as a diplomatic tool former base states use to isolate and regain control over claimant states, which is an early sign of military aggression, cognitive and cyber warfare, and socioeconomic coercion. It is an important indicator of an impending diplomatic war, with the potential to shatter a fragile peace and return states to situations of violent conflict. Moreover, the motives and politics behind derecognition by third countries are questionable. By renting or trading their right to recognize or derecognize other states for self-interest, third countries cause more harm than good to international order. Overall, the practice of state derecognition entraps all protagonists in a complex entanglement of dependent relations. Contrary to the official narratives, the process and act of derecognition do not contribute to conflict resolution between the former base state and the claimant state. It only deepens hostilities, distrust, and counter-peace (Richmond, Pogodda, and Visoka 2023). Among third states implicated in selling, renting, or transacting recognition and derecognition for self-interest, evidence shows the practice tends to destabilize political and economic effects. For other protagonist states encouraging state derecognition, the outcome tends to be more great power rivalry and regional hostility.

State Derecognition as an Ambiguous Concept

The first central theme discussed in this book was the meaning of state derecognition in theory and practice. The analysis showed state derecognition to be an essentially ambiguous concept, the interpretation and application of which is dubious. It has multiple meanings subject to various scholarly and policy interpretations. Although derecognition may seem to be a monolithic diplomatic practice or analytical concept, it is far more complicated. The concept of state derecognition captures a spectrum of different forms, semantics, and diplomatic actions undertaken by protagonist states to question, review, and reverse the recognition of claimant states. However, it is worth noting that this spectrum of meanings and variants of state derecognition is partially dictated by the limited diplomatic discourses describing the upgrading and downgrading of interstate relations while being partly determined by the diversity of contemporary cases under examination.

First, derecognition is often invoked interchangeably with concepts such as "withdrawal," "reversal," "rescinding," and "suspending" the previous recognition decision. When third countries invoke these concepts, they indicate they have moved backward to the previous status of nonrecognition. In this instance, formal and express derecognition can be considered both as discontinuing bilateral diplomatic relations and as a reversal of the original stance of nonrecognition. In this instance, derecognition essentially means reversing one or two steps back. One-step-back derecognition tends to involve severance and freezing of diplomatic relations where the claimant state continues to exist for the derecognizing states despite being diplomatically unrelated. In this instance, derecognition can be interpreted as downgrading of bilateral relations without formally taking a stance on the political and legal status of the claimant state. In other words, derecognition may entail recognition without engagement. It signifies moving from being diplomatic friends to being acquaintances or strangers. In this instance, while derecognition can best be described as a diplomatic practice or instrument consisting of multiple variants with distinct implications for all contender states, it doesn't question the existence of the claimant state. In short, derecognition is declarative, as the derecognizing state declares that it is reviewing and changing its diplomatic relations with the claimant state. This also resonates with the view of the scholarly community that considers recognition irreversible. Two-step-back derecognition entails the full recognition of the claimant state, which thus becomes nonexistent legally and diplomatically for the derecognizing state and becomes part of the former base state or disputant state. In this variant, derecognition would mean affirmative nonrecognition and implies dismantling of the claimant state's statehood attributes and international subjectivity. In short, derecognition would entail recognition afresh or transferring back to the former base state the sovereignty over the territory controlled by the claimant state. Here, derecognition is re-recognition of the former base state, and this understanding of derecognition tends to resonate with the constitutive theory of derecognition, which perceives the withdrawal of recognition as the unmaking of the attributes of independent statehood, namely, unraveling and reversing sovereign statehood and disregarding the legal and political existence of the claimant state.

These two meanings of derecognition correspond with the interpretation that all protagonist states give to the practice. Claimant states tend to prefer the first semantical variant of derecognition. Since derecognition—in any variant—is considered an assault on the sovereignty of the claimant states, they tend to handle such encounters with caution. When claimant states take note of the occurrence of derecognition, they consider such acts to be unilateral discontinuance of bilateral ties by third countries that do not influence their sovereign statehood. In frozen recognition without active diplomatic engagement, claimant states tend to avoid public friction and try to handle such encounters through secret diplomacy. On the other hand, former base states tend to treat the act and process of derecognition as an acknowledgment that the claimant state isn't a sovereign state, and that the sovereign entitlement has been returned to them. In other words, they treat derecognition as the gradual extinction of the claimant state and restoration of their territorial integrity. Even when derecognition takes the shape of suspension or freezing of bilateral relations, the former base states tend to consider such instances to be favorable and victorious moves that expand the international contestation of the claimant state. By withdrawing the recognition of the claimant state, the former base state satisfies some of its existential desires and hopes for regaining control over the lost territory. It represents a symbolic victory and recognition of its claim over the contested state. While such a recognition of symbolic sovereignty might not translate into physical reappropriation of the contested territory, it satisfies domestic political audiences in the short run. The act of derecognition can also enhance the bargaining power of the former base state in a conflict settlement process. Pragmatically, it can serve the domestic purpose of legitimizing the incumbent government. More broadly, instances of derecognition signal that counter-secession and counter-recognition diplomacy work and can restore damages following unilateral separation by the claimant state.

The meaning and significance that third countries, namely the derecognizing states, accord to derecognition, including the arguments they invoke, are related to the rewards they receive or the potential costs they incur. Derecognition is thus a transactional and measured response. Ultimately, derecognition helps third states actualize their sovereignty at the international level and helps generate external attention, aid, and benefits through trading, renting, and selling recognition to contender states. In their defense, by withdrawing the recognition of the claimant state, third countries reinforce their external sovereignty, namely the ability to determine their foreign affairs freely and according to their discretion, including which states they recognize as sovereign and independent. They enact the sovereign power to recognize others without much consideration for the factual situation and the negative consequences for the claimant state and the broader international system. As discussed in this book, derecognition is an effective instrument of prudent diplomacy to compensate for the lack of economic self-sufficiency in many postcolonial and impoverished states.

By suspending, freezing, or formally withdrawing their recognition, third countries commit an act of symbolic violence against the claimant state. The symbolic violence of derecognition lies in the third countries' ability to exert influence on and have advantages over the claimant states because of their status as recognized states with the discretionary power to recognize other states. When the capacity to recognize or derecognize other states is weaponized for self-interest and in a manner that causes harm to others, it becomes symbolically violent by preventing claimant states from accessing the club of sovereign nations with equal rights, opportunities, and privileges.

Thus, without a clear definition and policy consensus, the derecognition of states is both subject to scholarly disagreements and to abuse by protagonist states. Derecognition is what states make of it. The meaning and invocation of state derecognition largely depends on who the protagonists are and for what purpose they use it. For the claimant states, derecognition is a clear act of diplomatic aggression invoked by the former base state and third countries. It undermines their independent statehood, deepens interstate hostilities, and weakens conflict resolution efforts. For the former base state, derecognition is invoked as a diplomatic and nonviolent instrument to isolate the claimant state and thus derail the consolidation of its independent statehood. It is also an instrument for domestic political gains to compensate and recover from the humiliation suffered over the original loss of control over the territory of the claimant state. For former base states, derecognition is the pursuit of war by other (diplomatic) means. For third countries, mostly postcolonial and underdeveloped, derecognition is essentially a transactional tool in their limited foreign policy toolbox. For them, derecognition is not about upholding international norms, rules, and customs on statehood or contributing to international peace, security, and order. It is primarily driven by self-interest and a quest to fulfill immediate economic and security needs. The many meanings of state derecognition have far-reaching implications and harmful consequences for the stability and quality of diplomatic relations among all implicated states. Derecognition does, however, expose the existence of a parallel international diplomatic subsystem between countries that are members of the UN and other international organizations and countries that are excluded from and are struggling to enter the club of sovereign and recognized states.

State Derecognition as a Two-Way Process

Understanding of the politics and process behind the derecognition of states has been limited to date. Thus, one of the main purposes of this book has been the investigation of the process of state derecognition in practice, namely how the recognition is understood and perceived by protagonist states, who the key actors are, and what the main tactics and strategies are behind the derecognition of states. Far from being monolithic, the book showed that state derecognition in practice is a prudent two-way process consisting of multiple context-specific tactics and strategies that protagonist states deploy to reconsider, downgrade, or end their diplomatic relations with the claimant state. Although state derecognition is a multistage process and prone to failure, stagnation, or backsliding at each phase, in general the full reiterative process undergoes four distinct phases: (1) contesting the independence of the claimant state; (2) reconsidering the recognition of the claimant state; (3) freezing or suspending recognition; and (4) formally withdrawing recognition. Each phase of derecognition produces different outcomes and variants, ranging from de facto suspension and freezing of bilateral relations to formally withdrawing recognition and ending diplomatic relations.

These four phases, with the potential to also become variants of derecognition, have striking similarities to recognition efforts but in reverse order (Visoka 2018). In the first instance, third countries, unless directly involved in mediating the creation of the aspirant state, tend to have a default position of nonrecognition, which can be negative or positive. Negative nonrecognition entails proactive opposition to the recognition of the claimant state, whereas positive nonrecognition entails indifference or absence in terms of diplomatic activities or commentary regarding the independence of the claimant state. Usually, through diplomatic lobbying and persuasion, third countries tend to engage with the claimant state and offer de facto recognition through institutional cooperation or affirmative support within multilateral bodies. Finally, the recognition process is formalized and legalized when the third country grants formal and explicit recognition to the claimant state and proceeds to establish diplomatic relations.

In most instances, the process of derecognition is initiated by the former base state and takes place in parallel to the struggle of the claimant state to consolidate its independent statehood. Notably, the origins of state derecognition can be found on the path to the proclamation of independence itself. When the new state is created without the consent of the former base state and lacks universal recognition, its sovereignty and international standing remain contested. Recent practices, however, such as Russian Duma initiative to withdraw the recognition of Lithuania in 2022, show that even universally recognized and UN member states can be subject to potential derecognition by other states. The first step in the derecognition process is the former base state's continuous campaign to undermine the claimant state's domestic and international standing to weaken its capacity to act as a sovereign state at home and abroad. In this regard, by pushing for derecognition of the claimant state, the former base state ensures that countries that have not recognized the claimant state do not change their position. Thus, the derecognition process appears to have the effect of preventing or slowing down the recognition of the claimant state, especially among those that have signaled implicit recognition.

The former base state actively uses diplomatic, economic, and military instruments to expand international support and sympathy for its foreign policy of counter-secession and struggle to preserve claims of territorial integrity. However, contesting the sovereignty of the claimant state alone is insufficient on the international stage. Undermining the effective exercise of authority on the ground is crucial for keeping the territorial claims open over the claimant state. Domestic contestation entails deploying hybrid methods aimed at damaging the claimant state's political institutions, economy, and social fabric and portraying it as an illegal and illegitimate entity. Such mixed methods can also entail weaponizing kin minorities, prosecuting independence leaders, and not recognizing state symbols, identity, and jurisdiction. Keeping the territorial claims open helps the former base state constitute its foreign policy identity as a victim of secession and can thus generate global solidarity. It also affirms its claims by reconsidering the recognition of the claimant state. Thus, derecognition is a troublesome practice that intends to deepen hostilities and avoid accepting independence and normalization of relations.

The second phase in the state derecognition process consists of persuading third countries to reconsider their position on the claimant state, which could range from signaling the downgrading of diplomatic relations to taking proactive measures to freeze or suspend the previous decision for recognition. An initial sign of derecognition is when third countries issue antagonistic statements about the claimant state and flirt diplomatically with the former base state. Reconsidering the recognition of the claimant state most often comes in response to a lobbying campaign by the former host state, which includes a range of incentives from economic and development assistance, deeper bilateral military and security cooperation, and defense of mutual interests within multilateral organizations. Despite such incentives, this phase in the derecognition process can be lengthy, costly, and unpredictable. It can take many years of political and economic investment and the involvement of major powers to persuade third countries to rethink their decision and consider derecognition of another state.

As the discussion in the book has shown, this phase of state derecognition reveals that in some instances, the reconsideration of recognition is a by-product of weak bilateral ties between the claimant and the derecognizing state, while in other cases it may be determined by a former base state's diplomatic campaign. Countries such as Kosovo have long taken recognition by many global south countries for granted and have thus failed to nurture and cultivate bilateral relations. While this behavior was mostly driven by limited diplomatic resources and an inward-looking understanding of recognition, Serbia exploited this vulnerability at a critical point when Kosovo was undergoing domestic political instability (due to early elections and delays in government formation) to launch a derecognition campaign targeting third countries that had recognized Kosovo but did not cultivate bilateral ties. This shows that states' standing is not entirely determined by their self-perceived or self-recognized right to sovereign statehood, nor by their words, but by what they do to enact and perform their statehood. Diplomatic activity rather than passive claims over a territory often determine aspirant states' success and international standing. Yet this is not always the case. Taiwan, for instance, is proactive and resourceful in its diplomacy, with a vast informal diplomatic network. It dedicates almost all its foreign policy resources to preserving diplomatic allies. However, this is overridden by China's assertive diplomacy and economic and geopolitical incentives that convince third countries to stop recognition. Thus, the dynamics of derecognition are primarily determined by the power differential among the protagonist states. The case of Western Sahara is somewhere in between. Relying primarily on historical and ideological ties with several governments in Africa and Latin America, the SADR failed to cultivate active diplomatic ties with third countries due to limited diplomatic resources and an actual territorial base for the Polisario-run government. Morocco utilized this failure by launching a proactive diplomatic campaign, relying upon extensive economic incentives and alliance with Western powers, successfully persuading other countries to reconsider their position on Western Sahara.

On balance, the analysis in the book showed that global south and postcolonial states are more prone to reconsidering the recognition of other states, highlighting the indeterminacy of their foreign policy principles and practices and their willingness to trade their capacity to recognize in exchange for political and material goods. Third countries implicated in the derecognition of claimant states utilize their status as recognized states to benefit from conferring or withdrawing recognition to other states in exchange for economic assistance. As Nanen Prasad (2009: 53) bluntly puts it, "In this era of increased globalisation many small islands states sell their sovereignty to other countries in order to finance their budget or to get foreign aid." Such a quest for national development often comes at the expense of the claimant states' much-needed international recognition to secure their collective survival. Paradoxically, most derecognizing states are postcolonial states. Historically, Western colonial powers have amplified and utilized diplomatic recognition to exert control and determine who has the chance to become a sovereign state. By default, postcolonial states, through the acts of derecognition, now reproduce colonialist practices by undermining the claimant states' right to recognition and independent statehood.

The third phase of the state derecognition process entails instances when the lobbying campaign does not result in full and formal derecognition of the claimant state, but can result in the freezing of recognition and downgrading of bilateral relations. In contrast to the conventional, formulaic, and binary conception of diplomatic relations centered on the notion that states are either recognized or not recognized, or that states have diplomatic relations or not, this phase of state derecognition reveals the variety of relations that countries can form. The discursive invocations evident during the third phase highlight that third states have found creative ways to refer to the sensitive issue of state derecognition. For example, concepts such as freezing the recognition and taking a neutral stance or discontinuing and suspending diplomatic relations with the claimant state have become new, ambivalent methods of diplomatic disengagement without formally withdrawing the recognition of the claimant state. The practice of "recognition without engagement" mirrors in reverse order the practice of "engagement without recognition," both seen as optimal forms of developing relationships with the claimant state without formally establishing diplomatic ties or recognizing its sovereign statehood. Nonetheless, this diplomatic ambivalence leaves room to question whether derecognition has happened and creates uncertainties in the diplomatic relations between concerned states. Such ambivalent forms of derecognition often ensure that third countries continue to benefit from and exploit all concerned parties while avoiding potential accusations of causing diplomatic incidents and exposure to retaliatory measures from the claimant state and its global allies. The variant of frozen recognition can be seen as a balancing act governed by the principle of proportionality, namely the concern that full withdrawal of recognition of claimant state would cause harm to the derecognizing state, including adverse effects for the implicated states. Thus, there is a logic of proportionality in instances where countries have irregular diplomatic ties but refuse to end them. The diplomatic theology behind such rationales highlights the influence of entangled relations among states and the constraints such relations have on foreign policy conduct.

The fourth and final phase in the state derecognition process is the formal and explicit withdrawal of recognition of the claimant state. As the analysis in this book showed, following the guidance from the former base state, third countries tend to explicitly highlight in diplomatic notes that they have withdrawn recognition of the claimant state as a sovereign and independent state. In turn, they recognize the sovereignty and authority of the former base state over the contested territory, although the former base state cannot exercise such control on the ground. However, as discussed in this book, the ambiguity surrounding the authority and justification for state recognition among political leaders in derecognizing states allows them significant discretion to use and abuse the recognition of other states to suit their narrow self-interest with disregard for long-term national interests and status of the claimant state. It is worth noting that despite individual cases of derecognition, claimant states do not lose their independent statehood. The "absence of full membership of the international system of sovereign states does not destine de facto states to pariah status" (Caspersen 2015: 399). Unless it is collective derecognition that can severely impact a country's existence, these states continue to endure and benefit from their rights and obligations under international law. As Martin Riegl and Bohumil Doboš (2017: 234) stipulate, emerging "states may indeed establish their own complex political institutions mirroring their internal and external context." Taiwan is living testimony to the effects of derecognition. Regardless of how extensive it has been, the derecognition of Taiwan has not ended the country's international legal personality. Similarly, derecognition of Kosovo by two countries in 2017 and 2018 has not impacted its international standing. It has had the reverse effect of mobilizing Kosovo's and other partner states' diplomatic efforts to increase recognitions. In existentialist terms, state derecognition doesn't necessarily lead to state extinction. It may cause the state an injury, but not death. It is discontinuance of bilateral relations and reversion to the status of nonrecognition of one another's international legal sovereignty. In short, it is estrangement, not extinction.

Moreover, contemporary state practice shows that derecognition is a reversal too. In a significant number, derecognizing states have reinstated their previous decision for recognition. In other words, it is not only recognition that is reversible; derecognition is also reversible. As shown in the book, the re-recognition of Taiwan, Kosovo, or Western Sahara has taken place several times, largely because of three interlinked factors: a counter-derecognition campaign, a change of government in derecognizing states, and pressure from regional and global allies. The determinants of reversing derecognition are similar to those that explain the success of the initial recognition campaign. That combines a persuasive diplomatic narrative and a proactive performative diplomacy entangled with great powers, events, and developments (Visoka 2018).

It is common knowledge that countries with diplomatic presence in each other's capital are more likely to have more intense and active diplomatic relations. It can be assumed that they are less likely to derecognize one another unless there is a major diplomatic incident or breakage of diplomatic relations. The analysis in this book showed that in the case of Taiwan, almost all derecognizing states had diplomatic representation in Taipei, which did not stop them from switching recognition. In the case of Western Sahara, since the SADR doesn't have a physical state presence in the territory and mainly operates as a government-in-exile, countries that withdraw recognition did not have diplomatic representation in the Western Sahara, but in most of the cases were hosting diplomatic missions of SADR. Most countries that allegedly withdrew the recognition of Kosovo did not have diplomatic representation in each other's countries. Similarly, countries that withdrew Abkhazia's recognition had no diplomatic presence in Sokhumi. So, except Taiwan—a unique case in that is has to deal with a former base state that is a global power—it seems that claimant states that do not have diplomatic representation in third countries (derecognizing states) are more likely to be exposed to derecognition.

Tracing the derecognition process provides overwhelming evidence that this controversial diplomatic practice exists. It takes different shapes depending on the case and is prone to have far-reaching implications. The process of state derecognition shows not only that the act of recognition is reversible and subject to a reconsideration, but also that it follows the same steps, in reverse order, pursued by the claimant state and its allies in their quest for international recognition. Moreover, the process of state derecognition has several parallels to the process of severance or downgrading of bilateral relations among universally recognized states. It tends to be accompanied by suspending formal and diplomatic contacts or withdrawing bilateral cooperation projects. However, because the claimant state is in such a vulnerable position internationally, the derecognition process takes on a different connotation. For countries that have partial recognition, remained outside the UN system, and have open territorial disputes with other states, derecognition is an existential threat to their independent statehood and international standing. It is a reminder of the fragility of diplomatic relations and the possibility of interference by the former base state and its allies in persuading third countries to revisit and withdraw the previous decision of recognition. If recognition is reversible, as evidenced in contemporary diplomatic practices, then the next question is what normative, legal, political, and economic rationales drive the process.

State Derecognition through Discorded Justifications

There are currently two widely accepted truisms regarding the recognition of states in world politics. First, almost all states have inconsistent policies and practices regarding the recognition or derecognition of states. Second, states don't have a duty to recognize or derecognize other states. It is a discretionary and context-specific act, guided by different norms, principles, and justifications and stimulated by diplomatic incentives that protagonist states provide. One would expect the overwhelming rationale that drives the derecognition of states to be the disappearance of original conditions upon which the recognition was first granted. If the claimant state, for example, loses its core attributes of statehood or has merged with another state, then one would expect other countries to withdraw their recognition as unnecessary. We know from history that some countries under foreign occupation with a government-in-exile, such as the Baltic states, continue to claim legitimacy as states and enjoy external recognition. They are not subject to derecognition because they eventually restore their independent statehood. However, if we examine most cases of state derecognition in the last three decades, a significant mismatch appears between the original conditions for recognition, which in most cases have not changed, and the justifications invoked for reconsidering, suspending, freezing, or fully withdrawing the recognition of the claimant state. Thus, the derecognition of states represents an unfriendly act toward emerging states. It is used more like a foreign policy instrument for advancing self-interest than as one to uphold the norms and necessary conditions for independent statehood in contemporary world politics. In all the cases examined in this book, the conditions attached to derecognition are not exclusively normative, political, or legal, but primarily economic and geopolitical, such as the promise of financial and capital investment, trade preferences, and other humanitarian and technical assistance, as well as military aid. These inconsistencies notwithstanding, the arguments for derecognition are not much different from those invoked by states when initially recognizing new states. Often decisions for recognizing new states are presented in normative and legal language. Between the lines, however, they are driven by self-interest and other geopolitical considerations (Visoka, Doyle, and Newman 2020).

By the same logic, the book found that the justification for derecognition of states is guided by prudential ethics and arguments that aim to enhance the interest of the former base state and the derecognizing state at the expense of the claimant state. This means that legal, normative, and political arguments that third countries invoke to justify the derecognition of the claimant state are situational, one-sided, and intertextually linked to those propagated by the former base state. This makes state derecognition a diplomatic hypocrisy. The book demonstrated that a two-level game is frequently at work, in which the derecognizing states defend their choices using interchangeably inward- and outward-looking argumentations. When the domestic cost of state derecognition is significant, rulers of derecognizing states tend to invoke economic and geopolitical arguments as their rationales for state derecognition. Such rationales are also linked to the incentives they receive from the former base state in exchange for the derecognition of the claimant state. When derecognition is likely to have an international cost for the derecognizing state, we are more likely to see arguments related to upholding international law and norms on statehood, including peaceful conflict resolution of disputes. Despite instrumental and pragmatic justification of derecognition—often furbished with normative and legal justification—acts of derecognition tend to correspond with the international position of the former base state. The greater the international recognition of the claimant state and the weaker the international standing of the former base state, the stronger and more elaborate the justification for derecognition. And vice versa, the stronger the international standing and the claims of the former base state, the weaker the argumentation and less disguised the rationales for derecognition.

The reasons behind the derecognition of states only reveal the discursive hypocrisies that undermine the value of both recognition and derecognition as externally imposed and internally desired institutions in international relations. One could argue that the derecognition of states that fulfill statehood criteria and deserve self-determination for historical reasons also represents a severe assault on international legal principles, norms, and practices concerning the birth of new states. At a practical level, the derecognition of states driven by self-interest and by a marriage of convenience with former base states seriously undermines the international credibility of derecognizing states at the forefront of this controversial anti-diplomatic practice. Checkbook diplomacy and rental recognition are not sustainable practices. They turn the significant norm of international recognition into a tradable diplomatic commodity that can be shifted depending on self-interest, governmental change, or the highest bidder. As already mentioned, Chen (1951: 259–60) warned decades ago that there is "no greater threat to international legal order than the unrestricted notion of the revocability of recognition." Similarly, Lauterpacht (1947: 349) maintains that "the very idea that the legal personality of a State or the representative capacity of its government should be dependent on the continued goodwill of other States is deemed to be derogatory to the independence and the dignity of the State and inimical to the stability of international relations." Derecognition has also become a tradable asset for small and underdeveloped states that sell recognition to the highest bidder, be that the parent state and a great power ally or the emerging state and its great power ally.

The act of derecognition for domestic personal, political, or economic interests while blatantly disregarding the norms, values, and principles governing statehood in international politics may constitute an act of international delinquency, according to this line of reasoning (Lauterpacht 1944: 391). In other words, insofar as the state withdrawing recognition restricts other states' rights and obligations under international law, failing to uphold international law and causing international anarchy and conflict, derecognition of states resembles delinquent acts in international law. States that frequently rent diplomatic recognition as a result are pariah states and a source of unrest in global society. Derecognition is anti-diplomacy because it widens and deepens the gulf between societies. By putting personal interests ahead of the shared interests of peace, justice, and development, it fosters global disorder. Furthermore, it violates the conventions of proper diplomatic conduct by taking advantage of weaknesses, promoting unfair terms of relations, and disregarding the institutions, norms, and laws that govern diplomatic relations internationally. By questioning the effectiveness of international institutions, of which diplomacy itself is a particularly important one, pariah diplomacy "undermines international order" (Banai 2016: 657). Abuse of state derecognition runs the risk of transforming recognition from an important aspect of external certification and acceptance of new states into a politically and economically driven tool of states' foreign policy. In conclusion, it is abundantly clear that derecognition of states is based on unjustified legal and normative grounds and entails unnecessary interference and intervention in the internal affairs of the claimant state.

The Multiple Effects of State Derecognition

The derecognition of states produces multiple effects, which are often unintentional, unplanned, and detrimental. State derecognition's impact span political, economic, and security realms and affect not only the claimant state but also other protagonist states. Since the derecognition of states performs different functions for all implicated states, it tends to also produce different outcomes and effects. A narrow reading of its effects shows that the act of derecognition does not cause the factual and political existence of a claimant state to change or vanish, nor does it remove the state's international subjectivity. As in most cases the reasons for derecognition of claimant states contradict the original reasons for recognition, and if those original conditions for recognition are still in place, the act of derecognition is nothing but a declaration of the intent to discontinue relations between the claimant state and derecognizing state that does not threaten the existence of the claimant state. In other words, the claimant state can exist and perform almost all the key functions of independent statehood regardless of shrinking diplomatic relations. With the act of derecognition, the derecognizing state declares it is no longer ready to deal on a state-to-state basis with the claimant state, continue diplomatic relations, or exchange support in multilateral organizations. In ordinary circumstances, state recognition results in mutual respect and reciprocity. Derecognition involves a break in these fundamental principles of state relations. The sum of all derecognition instances results in the expansion of the estrangement between states—a contemporary prototype of anti-diplomacy. Thus, state derecognition can be conceived of as a political act that does not result in the extinction of the claimant state despite shifting recognition to another competing authority. Derecognition may result in the vanishing of the claimant state's legal existence only in relation to this particular (derecognizing) state. Its legal existence may continue in relation to other states that still recognize the claimant state as an independent and sovereign state. In this regard, state derecognition undermines the ability of the claimant state to enter diplomatic relations with other states, especially those that withdraw the recognition, thus diminishing its independence and capacity to enter into relations with other states, as prescribed in the Montevideo Convention (Lowe 2007: 157).

However, this narrow and bilateral effect of derecognition is only half the story. The broader negative impact of derecognition is its crippling of the claimant's statehood. Derecognition can create political conditions that inhibit the claimant state from exercising some of the core functions of sovereign statehood, especially in deterring the former base state from domestic interference and securing access to multilateral organizations. In this regard, like the process of recognition, which in specific instances has constitutive functions (Vidmar 2012: 362), derecognition can also play a role in ruining the statehood of the claimant state. Therefore, the derecognition of states is constitutive because it withdraws the claimant state's agency in international affairs. This takes the shape of disaffirming state identity, shrinking diplomatic allies, and narrowing access to multilateral organizations for the aspirant state. Derecognition can seriously affect a state's identity, self-esteem, and the public's perception of its status, even though it doesn't necessarily undermine the fundamental elements of statehood or the claimant state's actual existence as a sovereign entity. In other words, derecognition as counter-acknowledgment and disowning of the claimant state's place in international affairs can result in ontological insecurity for the derecognized state. Derecognition delegitimizes the claimant state's government and gives its opposition a pretext to push for no-confidence votes and early elections. For the claimant state, derecognition deepens disrespect, dissatisfaction, resentment, and anxiety. This discourages it from engaging in international mediation processes in good faith and ruins normalization and confidence-building measures, thus pushing both sides toward conflict. This runs contrary to external actors' desire to use derecognition for conflict ripeness, thus creating the necessary conditions for initiating negotiations and making mutual concessions toward resolving the self-determination dispute.

Derecognition narrows down the claimant state's opportunity to enjoy access to rights and goods provided by the international system and membership in multilateral bodies. It undermines the ability of the claimant state to perform its sovereign agency and equality in bilateral and multilateral affairs and to enjoy the many rights and benefits of admission to international treaty bodies, assistance programs, and, most important, much-needed protection from foreign intervention and breach of sovereignty. Therefore, derecognition as a manifestation of the exclusion of the claimant state from the goods provided by the international system reproduces state inequality. Lora Viola (2020: 73) defines inequality as "exclusion from formal membership in the system and its institutions, and exclusion from equal voice rights in the deliberations and decision-making processes undertaken by the political community." Inequality among states denies nonrecognized or derecognized states the ability to protect themselves against "arbitrary judgements"; they do not "enjoy the right of nonintervention and are not subject to the international laws of war" (Viola 2020: 75). Derecognition creates a distorted struggle for equality among states. It reproduces hierarchical orders where some states are more entitled and equal than others. Ultimately, derecognition results in the gradual closure of the claimant's international space because of the reduced scope to exercise international legal sovereignty and its inability to meet the required votes and thresholds set for membership and participation in international organizations (Viola 2020: 23). Moreover, with access to the international system denied, derecognized states may not get to enjoy the right of nonintervention and sovereignty. They become subject to interference both by the former base state and by other unfriendly states, thus weakening further claims to sovereign and independent statehood and foreign policy, which are considered important prerequisites for modern sovereign statehood.

For the former base state, the act of derecognition has mostly a positive impact both domestically and internationally. Since derecognition is perceived by the former base state as a reaffirmation of its sovereignty over the claimant state and thus respect for territorial integrity—at least symbolically—such moves tend to boost the domestic legitimacy of the incumbent government and strengthen its diplomatic position internationally. In some instances, as with Serbia, the campaign for the derecognition of Kosovo improved its bargaining power vis-à-vis Kosovo in the EU-led dialogue for normalization of relations. It also undermined Kosovo's ability to apply for membership in international organizations. In this case, together with the weaponization of its kin community within Kosovo, Serbia used derecognition as an important diplomatic instrument to curtail Kosovo's independence and sovereignty at home and abroad. Derecognition mainly serves as a reaffirmation of symbolic claims over Kosovo without formal and physical access to the territory. To a certain extent, this also applies to Taiwan, the derecognition of which has not resulted in expanding mainland China's empirical sovereignty over the territory. South Ossetia's and Abkhazia's situations are comparable. Georgia and its allies cannot enter these areas because of the military presence of Russia.

However, in instances where the former base state has physical control over certain parts of the claimant state, derecognition serves as external legitimation of the prolonged presence or a green light to expand control and occupation of the rest of the territory. State derecognition can be taken as a signal that derecognizing states are permitting the former base state to reassert control over the contested territory through invasion, use of force, or other violent methods. For instance, Morocco has perceived the derecognition of the SADR as legitimation of its prolonged occupation of Western

Sahara and as permission to continue to politically, economically, and militarily control the territory it occupies. Morocco has stepped beyond this, in fact, and exploited the derecognition of the SADR to consolidate its power in the occupied territories of Western Sahara. Morocco also encouraged the derecognizing states to open general consulates in major Western Saharan cities to symbolize Morocco's sovereignty over the occupied and contested territory. Diplomatically, Morocco was able to capitalize on the derecognition of the SADR to shape the UN agenda on the long-overdue referendum in Western Sahara. With the backing of the United States, a majority of European powers, and other regional actors, Morocco could limit the ability of the UN special envoy's access and scope of engagement in Western Sahara. Thus, the derecognition of the SADR has helped Morocco solidify its control over Western Sahara and shape international diplomatic efforts for conflict resolution. So, state derecognition—as much as it might be seen as a move to respect and restore the sovereignty and territorial integrity of the former base state over the contested territory—can also be a prelude to invasion and, thus, a breach of the norm against territorial conquest (Fazal 2022).

While these short-term gains benefit the former base state, the derecognition of the claimant state does not resolve the conflict. On the contrary, it deepens hostilities and sets back peacemaking efforts. In the Serbia and Kosovo dispute, the campaign for derecognition seriously undermined the process of normalization of relations and intensified unilateral actions on both sides of the border, deepening hostilities and returning to the rhetoric of war. In the Morocco-SADR dispute, the campaign for derecognition was crucial to ending the thirty-year ceasefire arrangement between them, causing them to return to low-intensity conflict in 2020. In the China-Taiwan dispute, derecognition negatively impacted cross-strait relations. China has openly threatened to use force to regain control over the contested island, whereas Taiwan has intensified militarization and preparations for eventual war. The conflict intensified—at least discursively for now—when the United States openly backed Taiwan's struggle for a distinct political existence and self-defense. Thus, contrary to the official policy discourse, third countries get implicated in self-determination disputes through their acts of derecognition and contribute to conflict escalation.

The act and process of state derecognition appears to also have double effects for third countries implicated in this controversial practice. On the one hand, derecognition is a profitable endeavor for third countries that use their capacity to recognize other states to generate foreign aid, strengthen security provisions, accrue personal profit, and compensate for the lack of domestic resources and self-reliance. In this sense, derecognition is an inexpensive diplomatic asset that brings high-value goods to derecognizing states. Yet this is only one side of the coin. The other side is grim. The practice of derecognition tends to trigger a negative chain effect on third countries. Dependency on the transactional culture of derecognition makes third states vulnerable to the sudden loss of diplomatic allies and the withdrawal of foreign assistance. For example, countries that have switched recognition from Taiwan to China have suffered from discontinued developmental projects and investments in local economy and society. The transactional nature of derecognition—centered on corruption and political favors—often results in domestic political competition for resources and power, which can end with early elections, the collapse of government, nonviolent or even violent coups. Therefore, derecognizing states not only export conflicts through their foreign policy decisions but also import them by risking domestic stability and political order.

Finally, states' derecognition tends to have systemic and global implications. Across all contemporary cases examined in this book, derecognition has bolstered rivalry among global and regional powers. The derecognition of states plays a crucial role in changing the geopolitical interests of major powers and signals shifts in political alliances and spheres of influence among the implicated states. Therefore, regional and global powers often engage in reactionary politics and intensify their diplomatic and military engagement to minimize and utilize such geopolitical changes. For instance, the derecognition of Taiwan by Latin American and Pacific states has deepened the hostility between the United States and China. Similarly, the derecognition of SADR has worsened the relationship between Algeria and southern European countries. In response, global and regional powers have deepened their strategic investment in constructing new regional alliances to protect their interests. This involves greater diplomatic and military investment in certain regions, as well as sanctioning actions to subvert the legitimacy and functionality of governments implicated in the derecognition saga. In such geopolitical constellations, claimant states tend to deepen their dependency on their regional and global allies and are often forced to make domestic decisions contrary to their national interests. Therefore, derecognition tends to produce double effects, which promote more disorder than order, encourage more counter-peace than peace, and enable vassal status more than independence among nations.

ESCAPING THE STATE DERECOGNITION TRAP

Considering the findings in this book, the final question that needs to be addressed concerns the pathways for escaping the derecognition trap. The derecognition of states is symptomatic of the lack of normative and institutional rules governing the granting, withholding, and withdrawing of recognition. As an uninstitutionalized and anti-diplomatic practice, state derecognition further erases rule-based international order. Most important, hypocrisy surrounding the derecognition of states plays a major role in weakening the political significance of state recognition as a diplomatic practice of acknowledging and legitimizing new states in the international system. If the lack of normative consensus and policy regulations play a role in permitting the use and abuse of derecognition with the discretionary right for granting, withholding, and withdrawing the recognition of states, what are the prospects and constrains for regulating it in the international system? Ultimately, responding to this question requires searching for solutions already present in international law and policy and envisaging new ones outside the existing normative, policy, and regulatory frameworks. There are three potential policy and institutional responses to state derecognition. They concern measures from needing new substantial rules and norms governing the derecognition of states to those requiring incremental norm-building measures.

This first option for escaping the derecognition trap is to fully regulate the recognition and derecognition of states through a collective legal and institutional mechanism. The case for regulating the recognition and derecognition of states is overwhelming. Diplomatic derecognition is symptomatic of the fact that as long as there is no consensual institutional regime governing the recognition of states, and for as long as it remains a matter left to the discretion of individual states, we are likely to see situations where states use and abuse their status as members of the club of sovereign countries to exclude other aspirant states. Derecognizing states tend to be selective law-abiders but exploit loopholes in the international system and exercise their sovereignty through them. So far, the international community has been unable to establish a regulatory regime (normative and institutional) on state recognition that would serve as an instrument for global conflict resolution (Dugard 1987). Instead, discretion on state recognition has become a platform for justifying and battling over conflicting interests and norms among existing sovereign states and newcomers (Takashi 2010).

The lack of precise normative and institutional regulatory mechanisms on state recognition and derecognition permits the commercialization of sovereignty and allows the perseverance of discorded conduct in world politics.

The need for regulating state recognition and derecognition becomes more obvious when considering that "the struggle for recognition takes place between unequal parties, in which the stronger party is in a position to grant or withhold recognition to the weaker one, and in which the stronger party is likely to perceive demands for recognition as challenges to its standing" (Bartelson 2013: 111). Thus, there is strong support for regulating state recognition. As Ryngaert and Sobrie (2011: 490) argue, "Legal norms . . . reduce the complexity of the choices with which states are confronted, thus further adding to international stability." Moreover, as exemplified by the current Russian aggression against Ukraine, unregulated state recognition practices serve the interests of dominant powers and systematically undermine the struggle to preserve the rules-based international order, which is under unprecedented threat. Regulating when and under what conditions new states should be recognized would provide legal predictability and political stability to the international system and constrain the arbitrary actions of dominant states that assault other states' sovereignty and territorial integrity.

As a solution to the arbitrary nature of state derecognition, scholars have proposed collective mechanisms to set principles and rules in place that regulate the recognition of states under international law (Lauterpacht 1944: 419; Peterson 1997: 51). The international law has the scope to open up again to the possibility of regulating state recognition through legal mechanisms, as it did with many other issues, including decolonization and nonuse of force (Orford 2012: 281). The UN has often been seen as the appropriate body to administer collective recognition of states. Paul Taylor (1999: 562) has proposed that "responsibility for the recognition and de-recognition of states . . . be transferred to the UN and exercised under a special procedure." This was attempted when the UN was founded but lacked wide international support. This could entail establishing a specially designated body within the UN responsible for dealing with state derecognition cases. However, international norms have usually emerged only after catastrophic events occur. This is the story with the prohibitory norms concerning genocide, war crimes, ethnic cleansing, and the arms race, as well as regulatory norms such as peacekeeping, protection of civilians, humanitarian intervention and the responsibility to protect, transitional justice, and peacebuilding. The emergence of the collective nonrecognition practice has been a response to the creation of new states with the use of force, as exemplified by Manchuria, Southern Rhodesia, Northern Cyprus, and Crimea more recently. With regard to state creation and recognition, such momentum has been missed despite the occurrence of wars for independence and escalation of violence following the recognition or nonrecognition of specific entities as sovereign states (as exemplified by the wars following the dissolution of Yugoslavia and in certain parts of the former Soviet Union). The renewed global rivalries between the West, Russia, and China could provide critical momentum for addressing the regulation of state recognition and derecognition in world politics. However, the existing setup and power-driven institutional setting with veto powers make the UN a less favorable venue for implementing the duty to recognize states unless fundamental changes take place (Weller 2009).

Regulating state recognition and derecognition inevitably involves addressing broader questions related to the right to self-determination, the procedure for secession and state creation, other issues related to power politics and institutional interventions, and the appropriate authority for granting, withholding, or withdrawing the recognition of states. Concerning the rules governing state recognition, Martti Koskenniemi (2005, 2011) highlights the difficulties in having a strict regulatory framework. He proposes a middle ground, a nuanced approach that combines elements of normativity (rule) and effectiveness (policy) as the most viable pathway for regulating state recognition. This entails developing normative instruments such as declarations, agreements, and guidelines that states can endorse and apply in guiding their foreign policy conduct. And it involves using existing international organizations and other treaty bodies to seek effective application and linkage with different international norms and legal rules. Allen Buchanan (1999: 59) has made a case for a justice-based approach to regulating the recognition and derecognition of states, claiming that such acts should be extended to "those entities that treat their own populations justly, and withholds those advantages from entities that fail to do so." Buchanan (2004: 260) argues for "a normativized practice of recognition according to which new entities ought to be incorporated into the society of states only if they satisfy justice-based criteria, that is, only if they do a credible job of protecting the basic human rights of their citizens and refrain from serious violations of the basic human rights of those beyond their borders." If these normative criteria of justice, democracy, and human rights were the basis of a regulatory framework for state derecognition, then derecognition would only be permitted when the claimant state failed to satisfy specific normative standards. Thus, when third countries derecognized a claimant state that met these normative standards, the decision would be considered null and a breach of the nonintervention principle (Jamnejad and Wood 2009: 373).

The second option would be to reject the derecognition of states as a norm and practice in world politics. The starting base for promoting an anti-derecognition position is to see recognition as irrevocable and irreversible unless original conditions for recognition disappear, and to agree to call derecognition "severance" or "break up of diplomatic relations" instead of labeling it a drastic step of ceasing or withdrawing recognition. In other words, the anti-derecognition consensus would entail disregarding the withdrawal of recognition, especially when the original conditions for recognition are still in place and the claimant state still satisfies statehood criteria, including viability and legitimacy as an independent state. Of course, third countries would be free to sever or discontinue bilateral relations in line with international diplomatic law, but such an endeavor would not be regarded as derecognition. Disregarding derecognition as a viable and credible practice enjoys broad scholarly support, as discussed in Chapter 2, and some state support, as demonstrated throughout the empirical chapters. Many states either remain silent or unwilling to get implicated in the derecognition of states. So the anti-derecognition practice already exists, but it requires greater scholarly and policy consensus to agree on the irreversibility of diplomatic recognition and the declaratory character of recognition in the first instance.

The norm-building on state derecognition could start with an international commission comprising influential global figures who would produce a landmark report offering intellectual and policy guidance. This could take the shape of a declaration or charter of principles governing the recognition and derecognition of states, whereby third countries would voluntarily endorse it to guide their future diplomatic practices on the subject matter. Although such a pledge would not have a legal and binding effect, it could promote self-restraint and set the practical and normative contours for an anti-derecognition norm. Only a few countries with long-standing diplomatic traditions have created guidelines and instructions for recognizing other states. States that are part of larger regional political and economic unions, such as the EU, are more likely to have their own or follow collective policies and guidelines on state recognition or derecognition. The EU's explicit guidelines on recognizing new states in the former Yugoslavia and Soviet Union are an example (Caplan 2005). The EU also has specific guidelines for nonrecognition of Abkhazia, South Ossetia, and Crimea (Newman and Visoka 2018a). The United States has passed special bills on the nonrecognition of Abkhazia, South Ossetia, and Crimea and against the derecognition of Taiwan. Thus, precedents exist that can be used to develop guidelines against the unprincipled and unjustifiable derecognition of states.

The third option for escaping or responding to derecognition hypocrisies is an extension to the second option. It can take the shape of scrutiny, including sanctioning, of premature and unprincipled withdrawals of recognition. Improvement of the justifications that third countries use for derecognition would be the first set of measures that could rectify the legal and political ambiguity and quandaries surrounding derecognition. Recognition of states is fundamental to administering the expansion of international law, acknowledgment of the collective right to self-determination, and affirmation of political emancipation of peoples who have been suppressed and denied freedom by the base state. Existing states are inadvertently abdicating their obligations to denounce international wrongdoing by refusing, delaying, or withdrawing their recognition of the claimant states that have experienced these illegal practices. Derecognition frequently raises questions about whether the claimant state actually meets the requirements for statehood, so the decision to deny recognition should also include a justification for the derecognizing state's decision. With few exceptions, as this book demonstrated, derecognition's process and result are still poorly understood. Thus, to ensure that derecognition is justifiable, derecognizing states must be transparent about the legal and political rationales behind the decision to reconsider. They must be transparent about their deliberative processes, and the domestic and international legal grounds upon which the decision to freeze, suspend, or fully withdraw the recognition of the claimant state must also be transparent. For example, a decision for derecognition would be more credible if it were accompanied by a detailed legal note outlining the breaches of bilateral agreements that the claimant state has committed and the objective evidence that justifies the discontinuance of diplomatic relations and withdrawal of recognition. The derecognition process would also be more credible if it were not entirely unilateral and arbitrary and if it showed that efforts had been made during the process to establish diplomatic relations and cultivate bilateral ties in good faith and in accordance with principles and norms of international law. Thus, derecognition should not be entirely driven and influenced by the diplomatic narrative and financial incentives the former base state and its allies provided. To put it another way, derecognition would be more accepted internationally if it were seen as a last resort, used only after all other attempts to forge bilateral ties with the claimant state had failed.

In most cases, the process, and the ultimate act of state derecognition

234 • *The Derecognition of States*

tends to legitimize the power of the occupying or former base state, which considers this act an external certification of its right to rule over the secessionist population seeking independent statehood. As Buchanan (2004: 270) maintains, "If we confer legal powers that support and enhance the unjust exercise of political power, we act wrongly." For example, the derecognition of Western Sahara and subsequent acceptance of Morocco's occupation of this territory represents a breach of international law on the obligation of states to nonrecognition of situations arising from the violation of peremptory norms of international law. The unjustified and unprincipled derecognition could amount to aggression toward the claimant state and broader international peace and stability. In an international environment where state derecognition goes unpunished and implicitly permitted, it allows states to violate other related international norms and principles without suffering reputational costs. Condemning or sanctioning the unjustifiable derecognition of states complements and nurtures the anti-derecognition norm outlined above. It could also prove to be an effective mechanism to mitigate the adverse effects of such a practice.

Under the third option discussed here, the international response to derecognition could take the shape of either bilateral or collective sanctions against the derecognizing states or more affirmative measures of suspending or removing them from global institutions. Calling out the derecognizing states and revealing the transactional aspects of selling, renting, or trading recognition would inflict reputational costs on those defecting states and discourage other states from following a similar path. Withdrawing bilateral cooperation or assistance and suspending their membership in regional and international organizations could equally play a role in indirectly constraining the abuse of the right to recognize other states. A handful of postcolonial states in Latin America, Africa, and Pacific islands are at the forefront of such abusive behavior. Their independence and international recognition have endowed them with the power to command domestic politics within their territory and the opportunity to shape international politics.

A more far-fetched option for sanctioning the irresponsible derecognition of states would be to withdraw recognition of states who abuse their discretionary right to recognize or derecognize other states. States that rent recognition for self-interest are not peace-loving nations, and, consequently, their own statehood and position within international organizations should be brought into question and potentially be outlawed by the wider international community. Grounds for derecognizing pariah states can be found in the very practice of collective nonrecognition of states complicit in aggressive acts. This option has already been proposed by other scholars, who have suggested withdrawing the recognition of nondemocratic and failed states that have abused unconditional international recognition, "reproducing the horrors of colonial-era domination under the guise of freedom" (Englebert 2009: 5–6). However, this option isn't without problems. As Robert Delahunty and John Yoo (2005: 149–50) point out, "The international community may fear that the derecognition of a particular failed state—i.e., the withdrawal of the recognition of its international legal sovereignty—risks 'domino' effects, leading to the derecognition of other states, and thus weakening the (fictitious, but arguably salutary) conception that the entire globe is and should be divided up into nation-states." Notwithstanding these dilemmas, creating a collective response to derecognition could contain the scope third countries have to abuse state recognition and derecognition by inflicting significant political and diplomatic reputational costs. Stephen E. Gent and Mark J. C. Crescenzi (2021: 36) show that "reputation costs tend to be greater when international rules are formalized, as the institutional commitments of the states are clearer and more visible and outside actors can more easily identify acts of noncompliance." In this regard, if there are more precise guidelines on state derecognition, third countries will likely avoid engaging in such a practice, significantly when the original recognition circumstances haven't changed, and such a decision would be identified as purely for self-interest.

While the first regulatory option might be hard to pursue, the two options discussed later in this section would be a suitable starting point to encourage states to make principles—not political expediency—their guide to exercising the right to recognition and derecognition of other states. Such norm-building practices form the basis of customary international law and could be a starting point for generating political consensus to develop a legal and binding norm. Since the derecognition of states manifests some of the most destabilizing features of contemporary world politics, it is symptomatic of broader global developments related to the rise of reversal politics and the unmaking of the current global order. Thus, there is not much room for optimism when it comes to regulating and constraining derecognition. Derecognition appears to be driven by the broader dynamics of transitional international order, where we see the rise of deglobalization, de-democratization, and counter-peace, among other tectonic shifts, reshuffling normative and geopolitical grounds and laying the foundations of a new and fragmented global order anchored by multiple regional hegemons and extralegal and arbitrary diplomatic practices.

Appendix

INDICATIVE DATA ON STATE DERECOGNITION
(BY COUNTRY AND YEAR) AS OF JANUARY 2024

Table 1. Taiwan

No.	Derecognizing state	Recognition	Derecognition 1	Re-recognition 1	Derecognition 2	Re-recognition 2	Derecognition 3
1	Afghanistan	1944	1950				
2	Argentina	1945	1972				
3	Australia	1941	1972				
4	Austria	1928	1971				
5	Bahamas (the)	1989	1997				
6	Barbados	1967	1977				
7	Belgium	1928	1971				
8	Bolivia	1919	1985				
9	Botswana	1966	1974				
10	Brazil	1928	1974				
11	Bulgaria	1947	1949				
12	Burkina Faso	1961	1973	1994	2018		
13	Cambodia	1953		1958		1970	
14	Cameroon	1960	1971				
15	Canada	1941	1970				
16	Central African Republic	1962	1964	1968	1976	1991	1998
17	Chad	1962	1972	1997	2006		
18	Chile	1931	1970				
19	Colombia	1941	1980				
20	Congo (the)	1960	1964				
21	Costa Rica	1944	2007				
22	Côte d'Ivoire	1963	1983				
23	Cuba	1929	1960				
24	DR Congo	1960	1961	1961	1972		
25	Denmark	1928	1950				

26	Dominica	1983	2004		
27	Dominican Republic	1941	2018		
28	Ecuador	1947	1980		
29	Egypt	1942	1956		
30	El Salvador	1961	2018		
31	Estonia	1921	1992		
32	Finland	1919	1944		
33	France	1928	1964		
34	Gabon	1960	1974		
35	Gambia	1968	1974	1995	2013
36	Germany	1955	1972		
37	Greece	1947	1972		
38	Grenada	1989	2005		
39	Guinea-Bissau	1990	1998		
40	Honduras	1985	2023		
41	India	1947	1949		
42	Indonesia	1945	1950		
43	Iran	1920	1971		
44	Iraq	1942	1958		
45	Italy	1928	1970		
46	Jamaica	1962	1972		
47	Japan	1930	1937	1952	1972
48	Jordan	1957	1977		
49	Kiribati	2003	2019		
50	Kuwait	1963	1971		
51	Laos	1953	1962		
52	Latvia	1923	1940	1992	1994
53	Lebanon	1954	1971		

Table 1—*Continued*

No.	Derecognizing state	Recognition	Derecognition 1	Re-recognition 1	Derecognition 2	Re-recognition 2	Derecognition 3
54	Lesotho	1966	1983	1990	1994		
55	Liberia	1957	1977	1989	1993	1997	2003
56	Libya	1958	1978				
57	Lithuania	1923	1992				
58	Luxembourg	1949	1972				
59	Madagascar	1960	1972				
60	Malawi	1966	2008				
61	Malaysia	1964	1974				
62	Maldives	1966	1972				
63	Malta	1967	1972				
64	Mauritania	1960	1965				
65	Mexico	1928	1971				
66	Myanmar	1948	1950				
67	Nauru	1980	2002	2005	2024		
68	Netherlands	1928	1950				
69	New Zealand	1912	1972				
70	Nicaragua	1930	1985	1990	2021		
71	Niger (the)	1963	1974	1992	1996		
72	North Macedonia	1999	2021				
73	Norway	1928	1950				
74	Pakistan	1947	1950				
75	Panama	1912	2017				
76	Papua New Guinea	1999	1999				
77	Peru	1931	1971				
78	Philippines (the)	1947	1975				

79	Poland	1929	1949				
80	Portugal	1928	1975				
81	Republic of Korea (the)	1949	1992				
82	Romania	1939	1949				
83	Rwanda	1962	1972				
84	Saint Lucia	1984	1997	2007			
85	Samoa	1945	1955				
86	Sao Tome and Principe	1997	2016				
87	Saudi Arabia	1946	1990				
88	Senegal	1960	1964	1969	1972	1996	2005
89	Sierra Leone	1963	1971				
90	Solomon Islands	1963	1971	1983	2019		
91	South Africa	1976	1998				
92	Spain	1928	1973				
93	Sri Lanka	1948	1950				
94	Sweden	1928	1950				
95	Switzerland	1913	1950				
96	Thailand	1946	1975				
97	Togo	1960	1972				
98	Tonga	1972	1998				
99	Türkiye	1934	1971				
100	United States of America	1928	1979				
101	Uruguay	1958	1988				
102	Vanuatu	2004	2004				
103	Venezuela	1941	1974				

Note: This list contains states that have switched recognition from Taiwan (Republic of China) to the People's Republic of China (PRC) at least once. It does not list the countries that have never recognized Taiwan or those that maintain diplomatic relations (as of January 2024).

Table 2. Western Sahara (Sahrawi Arabic Democratic Republic)

No.	Derecognizing state	Recognition	Derecognition 1	Re-recognition 1	De-recognition 2	Re-recognition 2	De-recognition 3
1	Afghanistan	1979	2002				
2	Albania	1987	2004				
3	Antigua and Barbuda	1987	2010				
4	Barbados	1988	2019				
5	Benin	1976	1997				
6	Burkina Faso	1984	2006				
7	Burundi	1976	2006	2008	2010		
8	Cape Verde	1979	2007	2012	2010		
9	Chad	1980	1997	2006			
10	Colombia	1985	2000	2022			
11	Congo	1978	1996				
12	Costa Rica	1980	2000				
13	Dominica	1979	2010				
14	Dominican Republic	1986	2002				
15	Ecuador	1983	2004	2006			
16	El Salvador	1989	1997	2009	2019		
17	Equatorial Guinea	1978	1980				
18	Eswatini	1980	1997				
19	Ghana	1979	2001	2011			
20	Grenada	1979	2010				
21	Guatemala	1986	1998				
22	Guinea-Bissau	1976	1997	2009	2010		
23	Guyana	2979	2020				
24	Haiti	2006	2013				
25	Honduras	1989	2000	2013			
26	India	1985	2000				

No.	Country						
27	Jamaica	1979	2016				
28	Kenya	2005	2007	2014	2022	2022	
29	Kiribati	1981	2000				
30	Liberia	1985	1997	2012	2020		
31	Madagascar	1976	2005				
32	Malawi	1994	2001	2002	2008	2014	2017
33	Mauritius	1982	2014	2015			
34	Nauru	1981	2000				
35	Nicaragua	1979	2001	2007			
36	Panama	1978	2013	2016			
37	Papua New Guinea	1981	2011				
38	Paraguay	2000	2000	2008	2014	2022	2023
39	Peru	1984	1996	2021	2022		
40	Saint Lucia	1979	1989	2010			
41	Sao Tome and Principe	1978	1996				
42	Serbia	1984	2004				
43	Seychelles	1977	2008				
44	Sierra Leone	1980	2003	2011	2021		
45	Solomon Islands	1981	1989				
46	South Sudan	2011	2018	2022			
47	St. Kitts and Nevis	1987	2010				
48	St. Vincent and the Grenadines	2002	2013				
49	Suriname	1982	2016				
50	Togo	1976	1997				
51	Tuvalu	1981	2000				
52	Vanuatu	1980	2000	2008			
53	Zambia	1979	2011	2112	2018		

Note: There is conflicting evidence whether Vietnam has withdrawn the recognition of SADR.

244 • *Appendix*

Table 3. Abkhazia

No.	Derecognizing state	Recognition	Derecognition
1	Tuvalu	2011	2014
2	Vanuatu	2011	2013

Table 4. South Ossetia

No.	Derecognizing state	Recognition	Derecognition
1	Tuvalu	2011	2014
2	Vanuatu	2011	2013

Table 5. Kosovo

No.	Derecognizing state	Recognition	Derecognition 1	Re-recognition 1
1	Sao Tome and Principe	2012	2013	
2	Suriname	2016	2017	
3	Guinea-Bissau	2011	2017	2018
4	Burundi	2012	2018	
5	Liberia	2008	2018	2018
6	Papua New Guinea	2012	2018	
7	Lesotho	2014	2018	
8	Comoros	2009	2018	
9	Dominica	2012	2018	2022
10	Grenada	2013	2018	2023
11	Solomon Islands	2014	2018	
12	Madagascar	2017	2018	
13	Palau	2009	2019	2022
14	Togo	2014	2019	
15	Central African Republic	2014	2019	
16	Ghana	2012	2019	
17	Nauru	2015	2019	
18	Sierra Leone	2008	2020	

Note: According to the president of Serbia in January 2023, the following states had withdrawn their recognition of Kosovo: Somalia, Burkina Faso, Gabon, Eswatini (formerly Swaziland), Libya, Guinea, Saint Lucia, Antigua and Barbuda, and the Maldives (Tanjug 2023). The MFA of Kosovo has refuted this assertion and argued that at least five of these nations have not derecognized it, providing documentation of meetings between Kosovo ambassadors and their counterparts from Somalia, Eswatini, Gabon, the Maldives, and Libya (Balkan Insight 2023).

References

ABC News. 2019. "'Alarming and Unacceptable': Kiribati Condemns US Charity's Decision to Pull Its Services." 15 October. https://www.abc.net.au/pacific/programs/pacificbeat/us-charity-pulls-out-of-kiribati-amid-taiwanchina-row/11606338

ABC News. 2020a. "Solomon Islands Discussed \$US100 Billion Loan from Chinese Businessman, according to Leaked Letters." 21 February. https://www.abc.net.au/news/2020-02-21/leaked-letters-solomon-islands-100billion-loan-chinese-business/11989270

ABC News. 2020b. "Chinese Charter Flight to Covid-Free Solomon Islands Fuels Independence Cries." 3 September. https://www.abc.net.au/news/2020-09-03/china-flight-to-covid-free-solomon-islands-independence/12626718

ABC News. 2021. "Solomon Islands Prime Minister Blames Foreign Powers for Civil Unrest That Prompted Call to Australia for Help." 25 November. https://www.abc.net.au/news/2021-11-26/solomon-islands-pm-blames-foreign-powers-for-civil-unrest/100652048

Abidde, S. O. 2022. *China and Taiwan in Africa: The Struggle for Diplomatic Recognition and Hegemony*. Cham, Switzerland: Springer.

Acharya, A. 2007. "State Sovereignty after 9/11: Disorganised Hypocrisy." *Political Studies* 55(2): 274–96.

Adler E. and Pouliot, V. 2011. "International Practices." *International Theory* 3(1): 1–36.

African Bulletin. 2013. "Barbados Freezes Recognition of So-Called SADR." 13 February. http://www.african-bulletin.com/6826-barbados-freezes-recognition-of-so-called-sadr-2.html

Agence Maghreb Arabe Presse. 2010. "Burundi Withdraws Recognition of 'SADR.'" 25 October. https://web.archive.org/web/20101027183913/http:/www.map.ma/eng/sections/politics/burundi_withdraws_re/view

Agence Marocaine de Presse. 2021. "Opening of Consulates of African Countries in Sahara Is Result of HM the King's Enlightened Vision: FM." 29 July. https://

246 • *References*

www.mapnews.ma/en/actualites/politics/opening-consulates-african-countries
-sahara-result-hm-king's-enlightened-vision

Al-Ahram. 2016. "The Egyptian Ambassador in Belgrade to Al-Ahram: Serbia Has Been Very Appreciative of Egypt and Supports It in Its War on Terror." 7 November. https://gate-ahram-org-eg.translate.goog/daily/NewsPrint/559923.aspx?_x_tr_sl=ar&_x_tr_tl=en&_x_tr_hl=en&_x_tr_pto=nui,sc

Albanian Post. 2022. "'Diplomacia e sheqerit'—Cilave shtete iu ofroi Serbia sheqer për ta çnjohur Kosovën?" [Sugar diplomacy—which states did Serbia offer sugar to derecognize Kosovo?]. 14 May. https://albanianpost.com/diplomacia-e-sheqer it-cilave-shtete-iu-ofroi-serbia-sheqer-per-ta-cnjohur-kosoven/

Al Jazeera. 2022. "US Approves $100m Support Deal for Taiwan Patriot Missiles." 8 February. https://www.aljazeera.com/news/2022/2/8/us-approves-support-de al-for-taiwan-patriot-missiles

Alexander, C. R. 2014. *China and Taiwan in Central America: Engaging Foreign Publics in Diplomacy*. New York: Palgrave Macmillan.

Alexandrowicz, C. H. 1958. "The Theory of Recognition in Fieri." *British Year Book of International Law* 34: 176–98.

Algeria Press Service. 2020. "Consulates Opened in Dakhla, Layun: Empty, Unreachable Premises." 10 November. https://www.aps.dz/en/world/36465-co nsulates-opened-in-dakhla-layun-empty-unreachable

All Africa. 2015. "Mauritius: Republic of Mauritius Recognizes SADR." 23 November. https://allafrica.com/stories/201511232970.html

Al Mayadeen. 2022. "Peru Withdraws Recognition of Polisario's SADR." 19 August. https://english.almayadeen.net/news/politics/peru-withdraws-recognition-of -polisarios-sadr

Anghie, A. 2004. *Imperialism, Sovereignty, and the Making of International Law*. Cambridge: Cambridge University Press.

Aqorau, T. 2021. "Solomon Islands' Foreign Policy Dilemma and the Switch from Taiwan to China." In G. Smith and T. Wesley-Smith, eds., *The China Alternative: Changing Regional Order in the Pacific Islands*. Acton: Australian National University Press, 319–48.

Arabic News. 2000. "Honduras Did Suspend Recognition of Polisario, FM Spokesperson Confirms." 3 March. https://web.archive.org/web/20060212082829/htt p:/www.arabicnews.com/ansub/Daily/Day/000302/2000030236.html

Arabic News. 2000. "Vanuatu No Longer Recognizes Whimsical SADR." 12 August. https://web.archive.org/web/20080725124510/http:/www.arabicnews.com/ans ub/Daily/Day/001208/2000120818.html

Arabic News. 2002. "Afghanistan Withdraws Recognition from So-Called Sahrawi Republic." 7 December. https://web.archive.org/web/20130808174924/http:// www.arabicnews.com/ansub/Daily/Day/020712/2002071222.html

Article 19. 2019. "Morocco Ready to Open New Page of Cooperation with El Salvador." 17 June. http://article19.ma/en/index.php/2019/06/17/morocco-ready-to -open-new-page-of-cooperation-with-el-salvador-video/

Assembly of Kosovo. 2018. "Committee on Foreign Affairs, Diaspora and Strategic Investments." 19 December.

Associated Press. 2022. "Taiwan Pays $900,000 for Ally Guatemala to Lobby Washington." 18 January. https://apnews.com/article/joe-biden-business-florida-dona ld-trump-taiwan-93a5ff9b52c52d5b50f49baf83cea4ba

Associated Press. 2022. "Explainer: Why Pelosi Went to Taiwan, and Why China's Angry." 3 August. https://apnews.com/article/taiwan-biden-asia-united-states-beijing-e3a6ea22e004f21e6b2a28b0f28ec4c5

Atalayar. 2021. "The President of Peru Appeals to 'the Principle of Self-Determination of Peoples' and Thaws Relations with the Polisario Front." 14 September. https://atalayar.com/en/content/president-peru-appeals-principle-self-determination-peoples-and-thaws-relations-polisario

The Australian. 2010. "If You're Willing to Pay, Nauru Can Be Amazingly Accommodating." 14 August. https://www.theaustralian.com.au/national-affairs/if-you re-willing-to-pay-nauru-can-be-amazingly-accommodating/news-story/849d6b 8eafa27aa86b2dcff0d697f559

The Australian. 2019. "Pacific Nations Set to Cut Ties with Taiwan." 11 September. https://www.theaustralian.com.au/nation/politics/pacific-nations-set-to-cut-ties -with-taiwan/news-story/482339d5099675be20828fa9e78f7315?fbclid=IwAR 1VA3od

B92. 2017. "South American country revokes recognition of Kosovo—FM." 31 October. https://www.b92.net/eng/news/politics.php?yyyy=2017&mm=10&d d=31&nav_id=102684

B92. 2018a. "Egypt Could Withdraw Decision to Recognize Kosovo—Report." 8 January. https://www.b92.net/eng/news/politics.php?yyyy=2018&mm=01&dd =08&nav_id=103213

B92. 2018b. "Egypt 'Edging Closer to Withdrawing Kosovo Recognition.'" 27 November. https://www.b92.net/eng/news/politics.php?yyyy=2018&mm=11& dd=27&nav_id=105617&fbclid=IwAR2EHQ8L8zspW1NVCYapPPSnZ-But TDAppafS4QeH6pFx50VeZPCZvTSZEc

B92. 2018c. "FM: This Isn't about Visas—Something Else Irks Them." 19 June. https://www.b92.net/eng/news/politics.php?yyyy=2018&mm=06&dd=19&n av_id=104429

B92. 2018d. "Latest Country to Revoke Recognition of Kosovo Revealed." 5 July. https://www.b92.net/eng/news/politics.php?yyyy=2018&mm=07&dd=05&n av_id=104566

B92. 2018e. "Lesotho Revokes Statements about Recognition of Kosovo." 16 October. https://www.b92.net/eng/news/politics.php?yyyy=2018&mm=10&dd=16 &nav_id=105307

B92. 2018f. "Mediji: SAD miniraju Dačića, šalju note pred posete" [Media: USA undermines Dačić, sends notes before visits]. 8 November. https://www.b92.net /info/vesti/index.php?yyyy=2018&mm=11&dd=08&nav_category=640&nav _id=1466835

B92. 2018g. "Solution for Kosovo and Resolution 1244 Inseparable." 18 December. https://www.b92.net/eng/insight/interviews.php?yyyy=2018&mm=12&dd=18 &nav_id=105790

B92. 2019. "It's Time for France, Too, to Withdraw Kosovo Recognition." 13 May. https://www.b92.net/eng/news/world.php?yyyy=2019&mm=05&dd=13&nav _id=106812

Balkan Insight. 2017. "Kosovo Says Suriname Can't Revoke Independence Recognition." 31 October. https://balkaninsight.com/2017/10/31/kosovo-claims-surina me-cannot-revoke-independence-recognition-10-31-2017/#sthash.cC81KwFz .uxfs

248 • *References*

Balkan Insight. 2021. "Serbia Strengthening 'Parallel Structures,' Kosovo Deputy PM Says." 7 December. https://balkaninsight.com/2021/12/07/serbia-strengthe ning-parallel-structures-kosovo-deputy-pm-says/

Balkan Insight. 2023. "Kosovo Debunks Serbian Claims about Derecognitions." 13 January. https://balkaninsight.com/2023/01/13/kosovo-debunks-serbian-clai ms-about-derecognitions/

Balkan Policy Research Group. 2023. "Kosovo: Unlocking Its Euro-Atlantic Path, the EU, Dialogue on Normalisation of Relations with Serbia, and the Prospects for Recognition by Five European Non-Recognisers." Prishtina: Balkan Policy Research Group. https://balkansgroup.org/en/kosovo-unlocking-its-euro-atlant ic-path-the-eu-dialogue-on-normalisation-of-relations-with-serbia-and-the-pro spects-for-recognition-by-five-european-non-recognisers/

Baltic Times. 2014. "Lithuania and Tuvalu Establish Diplomatic Relations." 24 December. https://www.baltictimes.com/lithuania_and_tuvalu_establish_diplo matic_relations/

Banai, H. 2016. "Pariah Diplomacy." In Constantinou, C. M., Kerr, P., and Sharp, P., eds., *The Sage Handbook of Diplomacy*. London: Sage, 654–65.

Barston, R. P. 2014. *Modern Diplomacy*. 4th ed. London: Routledge.

Bartelson, J. 2013. "Three Concepts of Recognition." *International Theory* 5(1): 107–29.

BBC. 2004. "Mbeki Backs W Sahara Independence." 16 September. http://news.bbc .co.uk/2/hi/africa/3664064.stm

BBC. 2018a. "Taiwan: How China Is Poaching the Island's Diplomatic Allies." 14 June. https://www.bbc.com/news/world-asia-40263581

BBC. 2018b. "Taiwan Loses Diplomatic Ally as Dominican Republic Switches Ties to China." 1 May. https://www.bbc.com/news/world-asia-china-43958849

BBC. 2021. "China-Taiwan Tensions: Xi Jinping Says 'Reunification' Must Be Fulfilled." 9 October. https://www.bbc.com/news/world-asia-china-58854081

Beha, A. 2015. "Disputes over the 15-Point Agreement on Normalization of Relations between Kosovo and Serbia." *Nationalities Papers* 43(1): 102–21.

Benabdullah, K. 2009. "The Position of the European Union on the Western Sahara Conflict." *Journal of Contemporary European Studies* 17(3): 417–35.

Berg, E. and Pegg, S. 2020. "Do Parent State Strategies Matter in Resolving Secessionist Conflicts with *De Facto* States?" In Griffiths, R. and Muro, D., eds., *Strategies of Secession and Counter-secession*. London: ECPR Press and Rowman and Littlefield, 52–68.

Berisha, B. 2019. *International Politics and Political Parties: Perceptions of Kosovo Citizens*. Prishtina: Prishtina Institute for Political Studies.

Besenyő, J., Huddleston, R. J., and Zoubir, Y. H., eds. 2023. *Conflict and Peace in Western Sahara: The Role of the UN's Peacekeeping Mission (MINURSO)*. London: Routledge.

Beta. 2018. "Ghana's Government to Reconsider Decision to Recognize Kosovo's Independence." 20 August. https://betabriefing.com/archive/news/6407-ghanas -government-to-reconsider-decision-to-recognize-kosovos-independence

Bjola, C. 2014. "The Ethics of Secret Diplomacy: A Contextual Approach." *Journal of Global Ethics* 10(1): 85–100.

Blanchette, J. and Hass, R. 2023. "The Taiwan Long Game: Why the Best Solution

Is No Solution." *Foreign Affairs*, January/February Issue. https://www.foreignaff airs.com/china/taiwan-long-game-best-solution-jude-blanchette-ryan-hass

Blic. 2019. "Dačić: Gana povukla priznanje Kosova, biće ih još do kraja godine" [Dačić: Ghana withdrew the recognition of Kosovo, there will be more by the end of the year]. 11 November. https://www.blic.rs/vesti/politika/gana-priznanje -kosova/r8823rr

Bloomberg. 2017. "Chinese Billions Fail to Sway Taiwan's Last Two Allies in Africa." 24 January. https://www.bloomberg.com/politics/articles/2017-01-24/chinese -billions-fail-to-sway-taiwan-s-last-two-allies-in-africa?

Bolton, G. and Visoka, G. 2010. "Recognizing Kosovo's Independence: Remedial Secession or Earned Sovereignty?" SEESOX Occasional Paper No. 11/10. https:// www.sant.ox.ac.uk/sites/default/files/recognizingkosovosindependence.pdf

Bolton, J. 2007. *Surrender Is Not an Option: Defending America at the United Nations and Abroad*. London: Threshold Editions.

Boukhars, A. and Roussellier, J., eds. 2014. *Perspectives on Western Sahara: Myths, Nationalisms, and Geopolitics*. Lanham, MD: Rowman and Littlefield.

Bouris, D. and Fernández-Molina, I. 2020. "Contested States and Their Everyday Quest for Recognition." In Visoka, G., Newman, E., and Doyle, J., eds., *Routledge Handbook of State Recognition*. London: Routledge, 333–43.

Bower, A. 2017. *Norms without the Great Powers: International Law and Changing Social Standards in World Politics*. Oxford: Oxford University Press.

Brady, A. and Henderson, J. 2010. "New Zealand, the Pacific and China: The Challenges Ahead." In Brady, A., ed., *Looking North, Looking South: China, Taiwan and South Pacific*. Toh Tuck: World Scientific Publishing, 189–226.

Braithwaite, J. et al. 2010. *Pillars and Shadows: Statebuilding as Peacebuilding in Solomon Islands*. Canberra: Australian National University E-Press.

Brown, P. 1942. "The Effects of Recognition." *American Journal of International Law* 36(1): 106–8.

Brownlie, I. 1983. "Recognition in Theory and Practice." *British Yearbook of International Law* 53(1): 197–211. https://doi.org/10.1093/bybil/53.1.197

Buchanan, A. 1999. "Recognitional Legitimacy and the State System." *Philosophy & Public Affairs*, 28(1): 46–78.

Buchanan, A. 2004. *Justice, Legitimacy, and Self-Determination: Moral Foundations for International Law*. Oxford: Oxford University Press.

Burcu, O. and Bertrand, E. 2019. "Explaining China's Latest Catch in Africa." 16 January. https://thediplomat.com/2019/01/explaining-chinas-latest-catch-in-af rica/

Bush, R. C. 2016. "China's Gambia Gambit and What It Means for Taiwan." Brookings Institution. 22 March. https://www.brookings.edu/blog/order-from-chaos /2016/03/22/chinas-gambia-gambit-and-what-it-means-for-taiwan/

Cabestan, Jean-Pierre. 2016. "Burkina Faso: Between Taiwan's Active Public Diplomacy and China's Business Attractiveness." *South African Journal of International Affairs* 23(4): 495–519.

Cancilleria Peru. 2022. Official Communication No. 003–22. 18 August. https://twi tter.com/CancilleriaPeru/status/1560288661337423875/photo/1

Caplan, R. 2005. *Europe and the Recognition of New States in Yugoslavia*. Cambridge: Cambridge University Press.

Caribbean News Now. 2017. "Suriname Revokes Kosovo Recognition, Heels Russia Visit." 2 November. https://www.caribbeannewsnow.com/2017/11/02/surin ame-revokes-kosovo-recognition-heels-russia-visit/

Caribbean News Now. 2018. "Serbian Foreign Minister: Suriname Expand Times." 12 February. https://www.caribbeannewsnow.com/2018/02/12/serbian-foreign -minister-suriname-expand-ties/

Casas-Zemora, K. 2009. "Notes on Costa Rica's Switch from Taipei to Beijing." Brookings Institution. 6 November. https://www.brookings.edu/on-the-record /notes-on-costa-ricas-switch-from-taipei-to-beijing/

Caspersen, N. 2012. *Unrecognized States: The Struggle for Sovereignty in the Modern International System*. Cambridge: Polity.

Caspersen, N. 2015. "The Pursuit of International Recognition after Kosovo." *Global Governance* 21(3): 393–412.

Caspersen, N. 2020. "Collective Non-recognition of States." In Visoka, G., Doyle, J., and Newman, E., eds., *Routledge Handbook of State Recognition*. London: Routledge, 231–40.

Cassese, A. 2005. *International Law*. 2nd ed. Oxford: Oxford University Press.

Cavanough, E. 2023. *Divided Isles: Solomon Islands and the China Switch*. Collingwood, Victoria: La Trobe University Press.

Chen, T. 1951. *The International Law of Recognition*. New York: F.A. Praeger.

Cheng, T. Y. 1994. "Foreign Trade in ROC Diplomacy." In Lin, B. and Myers, J. T., *Contemporary China and the Changing International Community*. Columbia: University of South Carolina Press, 176–77.

Chiang, H.-C. and Hwang, J.-Y. 2008. "On the Statehood of Taiwan: A Legal Reappraisal." In Chow, Peter C. Y., ed., *The "One China" Dilemma*. London: Palgrave Macmillan, 57–96.

Chirikba, V. 2013. *The International Legal Status of the Republic of Abkhazia*. Sukhum: Ministry of Foreign Affairs of the Republic of Abkhazia.

Choi, J. 2017. "The Costs of Not Being Recognized as a Country: The Case of Kosovo." Brookings Institution. https://www.brookings.edu/blog/future-develo pment/2017/11/16/the-costs-of-not-being-recognized-as-a-country-the-case-of -kosovo/

Chow, P. C. Y. 2022. "From Colony to Modern State: An Overview of Taiwan's Path of Development." In Chow, P. C. Y., ed., *A Century of Development in Taiwan: From Colony to Modern State*. London: Edward Elgar, 1–15.

Civil Georgia. 2011a. "Moscow Hails Tuvalu`s Abkhaz, S.Ossetia Recognition." 8 October. https://old.civil.ge/eng/article.php?id=24012

Civil Georgia. 2011b. "Vanuatu's UN Envoy Denies Abkhaz Recognition." 4 June. https://old.civil.ge/eng/article.php?id=23581

Civil Georgia. 2011c. "Vanuatu's Unsteady Abkhaz Recognition." 7 June. https://old .civil.ge/eng/article.php?id=23587

Civil Georgia. 2013. "Georgia, Vanuatu Establish Diplomatic Ties." 15 July. https:// old.civil.ge/eng/article.php?id=26273

Civil Georgia. 2014. "Tuvalu Retracts Abkhazia, S.Ossetia Recognition." 31 March. https://old.civil.ge/eng/article.php?id=27093

Civil Society Friends of Serbs in Kosovo and Metohija. 2018. "Petition—Invites the Government of the Czech Republic to Withdraw Recognition of the Self-

Proclaimed Albanian Quasi-State in Southern Serbia." http://www.kosovoonl ine.cz/index.php?option=com_content&view=article&id=1907%3A2018-02 -19-19-01-11&catid=55%3Aaktualne&Itemid=53&lang=cs/

Clark, C. 2008. "The Statehood of Taiwan: A Strange Case of Domestic Strength and International Challenge." In Chow, P. C. Y., ed., *The "One China" Dilemma*. London: Palgrave Macmillan, 81–96.

CNC. 2019. "Scandal of Corruption and Trafficking of False Documents at the Ministry of Foreign Affairs." 25 August. https://corbeaunews-centrafrique.org /scandale-de-corruption-et-du-trafic-des-faux-documents-au-ministere-des-affa ires-etrangeres/

Coggins, B. 2011. "Friends in High Places: International Politics and the Emergence of States from Secessionism." *International Organization* 65(3): 433–67.

Coggins, B. 2014. *Power Politics and State Formation in the Twentieth Century: The Dynamics of Recognition*. Cambridge: Cambridge University Press.

Colaresi, M. P., Rasler, K., and Thompson, W. R. 2007. *Strategic Rivalries in World Politics*. Cambridge: Cambridge University Press.

Colby, E. A. 2021. *The Strategy of Denial: American Defense in an Age of Great Power Conflict*. New Haven, CT: Yale University Press.

Cole, J. M. 2013. "Is China and Taiwan's Diplomatic Truce Over?" 18 November. https://thediplomat.com/2013/11/is-china-and-taiwans-diplomatic-truce-over/

Constantinou, C. M., Kerr, P., and Sharp, P., eds. *The Sage Handbook of Diplomacy*. London: Sage.

Cooper, A. F. and Shaw, T. M, eds. 2009. *The Diplomacies of Small States: Between Vulnerability and Resilience*. London: Palgrave.

Coppieters, B. 2020. "Engagement without Recognition." In Visoka, G., Doyle, J., and Newman, E., eds., *Routledge Handbook of State Recognition*. London: Routledge, 241–55.

Corbett, P. E. 1951. *Law and Society in the Relations of States*. New York: Harcourt, Brace.

Council of the EU. 2019. "Council Conclusions on Enlargement and Stabilisation and Association Process." Press release, 18 June. https://www.consilium.europa .eu/en/press/press-releases/2019/06/18/council-conclusions-on-enlargement-and -stabilisation-and-association-process/

Council on Foreign Relations. 2023. "U.S.-Taiwan Relations in a New Era: Respond- ing to a More Assertive China." Independent Task Force Report No. 82. 5 June. https://live-tfr-cdn.cfr.org/sites/default/files/2023-06/TFR81_U.S.-TaiwanRela tionsNewEra_SinglePages_2023-06-05_Online.pdf

Crawford, J. 2007. *The Creation of States in International Law*. Oxford: Oxford Uni- versity Press.

d'Aspremont, J. 2007. "Regulating Statehood: The Kosovo Status Settlement." *Leiden Journal of International Law* 20(3): 649–68. https://doi.org/10.1017/S0 92215650700430X

d'Aspremont, J. 2012. "Recognition in International Law." Oxford Biographies. http://www.oxfordbibliographies.com/view/document/obo-9780199796953 /obo-9780199796953-0009.xml

d'Aspremont, Jean. 2006. "Legitimacy of Governments in the Age of Democracy." *New York University Journal of International Law and Politics* 38(4): 877–917.

252 • *References*

Daase, C. et al., eds. 2015. *Recognition in International Relations: Rethinking a Political Concept in a Global Context.* Basingstoke: Palgrave Macmillan.

Darbouche, H. and Zoubir, Y. H. 2008. "Conflicting International Policies and the Western Sahara Stalemate." *International Spectator* 43(1): 91–105.

De Oliveira, V. S. M. 2023. "Statehood for Sale: Derecognition, 'Rental Recognition,' and the Open Flanks of International Law." *Jus Cogens* 5: 277–95. https://doi.org/10.1007/s42439-023-00075-y

De Vries, L., Englebert, P., and Schomerus, M., eds. 2019. *Secessionism in African Politics: Aspiration, Grievance, Performance, Disenchantment.* Cham, Switzerland: Palgrave Macmillan.

De Waal, T. 2010. *The Caucasus: An Introduction.* Oxford: Oxford University Press.

De Waal, T. 2018. *Uncertain Ground: Engaging with Europe's De Facto States and Breakaway Territories.* Washington, DC: Carnegie Endowment for International Peace.

De Waal, T. and von Twickel, N. 2020. *Beyond Frozen Conflict Scenarios for the Separatist Disputes of Eastern Europe.* London: Rowman and Littlefield.

Delahunty, R. J. and Yoo, J. 2005. "Statehood and the Third Geneva Convention." *Virginia Journal of International Law* 46(1): 131–64.

Demokracia. 2022. "Haziri thotë se Kurti dëshiron ta shtyjë dialogun me Serbinë: S'është i interesuar të negociojë" [Haziri says that Kurti wants to delay the dialogue with Serbia: He isn't interested in negotiating]. 25 August. https://demokracia.com/haziri-thote-se-kurti-deshiron-ta-shtyje-dialogun-me-serbine-seshte-i-interesuar-te-negocioje/

Denza, E. 2016. *Diplomatic Law Commentary on the Vienna Convention on Diplomatic Relations.* 4th ed. Oxford: Oxford University Press.

Der Derian, J. 1987. *On Diplomacy.* Oxford: Basil Blackwell.

Der Derian, J. and Wendt, A., eds. 2022. *Quantum International Relations: A Human Science for World Politics.* New York: Oxford University Press.

Deutsche Welle. 2020. "New African Consulates Cause Trouble for Western Sahara." 31 March. https://www.dw.com/en/new-african-consulates-cause-trouble-for-western-sahara/a-52967857

Dold, B. 2012. "Concepts and Practicalities of the Recognition of States." *Swiss Review of International and European Law* 22(1): 81–100.

Dominica News Online. 2012. "Dominica Recognizes Kosovo." 11 December. http://dominicanewsonline.com/news/homepage/news/politics/dominica-recognizes-kosovo/

Dugard, J. 2013. *The Secession of States and Their Recognition in the Wake of Kosovo.* Leiden: Brill.

Easton, I. 2022. *The Final Struggle: Inside China's Global Strategy.* Manchester: Eastbridge Books.

Eckart, C. 2012. *Promises of States under International Law.* Oxford: Hart.

Economic Normalisation Agreement. 2020. https://dialogue-info.com/economic-normalization/

Edmonds, K. 2012. "An Unexpected Ally: St. Lucia to Maintain Recognition of Taiwan." 28 September. https://nacla.org/blog/2012/9/27/unexpected-ally-st-lucia-maintain-recognition-taiwan

El-Amine Souef, M. 2018. Press Conference in Moscow. 9 November. https://www.youtube.com/watch?v=Xk630G2o9ko

Embassy of Kosovo in Japan. 2021. "Chargé d'Affaires ad Interim of the Embassy of the Republic of Kosovo in Japan, Mr. Arber Mehmeti Received for a Meeting Ambassador of the Republic of Palau to Japan, Hon. Mr. Francis Mariur Matsutaro." 26 April. https://www.facebook.com/KosovoinJapan/posts/553673 3336351920

The Embassy of the People's Republic of China in Australia. 2005. "A Rising China and the Flourishing China-Australia Relations Submission by the Embassy of the People's Republic of China in Australia to the Senate Foreign Affairs, Defence and Trade References Committee in relation to the Inquiry into Australia's Relations with China." June 2005. https://www.aph.gov.au/-/media/wo papub/senate/committee/fadt_ctte/completed_inquiries/2004_07/china/submi ssions/sub66_pdf.ashx

Emini, D. 2018. "Kosovo Security Barometer: De-constructing Public Perceptions Kosovo's Foreign Policy and Dialogue with Serbia." Prishtina: Kosovar Centre for Security Studies. https://qkss.org/images/uploads/files/KSB_Special_Editi on_-_De-constructing_public_perceptions_Kosovo's_foreign_policy_and_dial ogue_with_Serbia.pdf

Englebert, P. 2009. *Africa: Unity, Sovereignty, and Sorrow*. Boulder, CO: Lynne Rienner.

Epoch Times. 2019. "Pentagon Indo-Pacific Report Highlights China's Ambitions, Taiwan's Significance in US Strategy." 2 June. https://www.theepochtimes.com /pentagon-indo-pacific-report-highlights-chinas-ambitions-and-taiwans-signifi cance-in-us-strategy_2947673.html

Epstein, C., Lindemann, T., and Sending, O. 2018. "Frustrated Sovereigns: The Agency That Makes the World Go Around." *Review of International Studies* 44(5): 787–804.

Erikson, D. P. and Chen, J. 2007. "China, Taiwan, and the Battle for Latin America." *Fletcher Forum of World Affairs* 31(2): 69–89.

EuroNews Albania. 2021. "Një shtet është i gatshëm të njohë Kosovën falë punës sime." Behgjet Pacolli letër publike Kurtit. 19 December. https://euronews.al/raj oni/kosove/2021/12/19/nje-shtet-eshte-i-gatshem-te-njohe-kosoven-fale-punes -sime-behgjet-pacolli-leter-publike-kurtit/

European Parliament. 2008. Parliamentary Question No. E-4982/2008. 17 November. http://www.europarl.europa.eu/sides/getAllAnswers.do?reference=E-2008 -4982&language=EN

European Parliament. 2015. Parliamentary Question No. E-010478/2014. 2 March. http://www.europarl.europa.eu/sides/getAllAnswers.do?reference=E-2014-010 478&language=EN

European Parliament. 2018a. "Question for Written Answer E-006438/2018 to the Commission (Vice-President / High Representative) by Dominique Bilde (ENF)." https://www.europarl.europa.eu/doceo/document/E-8-2018-006438 _EN.pdf

European Parliament. 2018b. "Answer Given by Mr Hahn on Behalf of the European Commission." 17 March. https://www.europarl.europa.eu/doceo/docume nt/E-8-2018-006438-ASW_EN.pdf

European Parliament. 2022. "Answer Given by High Representative/Vice-President Borrell i Fontelles on Behalf of the European Commission." 21 June. https:// www.europarl.europa.eu/doceo/document/E-9-2022-001162-ASW_EN.html

254 • *References*

European Union. 2011. "EU Demarches for the Non-recognition of the Breakaway Regions of Abkhazia and South Ossetia, Georgia." Brussels. 15 June.

Evropa e Lirë. 2021. "Paqartësi rreth aplikimeve në organizata ndërkombëtare." Prishtina, 22 July. https://www.evropaelire.org/a/aplikimet-ne-organizata-nderk ombtare-njohjet-e-reja-/31372167.html

Exit Albania. 2020. "Kosovo and Serbia Signed Separate Pledges, Not an Agreement." 4 September. https://exit.al/en/kosovo-and-serbia-signed-separate-pledg es-not-an-agreement/.

Fabry, M. 2010. *Recognizing States: International Society and the Establishment of New States since 1776*. Oxford: Oxford University Press.

Fabry, M. 2012. "The Contemporary Practice of State Recognition: Kosovo, South Ossetia, Abkhazia, and Their Aftermath." *Nationalities Papers* 40(5): 661–76.

Fabry, M. 2020. "The Evolution of State Recognition." In Visoka, G., Doyle, J., and Newman, E., eds., *Routledge Handbook of State Recognition*. London: Routledge, 37-47.

Fakir, I. 2017. "Playing the Status Quo." Malcolm H. Kerr Carnegie Middle East Center. New York: Carnegie Foundation. https://carnegie-mec.org/diwan /74694

Fazal, T. 2007. *State Death: The Politics and Geography of Conquest, Occupation, and Annexation*. Princeton, NJ: Princeton University Press.

Fazal, T. M. 2022. "The Return of Conquest? Why the Future of Global Order Hinges on Ukraine." *Foreign Policy*, 6 April. https://www.foreignaffairs.com/arti cles/ukraine/2022-04-06/ukraine-russia-war-return-conquest?

Felgenhauer, P. 2009. "Venezuela's Multibillion Dollar Abkhazia and South Ossetia Recognition Fee." Jamestown Foundation. 17 September. https://jamestown.org /program/venezuelas-multibillion-dollar-abkhazia-and-south-ossetia-recogniti on-fee/

Fenwick, C. G. 1948. "The Problem of the Recognition of de Facto Governments." *Inter-American Juridical Yearbook* 1: 18–39.

Fernández-Molina, I. and Porges, M. 2020. "Western Sahara." In Visoka, G., Doyle, J., and Newman, E., eds., *Routledge Handbook of State Recognition*. London: Routledge, 376–90.

Financial Times. 2021. "The Moment of Truth over Taiwan Is Getting Closer." 11 October. https://www.ft.com/content/9833d499-07ce-40eb-84e7-436023c6 eb8b

Focus Taiwan. 2019. "Legislature to Vote on Anti-infiltration Bill." 30 December. https://focustaiwan.tw/politics/201912300013

Focus Taiwan. 2024a. "Nauru's financial demands key to breaking ties with Taiwan: Official." 15 January. https://focustaiwan.tw/politics/202401150026

Focus Taiwan. 2024b. "AIT chair disappointed by U.N.-resolution distortion in Nauru move." 16 January. https://focustaiwan.tw/politics/202401160005

Forbes. 2019. "U.S. Arms Sales to the Middle East Have Soared in Value This Year." 16 December. https://www.forbes.com/sites/dominicdudley/2019/12/16/arms -sales-middle-east-soar/?sh=6fcedf50fea8

Fowdy, T. 2019. "Why the Solomon Islands Switched Diplomatic Recognition to Beijing." 17 September. https://news.cgtn.com/news/2019-09-17/Why-the-So lomon-Islands-switched-diplomatic-recognition-to-Beijing-K3uxBwL2kU/ind ex.html

Freedom House. 2021. "Western Sahara." Freedom in the World Report. https://fre
edomhouse.org/country/western-sahara/freedom-world/2021

French, D., ed. 2013. *Statehood and Self-Determination: Reconciling Tradition and Modernity in International Law*. Cambridge: Cambridge University Press.

Fry, G. 2019. *Framing the Islands: Power and Diplomatic Agency in Pacific Regionalism*. Canberra: Australian National University.

Ganohariti, R. 2021. "Politics of Passportization and Territorial Conflicts." In Richmond, O. and Visoka, G., eds., *The Palgrave Encyclopedia of Peace and Conflict Studies*. Cham, Switzerland: Palgrave Macmillan, 1148–55

GAP Institute. 2023. "Migration of Kosovans to Germany: A Statistical Analysis." Prishtina: GAP Institute. https://www.institutigap.org/documents/72594_Migr
ation%20to%20Germany.pdf

Gazeta Express. 2019. "Serbia Accused of Waging Campaign to Stop Overturn Kosovo Being Independent State." 22 September. https://www.express.co.uk/ne
ws/world/1181127/serbia-campaign-kosovo-independent-state-behgjet-pacolli

Gazeta Express. 2021. "Osmani thotë se pranimi i moratoriumit në Washington ka cenuar rendin kushtetues të Kosovës." 12 December. https://www.gazetaexpress
.com/osmani-thote-se-pranimi-i-moratoriumit-ne-washington-ka-cenuar-rend
in-kushtetues-te-kosoves/

Gazeta Metro. 2022. "Kosova refuzoi të nënshkruajë marrëdhëniet diplomatike me Timorin Lindor." 31 January. https://gazetametro.net/kosova-refuzoi-te-nenshkr
uaje-marredheniet-diplomatike-me-timorin-lindor/

Geldenhuys, D. 2009. *Contested States in World Politics*. Basingstoke: Palgrave Macmillan.

Gent, S. E. and Crescenzi, M. J. C. 2021. *Market Power Politics: War, Institutions, and Strategic Delay in World Politics*. New York: Oxford University Press.

George, A. and Bennett, A. 2006. *Case Study and Theory Development in the Social Sciences*. Cambridge, MA: MIT Press.

German Bundestag. 2019. "On the Recognition of Foreign Heads of State." Research Services. 7 February. https://www.bundestag.de/resource/blob/827464/db8b83
88d02332c24bfc46e3e758de71/WD-2-014-19_EN-pdf-data.pdf

Gerring, J. 2016. *Case Study Research: Principles and Practices*. 2nd ed. Cambridge: Cambridge University Press.

Gerrits, A. and Bader, M. 2016. "Russian Patronage over Abkhazia and South Ossetia: Implications for Conflict Resolution." *East European Politics* 32(3): 297–313.

Giegerich, T. 2018. "Article 63: Severance of Diplomatic or Consular Relations." In Dörr, O. and Schmalenbach, K., eds., *Vienna Convention on the Law of Treaties: A Commentary*. Cham, Switzerland: Springer, 1183–99.

Global Taiwan Institute. 2022. "Taiwan Security Review, Episode 4: United States–Taiwan Defense Cooperation with Elbridge Colby." 28 January. https://anchor
.fm/global-taiwan/episodes/Taiwan-Security-Review--Episode-4-United-States
-Taiwan-Defense-Cooperation-with-Elbridge-Colby-e1dhuq4/a-a7aa8ch

Global Times. 2024. "China, Nauru to ramp up cooperation in agriculture, infrastructure construction and more: experts." 15 January. https://www.globaltimes
.cn/page/202401/1305413.shtml

Government of Bolivia. 2020. "Strengthening Diplomatic Relations between the Plurinational State of Bolivia and the Kingdom of Morocco." La Paz, 20 January. http://www.cancilleria.gob.bo/webmre/comunicado/3790

Government of Georgia. 2008. "The Law of Georgia on Occupied Territories." 23 October. https://smr.gov.ge/uploads/prev/The_Law_of_928ef0d7.pdf

Government of Kosovo. 2018. "Memorandum on the Imposition of Customs Tariffs Coming from Serbia and Bosnia and Herzegovina." 4 December. https://www.gazetaexpress.com/lajme-ekskluzive-haradinaj-u-dergon-leter-te-gjitha-shteteve-te-be-se-per-taksen-ndaj-serbise-602074/

Government of Kosovo. 2021. "The Programme of the Government of Kosovo 2021–2025." https://masht.rks-gov.net/wp-content/uploads/2022/06/Programi-i-Qeverise-se-Kosoves-2021-2025.pdf

Government of Lesotho. 2019. "Clarification of Lesotho's Position on the Question of Western Sahara." Press Release. 9 October.

Government of Lesotho. 2020. "Statement by the Minister of Foreign Affairs and International Relations, Honourable Matsepo Molise—Ramakoae on the Position of Lesotho Regarding the Question of Western Sahara." 1 June. https://www.gov.ls/wp-content/uploads/2020/06/Statement-Official-short-Hon-Matsepo-Ramakoae-Sahrawi-1-June-2020-2.pdf

Government of Maldives. 2024. "Statement by the Government of Maldives following elections in Taiwan region." 14 January. https://foreign.gov.mv/index.php/en/media-center/statements/statement-by-the-government-of-maldives-following-elections-in-taiwan-region

Government of São Tomé and Príncipe. 2012. "Resolution on the International Recognition of the Republic of Kosovo." 13 March.

Government of Serbia. 2009. Written Statement to the ICJ. 17 April. https://www.icj-cij.org/public/files/case-related/141/15642.pdf

Government of Serbia. 2018a. "Commonwealth of Dominica Suspends Recognition of Independence of 'Kosovo.'" 2 November. https://www.srbija.gov.rs/vest/en/133036/commonwealth-of-dominica-suspends-recognition-of-independence-of-kosovo.php

Government of Serbia. 2018b. "Dacic Appeals to the Comoros' Officials to Reconsider Decision to Recognize Independent Kosovo." 2 March. http://www.mfa.gov.rs/en/press-service/daily-news?year=2018&month=03&day=05&modid=62. Accessed 10 March 2018.

Government of Serbia. 2018c. "Comoros Withdraws Recognition of Kosovo." 7 November. https://www.srbija.gov.rs/vest/en/133283/comoros-withdraws-recognition-of-kosovo.php

Government of Serbia. 2018d. "Gratitude to Comoros for Support to Territorial Integrity of Serbia." 7 November. https://www.srbija.gov.rs/vest/en/133340/gratitude-to-comoros-for-support-to-territorial-integrity-of-serbia.php

Government of Serbia. 2020. "Antigua and Barbuda to Accept Results of Belgrade-Pristina Dialogue." Belgrade. 22 February. https://www.srbija.gov.rs/vest/en/150474/antigua-and-barbuda-to-accept-results-of-belgrade-pristina-dialogue.php

Government of Serbia. 2023. "Letter by the Prime Minister of Serbia to the EEAS's Deputy Managing Director" 13 December.

Government of Suriname. 2016. "Suriname Supports the UN efforts in Finding Peaceful Solutions to the Western Sahara Conflict." 3 March. https://web.archive.org/web/20171107025305/http://gov.sr/ministerie-van-buza/actueel/suriname-supports-the-un-efforts-in-finding-peaceful-solutions-to-the-western-sahara-conflict.aspx

Government of Taiwan. 2017. "Framework Co-operation Agreement between the Government of the Republic of China (Taiwan) and the Government of Solomon Islands." 31 January. https://law.moj.gov.tw/ENG/LawClass/LawAll.aspx?pcode=Y0010174

Government of the Republic of Nauru. 2024. "Nauru follows UN Resolution and moves to One-China principle." 15 January.

Government of Vanuatu. 2011. Press Release, Port Vila. 17 June. https://ic.pics.livejournal.com/suresnois/17886242/58974/58974_original.jpg

Gowan, R. 2020. "China's Pragmatic Approach to UN Peacekeeping." Brookings Institution. 14 September. https://www.brookings.edu/articles/chinas-pragmatic-approach-to-un-peacekeeping/

Grant, J. P. and Barker, J. C. 2009. *Parry and Grant Encyclopaedic Dictionary of International Law.* 3rd ed. Oxford: Oxford University Press.

Grant, T. D. 1999. *The Recognition of States: Law and Practice in Debate and Evolution.* Westport, CT: Praeger.

Griffiths, R. 2016. *Age of Secession: The International and Domestic Determinants of State Birth.* Cambridge: Cambridge University Press.

Griffiths, R. 2017. "Admission to the Sovereignty Club: The Past, Present, and Future of the International Recognition Regime." *Territory, Politics, Governance* 5(2): 177–89.

Griffiths, R. 2021. *Secession and the Sovereignty Game: Strategy and Tactics for Aspiring Nations.* Ithaca, NY: Cornell University Press.

Griffiths, R. and Muro, D., eds. 2020. *Strategies of Secession and Counter-secession.* London: ECPR Press and Rowman and Littlefield.

Grossman, D. 2021. "Taiwan Would Be Better Off Alone." *Nikkei Asia,* 23 December. https://asia.nikkei.com/Opinion/Taiwan-would-be-better-off-alone

Grossman, D. et al. 2019. *America's Pacific Island Allies: The Freely Associated States and Chinese Influence.* Santa Monica, CA: Rand Corporation.

Grzybowski, J. 2019. "The Paradox of State Identification: De Facto States, Recognition, and the (Re)production of the International." *International Theory* 11(3): 241–63.

The Guardian. 2019a. "Solomons' Government Vetoes Chinese Attempt to Lease an Island." 25 October. https://www.theguardian.com/world/2019/oct/25/solomons-government-vetoes-chinese-attempt-to-lease-an-island

The Guardian. 2019b. "Solomon Islands to Decide Soon on Whether to Cut Ties with Taiwan." 7 June. https://www.theguardian.com/world/2019/jun/05/solomon-islands-decision-ties-with-taiwan-or-china

The Guardian. 2020a. "Kosovan Acting PM Accuses Trump Envoy of Meddling." 20 April. https://www.theguardian.com/world/2020/apr/20/kosovan-acting-pm-accuses-trump-envoy-of-meddling

The Guardian. 2020b. "Pro-China Kiribati President Loses Majority over Switch from Taiwan." 24 April. https://www.theguardian.com/world/2020/apr/24/pro-china-kiribati-president-loses-majority-over-switch-from-taiwan

The Guardian. 2021. "Parliament Building and Police Station Burned Down during Protests in Solomon Islands." 24 November. https://www.theguardian.com/world/2021/nov/24/parliament-building-and-police-station-burned-down-during-protests-in-solomon-islands

258 • References

Hall, I. 2006. "Diplomacy, Anti-diplomacy and International Society." In Little, R. and Williams, J., eds., *The Anarchical Society in a Globalized World.* Basingstoke: Palgrave Macmillan, 141–61.

Heath, T. R., Lilly, S., and Han, E. 2023. "Can Taiwan Resist a Large-Scale Military Attack by China? Assessing Strengths and Vulnerabilities in a Potential Conflict." Rand Corporation. http://www.rand.org/t/RRA1658-1

Herbst, J. 2004. "Let Them Fail: State Failure in Theory and Practice." In Rotberg, R., ed., *When States Fail: Causes and Consequences.* Princeton, NJ: Princeton University Press, 302–18.

Hickey, D. 2007. *Foreign Policy Making in Taiwan: From Principle to Pragmatism.* London: Routledge.

Hoover Institution. 2021. "Taiwan in the Indo-Pacific Region." 27 September. https://youtu.be/MyAJxzgNIso

Hsieh, P. L. 2019. "The Quest for Recognition: Taiwan's Military and Trade Agreements with Singapore under the One-China Policy." *International Relations of the Asia-Pacific* 19(1): 89–115.

Huddleston, R. J. 2020. "Continuous Recognition: A Latent Variable Approach to Measuring International Sovereignty of Self-Determination Movements." *Journal of Peace Research* 57(6): 789–800.

Huddleston, R. J. 2021. "Foulweather Friends: Violence and Third Party Support in Self-Determination Conflicts." *Journal of Conflict Resolution* 65(6): 1187–1214.

Huddleston, R. J., Ghoorhoo, H., and Maquera Sardon, D. A. 2021. "Biden Can Backtrack on Trump's Move in Western Sahara." *Foreign Policy,* 9 January. https://foreignpolicy.com/2021/01/09/biden-can-backtrack-on-trumps-move-in-western-sahara/

Human Rights Watch. 2021. "Western Sahara: Harassment of Independence Activist." 5 March. https://www.hrw.org/news/2021/03/05/western-sahara-harassment-independence-activist

Igarashi, M. 2002. *Associated Statehood in International Law.* The Hague: Kluwer Law International.

IISS. 2021. "The End of the Ceasefire in Western Sahara." *Strategic Comments* 27(8): xi–xiii. https://doi.org/1080/13567888.2021.2006931

Ilyin, M. 2011. "Abkhazia, South Ossetia and Transdniestria: Secessions in the Post-Soviet Space." In Pavković, A. and Radan, P., eds., *The Ashgate Research Companion to Secession.* Farnham: Ashgate Publishing, 529–33.

Ing-wen, T. 2021. "Taiwan and the Fight for Democracy." *Foreign Affairs,* November–December. https://www.foreignaffairs.com/articles/taiwan/2021-10-05/taiwan-and-fight-democracy

Institut de Droit International. 1936. "Resolutions Concerning the Recognition of New States and New Governments." *American Journal of International Law* 30(4): 185–87.

International Alert. 2011. "The Politics of Non-recognition in the Context of the Georgian-Abkhaz Conflict." https://www.international-alert.org/publications/politics-non-recognition-context-georgian-abkhaz-conflict/.

International Crisis Group. 2021. "Time for International Re-engagement in Western Sahara." 11 March. https://media.africaportal.org/documents/b082-western-sahara-.pdf

Israel Law Review. 2019. "Recognition in the Context of the Israeli-Palestinian Conflict: Proceedings of an International Workshop Held at the Hebrew University of Jerusalem, 5 November 2018." *Israel Law Review* 52(3): 367–412.

Jackson, R. 2002. "Martin Wight's Thought on Diplomacy." *Diplomacy and Statecraft* 13(4): 1–28.

Jain, A. G. 2014. "Recognition of States in International Law: For Sale." EJIS Talk. 21 April. https://www.ejiltalk.org/recognition-of-states-in-international-law-for-sale/

James, A. 1999. "The Practice of Sovereign Statehood in Contemporary International Society." *Political Studies* 47(3): 457–73.

James, A. 2016. "Diplomatic Relations between States." In Constantinou, C. M., Kerr, P., and Sharp, P., eds., *The Sage Handbook of Diplomacy*. London: Sage, 257–67.

Jamnejad, M. and Wood, M. 2009. "The Principle of Non-intervention." *Leiden Journal of International Law* 22(2): 345–81.

Jornal de Angola. 2013. "Presidente de São Tomé e Príncipe vetou o reconhecimento do Kosovo." 9 January. https://www.pressreader.com/angola/jornal-de-angola/20130109/281621007683739

Kallxo. 2018. "Ngecjet në njohje, pasojë e konfuzionit politik brenda Kosovës." 7 November. https://kallxo.com/gjate/analize/ngecjet-ne-njohje-pasoje-e-konfuzionit-politik-brenda-kosoves/

Kelsen, H. 1941. "Recognition in International Law: Theoretical Observations." *American Journal of International Law* 35(4): 605–17.

Ker-Lindsay, J. 2012. *The Foreign Policy of Counter Secession: Preventing the Recognition of Contested States*. Oxford: Oxford University Press.

Kingsbury, D. 2015. "The Role of Resources in the Resolution of the Western Sahara Issue." *Global Change, Peace & Security* 27(3): 253–62.

Kiss, A. 2006. "Abuse of Rights." *Max Planck Encyclopedia of International Law*. https://opil.ouplaw.com/view/10.1093/law:epil/9780199231690/law-9780199231690-e1371

Koha. 2019a. "Hoxhaj për mediat boshnjake: Taksa mbetet në fuqi derisa nuk pushojnë arsyet që çuan në vendosjen e saj." 23 January. https://www.koha.net/arberi/141166/hoxhaj-per-mediat-boshnjake-taksa-mbetet-ne-fuqi-derisa-nuk-pushojne-arsyet-qe-shtyen-tek-vendosja-e-saj/

Koha. 2019b. "MPJ e cilëson të rremë lajmin për tërheqjen e njohjes së Kosovës nga Gana" [MFA considers the withdrawal of recognition of Kosovo by Ghana fake news]. 11 November. https://www.koha.net/arberi/193427/mpj-e-cileson-te-rreme-lajmin-per-terheqjen-e-njohjes-se-kosoves-nga-gana/

Koha. 2019c. "Serbia's 'Suitcase Diplomacy.'" 19 March. https://www.koha.net/arberi/151335/kofer-diplomacia-e-serbise/

Koskenniemi, M. 2005. *From Apology to Utopia: The Structure of International Legal Argument*. Cambridge: Cambridge University Press.

Koskenniemi, M. 2011. *The Politics of International Law*. Cambridge: Cambridge University Press.

Krasner, S. D. 1999. *Sovereignty: Organized Hypocrisy*. Princeton, NJ: Princeton University Press.

Krasner, S. D. 2013. "Recognition: Organized Hypocrisy Once Again." *International Theory* 5(1): 170–76.

Kyris, G. 2022. "State Recognition and Dynamic Sovereignty." *European Journal of International Relations* 28(2): 287–311.

Lakhal, M, Khalil, A., and San Martin, P. 2006. "Moroccan Autonomy for the Western Sahara: A Solution to a Decolonisation Conflict or a Prelude to the Dismantling of a Kingdom?" *Review of African Political Economy* 33(108): 336–41.

Lamb, K. 2015. "IKEA, Uber, and the Western Sahara: The Politics of Corporate Recognition." *Brown Political Review*, 1 November. https://brownpoliticalreview.org/2015/11/ikea-uber-and-the-western-sahara-the-politics-of-corporate-recog nition/

Lambert, M. 2020. "Consequences of the Diplomatic Recognition of Abkhazia by the Syrian Arab Republic (2018)." 17 March. https://russiancouncil.ru/en/analyt ics-and-comments/columns/military-and-security/consequences-of-the-diplom atic-recognition-of-abkhazia-by-the-syrian-arab-republic-2018/

Laoutides, C. 2020. "Self-Determination and the Recognition of States." In Visoka, G., Doyle, J., and Newman, E., eds., *Routledge Handbook of State Recognition.* London: Routledge, 59–70.

Lauterpacht, H. 1944. "Recognition of States in International Law." *Yale Law Journal* 53(3): 385–458.

Lauterpacht, H. 1945. "De Facto Recognition, Withdrawal of Recognition, and Conditional Recognition." *British Year Book of International Law* 22: 164–90.

Lauterpacht, H. 1947. *Recognition in International Law.* Cambridge: University Press.

Lee, M. M. 2020. *Crippling Leviathan: How Foreign Subversion Weakens the State.* Ithaca, NY: Cornell University Press.

Leff, R. S. 1977. "United States Policy Regarding Recognition of Foreign States." *Hastings International and Comparative Law Review* 1(1): 173–206.

Lesotho Times. 2018. "Lesotho: Fresh Controversy over Lesotho's Stance on Western Sahara." 18 December. https://allafrica.com/stories/201912180449.html

Lin, H. S., Wu, C. K. S., and Yeh, Y. 2022. "The Statehood of Taiwan." In Abidde, S. O., ed., *China and Taiwan in Africa: The Struggle for Diplomatic Recognition and Hegemony.* Cham, Switzerland: Springer, 37–54.

Lin, T.-C. and Lin, J. Y.-C. 2017. "Taiwan's Foreign Aid in Transition: From ODA to Civil Society Approaches." *Japanese Journal of Political Science* 18(4): 469–490. https://doi.org/10.1017/s1468109917000135

Long, T. and Urdinez, F. 2021. "Status at the Margins: Why Paraguay Recognizes Taiwan and Shuns China." *Foreign Policy Analysis* 17(1): 1–22.

Loo, J. T. 2014. "America's Security and Taiwan's Freedom." In Lee, S. and Williams, J. F., eds., *Taiwan's Struggle: Voices of the Taiwanese.* Lanham, MD: Rowman and Littlefield, 163–72.

Lowe, V. 2007. *International Law.* Oxford: Oxford University Press.

MacGibbon, I. C. 1958. "Estoppel in International Law." *International and Comparative Law Quarterly* 7(3): 468–513.

Madsen, B. A. 2001. The Struggle for Sovereignty between China and Taiwan." In Krasner, S., ed., *Problematic Sovereignty: Contested Rules and Political Possibilities.* Princeton, NJ: Princeton University Press, 141–93.

Maghess. 2007. "Sahara: Nairobi saisit l'UA au sujet de la RASD" [Sahara: Nairobi seizes AU on SADR]. 20 July. https://www.maghress.com/fr/aujourdhui/55842

Malay Mail. 2019. "Taiwan Warns Pacific Islands of China's "Empty Promises' on

Aid." 22 August. https://www.malaymail.com/news/world/2019/08/22/taiwan-warns-pacific-islands-of-chinas-empty-promises-on-aid/1783163

Mann, M. 1984. "The Autonomous Power of the State: Its Origins, Mechanisms and Results." *European Journal of Sociology / Archives européennes de sociologie* 25(2): 185–213.

March, J. G. and Olsen, J. P. 1998. "The Institutional Dynamics of International Political Orders." *International Organization* 52(4): 943–69.

Mario Díaz-Balart. 2024. "Taiwan Caucus Co-Chairs Introduce Resolution in Support of Democracy in Taiwan." 10 January. https://mariodiazbalart.house.gov/media-center/press-releases/taiwan-caucus-co-chairs-introduce-resolution-support-democracy-taiwan

Marin, J. and Paquin, J. 2018. *Foreign Policy Analysis: A Toolbox*. London: Palgrave Macmillan.

Martin, X. 2020. "Taiwan's Competition for Diplomatic Recognition with Mainland China." *Taiwan Insight*, 30 September. https://taiwaninsight.org/2020/09/30/taiwans-competition-for-diplomatic-recognition-with-mainland-china/

Masiky, H. 2017. "Strategy for New Approach to Moroccan Diplomacy in Mexico and Latin America." *Morocco World News*, 14 March. https://www.moroccoworldnews.com/2017/03/210928/strategy-new-approach-moroccan-diplomacy-mexico-latin-america/

McKercher, B. J. C., ed. 2022. *The Routledge Handbook of Diplomacy and Statecraft*. 2nd ed. London: Routledge.

MFA of Bolivia. 2021. Communiqué: "The Plurinational State of Bolivia Strengthens Diplomatic Relations with the Sahrawi Arab Democratic Republic." La Paz. 16 September. https://cancilleria.gob.bo/webmre/comunicado/4595

MFA of Burundi. 2008. "Note Sent to Diplomatic Missions and International Organization in Bujumbura." Doc. No. 204.01/242/RE/2008. 16 June.

MFA of Burundi. 2018. Note Verbale, Ref. 204.01/182/RE/2018 Bujumbura. 15 February.

MFA of China. 2016. "Joint Communiqué between the People's Republic of China and the Islamic Republic of the Gambia on Resumption of Diplomatic Relations." 13 March. https://www.fmprc.gov.cn/mfa_eng/zxxx_662805/t1348575.shtml

MFA of China. 2019. "Foreign Ministry Spokesperson Geng Shuang's Regular Press Conference on September 18, 2019." http://sc.china-embassy.gov.cn/eng/fyrth/201909/t20190918_5902250.htm.

MFA of Czech Republic. 2019. "Prohlášení MZV k uznání Kosovské republiky" [Foreign Ministry statement on the recognition of the Republic of Kosovo]. 12 September. https://www.mzv.cz/jnp/cz/udalosti_a_media/prohlaseni_a_stanoviska/archiv_prohlaseni_a_stanovisek/archiv_2019/x2019_09_12_prohlaseni_mzv_k_uznani_kosovske.html

MFA of Dominica. 2018. Note Ref. 21647–3856. 30 October.

MFA of Ghana. 2012. Note SCR.GH/KOS/RELS. 23 January.

MFA of Ghana. 2019. Note. 7 November. https://media.srbija.gov.rs/medeng/documents/odluka-povlacenje-gana-priznanje-kosova-eng.pdf

MFA of Grenada. 2018. Note No. 535/2018. 30 October.

MFA of Haiti. 2013. Communiqué, Port-au-Prince. 2 October.

262 • References

MFA of Kenya. 2022. "Kenya's Position on the Sahrawi Arab Democratic Republic (SADR)." MFA.REL/64 Vol. 1. 16 September.

MFA of Kosovo. 2018a. "MFA: Serbia through Fake News Is Misusing Also the Reputation of the Countries That Have Already Recognized Kosovo." Accessed November 7, 2018. http://mfa-ks.net/en/single_lajmi/3542

MFA of Kosovo. 2018b. "Note Verbal sent to the Ministry of Foreign Affairs and External Trade of Solomon Islands." 30 November.

MFA of Kosovo. 2018c. Press Release. Accessed October 16, 2018. http://www.mfa-ks.net/single_lajmi/3527

MFA of Kosovo. 2018d. Press Release. Accessed November 20, 2018. https://www.mfa-ks.net/al/single_lajmi/3551

MFA of Kosovo. 2018e. Press Statement. Accessed February 19, 2018. http://www.mfa-ks.net/single_lajmi/2580

MFA of Kosovo. 2018d. Press Statement. Accessed February 27, 2018. http://www.mfa-ks.net/single_lajmi/2567

MFA of Kosovo. 2019a. Diplomatic Note to Eswatini. 20 May.

MFA of Kosovo. 2019b. Nonpaper, no date but issued 2019.

MFA of Kosovo. 2019c. Note Verbale Ref. 520/2019. 26 August.

MFA of Lesotho. 2014. Note No. 1 (FR/CL/CTR/170). 12 February.

MFA of Lesotho. 2018a. Note No. 2 (FR/CL/CTR/140/2). 16 October.

MFA of Lesotho. 2019. Note No. 24 (FR/CL/CTR/31). 4 October.

MFA of Liberia. 2018. "Letter of Withdrawal of Kosovo's Independence." RL/MFA/2-1/249/18. Monrovia. 20 June.

MFA of Madagascar. 2018. Note Verbale No. 090/18-AE/M. 5 December.

MFA of Morocco. 2020. "The Gambia Opens a Consulate General in Dakhla." 13 January. https://www.diplomatie.ma/en/gambia-opens-consulate-general-dakhla-0

MFA of Panama. 2013. "Declaration of Suspension of Diplomatic Relations with the Sahrawi Arab Democratic Republic." 13 November.

MFA of Peru. 2022. "Official Communiqué of the Ministry of Foreign Affairs." 18 August. https://www.gob.pe/institucion/rree/noticias/642189-comunicado-oficial-del-ministerio-de-relaciones-exteriores

MFA of PRC. 2019. "Foreign Ministry Spokesperson Geng Shuang's Remarks on the Resumption of Diplomatic Relations between China and Kiribati." 28 September. https://www.mfa.gov.cn/ce/cegv//eng/fyrth/t1703326.htm

MFA of PRC. 2021. "Foreign Ministry Spokesperson Wang Wenbin's Regular Press Conference on October 22, 2021." https://www.fmprc.gov.cn/mfa_eng/xwfw_665399/s2510_665401/2511_665403/t1916229.shtml

MFA of Russia. 2017. "Foreign Minister Sergey Lavrov's Remarks and Answers to Media Questions at a Joint News Conference Following Talks with Surinamese Foreign Minister Yldiz Pollack-Beighle, Moscow, October 31, 2017." https://www.mid.ru/en/press_service/video/-/asset_publisher/i6t41cq3VWP6/content/id/2927121

MFA of Russia. 2018. "Foreign Minister Sergey Lavrov's Remarks and Answers to Media Questions at a News Conference Following Talks with the Minister of Foreign Affairs and International Cooperation of the Comoros, Mohamed El-Amine Souef, Moscow, November 9, 2018." https://www.mid.ru/en/web/guest

/meropriyatiya_s_uchastiem_ministra/-/asset_publisher/xK1BhB2bUjd3/conte
nt/id/3404241

MFA of Russia. 2023. "Press Release on Sergey Lavrov's Meeting with First Deputy
Prime Minister and Foreign Minister of the Republic of Serbia Ivica Dacic." 22
September. https://mid.ru/en/foreign_policy/international_safety/regprla/1905
862/

MFA of Russia. 2024. "Foreign Ministry Spokeswoman Maria Zakharova's answer
to a media question regarding Russia's position on the Taiwan issue". 13 January.
https://mid.ru/en/foreign_policy/news/1925467/

MFA of Serbia. 2017. "Principled Position of Sao Tome and Principe Concerning
the Respect of International Law and Non-recognition of Kosovo." 26 September. http://www.pretoria.mfa.gov.rs/odrzavanje/stampa.php?id=1506413433

MFA of Serbia. 2019a. "Gana povukla priznanje Kosova." 11 November. https://www
.mfa.gov.rs/lat/mediji/saopstenja/gana-povukla-priznanje-kosova

MFA of Serbia. 2019b. "Minister Dačić Met with President of Ghana." Accessed
May 20, 2019. http://www.mfa.gov.rs/en/press-service/statements/18734-minis
ter-dacic-met-with-president-of-ghana

MFA of Sierra Leone. 2008. Note Verbale 3079/132. Freetown. 1 June.

MFA of Sierra Leone. 2009. "Declaration of Support for the Independence of
Kosovo by the Government of the Republic of Sierra Leone." 15 April. https://
www.icj-cij.org/public/files/case-related/141/15672.pdf

MFA of Sierra Leone. 2020. Note Verbale 3079/39/DG. Freetown. 2 March.

MFA of Somalia. 2022. Press Statement. 6 August. https://twitter.com/RAbdiAnaly
st/status/1556532694624124929/photo/1

MFA of Taiwan. 2018. "The R.O.C. Government Has Terminated Diplomatic Relations with El Salvador with Immediate Effect in Order to Uphold National
Dignity." 21 August. https://www.mofa.gov.tw/en/News_Content.aspx?n=0E7B
91A8FBEC4A94&sms=220E98D761D34A9A&s=0DB8435E0E11485D

MFA of Taiwan. 2008. "To Maintain the National Dignity, Sovereignty and Interests of the Republic of China (Taiwan), the Government of Taiwan Is Terminating Diplomatic Relations with the Republic of Malawi and Suspending All Aid
Projects for That Country with Immediate Effect." 14 January. https://www.mo
fa.gov.tw/en/News_Content.aspx?n=0E7B91A8FBEC4A94&sms=220E98D7
61D34A9A&s=525F5DEA66142D6D

MFA of Taiwan. 2016. "Response to São Tomé and Príncipe's Re-establishment of
Diplomatic Ties with Mainland China." Press Release No. 004. 26 December.
https://en.mofa.gov.tw/News_Content.aspx?n=1330&s=34148

MFA of Taiwan. 2017. "The ROC Government Has Terminated Diplomatic Relations with Panama with Immediate Effect to Uphold National Dignity." 13 June.
https://en.mofa.gov.tw/News_Content.aspx?n=0E7B91A8FBEC4A94&sms=2
20E98D761D34A9A&s=CF11CEBE98E46573

MFA of Taiwan. 2018a. "The ROC Government Has Terminated Diplomatic Rela-
tions with the Dominican Republic with Immediate Effect to Uphold National
Dignity." 1 May. https://en.mofa.gov.tw/News_Content.aspx?n=0E7B91A8FB
EC4A94&sms=220E98D761D34A9A&s=E1732BD27CCB16CE

MFA of Taiwan. 2018b. "Statement by the Republic of China (Taiwan) on the
Resumption of Diplomatic Ties between Burkina Faso and China." 26 May.

https://en.mofa.gov.tw/News_Content.aspx?n=0E7B91A8FBEC4A94&sms=2 20E98D761D34A9A&s=8ADA4A4103ECE5AE

MFA of Taiwan. 2018c. "The ROC Government Has Terminated Diplomatic Relations with Burkina Faso with Immediate Effect to Uphold National Dignity." 24 May. https://www.mofa.gov.tw/en/News_Content.aspx?n=0E7B91A8FBEC4A 94&sms=220E98D761D34A9A&s=97A280F693D2020A

MFA of Taiwan. 2019a. "The Ministry of Foreign Affairs Clarification on the Solomon Islands Bipartisan Task Force Report." 13 September. https://en.mofa.gov .tw/News_Content.aspx?n=539A9A50A5F8AF9E&s=961E7B847A93B6B4

MFA of Taiwan. 2019b. "The R.O.C. (Taiwan) Government Terminates Diplomatic Relations with Solomon Islands with Immediate Effect to Uphold National Dignity." 16 September. https://en.mofa.gov.tw/News_Content.aspx?n=1EADDCF D4C6EC567&s=D9899CF130830D7B

MFA of Taiwan. 2024a. "MOFA response to false claims made by Russian Foreign Ministry following Taiwan's elections." 14 January. https://en.mofa.gov.tw/Ne ws_Content.aspx?n=1328&sms=273&s=116425

MFA of Taiwan. 2024b. "R.O.C. (Taiwan) government has terminated diplomatic relations with Republic of Nauru with immediate effect to uphold national dignity." 15 January. https://en.mofa.gov.tw/News_Content.aspx?n=1328&sms=27 3&s=116429

MFA of Vanuatu. 2011. Letter to the Minister of Foreign Affairs of Abkhazia. 1 July.

MFAT of Papua New Guinea. 2018. "Letter Addressed to First Deputy Prime Minister and Minister for Foreign Affairs of the Republic of Serbia." 27 June.

Middle East Eye. 2020. "Polisario Hopes Biden Will Cancel Trump's Western Sahara Deal. If Not, There's Always War." 17 December. https://media.africaportal.org /documents/b082-western-sahara-.pdf

Middle East Monitor. 2018. "Colombia Denies Having a Polisario Diplomatic Representation on Its Territory." 17 April. https://www.middleeastmonitor.com/201 80427-colombia-denies-having-a-polisario-diplomatic-representation-on-its-te rritory//

Miller, M. C. 2021. *Why Nations Rise: Narratives and the Path to Great Power*. New York: Oxford University Press.

Ministry of Defence of Serbia. 2017. "Strategy of National Security of the Republic of Serbia." https://www.mod.gov.rs/multimedia/file/staticki_sadrzaj/javna%20r asprava/strategije/Nacrt%20Strategije%20nacionalne%20bezbednosti.pdf

Minivan News. 2009a. "President Orders Bribery Investigation." 5 April. https:// web.archive.org/web/20090405010717/http:/www.minivannews.com:80/news _detail.php?id=6125

Minivan News. 2009b. "No Evidence of Bribery in Kosovo Investigation." 6 May. https://web.archive.org/web/20090529014902/http://www.minivannews.com /news_detail.php?id=6467

Mintz, A. and Redd, S. B. 2003. "Framing Effects in International Relations." *Synthese* 135(2): 193–213.

Morocco World News. 2015. "Crans Montana Forum: International Recognition of Morocco's Sovereignty over 'Western Sahara.'" 14 March. https://www.morocco worldnews.com/2015/03/153929/crans-montana-forum-international-recogni tion-moroccos-sovereignty-western-sahara

Morocco World News. 2019a. "El Salvador to Reconsider Its Recognition of Self-Proclaimed SADR." 7 June. https://www.moroccoworldnews.com/2019/06/27 5357/el-salvador-recognition-sadr-western-sahara/

Morocco World News. 2019b. "El Salvador Withdraws Its Recognition of Polisario's So-Called SADR." 15 June. https://www.moroccoworldnews.com/2019/06/275 934/el-salvador-recognition-sadr-polisario

Morocco World News. 2020. "FM: New Gambian Consulate in Dakhla Reflects Rabat-Banjul Strong Relations." 7 January. https://www.moroccoworldnews .com/2020/01/290647/gambian-consulate-dakhla-morocco

Morocco World News. 2021. "Malawi to Open Consulate in Morocco's Laayoune." 27 July. https://www.moroccoworldnews.com/2021/07/343610/malawi-to-op en-consulate-in-moroccos-laayoune

Mundy, J. 2017. "The Geopolitical Functions of the Western Sahara Conflict: US Hegemony, Moroccan Stability and Sahrawi Strategies of Resistance." In Ojeda-Garcia, R. et al., eds., *Global, Regional and Local Dimensions of Western Sahara's Protracted Decolonization.* Basingstoke: Palgrave Macmillan, 53–78.

Murray, M. 2019. *The Struggle for Recognition in International Relations: Status, Revisionism, and Rising Powers.* New York: Oxford University Press.

Murray, S. 2018. *Sports Diplomacy: Origins, Theory and Practice.* London: Routledge.

Musliu, V. and Gashi, K. 2009. "Kosovo Battle Moves to Maldives." *Prishtina Insight,* 13–26 March. https://prishtinainsight.com/wp-content/uploads/2016 /02/Prishtina-Insight-11.pdf

N1. 2018a. "Dačić: Burundi je povukao priznanje, a Priština teši svoje." 18 February. https://rs.n1info.com/vesti/a365427-dacic-burundi-je-povukao-priznanje-a-pri stina-tesi-svoju-javnost/

N1. 2018b. "Ghana to reconsider recognition of Kosovo." 28 May. https://n1info.rs /english/news/a391578-accra-to-look-into-decision-of-kosovo-recognition/.

N1. 2019a. "FM Denies Slovenia Will Withdraw Recognition of Kosovo." 20 March. https://rs.n1info.com/english/news/a469609-slovenia-wont-revoke-recognition -of-kosovo-fm-says/

N1. 2019b. "Dačić: Nadam se da će zločini OVK biti kažnjeni" [Dačić: I hope that the crimes of the KLA will be punished]. 22 July. https://rs.n1info.com/vesti/a5 01744-dacic-nadam-se-da-ce-zlocini-ovk-biti-kaznjeni/

N1. 2019c. "Vucic Calls Trump to Help Restart Kosovo Dialogue." 14 June. https:// rs.n1info.com/english/news/a491891-vucic-calls-trump-to-help-restart-kosovo -dialogue/

N1. 2019d. "Kosovo Foreign Ministry Says Belgrade Faked Diplomatic Notes." 26 August. https://rs.n1info.com/english/news/a520714-kosovo-foreign-ministry -says-belgrade-faked-diplomatic-notes/

N1. 2019e. "Zeman: It Would Be Tough, but Prague Could Withdraw Recognition of Kosovo." 6 September. https://rs.n1info.com/english/news/a523689-cze ch-president-says-his-country-could-revoke-its-recognition-of-kosovo-one-day/

N1. 2020. "Israeli Envoy to Serbia: We Recognised Kosovo on September 4; Not an Issue Anymore." 21 September. https://rs.n1info.com/english/news/a642039-is raeli-envoy-to-serbia-we-recognised-kosovo-on-september-4-its-not-issue-anym ore/

Naticchia, C. 2017. *A Law of Peoples for Recognizing States.* Lanham, MD: Lexington Books.

Naticchia, C. 2000. "Recognition and Legitimacy: A Reply to Buchanan." *Philosophy and Public Affairs* 28(3): 242–57.

National Parliament of Solomon Islands. 2019. "Report of the Inquiry into the Question of Severing Existing Ties with the Republic of China (Taiwan)." 26 November. https://www.parliament.gov.sb/sites/default/files/committees/foreig nrelations/2019/FRC%20Report%20November%202019.pdf

Neofotistos, V. P. 2012. *The Risk of War: Everyday Sociality in the Republic of Macedonia*. Philadelphia: University of Pennsylvania Press.

New Republic. 2014. "This Tiny Pacific Island Nation Just Gave Russia a Big Bruise." 2 April. https://newrepublic.com/article/117238/tuvalu-bruises-russia-establish ing-diplomatic-ties-georgia

New Times. 2017. "Malawi Withdraws Recognition of 'SADR.'" 10 May. https:// www.newtimes.co.rw/section/read/212129

New York Times. 2001. "Tiny Pacific Island Is Facing Money-Laundering Sanctions." 6 December. https://www.nytimes.com/2001/12/06/world/tiny-pacific -island-is-facing-money-laundering-sanctions.html

New York Times. 2007. "Reversal by Tiny St. Lucia Angers China." 2 May. https:// www.nytimes.com/2007/05/02/world/asia/02iht-island.1.5529756.html

New York Times. 2008. "Taiwan Foreign Minister Resigns over Diplomatic Blunder." 6 May. https://www.nytimes.com/2008/05/06/world/asia/06iht-taiwan .1.12605732.html

New York Times. 2018. "After Snubbing Taiwan, Burkina Faso Establishes Diplomatic Ties with China." 25 May. https://www.nytimes.com/2018/05/26/world /asia/burkina-faso-china-taiwan.html

New York Times. 2022. "Spain, Seeking Better Ties with Morocco, Shifts Stance on Western Sahara." 19 March. https://www.nytimes.com/2022/03/19/world/euro pe/spain-morocco-western-sahara.html

Newman, E. and Visoka, G. 2018a. "The European Union's Practice of State Recognition: Between Norms and Interests." *Review of International Studies* 44(4): 760–86.

Newman, E. and Visoka, G. 2018b. "The Foreign Policy of State Recognition: Kosovo's Diplomatic Strategy to Join International Society." *Foreign Policy Analysis* 14(3): 367–87.

Newman, E. and Visoka, G. 2023. "The Geopolitics of State Recognition in a Transitional International Order." *Geopolitics* 28(1): 364–91.

Nicholson, R. 2019. *Statehood and the State-Like in International Law*. Oxford: Oxford University Press.

Nincic, M. 2005. *Renegade Regimes: Confronting Deviant Behavior in World Politics*. New York: Columbia University Press.

Ninet, A. A., ed. 2024. *Constitutional Law and Politics of Secession*. London: Routledge.

Noutcheva, G. 2020. "Contested Statehood and EU Actorness in Kosovo, Abkhazia and Western Sahara." *Geopolitics* 25(2): 449–71.

Novinar. 2019. "Dačić: Gana povukla priznanje Kosova" [Dačić: Ghana withdrew recognition of Kosovo]. 11 November. https://www.novinar.rs/politika/dacic-ga na-povukla-priznanje-kosova/

Novosti. 2018a. "Pada Podrška Prištini: Klima se još 10 priznavanja Kosova." 22 June.

https://www.novosti.rs/vesti/naslovna/politika/aktuelno.289.html:734310-PA DA-PODRSKA-PRISTINI-Klima-se-jos-10-priznavanja-Kosova

Novosti. 2018b. "Pismo Amerike minira Beograd" [Letter of America undermines Belgrade]. 8 November. https://www.novosti.rs/vesti/naslovna/politika/aktuelno .289.html:759367-NOVOSTI-OTKRIVAJU-Pismo-Amerike-minira-Beograd

Novosti. 2019a. "Drecun: Nezavisnost Kosova besperspektivna" [Drecun: Independence of Kosovo without perspective]. 19 January. http://www.novosti.rs/vesti /naslovna/politika/aktuelno.289.html:772399-Drecun-Nezavisnost-Kosova-bes perspektivna

Novosti. 2019b. "Srbija otvara sedam ambasada i konzulata" [Serbia opens seven embassies and consulates]. 19 February. http://www.novosti.rs/vesti/naslovna/po litika/aktuelno.289.html:778187-Srbija-otvara-sedam-ambasada-i-konzulata

NPR. 2019. "Some Pacific Island Nations Are Turning to China. Climate Change Is a Factor." 23 November. https://www.npr.org/2019/11/23/775986892/some-pa cific-island-nations-are-turning-to-china-climate-change-is-a-factor?t=1577868 759261&t=1643191723424

Ó Beacháin, D. 2020. "Abkhazia and South Ossetia." In Visoka, G., Doyle, J., and Newman, E., eds., *Routledge Handbook of State Recognition*. London: Routledge, 430–45.

Office of the Prime Minister of Grenada. 2023. "Prime Minister Hon. Dickon Mitchell Met with H.E. Vjosa Osmani-Sadriu President of the Republic of Kosovo." 22 September.

Office of the Prime Minister of Kosovo. 2020. "Letter Dated 3 March 2020 Sent to Josep Borrel Fontelles, High Representative of the EU for Foreign Affairs and Security Policy." Doc. No. 047. Prishtina.

Oglesby, D. M. 2016. "Diplomatic Language." In Constantinou, C. M., Kerr, P., and Sharp, P., eds., *The Sage Handbook of Diplomacy*. London: Sage, 242–54.

Ojeda-Garcia, R., Fernandez-Molina, I., and Veguilla, V., eds. 2014. *Global, Regional and Local Dimensions of Western Sahara's Protracted Decolonization: When a Conflict Gets Old*. London: Palgrave.

Oltramonti, G. P. 2020. "Viability as a Strategy of Secession: Enshrining *De Facto* Statehood in Abkhazia and Somaliland." In Griffiths, R. and Muro, D., eds., *Strategies of Secession and Counter-secession*. London: ECPR Press and Rowman and Littlefield, 180–99.

Onuf, N. 2013. "Recognition and the Constitution of Epochal Change." *International Relations* 27(2): 121–40.

Oppenheim's International Law. 1996. 9th ed. Vol. 1, *Peace*. Edited by Jennings, R. and Watts, A. London: Longman.

Palmer, M. 2019. "Testimony by Deputy Assistant Secretary and Special Representative for the Western Balkans Matthew Palmer. Senate Foreign Relations Committee Subcommittee on Europe and Regional Security Cooperation Hearing on Successes and Unfinished Business in the Western Balkans." 23 October. https:// www.foreign.senate.gov/imo/media/doc/102319_Palmer_Testimony.pdf

Paquin, J. 2010. *A Stability-Seeking Power: U.S. Foreign Policy and Secessionist Conflicts*. Montreal: McGill-Queen's University Press.

Paris, R. 2020. "The Right to Dominate: How Old Ideas about Sovereignty Pose New Challenges for World Order." *International Organization* 74(3): 453–89.

268 • References

Pavković, A. and Radan, P., eds. 2011. *The Ashgate Research Companion to Secession*. Farnham: Ashgate.

Peralta, M. S. 2018. "A Test for Taiwan's Diplomatic Wisdom: Crisis in Nicaragua." Ketagalan Media. 26 July. https://ketagalanmedia.com/2018/07/26/a-test-for-taiwans-diplomatic-wisdom-crisis-in-nicaragua/

Permanent Mission of the Russian Federation to the OSCE. 2019. "Statement by Mr. Alexander Lukashevich, Permanent Representative of the Russian Federation, at the 1239th Meeting of the OSCE Permanent Council in Response to the Report by the Head of the OSCE Mission in Kosovo, Mr. Jan Braathu." 5 September. https://www.osce.org/files/f/documents/5/2/430559.pdf

Perritt, H. H. 2010. *The Road to Independence for Kosovo: A Chronical of the Ahtisaari Plan*. Cambridge: Cambridge University Press.

Peterson, M. J. 1997. *Recognition of Governments: Legal Doctrine and State Practice, 1815–1995*. New York: St. Martin's Press.

PIPS. 2019. "International Politics and Political Parties Perceptions of Kosovo Citizens." Pristina: Prishtina Institute of Political Studies. https://pips-ks.org/en/Detail/ArtMID/1446/ArticleID/3145/International-Politics-and-Political-Parties-The-perceptions-of-Kosovar-citizens.

Pogodda, S., Richmond, O. P., and Visoka, G. 2023. "Counter-peace: From Isolated Blockages in Peace Processes to Systemic Patterns." *Review of International Studies* 49(3): 491–512.

Ponzio, R. 2005. "The Solomon Islands: The UN and Intervention by Coalitions of the Willing." *International Peacekeeping* 12(2): 173–88.

Prasad, N. 2009. "Small but Smart: Small States in the Global System." In Cooper, A. F. and Shaw, T. M., eds., *The Diplomacies of Small States: Between Vulnerability and Resilience*. Basingstoke: Palgrave Macmillan, 41–64.

President of Kosovo. 2018. "President Thaçi Accepted Credential Letters from Ghana's Ambassador." 8 June. https://president-ksgov.net/en/president-thaci-receives-the-letters-of-credence-of-the-ghanaian-ambassador/.

President of Kosovo. 2022. "Joint Press Statement of the President of the Republic of Kosovo, Vjosa Osmani at the Beginning of the Meeting with the Secretary of State, Antony Blinken." 26 July. https://president-ksgov.net/en/speeches/joint-press-statement-of-the-president-of-the-republic-of-kosovo-vjosa-osmani-at-the-beginning-of-the-meeting-with-the-secretary-of-state-antony-blinken

President of Mozambique. 2004. "Speech by His Excellency Mr. Joaquim Alberto Chissano, President of the Republic of Mozambique on the Occasion of His Work Visit to the Saharawi Arab Democratic Republic." 12 December.

President of South Africa. 2004. "Letter of Thabo MBeki to Mohamed VI." 2 August. https://www.usc.gal/export9/sites/webinstitucional/gl/institutos/ceso/descargas/SA_Letter-MBeki-to-M6_en.pdf

President of Taiwan. 2008. "Presidential Office Statement on Termination of Diplomatic Relations with the Dominican Republic." 1 May. https://english.president.gov.tw/NEWS/5383

Prime Minister of Dominica. 2012. Letter dated 10 December 2012 addressed to the President of Kosovo.

Prishtina Insight. 2012. "Kosovo Oil Company Inks $800m Deal on Africa Refinery." 26 October. https://prishtinainsight.com/wp-content/uploads/2016/02/Prishtina-Insight-98.pdf

Prishtina Insight. 2018. "Burundi Revokes Kosovo Recognition, Leaving Kosovo PM Nonplussed." 4 April. https://prishtinainsight.com/burundi-revokes-kosovo-recognition-leaving-kosovo-pm-nonplussed/

Prishtina Insight. 2020. "Assembly Votes to Oust Kosovo Government." 25 March. https://prishtinainsight.com/assembly-votes-to-oust-kosovo-government/

Radan, P. 2020. "Recognition of States in International Law." In Visoka, G., Doyle, J., and Newman, E., eds., *Routledge Handbook of State Recognition*. London: Routledge, 48–58.

Radio Free Europe. 2014. "Tuvalu Retracts Recognition of Abkhazia, South Ossetia." 31 March. https://www.rferl.org/a/tuvalu-georgia-retracts-abkhazia-ossetia-recognition/25315720.html

Radio Free Europe. 2018. "Kosovo Fails for Third Time to Win Interpol Membership." 20 November. https://www.rferl.org/a/kosovo-fails-for-third-time-to-win-interpol-membership/29610709.html

Radio New Zealand. 2013. "Confusion Lingers over Vanuatu's Links with Abkhazia." 18 March. http://www.radionz.co.nz/international/pacific-news/210896/confusion-lingers-over-vanuatu's-links-with-abkhazia

Radio New Zealand. 2014a. "Tuvalu Joins Traditional Friends by Renewing Ties with Georgia." 16 April. https://www.rnz.co.nz/international/pacific-news/241800/tuvalu-joins-traditional-friends-by-renewing-ties-with-georgia

Radio New Zealand. 2014b. "Tuvalu Re-establishes Ties with Georgia." 18 April. https://www.rnz.co.nz/international/programmes/datelinepacific/audio/2593103/tuvalu-re-establishes-ties-with-georgia

Radio New Zealand. 2019. "Australia Says It Respects Solomons' Decision to Switch to China." 20 September. https://www.rnz.co.nz/international/pacific-news/399176/australia-says-it-respects-solomons-decision-to-switch-to-china

Radio New Zealand. 2024. "Marshall Islands reaffirms ties with Taiwan in wake of Nauru shift." 18 January. https://www.rnz.co.nz/international/pacific-news/507025/marshall-islands-reaffirms-ties-with-taiwan-in-wake-of-nauru-shift

Radio Slobodna Evropa. 2019. "'Ruska veza' u navodnom povlačenju priznanja Kosova?" [Russian "connection" in alleged withdrawal of Kosovo's recognition?]. 25 July. https://www.slobodnaevropa.org/a/30073173.html

Raič, D. 2002. *Statehood and the Law of Self-Determination*. The Hague: Kluwer Law International.

Razvani, D. A. 2014. *Surpassing the Sovereign State: The Wealth, Self-Rule, and Security Advantages of Partially Independent Territories*. Oxford: Oxford University Press.

Reisigl, M. and Wodak, R. 2009. "The Discourse-Historical Approach (DHA)." In Wodak, R. and Meyer, M., eds., *Methods of Critical Discourse Analysis*, 2nd ed. London: Sage, 87–121.

Republic of Ghana. 2009. Letter dated 28 May 2009 addressed to the President of the Republic of Kosovo. Accra. 28 May.

Republic of Maldives. 2009. Kosovo Recognition Letter. 19 February.

Republic of Nauru. 2019. Note No. 702/2019. 13 November.

Reuters. 2016. "With Gambia Move, China Ends Diplomatic Truce with Taiwan." 17 March. https://www.reuters.com/article/us-china-gambia-idUSKCN0WJ1DT

Reuters. 2018a. "China Opens Embassy in Dominican Republic after Break with Taiwan." 21 September. https://www.reuters.com/article/us-dominican-diploma

270 • *References*

cy-china/china-opens-embassy-in-dominican-republic-after-break-with-taiwan-idUSKCN1M12IF

Reuters. 2018b. "China Pledges $150 Million Aid to El Salvador as Relationship Deepens." 8 November. https://www.reuters.com/article/us-elsalvador-china/china-pledges-150-million-aid-to-el-salvador-as-relationship-deepens-idUSKCN1ND0IT

Reuters. 2019a. "Loan of $100 Million from Taiwan Gives Lifeline to Nicaragua's Ortega." 20 February. https://www.reuters.com/article/us-nicaragua-protests-taiwan/loan-of-100-million-from-taiwan-gives-lifeline-to-nicaraguas-ortega-idUSKCN1Q903T

Reuters. 2019b. "Solomon Islands Look beyond Taiwan Alliance as Election Looms." 20 March. https://www.reuters.com/article/us-pacific-china-solomonislands/solomon-islands-look-beyond-taiwan-alliance-as-election-looms-idUSKCN1R12TR

Reuters. 2019c. "Taiwan Says China Is an 'Authoritarian' Threat in the Pacific." 7 October. https://www.reuters.com/article/us-taiwan-diplomacy-idUSKBN1WM0NL

Reuters. 2020. "Fierce Presidential Election Erupts in Pacific amid China-Taiwan Tussle." 19 June. https://www.reuters.com/article/us-china-kiribati-idUSKBN23Q0ZN

Reuters. 2022. "U.S. Should Recognise Taiwan, Former Top Diplomat Pompeo Says." 4 March. https://www.reuters.com/world/asia-pacific/us-should-recognise-taiwan-former-top-diplomat-pompeo-says-2022-03-04/

Reymond, M. 2019. *Social Practices of Rule-Making in World Politics*. New York: Oxford University Press.

Rich, T. and Dahmer, A. 2018. "Taiwan's Diplomatic Recognition Challenge in 2018." *Taiwan Sentinel*, 31 October. https://sentinel.tw/tw-diplo-recognition-challenge-2018/

Rich, T. and Dahmer, A. 2020. "Taiwan." In Visoka, G., Doyle, J., and Newman, E., eds., *Routledge Handbook of State Recognition*. London: Routledge, 363–75.

Rich, T. and Dahmer, A. 2022. "Should I Stay or Should I Go? Diplomatic Recognition of Taiwan, 1950–2016." *International Journal of Taiwan Studies* 5(2): 353–74.

Richmond, O. P, Pogodda, S., and Visoka, G. 2023. "The International Dynamics of Counter-peace." *European Journal of International Relations*. https://doi.org/10.1177/13540661231168772

Richter, D. 2013. "Unfriendly Act." In R. Wolfrum, ed., *The Max Planck Encyclopedia of Public International Law*. https://opil.ouplaw.com/view/10.1093/law:epil/9780199231690/law-9780199231690-e423

Riegl, M. and Doboš, B. 2017a. "(Super)power Rule: Comparative Analysis of Parent States." In Riegl, M. and Doboš, B., eds., *Unrecognized States and Secession in the 21st Century*. Cham, Switzerland: Springer, 85–108.

Riegl, M. and Doboš, B. 2017b. "Conclusion: Future of International Recognition?" In Riegl, M. and Doboš, B., eds., *Unrecognized States and Secession in the 21st Century*. Cham, Switzerland: Springer, 223–24.

Ringmar, E. 2014. "Recognition and the Origins of International Society." *Global Discourse* 4(4): 446–58.

Risse, T., Ropp, S. C., and Sikkink, K., eds. 1999. *The Power of Human Rights: International Norms and Domestic Change*. Cambridge: Cambridge University Press.

Roberts, I. 2009. *Satow's Diplomatic Practice*. Oxford: Oxford University Press.

Roth, B. 2020. "Bilateral Recognition of States." In Visoka, G., Doyle, J., and Newman, E., eds., *Routledge Handbook of State Recognition*. London: Routledge, 191–204.

Roussellier, J. 2018. "A Role for Russia in the Western Sahara?" Carnegie Endowment for International Peace. 5 June. https://carnegieendowment.org/sada/76532

RTS. 2018. "Šukri: O Kosovu u skladu sa međunarodnim pravom" [Shukri: On Kosovo in accordance with international law]. 28 November. https://www.rts.rs/page/stories/sr/story/9/politika/3337484/sukri-o-kosovu-u-skladu-sa-medjuna rodnim-pravom.html

RTS. 2019a. "Dačić: Šta Priština slavi i šta su uradili za 11 godina?" 17 February. https://www.rts.rs/page/stories/sr/story/9/politika/3423358/dacic-sta-pristina -slavi-i-sta-su-uradili-za-11-godina.html

RTS. 2019b. Dačić za RTS: Cilj je da nijedna zemlja više ne prizna Kosovo" [Dačić for RTS: The goal is for no country to recognize Kosovo any longer]. 24 May. https://www.rts.rs/page/stories/sr/story/9/politika/3533144/dacic-za-rts-cilj-je -da-nijedna-zemlja-vise-ne-prizna-kosovo.html

RTV Dukagjini. 2021. "InfoBox." 20 December. https://www.youtube.com/watch ?v=tveYqiWFFK0&t=146s

Ryngaert, C. and Sobrie, S. 2011. "Recognition of States: International Law or Realpolitik? The Practice of Recognition in the Wake of Kosovo, South Ossetia, and Abkhazia." *Leiden Journal of International Law* 24(2): 467–90.

Sahara Press Service. 2020. "SMACO: Moroccan Army Plants Thousands of Landmines around Newly Built Berm in Guergarat." 22 November. https://www.spsr asd.info/news/en/articles/2020/11/22/28868.html

Sahara Press Service. 2021. "Russia Supports a Consensual Solution to the Conflict in Western Sahara on the Basis of UNSC Relevant Resolutions." 20 October. https://www.spsrasd.info/news/en/articles/2021/10/20/35882.html

Samorukov, M. 2019. "A Spoiler in the Balkans? Russia and the Final Resolution of the Kosovo Conflict." Washington, DC: Carnegie Endowment for International Peace. https://carnegieendowment.org/files/WP_Samorukov_Balkans_v2.pdf

SBS News. 2022. "Solomons Police Fire Warning Shots to Disperse Protesters, as Australian Peacekeepers Arrive." 26 November. https://www.sbs.com.au/news /solomon-islands-pm-urges-calm-refuses-to-step-down-as-violent-protests-eru pt/7e726921-03ba-49c7-bb05-5241189db0c5

Schwarzenberger, G. 1955. "The Fundamental Principles of International Law." Vol. 87 in *Collected Courses of the Hague Academy of International Law*. http://dx.doi .org/10.1163/1875-8096_pplrdc_A9789028612426_03

Senate Foreign Affairs. 2005. "Defence and Trade References Committee Opportunities and Challenges: Australia's Relationship with China." Commonwealth of Australia. https://www.aph.gov.au/Parliamentary_Business/Committees/Sen ate/Foreign_Affairs_Defence_and_Trade/Completed_inquiries/2004-07/china /report01/index

Shaomin, X. and Jiang, L. 2020. "The Emergence and Fallacy of 'China's Debt-Trap Diplomacy' Narrative." *China International Studies* 81: 69–84.

Sharman, J. C. 2017. "Sovereignty at the Extremes: Micro-states in World Politics." *Political Studies* 65(3): 559–75.

Sharp, P. 2009. *Diplomatic Theory of International Relations*. Cambridge: Cambridge University Press.

Shattuck, T. J. 2020. "The Race to Zero? China's Poaching of Taiwan's Diplomatic Allies." *Orbis* 64(2): 334–52.

Shaw, M. 2017. *International Law*. 8th ed. Cambridge: Cambridge University Press.

Shaw, M. 2021. *International Law*. 9th ed. Cambridge: Cambridge University Press.

Shen, S. 2015. "From Zero-Sum Game to Positive-Sum Game: Why Beijing Tolerates Pacific Island States' Recognition of Taipei." *Journal of Contemporary China* 24(95): 883–902.

Simpson, G. 2004. *Great Powers and Outlaw States*. Cambridge: Cambridge University Press.

Sjursen, H. and Smith, K. E. 2004. "Justifying EU Foreign Policy: The Logics Underpinning EU Enlargement." In Tonra, B. and Christiansen, T., eds., *Rethinking European Union Foreign Policy*. Manchester: Manchester University Press, 126–41.

Slonim, Sh. 2022. "Derecognition is a serious matter in diplomatic relations – opinion", The Jerusalem Post, 15 November. https://www.jpost.com/opinion/article-722387.

Smith, J. J. 2015. "The Taking of the Sahara: The Role of Natural Resources in the Continuing Occupation of Western Sahara." *Global Change, Peace & Security* 27(3): 263–84.

Smith, N. 2019. "Fears of Military Build Up as China Secretly Leases Entire Island." *The Telegraph*, 17 October. https://www.telegraph.co.uk/news/2019/10/17/fears-military-build-up-china-secretly-leases-entire-island/

Solomon, T. and Steele, B. J. 2017. "Micro-moves in International Relations Theory." *European Journal of International Relations* 23(2): 267–91.

Solomon Islands Government. 2020. "Suidani's Referendum Illegal." 6 September. https://solomons.gov.sb/suidanis-referendum-illegal/

Solomon Islands High Commission in Australia. 2018. Note 2018/228. Canberra. 28 November.

Solomon Star. 2019. "Malaita Launches 2019 Communique." 18 October. https://www.solomonstarnews.com/malaita-launches-2019-communique/

Solomon Times. 2011. "Political Watchdog Voices Concern." 16 November. https://www.solomontimes.com/news/political-watchdog-voices-concern/6646

Solomon Times. 2019a. "Sogavare Pressured to Switch Recognition." 20 May. https://www.solomontimes.com/news/sogavare-pressured-to-switch-recognition/9076

Solomon Times. 2019b. "Statement by the Prime Minister Hon. Manasseh Sogavare on Switch to China." 20 September. https://www.solomontimes.com/news/statement-by-the-prime-minister-hon-manasseh-sogavare-on-switch-to-china/9362

Solomon Times. 2019c. "Switching to China Is High Risk: CBSI." 16 September. https://www.solomontimes.com/news/switching-to-china-is-high-risk-cbsi/9342?fbclid=IwAR1VD3LBCwjf0W7_9m-pmnxg7io2HZlgoHI5vsaIgAh-xogUchRNgwQiXGA

Somers, W. 2023. *The State of Taiwan: From International Law to Geopolitics*. Leiden: Brill.

South China Morning Post. 2014. "El Salvador's Ex-president Francisco Flores Admits Payments from Taiwan." 8 January. https://www.scmp.com/news/wor ld/article/1400906/el-salvadors-ex-president-francisco-flores-admits-payments -taiwan

South China Morning Post. 2018a. "China's New Alliance Stirs US Worries over Possible 'Military Base' in El Salvador." 22 August. https://www.scmp.com/ne ws/china/diplomacy-defence/article/2160731/chinas-new-alliance-stirs-us-worr ies-over-military-base

South China Morning Post. 2018b. "El Salvador Corruption Probe Investigates US\$10 Million in Taiwan Donations, 'Diverted to Ruling Party.'" 14 September. https://www.scmp.com/news/world/americas/article/2164158/el-salvador-corr uption-probe-investigates-us10-million-taiwan

South China Morning Post. 2018c. "Should Taiwan Be Worried If It Loses All Its Allies?" 1 September. https://www.scmp.com/news/china/diplomacy/article/216 2316/can-defiant-taiwan-hang-its-allies-and-sovereignty-beijing-puts

South China Morning Post. 2019a. "Solomon Islands Leader May Miss UN Summit amid Fallout over Taiwan Decision." 19 September. https://www.scmp.com/ne ws/china/diplomacy/article/3028123/solomon-islands-leader-may-miss-un-su mmit-amid-fallout-over

South China Morning Post. 2019b. "Taiwan Ends Relationship with Solomon Islands after It Votes to Cut Ties." 16 September. https://www.scmp.com/news /china/diplomacy/article/3027420/taiwan-tries-stop-solomon-islands-diplomat ic-switch-beijing

South China Morning Post. 2019c. "US and Taiwan Hold Forum to Shore Up Support for Taipei in Pacific." 7 October. https://www.scmp.com/news/china/dipl omacy/article/3031891/us-and-taiwan-hold-forum-shore-support-taipei-pacific

South China Morning Post. 2019d. "US Cancels Solomon Islands Meeting after 'Disappointment' at It Switching Ties from Taipei to Beijing." 18 September. https://www.scmp.com/news/china/diplomacy/article/3027827/us-cancels-solo mon-islands-meeting-after-disappointment-it

Southerland, M. 2017. "As Chinese Pressure on Taiwan Grows, Beijing Turns Away from Cross-Strait 'Diplomatic Truce.'" U.S.-China Economic and Security Review Commission. 9 February. https://www.uscc.gov/sites/default/files/Rese arch/Issue%20Brief_As%20Chinese%20Pressure%20on%20Taiwan%20Gro ws%20Beijing%20Turns%20Away%20from%20Cross-Strait%20Diplomatic %20Truce.pdf

Spies, Y. K. 2019. *Global Diplomacy and International Society*. Cham, Switzerland: Palgrave Macmillan.

State News Agency RES. 2014. "The Ministry of Foreign Affairs of South Ossetia Has No Information about the Change of Positions in Diplomatic Relations between South Ossetia and Tuvalu." 1 April. https://cominf.org/node/116650 1463

Stilwell, D. 2019. "Statement of Assistant Secretary David Stilwell, Bureau of East Asian and Pacific Affairs U.S. Department of State before the Senate Foreign

Relations Committee." 18 September. https://www.foreign.senate.gov/imo/media/doc/091819_Stilwell_Testimony.pdf

Strang, D. 1991. "Anomaly and Commonplace in European Political Expansion: Realist and Institutional Accounts." *International Organization* 45(2): 143–62.

Stratfor. 2019. "Solomon Islands: Government Cuts Diplomatic Ties with Taiwan." 16 September. https://worldview.stratfor.com/situation-report/solomon-islands-government-cuts-diplomatic-ties-taiwan

Stringer, K. D. 2006. "Pacific Island Microstates: Pawns or Players in Pacific Rim Diplomacy?" *Diplomacy & Statecraft* 17(3): 547–77.

Stuttgarter Zeitung. 2020. "Ein großer Verlust für unser Land" [A great loss for our country]. 17 February. https://www.stuttgarter-zeitung.de/inhalt.kosovaren-im-ausland-ein-grosser-verlust-fuer-unser-land.aa617e51-854e-4db2-9bac-d40d10aa343a.html

Sunshine State News. 2018. "Marco Rubio: U.S. Needs to Keep China from Bullying Other Nations to Cut Ties with Taiwan." 8 September. http://sunshinestatenews.com/story/marco-rubio-us-needs-keep-china-bullying-other-nations-cut-ties-taiwan

Swarajya. 2018. "China in Talks with Island Nation of Vanuatu to Build a Military Base, Says Report." 10 April. https://swarajyamag.com/insta/china-in-talks-with-island-nation-of-vanuatu-to-build-a-military-base-says-report

Sydney Morning Herald. 2018. "China Cements Fresh Burkina Faso Ties with Hospital and Highway." 8 August. https://www.smh.com.au/world/asia/china-cements-fresh-burkina-faso-ties-with-hospital-and-highway-20180808-p4zw4e.html

Taiwan Focus. 2019a. "Recognizing Beijing Imperils Taiwan Allies' Sovereignty: U.S. Official." 12 October. https://focustaiwan.tw/cross-strait/201912100009

Taiwan News. 2017. "Burkina Faso Rejects US$50 Billion from China to Ditch Taiwan." 25 January. https://www.taiwannews.com.tw/en/news/3081895

Taiwan News. 2018. "US Senator Urges Guatemala to Maintain Taiwan Diplomatic Ties." 31 August. https://www.taiwannews.com.tw/en/news/3519280

Taiwan News. 2019a. "Taiwan Deputy Foreign Minister to Visit Tuvalu after Government Change." 31 October. https://www.taiwannews.com.tw/en/news/3807295

Taiwan News. 2019b. "Taiwan Invites Solomon Islands Leadership to Visit." 6 June. https://www.taiwannews.com.tw/en/news/3718789

Talmon, S. 1998. *Recognition of Governments in International Law.* Oxford: Oxford University Press.

Talmon, S. 2005. "The Constitutive Versus the Declaratory Theory of Recognition: Tertium Non Datur?." *The British Year Book of International Law* 75(1): 101–81.

Tanjug. 2023. "Vucic: Further Nine Countries Have Derecognised So-Called Kosovo." 4 January. https://www.tanjug.rs/english/politics/6656/vucic-further-nine-countries-have-derecognised-so-called-kosovo/vest

TASS. 2022. "A Draft Law on the Abolition of the Resolution of the USSR State Council on the Independence of Lithuania Was Submitted to the Duma." 8 June. https://tass.ru/politika/14857607

Taylor, I. 2002. "Taiwan's Foreign Policy and Africa: The Limitations of Dollar Diplomacy." *Journal of Contemporary China* 11(30): 125–40.

Taylor, P. 1999. "The United Nations in the 1990s: Proactive Cosmopolitanism and the Issue of Sovereignty." *Political Studies* 47(3): 538–56.

Tela Non. 2013a. "Patrice Trovoada, Kosovo and Sao Tome and Principe." 16 February. https://www.telanon.info/politica/2013/02/16/12492/patrice-trovoada-kos ovo-e-sao-tome-e-principe/

Tela Non. 2013b. "PCD exige esclarecimento urgente do caso Kosovo." 11 January. https://www.telanon.info/politica/2013/01/11/12241/pcd-exige-esclarecimen to-urgem-do-caso-kosovo/

Telegraf. 2019. "The French Government under Pressure to Withdraw the Recognition of Kosovo: People Started the Petition." 7 May. https://www.telegraf.rs/eng lish/3058562-the-french-government-under-pressure-to-withdraw-the-recognit ion-of-kosovo-people-started-the-petition

Telegrafi. 2021. "Osmani: Synim primar i Kosovës anëtarësimi në BE, NATO, Interpol dhe organizata të tjera ndërkombëtare." 29 October. https://telegrafi.com/os mani-synim-primar-kosoves-anetaresimi-ne-nato-interpol-dhe-organizata-te-tje ra-nderkombetare/

Telesure. 2019. "El Salvador: Bukele Breaks Off Relations with Sahrawi Republic." 16 June. https://www.telesurenglish.net/news/El-Salvador-Bukele-Breaks-off-Re lations-with-Sahrawi-Republic-20190616-0009.html

Thompson, W. R., ed. 1999. *Great Power Rivalry*. Columbia: University of South Carolina Press.

Thorhallsson, B. and Bailes, A. J. K. 2016. "Small State Diplomacy." In Constantinou, C. M., Kerr, P., and Sharp, P., eds., *The Sage Handbook of Diplomacy*. London: Sage, 294–307.

Tierney, S. 2013. "Legal Issues Surrounding the Referendum on Independence for Scotland." *European Constitutional Law Review* 9(3): 376–77.

Tiezzi, S. 2020. "Kiribati President Makes First Trip to China after Switch from Taiwan." 7 January. https://thediplomat.com/2020/01/kiribati-president-makes -first-trip-to-china-after-switch-from-taiwan/

Titscher, S., Meyer, M., Wodak, R., and Vetter, E. 2000. *Methods of Text and Discourse Analysis*. London: Sage.

Tomuschat, C. 2012. "Recognition of New States—the Case of Premature Recognition." In P. Hipold, ed., *Kosovo and International Law: The ICJ Advisory Opinion of 22 July 2010*. Leiden: Martinus Nijhoff, 31–45.

Tubilewicz, C. 2004. "Taiwan's 'Macedonian Project,' 1999–2001." *China Quarterly* 179: 782–803.

Tubilewicz, C. 2015. "State Transformation and the Domestic Politics of Foreign Aid in Taiwan." *Pacific Review* 29(1): 45–66.

Tudoroiu, T. 2017. "Taiwan in the Caribbean: A Case Study in State De-recognition." *Asian Journal of Political Science* 25(2): 194–211.

UN General Assembly. 1981. "Annex: Declaration on the Inadmissibility of Intervention and Interference in the Internal Affairs of States." UN Doc. A/36/102. 9 December.

UN General Assembly. 2010. Resolution 64/298. UN Doc. A/RES/64/298. 13 October.

UN Secretary-General. 2010. "Letter dated 27 July 2010 from the Permanent Representative of Serbia to the United Nations addressed to the Secretary-General." UN Doc. A/64/876. 28 July.

UN Secretary-General. 2021. "Situation Concerning Western Sahara." UN Doc. S/2021/843. 1 October.

276 • *References*

UN Security Council. 1999a. "Provisional Verbatim of 3982nd Meeting." UN Doc. S/PV.3982. 25 February.

UN Security Council. 1999b. Resolution 1244, UN Doc S/RES/1244(1999). 10 June. Https://Peacemaker.Un.Org/Sites/Peacemaker.Un.Org/Files/990610_Scri 244%281999%29.PdfUN Security Council. 2019a. "Provisional Verbatim of the 8541st Meeting." UN Doc. S/PV.8541. 10 June.

UN Security Council. 2019b. "Provisional Verbatim of the 8618th Meeting." UN Doc. S/PV.8518. 30 April.

UN Security Council. 2019c. "Provisional Verbatim of the 8655th Meeting." UN Doc. S.PV.8655. 31 October.

UN Security Council. 2020. "Provisional Verbatim." UN Doc. S/2020/339. 29 April.

UNMIK Media Observer. 2019. "Representatives of Washington and Moscow Answered Three Questions of Vecernje Novosti Daily." 24 October. https://med ia.unmikonline.org/?p=106363

US Attorney for the Southern District of New York. 2014. "Former President of Guatemala, Alfonso Portillo, Sentenced in Manhattan Federal Court for Laundering Millions of Dollars through United States Banks." 22 May. https://www .justice.gov/usao-sdny/pr/former-president-guatemala-alfonso-portillo-sentenc ed-manhattan-federal-court

US-China Economic and Security Review Commission. 2019. "2019 Report to Congress of the US-China Economic and Security Review Commission." https:// www.uscc.gov/sites/default/files/2019-11/Chapter%204%20Section%204%20 -%20Changing%20Regional%20Dynamics%20-%20Oceania%20and%20Sin gapore.pdf

US Congress. 2017. Consolidated Appropriations Act. 30 September. https://www .gpo.gov/fdsys/pkg/BILLS-115hr244enr/pdf/BILLS-115hr244enr.pdf

US Congress. 2019a. "Georgia Support Act." 23 October. https://www.congress.gov /bill/116th-congress/house-bill/598/

US Congress. 2019b. "An Act to Express United States Support for Taiwan's Diplomatic Alliances around the World." 29 October. https://www.congress.gov/116 /bills/s1678/BILLS-116s1678es.pdf

US Department of State. 2022. "Kosovo National Day." 17 February. https://www.st ate.gov/kosovo-national-day-2/

US Department of State. 2024. "Nauru Officially Breaks Ties with Taiwan." 15 January. https://www.state.gov/nauru-officially-breaks-ties-with-taiwan/

US Embassy in Kosovo. 2020. "Statement from the U.S. Embassy on the Tariffs." 1 April. https://xk.usembassy.gov/april01st/

US Embassy in Morocco. 2021. "The Ambassador's Historic Visit to Dakhla." 10 January. https://ma.usembassy.gov/historical-visit-of-the-ambassador-of-the-un ited-states-of-america-to-dakhla/

US Embassy Pristina. 2019. "Statement from U.S. Embassy Pristina." 25 January. https://xk.usembassy.gov/statement-from-u-s-embassy-pristina-2/

US Government. 2019. "Letter Sent to the Leaders of Kosovo." 11 February.

US House of Representatives. 2018. "Reinforcing the U.S.-Taiwan Relationship— Hearing before the Subcommittee on Asia and the Pacific of the Committee on Foreign Affairs House of Representatives." 17 April. Washington DC: US Government Printing Office. https://docs.house.gov/meetings/FA/FA05/20180 417/108170/HHRG-115-FA05-Transcript-20180417.pdf

US Mission to the United Nations. 2020. "Explanation of Vote on the Mandate Renewal of the UN Mission for the Referendum in Western Sahara." 20 October. https://usun.usmission.gov/explanation-of-vote-on-the-mandate-renewal-of-the-un-mission-for-the-referendum-in-western-sahara-via-vtc/?_ga=2.1240 85898.1668525927.1643208251-1700242002.1643208251

Van Fossen, A. 2007. "The Struggle for Recognition: Diplomatic Competition between China and Taiwan in Oceania." *Journal of Chinese Political Science* 12(2): 125–46.

Venediktova, N. 2011. "The West's Policy of Non-recognition of Abkhazia's Independence: Consequences and Prospects." *International Alert*, March, 10–13.

Vidmar, J. 2012. "Explaining the Legal Effects of Recognition." *International and Comparative Law Quarterly* 61: 361–87.

Vidmar, J. 2013. *Democratic Statehood in International Law: The Emergence of New States in Post–Cold War Practice*. Oxford: Hart.

Vidmar, J., McGibbon, S., and Raible, L., eds. 2022. *Research Handbook on Secession*. London: Edward Elgar.

Viola, L. A. 2020. *The Closure of the International System: How Institutions Create Political Equalities and Hierarchies*. Cambridge: Cambridge University Press.

Visoka, G. 2018. *Acting Like a State: Kosovo and the Everyday Making of Statehood*. London: Routledge.

Visoka, G. 2019. "Metis Diplomacy: The Everyday Politics of Becoming a Sovereign State." *Cooperation and Conflict* 54(2): 167–90.

Visoka, G. 2020a. "Kosovo." In Visoka, G., Newman, E., and Doyle, J., eds., *Routledge Handbook of State Recognition*. London: Routledge, 402–16.

Visoka, G. 2020b. "The Derecognition of States." In Visoka, G., Newman, E., and Doyle, J., eds., *Routledge Handbook of State Recognition*. London: Routledge, 316–32.

Visoka, G. 2020c. "Towards a Critical Agenda on State Recognition." In Visoka, G., Newman, E., and Doyle, J., eds., *Routledge Handbook of State Recognition*. London: Routledge, 473–94.

Visoka, G. 2022. "Statehood and Recognition in World Politics: Towards a Critical Research Agenda." *Cooperation and Conflict* 57(2): 133–51.

Visoka, G. 2023. "A New (Dis)agreement on the Path to Normalization between Kosovo and Serbia." DCU Brexit Institute Blog. 29 March. https://dcubrexitin stitute.eu/2023/03/a-new-disagreement-on-the-path-to-normalization-between-kosovo-and-serbia/

Visoka, G. and Doyle, J. 2016. "Neo-functional Peace: The European Union Way of Resolving Conflicts." *Journal of Common Market Studies* 54(4): 862–77.

Visoka, G., Doyle, J., and Newman, E., eds. 2020. *Routledge Handbook of State Recognition*. London: Routledge.

Visoka, G. and Musliu, V. 2023. "Kosovo and Serbia: Synchronising the Timing for Peace." EurActiv. 31 January. https://www.euractiv.com/section/enlargement-ne ighbourhood/opinion/kosovo-and-serbia-synchronising-the-timing-for-peace/

Visoka, G., Newman, E., and Doyle, J. 2020. "Introduction: Statehood and Recognition in World Politics." In Visoka, G., Doyle, J., and Newman, E., eds., *Routledge Handbook of State Recognition*. London: Routledge, 1–22.

Voice of America. 2018. "Taiwanese to Take to Streets Saturday, Protest China 'Bullying.'" 19 October. https://www.voanews.com/a/taiwanese-to-take-to-streets-sa turday-protest-china-bullying/4620212.html

Von Glahn, G. and Taulbee, J. L. 2017. *Law among Nations: An Introduction to Public International Law*. London: Routledge.

Warbrick, C. 1981. "The New British Policy on Recognition of Governments." *International and Comparative Law Quarterly* 30(3): 568–92. https://doi.org/10.1093 /iclqaj/30.3.568

Washington Examiner. 2018. "Lawmaker: Chinese Navy Seeks to Encircle US Homeland." 24 August. https://www.washingtonexaminer.com/policy/defense -national-security/lawmaker-chinese-navy-seeks-to-encircle-us-homeland

Weber, C. 1994. *Simulating Sovereignty: Intervention, the State and Symbolic Exchange*. Cambridge: Cambridge University Press.

Wei, Y. 2000. "Recognition of Divided States: Implication and Application of Concepts of 'Multi-system Nations,' 'Political Entities,' and 'Intra-National Commonwealth.'" *International Lawyer* 34(3): 997–1011.

Weill, R. 2020. "Global Constitutional Strategies to Counter-secession." In Griffiths, R. and Muro, D., eds., *Strategies of Secession and Counter-secession*. London: ECPR Press and Rowman and Littlefield, 84–99.

Weller, M. 2009. *Escaping the Self-Determination Trap*. Leiden: Martinus Nijhoff.

Weller, M. 2010. *Contested Statehood: Kosovo's Struggle for Independence*. Oxford: Oxford University Press.

Weller, M. and Metzger, B. 2008. *Settling Self-Determination Disputes: Complex Power-Sharing in Theory and Practice*. Leiden: Martinus Nijhoff.

Welt, C. 2019. "Georgia: Background and U.S. Policy." Congressional Research Services Report No. R45307. 17 October. https://fas.org/sgp/crs/row/R45307.pdf

White House. 2018. "Statement from the Press Secretary on El Salvador." 23 August. https://ht.usembassy.gov/statement-from-the-press-secretary-on-el-salvador/

White House. 2020a. "President Donald J. Trump Has Brokered Peace between Israel and the Kingdom of Morocco." 11 December. https://trumpwhitehouse .archives.gov/briefings-statements/president-donald-j-trump-brokered-peace-isr ael-kingdom-morocco/

White House. 2020b. "Proclamation on Recognizing the Sovereignty of the Kingdom of Morocco over the Western Sahara." 10 December. https://trumpwhiteh ouse.archives.gov/presidential-actions/proclamation-recognizing-sovereignty-ki ngdom-morocco-western-sahara/

Wikileaks. 2019. "Serbia Lobbying Maldives to Reverse Kosovo Recognition." 9 March. https://wikileaks.org/plusd/cables/09COLOMBO264_a.html

Wilson, A. 2016. *Sovereignty in Exile: A Saharan Liberation Movement Governs*. Philadelphia: University of Pennsylvania Press.

Wise Afri. 2019. "El Salvador Withdraws Its Recognition of Polisario's So-Called SADR." 17 June. https://wiseafri.wordpress.com/2019/06/17/el-salvador-withd raws-its-recognition-of-polisarios-so-called-sadr/

Wooldridge, F. 1979. "The Advisory Opinion of the International Court of Justice in the Western Sahara Case." *Anglo-American Law Review* 8(2): 86–122.

Wu, C. and Laio, P. 2021. "Treaty Validity after Diplomatic Cutoff: The Case of the Taiwan-Panama Free Trade Agreement." *Indiana Journal of Global Legal Studies* 28(1): 293–324.

Wyeth, G. 2017. "The Sovereign Recognition Game: Has Nauru Overplayed Its Hand?" 17 May. https://thediplomat.com/2017/05/the-sovereign-recognition-game-has-nauru-overplayed-its-hand/

Xinhua Net. 2019. "China, Solomon Islands Establish Diplomatic Ties." 21 September. http://www.xinhuanet.com/english/2019-09/21/c_138410830.htm

Yang, J. 2011. *The Pacific Islands in China's Grand Strategy*. New York: Palgrave Macmillan.

Yemelianova, G. and Broers, L., eds. 2020. *Routledge Handbook of the Caucasus*. London: Routledge.

Yinglung, Y. 2021. "Taiwanese National Identity and the Shifts in Support for Unification vs. Independence." Taiwanese Public Opinion Foundation. 11 August. https://bit.ly/3BefUhG

You, J. 2006. "China's Anti-secession Law and the Risk of War in the Taiwan Strait." *Contemporary Security Policy* 27(2): 237–57.

Yusuf, A. A. 2012. "The Role That Equal Rights and Self-Determination of Peoples Can Play in the Current World Community." In Cassese, A., ed., *Realizing Utopia: The Future of International Law*. Oxford: Oxford University Press, 375–91.

Zambian Watchdog. 2017. "Lungu Revokes Recognition of Western Sahara after Meeting King of Morocco." 26 February. https://www.zambiawatchdog.com/lungu-revokes-recognition-of-western-sahara-after-meeting-king-of-morocco/

Zartman, I. W. 2003. "The Timing of Peace Initiatives: Hurting Stalemates and Ripe Moments." In Darby, J. and Ginty, R. M., eds., *Contemporary Peacemaking*. London: Palgrave Macmillan, 19–29.

Zëri. 2019a. "15 muaj zero njohje, Ministria e Jashtme mburret me ndaljen e çnjohjeve." 23 May. https://zeri.info/aktuale/262147/15-muaj-zero-njohje-ministria-e-jashtme-mburret-me-ndaljen-e-cnjohjeve/

Zëri. 2019b. "Ankthi i çnjohjeve të Kosovës." 10 September. https://zeri.info/aktuale/286338/ankthi-i-cnjohjeve-te-kosoves/

Zëri. 2019c. "Çnjohje po, taksë jo!" [Derecognition yes, tax no!]. 21 January. https://zeri.info/aktuale/235681/cnjohje-po-takse-jo/

Zëri. 2019d. "Hoti: Politika e jashtme e Kosovës është jo ekzistente." 8 April. https://zeri.info/aktuale/251132/hoti-politika-e-jashtme-e-kosoves-eshte-jo-ekzistente/

Zëri. 2019e. "Qeveria e Çekisë: Nuk kemi arsye të tërheqim njohjen e Kosovës" [Czech government: We have no reason to withdraw the recognition of Kosovo]. 11 September. https://zeri.info/aktuale/286941/qeveria-e-cekise-nuk-kemi-arsye-te-terheqim-njohjen-e-kosoves/

Zëri i Amerikës. 2018. "Intervistë me kryeministrin e Kosovës, Ramush Haradinaj." 18 December. https://www.zeriamerikes.com/a/kosovo-pm-interview/4705698.html

Zoubir, Y. H., ed. 2020. *The Politics of Algeria: Domestic Issues and International Relations*. London: Routledge.

Zunes, S. and Mundy, J. 2010. *Western Sahara: War, Nationalism, and Conflict Irresolution*. New York: Syracuse University Press.

Zunes, S. and Mundy, J. 2022. *Western Sahara: War, Nationalism, and Conflict Irresolution*. 2nd ed. New York: Syracuse University Press.

Index

Abkhazia, 3–5, 7–8, 63–65, 79–80, 83–84, 88, 95–97, 106–7, 120–21, 126, 133–34, 136, 171–72, 201–2, 205–6, 209, 220, 226. 232, 244
act of aggression, 30, 146
African Union, 75–76, 204
Algeria, 8, 64–65, 75, 134–35, 138–39, 149–50, 152, 179, 181, 203–6, 228
anti-derecognition norm, 65, 232, 234
anti-diplomacy, 22, 55, 223–24
Anti-Secession Law, 72
Australia, 26, 65, 72, 74, 98–100, 132–34, 195, 199
autonomy, 12, 51, 75–77, 86, 96, 110, 113, 122, 132, 135, 139–42, 155, 172, 180–81, 186, 191

Balkans, 1, 86, 89, 137, 143, 183, 185, 191, 202–3
Baltic states, 221
bilateral cooperation, 13, 31, 59, 97, 111, 133, 151, 192
Bolivia, 85, 94, 110, 125
Bourita, N., 179–180
Brownlie, I., 38, 58
Buchanan, A., 231, 234
Burkina Faso, 1, 7, 82–83, 91, 102, 109, 119–20, 125, 131, 173

Caplan, R., 137, 232
Caribbean, 7, 74, 81, 117, 122, 133
Caspersen, N., 2, 24, 64, 175, 219
Cassese, A., 38, 41, 49
Central African Republic, 7, 82, 118, 123, 125
checkbook diplomacy, 26, 83, 85, 112, 119, 133, 191

Chen, T., 9, 11, 37, 40, 46, 48–49, 51–52
claimant states, 6–10, 12–13, 16–18, 20, 24–26, 28, 31–32, 34, 38, 47, 53, 56–57, 64, 70–72, 80, 84, 86, 88, 100–102, 114, 124, 130, 147–48, 152, 160–61, 164, 166–67, 171–73, 175, 186–87, 191
Coggins, B., 2, 8, 28, 163
Cold War, 44, 85, 124–25
collective anxiety, 20
collective derecognition, 38, 219
collective recognition, 3, 7, 34
Comoros, 75, 86, 104, 122, 128–29, 155
conditionality, 132, 134
conflict resolution, 4, 10, 12–13, 21, 25, 32, 45, 114–16, 137–38, 141–42, 161, 164, 186, 204–8, 210–14, 222, 227–29
conflict ripeness, 116, 138, 225
contender states, 6, 12–16, 31, 62, 70, 80, 83, 85, 90, 111–14, 124–26, 130, 137, 162–64, 186–88, 197, 205–7, 212–13
contestation, 3, 8, 17, 20–21, 24, 31, 47, 57, 64, 67, 70–74, 76, 79–81, 137, 147, 171, 176, 197, 203, 205, 213, 216
contested states, 3, 7, 26, 64, 81
corruption, 18, 22, 25–26, 118, 112–123, 133, 160, 175, 187–91, 195, 207, 228
counter-peace, 25, 211, 228, 235
counter-secession, 17, 21, 59, 213, 216
Crawford, J., 2, 4–5, 39
Crimea, 22, 231–32
criteria for statehood, 12, 30, 46, 48, 53, 61, 148–49
cross-strait, 72, 74, 179, 199–200, 227

281

282 ◆ *Index*

customary international law, 42, 148, 235
Cyprus, 86, 231

Dačić, I., 78, 85–86, 94, 123, 129, 142, 147, 151, 182
Dakhla, 75–76, 179, 181
de facto recognition, 50–51, 58, 186, 215
de facto statehood, 35
democratic legitimacy, 148, 159
derecognition campaign, 17, 57, 62, 65, 87, 97, 105, 135, 140, 142, 168–71, 182–86, 217, 220
derecognized state, 2, 6, 10, 14, 22, 25–27, 31, 40, 47–48, 59, 61, 95, 98, 101, 103–4, 109, 225–26
derecognizing state, 9, 19, 24, 26, 32, 35, 38, 40, 51, 95, 101–3, 116, 146, 163, 165, 212, 217, 219, 222, 224
diplomacy, 8, 18, 21–24, 27, 45, 55, 58, 62–63, 67, 80, 82–83, 85, 102, 104, 112, 116–17, 119, 121, 132–33, 138, 147, 152, 168, 174, 177, 187, 189, 191–92, 203, 213, 217, 220–24
diplomatic aggression, 21, 138, 176, 182, 207, 214
diplomatic allies, 7–8, 65, 73–74, 81, 83, 87, 90, 102, 108, 118, 124–25, 130, 135, 166–68, 173–74, 177–78, 187–88, 190, 206, 217, 225, 228
diplomatic cultures, 14, 113
diplomatic discourse, 19, 45, 54, 55, 63, 66, 142–43, 159–61, 211
diplomatic disengagement, 16, 19, 218
diplomatic equality, 15
diplomatic hypocrisy, 14, 16, 161
diplomatic isolation, 24, 126, 173
diplomatic lobbying, 81, 89, 215
diplomatic practice, 2, 4–6, 15, 21, 34, 36, 40, 45, 47, 53, 55–57, 62–63, 67–69, 81, 90, 108, 114, 116, 119, 124, 162, 187, 211–12, 220–23, 229, 232
diplomatic pressure, 32, 87, 124, 138
diplomatic strategy, 147
diplomatic theology, 219
domestic legitimacy, 162, 173, 206, 216
Dominican Republic, 1, 7, 82, 88, 91, 102, 108, 120, 177

economic interests, 14, 27, 134, 137, 223
effective statehood, 51, 145, 154
Egypt, 93
empirical sovereignty, 17, 71, 226
estrangement, 16, 22–23, 27, 55, 112, 210, 219, 224
European Parliament, 135–36, 184
European Union (EU), 1, 91, 98, 123, 136–37, 156, 184

Fabry, M., 58, 115, 166
failed states, 52, 150, 235
Fazal, T., 172, 227
foreign policy, 5–10, 13, 15–16, 18, 20, 22, 25, 27, 29–30, 32, 26, 46–47, 54–60, 65–68, 74, 77, 79, 81–84, 89, 98, 105, 113–14, 117, 124–33, 143–46, 170–74, 191, 206–8, 214–19, 221–23
former base state, 2–3, 5, 7, 11, 13–15, 17–21, 24–25, 40, 49–50, 56, 59, 62, 64–65, 71–72, 79–84, 87, 95, 97–98, 112, 115–17, 123, 129, 138, 145, 147–48, 151, 160–62, 165, 172–73, 176, 186, 207, 211–16, 219–27
Freedom House, 175
frozen recognition, 90, 93, 95, 213, 218

Gambia, 7, 75, 82–83, 96, 119, 125, 168, 179
geopolitical rivalries, 4, 11, 68, 205
Georgia, 4, 8, 64–65, 79–80, 84, 96–97, 106–7, 121, 126–27, 134, 136, 172, 202, 206
Germany, 44, 49, 64, 93, 183
Gërvalla, D., 110
Ghali, B., 180
global powers, 1, 8, 12, 21, 57, 84, 87, 113, 130, 162–63, 197, 205–8
Golan Heights, 22
Government of Vanuatu, 95, 106
government-in-exile, 64, 149, 175, 220–21
Grant, T. D., 5, 12, 21, 39, 48, 145–46, 203
great powers, 8, 10, 28, 57, 87, 163, 197, 220
Griffiths, R. D., 2–3, 7, 17, 57, 64

Helsinki Final Act, 143, 154–55
Huddleston, R. J., 8, 58, 71, 75, 77, 164, 182
human rights abuses, 51–52, 115
humanitarian crisis, 12, 26, 192
hybrid warfare, 21, 73
Hyseni, S., 174

ICJ Advisory Opinion, 141, 146, 154, 156–58
incomplete state, 24
informal diplomatic relations, 70
institutional engagement, 16, 112
interest groups, 61, 84, 86
International Court of Justice, 76–77, 156–58
International Crisis Group, 180–81
international isolation, 79, 153, 162, 172, 174
international law, 2, 4–5, 8, 9, 12–13, 22–26, 29, 31, 34–35, 37–52, 54, 73, 75, 77–78, 86, 90, 93, 104–7, 125, 128–29, 135, 143, 145–46, 148–58, 160–65, 180–83, 189, 195, 219, 222–23, 229–35
international norms, 13–15, 21–23, 26–29, 32, 42,

78, 94, 99, 113–17, 142, 147–48, 152–53, 156, 159, 161, 170, 180, 197, 214, 230–34
international order, 4–5, 10, 12, 21, 32, 56, 103, 173, 199, 201, 205, 208
international organizations, 3, 6, 18, 24, 27, 52, 71, 74, 78–79, 93, 107, 109, 118, 137, 156, 165–71, 174, 177, 179, 182–83, 186, 206, 214, 226, 231, 234
international recognition, 3, 7, 26, 28, 31, 53, 56, 64, 75, 77, 79–80, 83, 142, 147, 154, 167, 171, 174, 186, 202, 208, 218, 220, 222–25
international society, 9, 14, 26–27, 30, 52, 147
international system, 2, 8, 19, 21, 23, 27–28, 41, 46–47, 57, 60, 78, 80, 82, 117, 130, 143, 161, 166, 206, 210, 213, 219, 225–26, 229–30
international trusteeship, 171
internationalization, 25, 171
INTERPOL, 111, 169, 171, 174, 183
inward-looking rationales, 14, 32, 114–117, 163
irrevocability, 35–37

James, A., 11, 23, 40, 98

Ker-Lindsay, J., 3, 10, 17, 38, 51, 58, 65, 71–72, 78
Koskenniemi, M., 231
Krasner, S., 47, 51, 54
Kurti, A., 105, 185

Laayoune, 76, 180
Latin America, 26, 28, 84–85, 113, 117, 124–25
Lauterpacht, H., 4–5, 9, 11–12, 38–39, 42–43, 48–50, 223, 230
League of Nations, 29
legal personhood, 47
legitimization, 13, 60–61, 152, 178, 180
Lesotho, 7, 82, 88–89, 97, 104, 144, 154, 158
Liberia, 7, 75, 82, 91, 118, 125, 190
Limited recognition, 172
Lotus principle, 46
Lowe, V., 37, 51, 145, 164, 166, 224

Macedonia, 131, 195–96
Malaita, 193–95
Malawi, 7, 82–83, 94, 102, 109, 140, 192
Mayotte, 128–29
membership in international organisations, 182
MFA of China, 96, 200
MFA of Dominica, 158
MFA of Ghana, 155, 157
MFA of Grenada, 92, 143
MFA of Kenya, 92

MFA of Kosovo, 84, 104–06, 110, 123, 143, 146, 157, 170–71, 182
MFA of Liberia, 91
MFA of Madagascar, 143–44
MFA of Peru, 96, 125
MFA of Russia, 87, 155, 192, 200
MFA of Serbia, 94, 97, 128, 142, 151
MFA of Taiwan, 91, 100–103, 119, 125, 173, 201
MFAT of Papua New Guinea, 92, 97,
military provocations, 72, 177
Montevideo Convention, 37, 105, 108, 148
Morocco, 1, 8, 64–65, 74–77, 83, 85, 89, 92, 94, 96, 98, 121–25, 134–35, 138–41, 149–50, 179–82, 196, 204–5, 217, 226–27
Movement for Self-Determination, 174
multilateralism, 22, 29
multiplicity, 16, 57, 90, 112
mutual derecognition, 101–2
mutual recognition, 21, 58, 111, 142, 146, 185

Naticchia, C., 28, 52
National Parliament of Solomon Islands, 99–100, 119
Nauru, 7, 74, 82–84, 102, 109, 118, 120, 123, 134, 144, 153, 164, 200
New Zealand, 195, 199
Newman, E., 2, 4, 8, 16, 77–78, 136–37, 197, 222, 232
Nicaragua, 44, 118, 133, 190
non-intervention principle, 46
non-recognition, 28, 46, 103, 128
normalization, 21, 77, 79–80, 88, 142, 144, 146–77, 158, 169, 176, 181–82, 185–86, 216, 225–27
normative institutions, 6
Northern Cyprus, 231

Ó Beacháin, D., 8, 64, 80, 88, 134, 172
occupation, 1, 3, 22, 75, 121, 134, 149, 152, 177, 180–81, 204, 221, 226
One-China Principle, 96, 153, 200
ontological security, 24, 173
original conditions of recognition, 2, 35, 67, 130, 146, 152, 160
Osmani-Sadriu, V., 169–70
outward-looking justification, 114, 116, 137, 147

Pacific, 7, 26, 28, 72, 74, 85, 99–100, 103–8, 113, 117–18, 124, 127, 131–34, 166, 187–89, 191–93, 198–200, 234
Pacolli, B., 104, 123, 190
Palau, 83, 111

Index

Panama, 1, 7, 82, 84, 91, 102, 139, 149–50, 198
Papua New Guinea, 92, 97, 99, 103, 111, 188–89
partially recognized states, 10
Pavković, A., 4
People's Republic of China, 64, 72, 96, 153, 178, 195, 200
performative diplomacy, 220
performativity, 55
Peterson, M.J., 44, 51, 145, 230
Polisario Front, 64, 74–76, 92, 124–25, 135, 138–40, 150, 175, 179–81, 204, 217
political corruption, 187
political culture, 15
political self-interest, 14, 27, 115
population, 11, 25, 35, 38, 50–52, 64, 74, 77, 109, 115, 118, 121, 128, 134, 138, 142, 145, 148–49, 165, 167, 193
powerful states, 14, 28, 32, 81, 131
premature recognition, 35, 145
principle of estoppel, 40, 42

Radan, P., 4, 24, 48, 64, 149
recognition-without-engagement, 19, 90, 95, 212, 218
referendum, 64, 75, 77, 92–93, 121, 128, 138, 140–41, 174, 194, 204, 227
regional powers, 7, 11, 32, 56, 65, 78, 81, 108, 205, 228
regional security, 132–33
renting recognition, 15, 18, 19
reputation, 18, 235
re-recognition, 2, 7, 16, 40, 57, 59, 63, 70, 96–97, 103, 108, 109, 124, 212, 219
reversal politics, 4, 67, 209, 235
reverse order, 16, 31, 91, 112, 210, 215, 218
reversibility, 21
revocation of recognition, 4, 37, 40, 137
Rich, T., 137, 167, 188
right to self-determination, 2, 29, 115, 129, 138, 141, 155, 164, 175, 180, 231, 233
rivalry, 12, 14, 25, 30, 81–82, 124, 127, 134, 137, 187, 197, 202–4, 208
Roth, B., 29, 145
rules-based order, 30
Russia, 8, 28, 65, 78–80, 87–88, 120–21, 133–34, 136, 150–51, 155, 171–73, 181, 192, 200–205, 226, 231

Sahrawi Arabic Democratic Republic (SADR), 1, 64, 74
São Tomé and Príncipe, 1, 83, 103, 127–28

secession, 4, 17, 21, 59. 72, 78. 129, 136, 163, 176, 213, 216, 231
secret diplomacy, 18, 83, 213
Senegal, 75, 110, 132
Serbia, 1, 4, 8, 64–65, 77–79, 83–95, 97, 104–5, 110, 122–23, 127–29, 141–44, 146–47, 150–51, 154, 156, 158, 168–71, 174, 182–86, 190, 192, 203, 217, 226–27
severance of diplomatic relations, 39, 90, 107, 113
shared sovereignty, 148
Shaw, M., 4, 45, 60, 160, 176
small states, 22, 46, 82, 110, 117, 191, 207
Sogavare, M., 100, 195
Solomon Islands, 1, 7, 82–83, 96, 98–108, 118–19, 125, 131–33, 152–53, 166, 173, 187, 191, 193–96, 199
South Caucasus, 79
South Ossetia, 3–5, 7–8, 63–65, 79, 83–84, 96–97, 106–7, 120–21, 126, 133–34, 136, 171–72, 202, 205–6, 226, 232
sovereign equality, 12, 23, 41–42, 55, 73, 106, 161, 176, 210
sovereign statehood, 11, 15, 28, 35–36, 51, 73, 77, 84, 105, 132, 148, 150, 158, 161–62, 171, 173, 212–13, 217–18, 226
sovereignty dispute, 19
spillover effect, 26–27, 103
stability, 10, 12, 24–26, 30, 38, 44–45, 53, 67, 72–73, 88, 113, 133, 136–37, 142, 156, 163–65, 174, 176, 180, 182, 186, 190, 195–96, 199–201, 206–7, 210, 214, 223, 228, 230, 234
state contestation, 17, 67, 71, 80–81
state creation, 3–4, 10, 21, 231
state discourse, 6
statecraft, 4, 14, 82
state-like entity, 12, 14, 48
Sterio, M., 58, 164
subversive diplomacy, 22
Suriname, 7, 82, 87, 98, 111, 122, 133, 140, 151
symbolic sovereignty, 9, 23, 76, 213
symbolic violence, 214

Taipei, 73, 87, 102, 117, 119, 129, 173, 175, 179, 200, 220
Taiwan, 1, 3, 5, 7–8, 11, 24, 63–65, 70, 72–74, 83–89, 91, 96, 99–103, 108–9, 117–20, 124–33, 153, 159, 164, 166–68, 173–75, 177–79, 187–96, 198–201, 206, 209, 217, 219–20, 226–28
Taiwan Allies International Protection and Enhancement Initiative (TAIPEI) Act, 87, 200

Index • 285

Talmon, S., 87, 200
territorial integrity, 2, 11, 13, 17, 28, 72, 74, 77–78, 80, 84, 89, 94–97, 107, 115, 125, 128–29, 136, 141, 143, 148, 150–51, 154–55, 161, 178–80, 182, 197, 202, 213, 216
territory, 2–3, 5, 9, 11–12, 17, 19, 22–24, 35, 38, 40, 50–51, 65, 71–72, 74–77, 96, 98, 115, 120, 122, 128, 139, 141, 145, 148–52, 154, 157, 164–65, 172, 175, 179–80, 198, 201–2, 204, 212–14, 217, 219–20, 226–27, 234
titular sovereignty, 11
Togo, 75
Trump, D., 76, 169, 181, 184
Tubilewicz, C, 117, 119, 195
Tuvalu, 7, 82, 85, 96, 103, 106–07, 126, 136, 172

Ukraine, 26, 171–72, 192, 230
UN Mission for Referendum in Western Sahara (MINURSO), 77, 138, 180, 204
UN peacekeepers, 131, 195–96
unaccountable practices, 187
unbecoming a sovereign state, 209
UNESCO, 78, 174
unfriendly act, 42, 163–64, 221
ungoverned territories, 12
Unilateral Acts of States, 42–43
United Nations Secretary-General, 89, 140
United Nations Security Council, 135, 139
universal recognition, 56, 65, 209, 215
use of force, 12, 50, 71, 178, 226, 231

Van Fossen, A, 5, 65, 117–19, 189
Vanuatu, 7, 82, 95, 97, 99, 106–7, 109, 121, 126, 172, 188, 193
Venezuela, 44, 133
Vidmar, J., 4, 11, 37, 148, 154
Vienna Convention on Diplomatic Relations, 105, 158
Viola, L., 225–26
visit diplomacy, 83
Visoka, G., 2, 4, 7–8, 10, 16, 24, 26, 56, 58–59, 63, 65–66, 77–78, 136–37, 141, 150, 154, 156, 185, 197, 211, 215, 220, 222, 232
vulnerability, 8, 57, 82, 172, 217

weak states, 14, 73
Weller, M., 64, 77, 137, 154, 156, 231
Western Sahara, 1, 3, 5, 7–8, 22, 24, 63
withdrawal of recognition, 1–6, 9, 12, 14–15, 19–20, 23–35, 28, 30–32, 35–51, 56, 59, 62, 65, 70, 83, 88, 93–96, 98, 101, 105–8, 113, 119, 128, 143, 146, 150, 152, 160, 164, 166, 170, 174, 206, 209, 210, 112, 218–29, 232–33
World Trade Organization, 166
Wu, J., 108, 173, 177

Yugoslavia, 37, 49, 65, 85–86, 154–55, 231–32

Zëri i Amerikës, 182
Zunes, S., 64, 75, 125, 152, 204